Presented

to

Buena Vista University Library

by the

Family

of

Wayne B. Jensen

THE SECRETS OF THE SERVICE

by the same author
EXILE POLITICS DURING THE SECOND WORLD WAR

THE SECRETS OF THE SERVICE

★

A story of Soviet Subversion of Western Intelligence

ANTHONY GLEES

Carroll & Graf Publishers, Inc.
New York

for my parents Eva and Paul Glees

First Carroll & Graf edition 1987

Carroll & Graf Publishers, Inc.
260 Fifth Avenue
New York, NY 10001

Library of Congress Cataloging-in-Publication Data

Glees, Anthony, 1948–
  The secrets of the service.

  Bibliography: p. 9
  Includes index.
  1. Great Britain.   Secret Intelligence Service—
History.   2. Espionage—Soviet Union—History—20th
century.   I. Title.
UB271.R9G58   1987   327.1'2'0941   87-20862
ISBN 0-88184-375-X

Manufactured in the United States of America

Contents

Contents   *vii*

Illustrations

Acknowledgments

The author and publishers are grateful to the following for permission to reproduce copyright material: to BBC Enterprises Ltd for extracts from *SOE* by M. R. D. Foot; extracts from *Approach March* © Julian Amery 1973 by permission of Curtis Brown Ltd; to Macmillan, London & Basingstoke, and the University of Toronto Press for extracts from *Britain and European Resistance* by David Stafford.

They would also like to thank the following for permission to reproduce illustrations: the Rt Hon. Julian Amery, MP (no. 2); Fritz Heine (no. 4); Adrian Hollis (nos 13, 14, 15 and pp. 374–5); Imperial War Museum (no. 1); The Photo Source Ltd (nos 3, 5, 6, 7, 8, 9 and 12); Public Record Office (no. 16 and p. 293).

I remember saying to Roger [Hollis] on one of those occasions after the Russians had come in against the Germans, 'You know, I think we spend too much time worrying over the Russians. What do you say?' He answered, 'I do not think that I should think that if I were you' ... The points to notice carefully are these. Roger was thoroughly grounded in the position of the office under dear Sir Vernon Kell who was wantonly sacked by Churchill. Kell was a very fine man and very carefully guarded the secrets of the Service. Roger Hollis – and I remember this very well – acknowledged these traditions as the main block of the Service.

(Note prepared for me by the late Sir Roger Fulford, March 1982.)

Preface

This is the history of a problem. It has to do with secrets; with keeping them and discovering them; with not keeping them and, indeed, with failing to discover them. This is not a book about James Bond or the apparent glamour of espionage, but it does concern spies, moles and, ultimately, traitors. Although there is blood here, there is rather less thunder.

My chief concern is with the impact of secrets and of intelligence upon the making of British policy at a very dramatic and critical time for this country. From 1939 until 1951, Britain was forced first to fight for its survival against the Nazi menace and then to adapt to a new role in a changed world divided between Soviet Russia and the West. Many factors influenced the course Britain chose to pursue both during the war and after it. One of them was intelligence – and the lack of it.

Its role should not be overdone. Nevertheless, there is much to be said for the view put to me by one former officer that, in the final analysis, it *is* an understanding of intelligence, its successes and its failures that provides what Sir Alec Cadogan called the 'missing dimension' to why what happened actually did happen. Yet the role played by British Intelligence at this time is highly controversial, particularly in terms of its effectiveness against Communist subversion. Its apparent shortcomings in this area have, for over thirty years, occupied the minds of considerable numbers of people, many of them at the top of Britain's political establishment. Intelligence was one pillar of foreign policy; it was meant to alert policy-makers to the secrets of their opponents, in short, to subversion. Yet the intelligence services themselves proved to be subverted. What impact this had on policy is the problem to which this book addresses itself.

This historical problem also involves a whole series of spy cases, and particularly intriguing ones at that. As an intelligence story the book's conclusions are inevitably interim. Espionage and counter-espionage are activities conducted in a 'wilderness of mirrors'. People 'positively identified' as Communist moles may turn out to have been double agents working for the West (turning spies was one of MI5's fortes in respect of German agents).

Britain's concern with Communist subversion, often in danger of becoming an obsession, began on a Friday in the early summer of 1951 when two British diplomats took their leave of Whitehall. It was rekindled in the autumn of 1955. Further developments took place in February 1956 and 1963, with the reappearance of the diplomats in Moscow and the disappearance of Kim Philby from Beirut. But not only does the story not end there; it in fact begins again, this time in November 1979 (when Blunt was publicly named), and yet again in 1981 when the British people learned for the first time that the Director General of MI5 from 1956 until 1965, Sir Roger Hollis, had come under suspicion of being a Soviet mole.

For those seeking an answer to certain aspects of British intelligence and its impact on British foreign policy from 1939 to 1951, this book shines a searchlight over a number of key issues. For those more interested in exploring the allegations made against MI5 and MI6, I have set them in context and, in particular, I have made a judgment upon the career and the reputation of Roger Hollis who was intimately connected with MI5's anti-Communist activities from 1939 until his retirement as Director General.

At all stages detailed evidence, both verbal and documentary, is provided so that readers can re-create the process of intelligence analysis for themselves. This material provides the facts upon which my own comments are based. My aim is to examine the past through the perspectives of the time; to add insights gleaned from the present, and, especially important where a controversial case is being put, to provide the necessary evidence, not least because so much of it is circumstantial. If decisive documentary proof of subversion had been available, this study would not have needed to be written.

In every possible case, a source for a statement or a document has been provided; yet not every written or verbal statement can be attached to an identity. This is simply because many of those who have made such statements believe that, even though most of the events in this study happened more than thirty years ago, they were charged with keeping them secret, and to disclose them now would be tantamount to betraying their professional integrity. Hence communications from and by them are signified by the dates when they wrote to me or when they agreed to be interviewed. The reader will have to accept that they are genuine accounts of what I have been told (there would be no sense in my falsifying them), even though their anonymity means they cannot be cross-checked.

Since it is my argument that the question of subversion can neither be properly put nor properly answered without an adequate understanding of Britain's foreign policy, especially towards the Soviet Union, this book investigates the subject after exploring the nature of the intelligence problem that presents itself. We then turn to specific examples of apparent Communist subversion within British Intelligence, looking first at the Special Operations Executive (SOE), and then at MI6 and MI5. Although the extent of subversion should never be exaggerated, we shall see clear evidence of the damage it caused. Finally, we pose the most intriguing question of all: why those involved in intelligence failed to perceive this damage, and thus why they failed to act against it. Any reader who is not interested in British foreign policy, but is concerned about MI5 and Roger Hollis, may, of course, read those particular sections only, and, I hope, with profit.

Until the records of SOE, MI6 and MI5 are made public, any study of their history is bound to be provisional. Yet this does not mean a serious study cannot be attempted: many of those who participated in these matters are now prepared to discuss them, and the occasional intelligence document does slip through the net. There are, in addition, a number of primary and secondary studies dealing with these topics. A list of them is given at the back of this book.

Many people have helped me in countless ways to produce this study. Some have asked me not to reveal their names for very obvious reasons, which I respect. They know how grateful I am to them. Those whose assistance I am able to acknowledge are listed below: the Rt Hon. Julian Amery, MP; the Hon. David Astor; the Hon. Hugh Astor; Professor Michael Balfour; Major Axel von dem Bussche-Streithorst; Raymond Carr; Robert Cecil; Clifton Child; Cora Creutzfeldt; Sir William Deakin; Professor David Dilks; Felix Erith; Professor M. R. D. Foot; Henry Fowler; the late Sir Roger Fulford; Lord Gladwyn; Dr John Glees; Professor Margaret Gowing; Mandy Greenfield; Ludwig von Hammerstein-Equord; Fritz Heine; Christopher Hill; Professor F. H. Hinsley; Adrian and Margaret Hollis; Marcus Hollis; the late Bishop Michael Hollis; Professor Michael Howard; Inter Nationes; Ann Jefferson; Phillip Knightley; Professor Richard Loewenthal; Tony and Christine Nicholls; Professor Gottfried Niedhart; Dr Ben Pimlott; Alice Prochaska; the staff of the Public Record Office, Kew; Alan Quilter; Professor Joachim Radkau; Sir Patrick Reilly; Sir Frank Roberts; Colonel T. A. Robertson; Dr Graham Ross; Lord Sherfield; Jack Swayne; Fritz Tobias; Professor D. C. Watt; Nigel West; Phillip Whitehead; the late Philip Williams; Professor Robert Williams and Sir Geoffrey Wilson.

Thanks are also due to my students and colleagues at Brunel University. I am, in particular, indebted to David Shapiro, whose friendly interest in the subject and bibliographical skills were an enormous help; to Harry Chapman Pincher who, knowing I took a very different view from his own, nevertheless went out of his way to assist me on many occasions and, perhaps most of all, to Graham C. Greene for his constant encouragement and practical assistance.

Brunel University, London   ANTHONY GLEES
1987

Abbreviations

ASIO	Australian Security Intelligence Organisation
ASIS	Australian Secret Intelligence Service
BfV	Bundesamt für Verfassungschutz (Federal Office for the Protection of the Constitution – West German equivalent of MI5)
BND	Bundesnachrichtendienst (Federal Intelligence Agency – West German equivalent of MI6)
CDU	Christlich-Demokratische Union (German Christian Democrats)
CPGB	Communist Party of Great Britain
DSIR	Department of Scientific and Industrial Research
FCO	Foreign and Commonwealth Office
FORD	Foreign Office Research Department
GCHQ	Government Communications Headquarters (previously the Government Code and Cipher School)
GC&CS	Government Code and Cipher School
GRU	Glavnoe Razvedyvatelnoe Upravlenie (Soviet Military Intelligence)
ISRB	Inter-Services Research Bureau
JIC	Joint Intelligence Committee
KGB	Komitet Gosudarstvennoi Bezopastnosti (Soviet Committee of State Security)
KPD	Kommunistische Partei Deutschlands (German Communist Party)
MEW	Ministry of Economic Warfare
MI5	British domestic security service
MI6	British secret intelligence service
NKVD	Narodny Komitet Vnutrennikh Del (Soviet People's Commissariat for Internal Affairs)
OGPU	Otdelenie Gosudarstvenny Politicheskoy Upravy (Soviet Department of State Political Directorate)
OPC	Office for Policy Coordination

OSS	Office of Strategic Services (US)
OWI	Office of War Information (US)
PID	Political Intelligence Department
PWE	Political Warfare Executive
RCMP	Royal Canadian Mounted Police
SHAEF	Supreme Headquarters of the Allied Expeditionary Force
SOE	Special Operations Executive
SPD	Sozialdemokratische Partei Deutschlands (German Social Democratic Party)
WO	War Office

1

A National Obsession

The missing diplomats: the making of a national obsession

Late in the evening of Friday 25 May 1951 two British diplomats fled the country. Their employers did not find out until the following Monday and their country was not told until 7 June. One of the diplomats, Donald Maclean, was the Head of the American Department of the Foreign Office in Whitehall. He was thirty-eight years old and married, with two children. The other diplomat had been a Second Secretary at the British Embassy in Washington. He was an unmarried homosexual called Guy Burgess.

On 7 June 1951 an announcement was made by the Foreign Office that two of its men had disappeared and that both of them had been suspended with effect from 1 June for being absent from their posts without leave. But what was really going on? Those who knew did not want to say; those who did not know were not going to be told.

To judge by apparent official concern, the affair was of little consequence. Indeed, *The Times*, that mouthpiece of the British Establishment (it does not seem an unfair description), evidently considered it so unimportant that it barely reported the issue at all (there were only three references to it for the whole of that year). The Britain of 1951 soon forgot about the missing men (murdered, runaway lovers, lunatics, or all three) and turned its mind instead to the Communist advance in Korea, the health of the King, and the crisis in Persia. One unwanted clue that something rather important had happened was, however, given to the readers of the *Daily Express*, who were told that Sir Percy Sillitoe, then Director General of MI5, paid an unexpected visit to the United States from 11 to 17 June.

It is true that the matter was raised very briefly in Parliament on 7 and 18 June, and again on 10 July, but anyone seeking enlightenment from this was not going to be any the wiser. There was no suggestion in the parliamentary discussions of 1951 that the case of the 'missing diplomats' would prove, four years later, to make Britain's blood run cold, something it has continued to do since then. Ordinary British people and successive British Governments were soon to be as horrified and unsettled by Burgess and Maclean as their ancestors had been by allegations of witchcraft.

There was, however, a hint, even in 1951, that something sinister lay behind the disappearance of Burgess and Maclean. In June, for example, Duncan Sandys, then a Conservative (Opposition) MP, asked whether the Government had not known that Burgess had possessed 'strong Communist views' when put on the Foreign Office Establishment in 1944. The junior Foreign Office minister Mr Younger replied that the then Government had not been aware that Burgess had 'an association with Communist circles of a kind which threw doubt on his reliability'. Furthermore, Sandys was warned that 'speaking of strong Communist views is using a phrase which is very vague and liable to be misinterpreted'.

Burgess had been subject to a 'security check' but he was not positively vetted, and the minister added:

> Frankly, I do not see why he should have been. He had already been in the Foreign Service and other forms of Government employment some time before that. His establishment did not give him a more confidential position than he had before and a check was not made at the time ...[1]

Anthony Eden, who had been Foreign Secretary during the critical period, added, 'Has it not been the assumption by all of us that the Civil Service has no part in political views?'[2] Eden seemed to imply that in some senses it did not matter whether a civil servant was a Communist or not, because his or her party politics would never be permitted to enter into the policy-making process. Younger agreed, saying he had known many people accused of having Communist sympathies who had been perfectly ordinary liberals.

Eden's remarks could, however, have been taken to mean that the Foreign Office staff had to be apolitical and that, if they were not keeping out of party politics, this was cause for great concern. Indeed, this interpretation reflected the position of the Government and of the then Prime Minister, Clement Attlee, who had stated in 1948 that:

> It is the policy of the Government that no one who was known to

be a member of the Communist Party or to be associated with it in such a way as to raise legitimate doubts about him or his reliability is to be employed in connection with work, the nature of which is vital to the security of the State.[3]

In other words, a distinction was to be drawn between those civil servants who supported or were members of the democratic political parties, and those who supported parties pledged to overthrow liberal democracy. What this meant to the man in the street in 1951 is hard to judge, but one thing must have been very clear: that, at least since 1948, the Government had screened its officials (for how else could it discover who was disloyal?), but that Burgess and Maclean had none the less escaped detection. This, in turn, begged the question: why? Not surprisingly, the Government was obliged to have another go at reassurance. On 10 July 1951 Herbert Morrison, the then Foreign Secretary, restated the official line:

The Government of that time was not aware of Mr Burgess having associations with Communist circles of a kind which threw doubt on his reliability and the same applied to Mr Maclean.[4]

This could, of course, have implied that MI5 *had* known that Burgess and Maclean had associated with Communists, but that this did not throw any doubt on their reliability, about which, Morrison might have added but did not, MI5 was entirely wrong.

Morrison countered criticism by pointing out on 11 July that there was no cause for any public alarm. While accepting that MI5 had got it wrong in the case of Burgess and Maclean, he went on to state that:

Forty-three civil servants were suspended during 1950; 7 were reinstated, 17 transferred to other work, 4 given special leave, 4 resigned and 11 dismissed.[5]

In short, MI5 had spotted forty-three likely Communists, even if they had not spotted the two missing diplomats. Many officials believed that Morrison had made matters worse. For one thing, the figures given previously of the number expelled from Government service had been considerably less. It had always been understood that only three people had been removed on the grounds of their Communist affiliations as a result of Attlee's 1948 ordinance; now it was forty-three. Some evidence of the tension this announcement generated emerged in a comment made by a back-bench Tory, Sir W. Smithers, who asked:

> If the Government are sincerely anti-Communist, will they now prosecute the Dean of Canterbury and, when he has been convicted, ensure he is publicly hanged?[6]

Those who had urged discretion on this issue seemed to win the day: too much information had merely succeeded in making the public anxious. Important questions about MI5's competence had been raised; they had been answered only to raise deeper questions about the true number of Communists in the Civil Service. While public hangings were not on in Britain (yet), Morrison must have viewed with alarm the debate then raging in Australia, where a referendum was to be put to the country that very September giving the Government the power to dissolve the Communist Party and enact specific pieces of anti-Communist legislation for security reasons.

In some ways, then, it would be correct from a liberal standpoint to argue that secrecy on this issue was not intrinsically evil. What was wrong was to fail to comprehend how deeply the defection would concern people and that, since damage would be done in any case, the best thing was to make a clean breast of things. Indeed, it was the unwillingness to accept this which, somewhat paradoxically, threw doubt not just on the competence of successive Labour and Conservative Governments, but also on their commitment to liberal values. For the public's right to know is as important a civil liberty as a diplomat's right to be presumed innocent unless proven guilty. What is more, this secrecy may have prevented a witch-hunt being pursued by the civil servants, but it did not prevent one being pursued by others, often less scrupulous. All sorts of doubtful 'investigations' were carried out by people claiming to act in the interests of providing 'the facts' but actually after 'the names'.

The question of how much to reveal and when to reveal it is, like all political decisions, a matter of finely balanced judgment. The record seems to suggest that although those who wanted to suppress this issue did so for the best liberal motives, they were wrong to do so. Liberalism would have been better served by a full account early on. Too much secrecy has proved counter-productive. It *has* led to witch-hunts and, by undermining faith in British security, it has damaged the morale and the work of both MI5 and MI6.

In September 1955, a new twist to the tale was produced by the revelation made by a Soviet defector, Vladimir Petrov, that Burgess and Maclean had both been long-term Communist agents and that they were alive and well and living in Moscow. Two years previously Melinda Maclean, Donald's unfortunate wife, had also disappeared; once again, the Government had pointed out that it did not know where the diplomats were. They were still absent without leave.

Petrov's allegations made a further Government statement inevitable. This came in the White Paper of September 1955 and the subsequent debate, yet no one was much wiser as a result, which was precisely the Government's intention. As in 1951, the question was begged: did the political establishment have something to hide? Or was it simply that in a nation as secretive as Britain, any information, however harmless, about a problem to do with the governing of the country was likely to remain hidden for as long as possible?

The Government's appointed mouthpiece was the then Foreign Secretary, Harold Macmillan. He based his submission on the firmly stated conviction that individual liberties were paramount in a free society and no one, not even a Government, had the right to take action against individuals simply because they were suspected of being Communists. Unwillingly indicating a certain incompetence on the part of those charged with knowing these things, he added that there was still no definite proof of where the diplomats had gone, even if their reasons for going were now plain.

Indeed, Macmillan obviously hoped to be able to dispel any suspicions that MI5 had been inept. Although Maclean (but not Burgess, as he pointed out) had been under suspicion and was being observed by MI5, that surveillance did not extend beyond London. There had been insufficient evidence to detain Maclean; this naturally meant that it was possible for him to escape. As to the assertion that there might have been a cover-up, or even a 'tip-off' to enable Maclean to slip away, Macmillan utterly rejected the first notion and gave a categorical assurance that, even if there had been a 'tip-off' by a third man, which he seemed inclined to doubt, there was no evidence to suggest that H.A.R. 'Kim' Philby had been the culprit:

Whilst in Government service, Philby had carried out his duties ably and conscientiously and [there was] no reason to conclude that he had at any time betrayed the interests of Britain or to identify him as the 'Third Man', if there ever was one ...[7]

Philby's sang-froid following his exoneration by Macmillan was remarkable. At his press conference, he said that the 'last time' he had 'spoken to a Communist, knowing he was a Communist was in 1934'. 'The last time' he had spoken to one 'not knowing he was a Communist was in April 1951 when Burgess was staying in my house'. Philby added:

I have never been a Communist although I have always been a bit to the Left. My own politics are not very interesting ...[8]

A minute prepared for the Cabinet by Harold Macmillan before the Government debate, released in 1986, shows clearly that, despite quite inappropriate flippancy, he had a genuine moral objection to using security requirements to curtail civil liberties. Indeed, this minute shows his considerable distaste at having to deal with the matter at all. Dated 19 October 1955, Macmillan wrote:

I have been considering how to deal with this debate ... there are certain questions which have been pushed hard, especially by the Press, which have to be answered. It will not be very easy to make a wholly convincing defence of what has happened in the Past. At the same time, I think it would be possible to show some of the inherent difficulties in a situation where the principles of security and freedom appear to be in conflict.
Nothing would be worse than a lot of muckraking and innuendo ... nevertheless I think we must make some suggestion. I therefore propose we should have an enquiry not into the Past but into the Future ... the advantages of the enquiry would be twofold. First, on the principle of Albert and the Lion 'someone had to be summoned so that was decided upon' and the Public would feel that something is being enquired into and, secondly, the Public will be brought up against the dilemma of security in a free society. Almost all of the accusations of the Press against the laxity of the authorities are really demands for changing English Common Law.[9]

The points Macmillan had in mind are listed by him. They include the need to arrest people without legal grounds and thus without fear of Habeas Corpus or proceedings for false imprisonment, the power to stop a person and his relatives from leaving the country if they had access to secret information and were under suspicion, and the power to dismiss civil servants who had held or still held Communist views or opinions.

Macmillan did treat the whole issue as something of a joke. It is clear from this minute that he would have preferred to do nothing, and that the enquiry he proposed to set up was established for the chief purpose of reassuring the public rather than properly investigating the past. For all this he must be condemned: had he taken the matter more seriously in 1955, Philby might have been caught and many reputations, including those of MI5 and MI6, would have been less tarnished. Yet we should not ignore Macmillan's reasons for failing to act, reasons shared by many within the security service. Indeed, some very important issues had been evaded.

For a start, why had the two men defected immediately after a decision to arrest Maclean had been taken by the Foreign Secretary? Had they made an inspired guess? Or had somebody indeed told them they were about to be picked up? Individual liberties needed to be protected, but could one be certain that civil servants were sufficiently professional to repress their own political beliefs, particularly when the cause they supported, namely Communism, was sworn to destroy the system of liberal democracy which employed them? Was it right that their Communist sympathies had not disqualified them from office? Why had they been steadily promoted? Was someone protecting them? Was that someone MI5? The Foreign Office? The Government?

Thus it was that the case of Burgess and Maclean became a national obsession. The discovery that there existed Englishmen (the women were not yet known about) who possessed two quite different identities, at once members of Britain's governing élite and at the same time long-term penetration agents of the Soviet Union, horrified an innocent nation.

The British public had, it may reasonably be thought, assumed that men such as Burgess and Maclean represented the best and the brightest that Britain could produce; they were the cream of British education, of its middle class and its culture. Yet these things had secretly been rejected by them, for their real master, whom they loyally served, was Stalin. To many it must have seemed that they betrayed not simply the interests of their country, but also its values. If Burgess and Maclean ought not to have been trusted, who could be?

There were others, however, who took a different view. They argued that the whole affair had been exaggerated and that it was vital to try to regain some sense of proportion. Errors had perhaps been made but, and this was an important point, the things that were often perceived as errors at the time were, in reality, not so at all. There had, for example, been considerable disquiet that Donald Maclean had, after falling under suspicion, been made Head of the American Department of the Foreign Office, but people privy to the nation's secrets knew that this had been done in order to keep him under close observation without his knowledge (see p. 363). For such people the really important goal now was to prevent the public from over-reacting. Unless this were done, they feared the affair would soon engender British McCarthyism with all its unwanted repercussions.

While they accepted that Burgess and Maclean and other moles were traitors, they also believed that no national good would be served by what they saw as a potential witch-hunt. Perhaps, at the back of their minds, some of them believed that Burgess and Maclean were simply the casualties of history; they had been caught out by the political sea-change that had followed the collapse of the alliance with the Soviet Union after 1945. For by 1948 the alliance had been destroyed by the Cold War and had become a deadly combat between two conflicting political systems, making those who had previously passed for deluded idealists into dangerous traitors.

Those who held this view believed it was best to quieten things down, in the hope that the whole issue would in due course go away. Of course, they were wrong. It did not go away and those who had hoped it would soon found themselves the subject of questions concerning their own political loyalties. Indeed, the quintessential suspicion that a deep Establishment cover-up was being put into operation is still capable of causing major political upsets today. For although some people could see that the attempts to play down the defection of Burgess and Maclean might be necessary to avoid wide-scale hysteria, others declared that they were part of an elaborate and sinister plot, more far-reaching than had hitherto been supposed.

The wish to avoid McCarthyite purges could, of course, stem from two quite contradictory motives: a legitimate desire to maintain the principles of a politically free and pluralistic society or to prevent the security service from quietly removing Communists from positions where they could do damage both to themselves and their country. There was also a distinction to be drawn between knowing about Communist infiltration and choosing to ignore it (for whatever reasons), and not knowing about it in the first place. The British authorities followed both paths at different periods, thus inevitably raising questions, in the one instance about MI5's loyalty and, in the other, about its competence.

Where both the politicians and the mandarins made a misjudgment was not in wanting to eschew witch-hunts, but in not admitting at the earliest opportunity the full implications of the deep changes in the perception and understanding of Communism which had taken place since 1945 and the advent of the Cold War. To have done so would naturally have required great courage, since it implied the admission of intelligence errors. But the fact that it was not done has caused far more damage and for far too long. In any case, successive Governments were forced to be less easy-going about security, which served simply to confirm the beliefs of those who suggested that Britain's security policies were not liberal but merely incompetent. The truth, of course, was far more complex: incompetence did play its part but so did decency. The main culprit, however, was historical change.

That a certain amount of covering-up went on can hardly be denied; and in one way the official secrecy, which still prevents the release of documentary evidence concerning Communist penetration and subversion that occurred thirty and more years ago, is part of that cover-up. Documentary records concerning these affairs are still kept under lock and key, with the exception of isolated papers (such as Macmillan's minute) or papers which have somehow slipped through the net (such as those dealing with Otto John, considered later). The real question, therefore, is not whether covering-up took place, but whether it was done to protect the values of British political life and the effectiveness of British security, or to keep from the British public some appallingly terrible truth.

The White Paper on Burgess and Maclean

The 1955 Government led by the hapless Anthony Eden decided to produce a White Paper on the disappearance of the two men and promised to have a debate upon it. The Paper was published on 23 September 1955 and it may be said to have been the first time the full impact of the affair was felt in Britain. Yet the White Paper[10] was soon dismissed as a whitewash which, in the circumstances surrounding its inception, was a foregone conclusion.

The Paper stated that neither Burgess nor Maclean had given anyone any reason to doubt their loyalty. It was true that in 'late 1949', while on holiday abroad, Burgess had been 'indiscreet'. But MI5 had got to hear about this and the Foreign Office had 'severely reprimanded him'. In January 1949, however, MI5 had received reports about 'certain Foreign Office information' leaked to Russia four years earlier. It was this information which by April 1951 had been narrowed down to two or three people. It should be noted that the Paper did not, for security reasons, explain precisely what this information was (it is discussed in detail later; see p. 359).

Maclean then became the prime suspect, but the report stated that there was no evidence with which to prosecute him under the Official Secrets Act. On 25 May Morrison agreed to Maclean's interrogation. That night both Maclean and Burgess disappeared. Since that time, the Government declared, it had received no information as to their whereabouts. In June 1951 Burgess's and Maclean's mothers had received telegrams from France. In August of that year Mrs Maclean received a letter from Donald posted in Reigate, and in November Burgess wrote to his mother – ostensibly from Poplar in East London. By 1955 Petrov claimed they were established in Moscow.

The White Paper insisted that when both men had been appointed 'nothing was on record to show anything unsuitable for public service'. This suggested that the records that the Government had were obviously not very satisfactory and so, as a direct consequence of this, the then minister with responsibilities in this area, Herbert Morrison, ordered an investigation into vetting procedures in July 1951, which reported in November 1951 and introduced positive vetting (where individuals were not simply checked against records but actively investigated; see p. 337).

This explanation seemed plausible enough, on paper. However, in the celebrated debate on the White Paper on 7 November 1955, the Government was bitterly attacked. This debate was to prove a turning point, in several ways, in the history of Communist subversion. First, as we have seen, Harold Macmillan totally exonerated Philby; second, the charge of a cover-up was made far more openly than ever before, a charge which has persisted to the present day. Third, procedures were adopted which changed the basis on which the British Civil Service was run. But was it fair to attack the Government? Had there been a cover-up? And why did Macmillan go out of his way to exonerate Philby?

Macmillan went over the top in his defence of Philby. For the fact was that many senior figures in Whitehall were by now privately convinced that Philby was a traitor; indeed, he had been forced to resign from MI6 (only then to be secretly re-employed on a part-time basis at the personal order of the then 'C' or Head of MI6). It was therefore untrue to say that the Government had 'no reason to conclude' that he was the Third Man – because there was reason; there was simply no proof.

On the other hand, Macmillan believed very strongly that people who were not found guilty should be declared innocent and that they, rather than their country, should be given the benefit of the doubt. The Government as a whole was soon to contradict this policy within the hidden corridors of power, for it was to decide that, behind locked doors, a different set of standards should apply; but it seems hard not to recognise that Macmillan was both justified and right in stressing what might be called the libertarian aspects of the matter. For Britain was a parliamentary liberal democracy which upheld the rule of common law, and it had a security service, rather than a secret police. The price of that was the occasional mistake.

In Parliament, however, the Government had a rough ride. Richard Crossman, who had himself worked in intelligence during the war and almost certainly knew both Burgess and Philby, said:

If after four years, a tissue of palpable half-truths and contradictions is the best the Government can do, the impression of a cover-up is more substantiated than ever.[11]

Herbert Morrison said, rather weakly, that he did think there had been a Third Man, because it had always seemed rather odd that he had signed the order for Maclean's interrogation on 25 May and 'both men went missing the same night'. He added that he found the incident 'beastly and unhappy'.

Other MPs were fiercer than Morrison. One back-bencher accused the Foreign Office of 'covering up for its friends'. How else could one explain that 'a couple of drunks, a couple of homosexuals could for so long have occupied important posts in the Foreign Office'? And in the Lords, Viscount Astor (who was later to host parties for John Profumo and Christine Keeler) railed against:

A Government more concerned to hide the truth than uncover it. Maclean was twice engaged in drunken brawls with his left-wing friends. Burgess was a dirty, drunken, sexual inebriate. It is remarkable how slow Britain had been in realising the importance of the theory of Communism. For the first time since the reign of Elizabeth I, there exists a Fifth Column in Britain, which has permeated to the highest ranks of the Civil Service, Science and the Church ...[12]

The talk of a Fifth Column was a crazy device to generate public disquiet. Yet the Conservative Government's ineptitude seemed to encourage unrest in the same way that its Labour predecessor's bungling had done. Clearly, too, party politics played its part in escalating the conflict which was not, in reality, a party political issue at all.

The unfortunate Government was forced to accept a further humiliation when on 11 February 1956 Guy Burgess and Donald Maclean decided to come out into the open. They gave a press conference in Moscow and it was clear that the Kremlin had decided that the time had come to start rubbing the salt in.

They both declared that they had gone to work for Russia because they were 'convinced from official knowledge in our possession that neither the British, nor still more the Americans, were at that time' seriously trying to co-operate with the USSR. They had been straightforward Marxists, but they realised that they could 'do more to put Marxist ideas into practical effect' by entering the public service. Somewhat strangely they added 'neither of us were Communist agents'. Guy Burgess went on to say that he had never, at any time, made any secret of his Communist beliefs, and he added that he had worked for MI6 as well as MI5.

In the best traditions of Communist propaganda, Burgess and Maclean had succeeded not merely in muddying the waters even more, but in raising a whole new series of allegations, all of which put the British Government in an even more embarrassing position.

One of the major causes of Government red faces was, of course, the defectors' very appearance in Moscow, for until that time their whereabouts were unknown; an ignorance which was compounded by the fact that Harold Wilson, then a front-bench Labour MP, had gone to Moscow in January 1956 and had been requested to ask the Soviet leader Nikita Khrushchev where Burgess and Maclean were. Khrushchev had replied:

I have not heard anything of them from any Soviet officials, nor have I ever met them so it stands to reason that I don't know what they are doing.

Wilson duly reported this only to find, in under a month, Burgess and Maclean themselves telling everybody where they were. Indeed, it is tempting to think that Wilson's curiosity encouraged Khrushchev to order them into the open.

The Government reacted in two ways. First, it officially denied that Burgess had worked for MI5 or MI6. Mr Selwyn Lloyd stated that Burgess:

Had been in a Department which on the outbreak of war dealt with propaganda to neutral countries, an organisation which later came to be known as SOE. The only connection with MI5 had been [that] whilst working for the BBC he had from time to time reported to an informant information about Germany received by him from a contact ...[13]

What this misinformation actually meant is discussed later. SOE had, of course, done rather more than dabble in propaganda to neutral countries; it was a subversive organisation designed to undermine Nazi-occupied Europe in the British interest. Ordinary British citizens did not know this at the time, so they also could not know that Selwyn Lloyd was actually admitting that Burgess *had* worked for British Intelligence, as well as giving some indication of the specific issues in which the Kremlin instructed Burgess to take an interest (see p. 138).

The second reaction was to permit what could be seen as the thin end of the McCartyite wedge to enter British public life. It was the simple outcome of the Government's belief that it would have to do something to try to win back its reputation as a responsible guardian of the nation's security. Although this was probably the first time this had happened, it was by no means the last. Now, at the beginning of 1956, the Government decided to publish the recommendations of a special Privy Councillors' Conference on Security in the Public Services.[14] They are significant because they show the extent to which senior figures now believed harsher security measures were called for. The Government was clearly bound to accept them. Although Harold Macmillan had intimated that a few mistakes were an acceptable price for having a liberal secret service, the Government now rejected this idea. From this point on, it was the country that was to be given the benefit of the doubt and not the individual, or so the public was told. Rather than supply more documentary evidence to back up its case, to show how MI5 could have failed repeatedly to identify Burgess and Maclean, and why it had been possible for the Communists to achieve such a massive penetration in British political institutions after 1939, the Government simply accepted the Privy Councillors' proposals, some of which were really very far-ranging.

The recommendations, published on 8 March 1956, stated that individuals who, for one reason or another, were subject to Communist loyalties were always to be considered a major risk, because 'the Communist faith overrides a man's normal loyalties to his country and induces the belief that it is justifiable to hand over secrets'. It should be noted that although the report dealt principally with Communism, in order to avoid appearing biased it also wished its recommendations to be applied to Fascism (it stated that 'the term Communism is used to cover both Communism and Fascism alike').

It was also decided to recommend that a Communist affiliation should bar a civil servant from employment not simply on secret duties but also on non-secret ones, as well as unfavourably affect his or her promotion. Where officials were not Communists themselves but had wives or husbands who were, they were to be removed from secret work. Furthermore, in order to protect sources, decisions would have to be taken about civil servants without revealing the evidence against them. Alternative work would be sought for such people but it could not be guaranteed.

Finally, the Privy Councillors accepted that 'some of these measures, to which the State is driven, are alien to our traditional practices'; its answer was to give people suspended the right to a hearing by the 'Three Advisers', a tribunal set up in 1948 to deal with Attlee's first purge.

It is not the historian's task to express a view on whether such measures were really necessary. His job is confined to pointing out that changes had taken place and that there was some justification for them, bearing in mind the penetration that had been achieved by Communists after 1939. Whether such measures really made sense by 1955, when a completely different political perspective obtained, is another matter, for there is some reason to believe that what had happened in 1939 and 1940 was a one-time thing. Yet what had passed for legitimate security activity in 1939 and 1940 was no longer held to be tight enough in 1948. By 1956 it was required to be even tighter. It can be argued that the British had been too lax about security, and doubtless they had been, but it is also important not to exaggerate the effect of that laxness. This is why some believed the Government had over-reacted to reasonable anxieties about the role of MI5 and the role of the intelligence services more generally.

Some of the criticisms of the Government were merely party political hot air. When Labour had been in Government in 1951, the Conservatives criticised them for covering up the true facts of Burgess and Maclean's security clearance. Then, in 1955 and 1956, it was the turn of Labour and men such as Crossman to attack the Conservatives for exactly the same offence. What both parties appeared to forget was that most of the errors or worse had been committed during the Second World War when a coalition had governed Britain.

Successive Governments ought to have explained about the role of a security service in a free society; they should have discussed the historical implications of policy-making in the Second World War and stressed that Burgess and Maclean were, in part at any rate, relics of the Second World War era. Even if in 1939 and 1940 it would have been right to see them as part of an intensive Communist drive to take over Britain (which is how they saw themselves but not necessarily what they actually were), by 1951 their chances of doing this were hopeless. Although the Russians would always try to get their moles into position and would sometimes succeed, the objective situation was never again going to be as favourable for them as it had been immediately after 1939.

Today, however, it has become possible to begin the process of answering the questions which refused to go away. They have grown in intensity rather than diminished, and they have been fuelled by new names, by fourth, fifth, even tenth men (and women). As early as 1951 there was a suggestion that MI5, the institution charged with protecting British security, had not done its job properly during the war years and that dangerous Communists had been able to penetrate British public life.

One explanation for the increase in anxiety was Burgess's declaration that he had himself worked for British Intelligence. The implications were obvious and have continued to generate unease. In due course Philby was uncovered, then Blunt was shown to have worked as a mole in MI5. Now, finally, the debate has moved into a totally new sphere with the suggestion that there was a 'supermole' within MI5 whose job it was to prevent the Communist moles from ever being detected in the first place. The fingers pointed to an

individual of whom very few people had even heard. This was the
person who during the war had been charged with keeping a watch
on Communist activities. His name was Roger Hollis.

There is absolutely no doubt that during the Second World War
Britain, and that includes British Intelligence, dropped its guard
against Communist subversion. So, of course, did the United States.
The real questions to be addressed are very different. The first is to
discover why this happened; the second to estimate the amount of
damage that was caused. We shall see that the main reason for
Britain's lack of proper security emerged out of the political context
of Britain's alliance with the Soviet Union after 1941 (which today
must be called its historical context). There seems absolutely no
reason to believe that Roger Hollis himself was in any way guilty of
treachery, although he clearly made mistakes.

Second we shall see that in general terms the amount of damage
that the moles caused has been grossly exaggerated. Their activities
were serious, but there is no evidence to suggest that, except in very
detailed areas, matters would have been very different had the moles
loyally served the Crown rather than Stalin. That they had been in
a position to do grave harm, however, cannot be doubted. For by
virtue of their posts, they were not simply privy to Britain's official
secrets but also, and more sinisterly, were able actually to help with
the making of British policy. They were far more than mere spies.

Even so, the truth is that Stalin's aims were chiefly served by the
might of the Red Army and only in a very secondary sense by the
machinations of the moles. Perhaps the most damning, and ultimately most accurate, verdict upon the damage caused by the moles
comes from the fact that in many cases it is still impossible to be
absolutely certain about its extent. What the moles tried to do, what
the British Government tried to do, and what Stalin managed to
achieve all merged into each other so closely that it is, quite simply,
very difficult to be certain where the one activity ended and another
began. Indeed, one suspects that many of the diplomats and intelligence officers would, on looking back, accept that this was so.
Naturally such a verdict can be taken two ways: to imply that great
damage was done or that comparatively little damage occurred.

This book offers no comfort to those who argue that subversion
mattered a great deal; but it also will not satisfy those who argue
that it was entirely irrelevant. Both propositions are patently false.
Communist subversion almost certainly did have a serious effect in
very detailed and specific areas; the plain truth that what happened

there would probably have happened in any case, even if there had been no subversion, is an argument for not exaggerating its impact. It is not an argument for ignoring its existence.

The evidence suggests that MI5, MI6 and SOE do have a case to answer. Yet, at the end of the day, the role played by British Intelligence was by no means as disastrous as has been claimed. Not only are many of the criticisms levelled against British Intelligence unjustified, but it is also important never to forget that this whole matter can be properly understood only if due attention is paid to the historical context of this period.

Why was it that such a major Communist penetration took place after 1939? Why, apparently, did so much (but not all) of it remain undetected for so long? In short, why did MI5 not catch the British moles? Did it not know of their existence? Or did it let them get away? These, then, are the secrets of the service which we now must explore.

First of all, let us turn to two of the problems implicit in this study: how much was known about Russia and Communism before the outbreak of war, and were the moles 'traitors' or simply misguided agents of Russia as well as servants of the Crown?

The problem of knowledge

What people knew is a factor that repeatedly enters into this study. For it is the duty of an intelligence service to be knowing, and whether it is regarded as good or bad depends in large measure on how much it knows. Similarly, our attitude towards the activities of the moles is conditioned by an assessment of the state of their knowledge. Ironically, the decisive issue here is how much both British Intelligence and Stalin's English agents really knew about the aims and interests of Russia from 1939 to 1951.

The point is straightforward. If it can be shown that the moles were ignorant of the true nature of Stalinism and the role that Soviet-inspired Communism was set to play in post-war Europe, then it becomes difficult to condemn Stalin's Englishmen and women as evil and sinister subversives. Indeed, subversion itself becomes a questionable term, since it implies the surreptitious undermining of British public life by people who might justify their actions by claiming they were acting wholly in accord with democratic principles, unaware they were undermining anything. Equally, it would not be easy to convict them of treason if they could prove they had not known that Stalin and the Crown were incompatible masters and that, in serving the former, they could not, at the same time, have been serving the latter. This is something the moles themselves understood, for did not Anthony Blunt argue that during his period of service for Stalin he was wholeheartedly committed to Britain's cause?

In the same way, if it can be demonstrated that MI5 could not possibly have known of the existence of British moles at the time when they were able to penetrate the high offices of the British State, then its apparent incompetence in tracking them down is a charge which can barely be sustained.

It is, therefore, important to try to establish the state of knowledge that existed in 1939 and 1940 about the aims and strategies of Communist subversion. We shall see that there is no truth in the moles' assertion that they could not have known then what Stalinism really consisted of. If the moles chose none the less to ignore or discount the realities of Stalin's politics, their historical responsibility for helping him is not thereby diminished, even if their own consciences were salved (although it seems to me that wilful ignorance is not a very satisfactory defence for serving a totalitarian dictator, whether Communist or Nazi).

The full extent of MI5's knowledge of these matters is dealt with later (see p. 336). Here, however, it may be pointed out that MI5 was fully aware that Communist moles might exist within the wider government of Britain and, were it to plead that it chose to ignore this knowledge, this would of course be no defence at all.

Anthony Blunt has, perhaps, provided us with the most representative account of what the moles wished us to believe about their knowledge of Soviet Russia and its aims in the 1930s and 1940s.[15] We should begin by considering those views in detail and then contrast them with other left-of-centre ones; for in wishing to decide whether the moles were befuddled, if humane, idealists, or a group of dedicated and highly organised subversives, it is important to take on board the testimony of those on the left who chose to oppose Stalinism.

Blunt appeared to fit easily into the well-established thought patterns of left-wing intellectuals in Britain in the 1930s. Many of them held that democracy was threatened by only one enemy and that was Fascism. Most university clubs in Oxford and Cambridge which had a political concern were well-stocked with Communists and Fellow-Travellers, and all shared the view that it was necessary to prepare for the coming struggle with Hitler. Blunt said:

> I became a Communist and more particularly a Marxist in 1935–36. I had a sabbatical leave from Cambridge in 1933–34 and when I came back in October 1934 I found that all my friends and almost all the intelligent and bright young undergraduates who had come to Cambridge had suddenly become Marxists under the impact of Hitler coming to power and that there was this very powerful group of Communist intellectuals in Cambridge of which Guy Burgess was one, James Klugman another, John Cornford another [still].
>
> I became convinced that the Marxist interpretation of history was right and that therefore this was where the logical break took place and that one ought to be a Communist at that moment. And when Guy put it to me that the best way to help anti-Fascism was to help in his work for the Russians, I agreed.
>
> I did go for a holiday to Russia, not with Guy, in 1935 or 1936. It was one of the ordinary Intourist visits. I went with a group of enthusiastic young left-wingers, mainly Communists. I cannot [put a precise date on when Burgess enrolled me], it was late 1935, early 1936.[16]

If Blunt ever felt the slightest guilt about working for the Russians (his interview suggests he did not), life became much easier once Russia entered the war on the side of Britain in 1941. Unlike some others, Blunt had not abandoned Communism when Ribbentrop, Hitler's Foreign Minister, flew to Moscow in 1939 to agree to carve up Poland with Stalin. Blunt said he believed the Non-Aggression Pact with the Nazis had been nothing more than a 'tactical necessity to gain time'. What he would have said about this tactical necessity if Hitler had been able to defeat Britain in 1940, as he almost did, is of course unknown. It is a point to which we shall return.

Blunt was then asked when he had changed his mind about Communism. He replied:

> It was a gradual process, and I find it very difficult to analyse. It is, after all, more than 30 years ago. But it was the information that came out after the war. During the war one was thinking of the Russians as Allies but then the information about the camps

... By 1951 I was clear. In 1937 I thought that Russia was following the true principles of Marxism. By 1951, I realised this was quite false. The British Way of Life and British constitutionalism, whatever it is, are best.[17]

As we can see, it was knowledge which converted Blunt to Communism, and it was further knowledge which turned him away from it.

Mrs Jennifer Hart has offered a very similar testimony.[18] She has stated quite clearly and categorically that from 1935 until 1938 or 1939 she was a Communist mole, although she emphasised that she had never been activated. For her, the 'great enemy was Fascism'. She did not know much about the Communist Party in 1935 but a fellow-undergraduate 'persuaded' her to attend a summer camp organised by an unemployed workers' group.

Mrs Hart became a 'secret' member of the Communist Party; she was never given a membership card and was told not to associate with known Communists. She was then ordered to infiltrate the Civil Service (in her case, the Home Office was the target). According to Michael Straight (another 'secret' Communist), she was one of about fifty moles laid down at this time.

The significance of her 'secret' membership should not be ignored, not least because it plays a critical part in any assessment of MI5's counter-subversive efforts (or the lack of them). A 'secret' Communist was very hard to detect; the Soviet controllers of the British Communist élite appeared to know that by injecting such members into the high offices of the British State, their presence would be virtually secure. 'Open' Communists, on the other hand, whose names were recorded in the King Street headquarters of the CPGB, could be identified with comparative ease (not least because MI5 appears to have had copies of the names on file. For the implication of this, particularly in respect of vetting, see p. 338).

In due course, Mrs Hart was passed on to a Russian controller:

At first it was exciting then it palled ... it was sinister. The Russian seemed creepy ... he tried to reassure me about the trials in Russia but I was worried that the Party did not like differences of view.[19]

Mrs Hart was worried about the excesses of Stalinism, particularly the show trials of the mid-1930s, but unlike Blunt, she lost faith in Communism before the outbreak of war.

Both of them, by their own admission, accepted that for a specified period they had served 'the Party' and Stalin, and they were both prepared to serve him even before 1941 when the interests of Russia and the interests of Britain were patently not the same. The view that Stalin's pact with Hitler was merely a tactical necessity did not just imply that the destruction of Poland was accepted by Blunt and his fellow-moles, but that if the result of that pact had been that Hitler could have destroyed Britain in 1940, this too would probably have been perfectly acceptable to them.

We should, of course, not assume that all left-of-centre intellectuals took this line. George Orwell, for example, saw from the Spanish Civil War that the Soviet Union was not the revolutionary force he had hoped it would be. By September 1937 Orwell could write:

All the Popular Front stuff [a coalition of Communists and Social Democrats to defeat Fascism] that is now being pushed by the Communist press and the Party, Gollancz and his paid hacks etc. only boils down to saying that they are in favour of British Fascism ... The Popular Front baloney boils down to this: when war comes, the Communists, Labourites etc. instead of working to stop the war and overthrow the Conservative Government will be on the side of Government ... the grotesque feature of the Communists [in Spain] is that they stood furthest to the Right and were even more anxious than the liberals to stamp out revolutionary ideas ...[20]

Later on in 1938 Orwell expressed his disgust at the trials. He wrote:

The OGPU are everywhere, everyone lives in constant fear of denunciation, freedom of speech and of the press are obliterated to an extent we can hardly imagine. There are periodical waves of terror, sometimes the liquidation of Kulaks and New Economic Policy men, sometimes some monstrous state trial at which people who have been in prison for months are dragged forth to make incredible confessions ...[21]

The issue is, of course, not whether Orwell was right to want revolution or not, but that Orwell was able to see that the reality of Soviet Communism was quite different from the image the Communists themselves tried to purvey.

For the fact was that there was considerable evidence available at

the time to suggest that the Soviet Union was not the model state
that it appeared to be. One widely read book making this very point
was written by the trade union leader, Lord Citrine.[22]

Citrine identified armed political police in Russia. While arguing
that it was less evil than Nazi Germany or Fascist Italy, he pointed
out that Russia was a dictatorship (indeed, that this was something
of which Communists were inordinately proud). Citrine noted that
when he had tried to intercede for fairness in Zinoviev's trial, he had
been 'met with a torrent of abuse and stigmatised as an ally of the
Gestapo'. This merely confirmed his condemnation of the 'orgy
of arrests and denunciations, the many thousands imprisoned ...
denounced as venomous reptiles, Trotskyist wreckers or Gestapo
agents'.[23] He said that he knew that evidence used against Stalin's
enemies was often totally fictitious and that even someone relying
on the Soviet press would become suspicious on reading, for example,
that up to July 1937, 167 people had been executed for 'wrecking,
spying and sabotage'; and that from July until September 1937, 501
others had been executed for 'wrecking, spying, Trotskyism, infecting
grain with insect pests and poisoning sausages'.

Lord Citrine's search for truth in Russia was not a rabid attack
on Communism, even if it suggested that Stalinism was a perversion
of Socialist ideals; Citrine himself was a respected trade unionist and
Labour leader and hardly a Capitalist stooge. If he could perceive
several essential truths about Stalinism, proving that it was incompatible with any sort of democratic practice and that it was maintained, in part at any rate, by the rule of terror, it is very hard to see
why Blunt and his colleagues were blind to these facts.

If, however, it is held to be unfair to expect a down-to-earth
trade unionist such as Citrine to be convincing to young Oxbridge
intellectuals, it is worth recalling that others of an altogether different
cast, to whom intellectuals might have listened with greater ease,
were saying very similar things. In 1937 the celebrated writer (and
homosexual) André Gide published his own account of Stalinism.[24]
He must have been a member of the reference group of men such as
Blunt and Burgess, and it is hard to imagine that they did not read
his book.

Gide, not an anti-Russian bigot by any means, was forced to
declare that his earlier enthusiasm for Russia was evaporating:

Was I mistaken? ... Is it I who have changed or the Soviet Union?
And by Soviet Union I mean the man at its head ... In the USSR

everyone knows beforehand once and for all, that on any and every subject there can only be one opinion ... the smallest protest is liable to the severest penalties ... And I doubt whether in any country in the world, even Hitler's Germany, thought is less free, more bowed down and more terrorised.[25]

There were of course many other accounts of what was happening in Russia. *The Times*, for example, carried fairly full reports of the show trials. But the moles, of course, would have dismissed such tales as anti-Communist propaganda. That is why the testimonies of men such as Lord Citrine are so important: they could not be ruled out of order on ideological grounds.

What does all this imply? The answer seems simple enough: whatever else the moles may have believed they were doing by working for Stalin, they cannot for one minute have thought that they were advancing the cause of British liberal democracy. Furthermore, by accepting even one of Stalin's tactical necessities, they signified their complete commitment to his cause. In short, they were Communists. It might be said that everyone now knows this, and that it does not have to be emphasised, but this is not the point as far as our present study is concerned. For both during the Second World War and subsequently, the moles tried to conceal from others what their Communism actually entailed. They pleaded ignorance of the excesses of Soviet totalitarianism; yet that they were in a position to know about at least some of them cannot be seriously doubted. As we have seen, evidence of the real nature of Stalin's regime, which by 1939 simply could not be dismissed as 'capitalist propaganda', was readily available to the general reading public, and it may be supposed that the moles were privy, as Party members, to even more information than the man or woman in the street.

To suggest, as Blunt did, that information about 'the camps' filtering out after 1945 was sufficient to turn him from Communism, but that the information about the organised outrages of the 1930s did not do so, is to stretch credibility to ridiculous limits. 'Ignorance' is thus a plea which cannot be sustained (in any case, it is a very curious excuse to emanate from the lips of people so utterly convinced of their own intellectual brilliance).

By the same token, Blunt's claim that before 1945 he thought of the Russians as 'allies' is equally unconvincing. The fact was that the relationship between the moles and Russia was rather more than just one of alliance (from which one might infer that serving Stalin was consistent with serving the Crown). For the moles were Communists, by definition opposed to the British liberal system, seeking ultimately to destroy it. As Blunt himself said, it was only after 1951 that he came to realise that 'the British Way of Life and British constitutionalism' were 'best'. Before that time, then, he and his colleagues may have shared with British liberals the aim of defeating Hitler (although this was true only after the German attack on the Soviet Union in June 1941) but that was all. In domestic terms, their political aims were quite incompatible with those of their non-Communist colleagues; indeed, as we shall see, this incompatibility was the very reason why moles were utilised in the first place and, more than once, was the cause of deep and sometimes deadly conflict. Those who seek to minimise the moles' activities by suggesting that there was nothing wrong with their being Communists, indeed that they may well have been lofty and brilliant idealists, must explain why, if this is so, the moles went to such lengths to keep their activities secret. The fact that a liberal system allows its opponents considerable freedom to oppose that system should not cause one to forget that such opposition had, as its end, the destruction of liberalism.

We are not concerned here with the morality of the moles' actions but with their political objectives and the impact that they had. It does not therefore seem unfair to brand them as true subversives, even fanatics, intent on fighting for their chosen cause. From a liberal standpoint, then, they were dangerous agents of a regime which sought to undermine British policy in its own Communist interest and destroy traditional British political values and institutions. Their orders were clear: where British policy was seen to work in favour of Communist ends, it was to be sustained; where it ran counter to them, it was, if at all possible, to be subverted.

2

The Historical Context of Subversion

British foreign policy towards the Soviet Union

Why is an examination of British foreign policy towards the USSR crucial for any study of British Intelligence and Communist subversion? The answer to this question is twofold. On the one hand, British foreign policy circumscribed the precise conditions which governed the gathering of secret information about the Soviet Union by British Intelligence. On the other, however, British foreign policy was itself the chief client of British Intelligence, since both MI6 and MI5 were charged with the provision of secret material which could influence British policy.

Thus British foreign policy did not merely call the tune to be played by British Intelligence, but the nature and frequency of the call itself was in part the outcome of secret intelligence. This complex interrelationship of input and output is a factor to which we shall often return.

From 1941 until 1945 it was British public policy to offer close friendship to Russia, a friendship made concrete in 1942 by the Anglo-Soviet Alliance which, it was hoped, would last for at least twenty years (see p. 41). The most important result of this alliance was that it enabled Britain, the Soviet Union and then the United States to overthrow the Third Reich, Fascist Italy and Japan – the most hideous political tyrannies that the world had so far seen. By June 1945, then, the alliance may be said to have fulfilled its major task.

Yet today we know that it was during this very period that the Soviet Union proved most successful in installing its moles and agents in Britain's high places. Its purpose was to establish an intelligence network which would not only supply Russia with most of the United Kingdom's secrets, but also, by virtue of the position the moles were able to take up, play some part in the formulation of British policy itself. Furthermore, British Intelligence appears to have failed either to alert British policy-makers that this process was under way or to take effective measures to counter this subversion by the Soviets.

Like everyone else in Britain, SOE, MI6 and MI5 were obliged to abide by Government policy, and in their dealings with Russia that policy was foreign policy. After 1940, and most certainly after 1941 and Hitler's attack on Russia, the keynote of this policy was co-operation. There were, perhaps surprisingly, very few exceptions to this rule, of which the most important was the Anglo-American decision not to pass on any information about the development of the atom bomb to either the Soviet Union or to France, a decision formally written into the 1943 Quebec Treaty on nuclear develop-ment. MI5, it should be noted, was thus given a very special role to play, since it was charged with the security of the nuclear secret (this is examined in detail later; see p. 348).

Intelligence was not concerned, however, solely with keeping Bri-tain's secrets. Britain's policy-makers also required it to discover the secrets of the other side. For all the belligerents of the Second World War possessed secrets; some so covert that they truly were 'most secret' secrets. Thus, while Britain and America, in addition to their pioneering work on the atom bomb, maintained the greatest secrecy over Britain's ability to crack the ciphers of German military wireless traffic, Nazi Germany put into effect the 'final solution of the Jewish problem in Europe'. This was the Nazis' code word for the physical extermination of Europe's Jews, a plan which was so secret that Hitler appears never even to have given a written order for it.

Finally, as we shall investigate, Stalin, too, had his 'secret' secrets. Rather ironically, one of his chief ones was his discovery, virtually from the moment that the USA and Britain took the decision in 1941, that they were developing nuclear weapons and were excluding him from the process. In addition, the Russians produced, during the war itself, what may be called a secret blueprint for the political domination of as much of the continent of Europe as they could lay their hands on. It must be said at once that there are those who dispute that Stalin had such a plan at all or, at any rate, that he had such a plan before 1945. It is, however, my argument that Stalin and his closest advisers did have a blueprint of this nature (the evidence for and against this assertion is discussed in detail later; see p. 181).

Indeed, it was the realisation after 1945 by Britain and America that Stalin had possessed a secret blueprint for Europe, by which time it was too late to do anything about it, that engendered many of the deep doubts about him which produced the Cold War. For the deception that the Soviet Union had wrought totally contradicted the treaty obligations concerning Europe into which it had freely entered during the war. This realisation was to be as much of a turning point in contemporary history as the defeat of Hitler himself.

Furthermore, the Cold War did not merely increase the chances of a nuclear holocaust, but also brought about a dramatic change in the relationship between Britain and Russia. One immediate effect of this change was that the West suffered an attack of amnesia; because Britain and America now distrusted the Russians, they both appeared to forget that they had ever been Russia's close allies. Yet close allies they certainly had been; so close, in fact, that Communist subversion could flourish apparently unnoticed: the true 'climate of treason' (to use Andrew Boyle's phrase) did not occur in Cambridge in the 1930s but in Whitehall in the 1940s, if by 'climate of treason' we mean the creation of conditions favourable to the moles' penetration of British institutions rather than any conscious act of treachery on the part of those who legitimately sought to co-operate with the Soviet Union.

We have thus a situation where, during the war itself, Britain and America believed that they were acting in close concert with Russia, concealing only what they considered their most vital secrets. Russia, on the other hand, not only knew that the West genuinely wanted to work together with it (save in the aforementioned areas), but also that the West had been successfully deceived about the true nature of its post-war plans for Europe. Russia also knew that the West was patently unaware that it possessed a secret network of moles and agents whose purpose was both to pass information to the Kremlin about these matters and, wherever possible, to promote Soviet interests from within the West itself.

One excuse that has been made on the Soviets' behalf has been that the West had never truly wished to co-operate with Russia. The Cold War, it is alleged, did not begin in 1945 but had been under way ever since 1917. Thus, it has been argued, the Soviet Union was justified in hiding its aims from Britain and America.[1] This excuse is hardly satisfactory, not least because Stalin broke many of his treaty obligations, whereas the West honoured them faithfully. Excluding Russia from the nuclear secret – not an easy decision – did not mean the West was not genuine in wanting to work together with Russia in almost every other sphere. Another apology for Soviet policy after 1945 rests on the plea that Russia's exclusion from the atomic project entitled it not to tell the West about its plans for the continent of Europe. What is more, or so the argument goes, realising that the West might have a new and very powerful strategic weapon actually forced the Russians to dominate as much of Europe as they could in order to defend themselves against such a weapon. The British and the Americans, it may have been surmised, might readily drop the bomb on the USSR, but if the Red Army were dispersed throughout central and eastern Europe, Soviet forces would be safe, since the West could hardly destroy the inhabitants of those areas.

This strategic argument undoubtedly has something to commend it. Its critical point, however, lies in its dating. If we argue that Stalin and his chief advisers developed this blueprint only after 1945 and the destruction of Hiroshima and Nagasaki, their proposed domination of Europe could be seen as being chiefly defensive. If, on the other hand, we prefer to argue that their blueprint was developed before, say, 1941, then it was chiefly offensive, since they could not have known at this time that the West would possess the nuclear secret. Those who would categorise this blueprint as predating 1945 but postdating 1941 could, of course, still hold that it was essentially defensive, since after 1941 Klaus Fuchs and Alan Nunn May had already started to tell the Russians about nuclear weapons.

The evidence, however, suggests that all these theories are somewhat over-elaborate (although until the Kremlin opens its archives we shall not know for certain). There was, it appears, no direct correlation between Stalin's blueprint for Europe, originally conceived almost certainly before 1941, and the atom bomb project. Equally, we can be sure that the development of the atom bomb had nothing to do with Western fears about Stalin's plans, because the West never discovered their existence (see pp. 244 ff.).

British foreign policy towards the Soviet Union from 1940 until 1945 immediately presents us with three vital implications for the study of British Intelligence and Communist subversion. The first is that if high policy ordained co-operation with the Soviet Union, this was bound to affect the activities of the intelligence community. Second, since this high policy endured unchanged until the end of the war, and since it can be shown that the British authorities were genuinely ignorant both about the 'climate of treason' within Britain and about Stalin's secret blueprint for Europe, it must follow that British Intelligence appears, on the face of it, not to have been terribly competent at this time.

Third, however, since Communist penetration was so widespread (we have already noted that during 1950 forty-three civil servants were suspended from their duties on suspicion of Communist activities), it must in theory be possible that British high policy may itself have been subverted, either directly due to the activities of moles and agents inside the Foreign Office itself, or indirectly thanks to the penetration and subversion of British Intelligence.

Having posed these questions, we must proceed to answer them carefully. They are obviously highly complex and, given the suspicions and doubts of the past thirty odd years, there will be many who will assume the very worst straight away. 'Ah yes,' they will say, 'the whole of British foreign policy towards Russia was subverted.' They might even assume that everyone from Roger Hollis in MI5 to Winston Churchill in Downing Street was a Soviet agent.

Assertions like these are, of course, completely ridiculous. Undoubtedly, like all the other high offices of State, the British Foreign Office was a natural target for Communist subversion (because the Russians wanted both to know about Britain's foreign policy secrets and to try to influence policy itself, if they could). Having said this, however, it must immediately be added that there is no evidence of any widespread subversion within the Foreign Office.

It is important to stress this point, not merely to prevent this issue from being exaggerated out of all proportion, but also to make it clear that the limits of British foreign policy towards Russia were defined by policy decisions taken at the very highest level. They were, furthermore, made for an excellent and vital reason, namely the defeat of Hitler, and were not at this high level in any way the outcome of subverted inputs. Where Foreign Office and other moles may have had some effect was in the 'second division' of issues, at the fringes of policy. While these fringes were undoubtedly of great importance to those affected by them, they were of lesser significance to a Britain fighting to avoid the Nazi jackboot. Finally most of the time the moles were knocking at doors which were already open; open because of the implications of high policy and not because of subversion itself.

As the record indicates, high policy was made by those at the top of British political life (the Prime Minister, the Foreign Secretary, the leading officials in the Foreign Office) and not by the moles either in the Foreign Office or in British Intelligence.

Having said this, however, there is one last point to note. Although one of the keynotes of this policy was co-operation with the USSR, it was to a certain extent undermined by another keynote – ignorance, and a deep lack of knowledge about Russia. British policy-makers were indeed remarkably ignorant about Russian aims and ambitions during the Second World War. The most important reason for this, it should be stressed, had nothing to do with subversion, even though moles may have done their best to ensure that this ignorance endured for as long as possible.

Did Yalta really validate the carve-up of Europe?

In our examination of British foreign policy we must first of all seek to substantiate the charge that it was, in many respects, an ignorant policy. We must then proceed to explain the causes for that ignorance. This is, of course, a weighty matter since it touches, in part, on the vexed issue of the origins of the Cold War.

There are those who argue that the Cold War between Russia and the West was already under way by 1944, since it was the outcome of Stalin's take-over of central and eastern Europe, which was itself the inevitable consequence of the westward drive of the Red Army, and part of the Grand Strategy to destroy Hitler's Germany. Thus, the argument goes, the West knew this take-over would happen but was powerless to prevent it and had to accept it, while altering its perception of its Soviet ally. Others, however, prefer to suggest that the Cold War really began well after 1945, when the empirical evidence of Stalinist domination was fully apparent. Before then, even during 1945 itself, the West simply did not realise Stalin had any such plans.

The issue is important, because if we believe that Britain and America knew what Stalin would do with that part of Europe which was liberated by the Red Army, then their policy during the war, particularly during its final two years, becomes either one of base appeasement or wholly irrational (for a discussion of the appeasement theory, see p. 44). If, on the other hand, the West genuinely did not know about these plans, their policy becomes infinitely more intelligible, and honourable too.

The Yalta Conference of February 1945 has often been seen as a symbol of Roosevelt's and Churchill's inability to counter the westward expansion of Stalinist Communism, in short, as a disgraceful 'sell-out' of central and eastern Europe. By agreeing to border revisions in respect of Poland and Germany, and to conditions on a provisional Government for Poland which, it is alleged, they knew Stalin would not keep, the two Western leaders effectively set the seal on the Russian domination of that unhappy nation.[2]

Yet there is no real evidence to suggest that Churchill, Roosevelt, or their officials knew that Stalin was determined to break his word on the political independence of the peoples he liberated. Yalta did not, therefore, legitimise Stalin's policies and, whatever else it was that led to the Yalta agreement, it was not Western consent to 'sell out' to Stalin.

Indeed, recent comments by two senior British diplomats, Lord Gladwyn and Sir Frank Roberts (both of whom were at Yalta) confirm this. The former has argued that it was not the conference at Yalta which divided Europe, but the presence in central and eastern Europe of Soviet armies of occupation which, after 1945, imposed Communist regimes on unwilling populations.[3] Elsewhere, Lord Gladwyn has gone into greater detail about what Yalta stood for:

The suggestion that Europe was carved up at Yalta is an illusion. It wasn't carved up at Yalta, it was carved up by the advance of the Soviet armies into eastern Europe ... At Yalta efforts were made to make the situation less intolerable, as far as we could, for the Poles and other nationalities. We didn't succeed but I don't think you can criticise Yalta for having carved Europe up ...[4]

If Lord Gladwyn's interpretation is correct, it must follow that since Europe was divided after Yalta (but not because of it), then the British and Americans, both at Yalta and before, were genuinely ignorant about Stalin's intentions. Indeed, they clearly continued to be deluded during the conference itself, since Gladwyn says the West hoped to ameliorate the position for the Poles and others, something which was certainly no longer possible at this time. From the Russian viewpoint, the die had already been cast.

It is thus clearly not the case, as is often claimed, that everyone knew, well before the war had ended, that Stalin would ultimately be in a position from which to control politically half of Europe; that an agreement that he should do this was in some way the necessary price which the West had to pay for the defeat of the Third Reich. Europe may indeed have been effectively divided on VE Day in May 1945, but it would be quite wrong to believe British and

American policy-makers assumed this beforehand, whatever private doubts they may have had at various stages of the war.

Those suggesting that the West acquiesced in a 'sell-out' must therefore believe the Western leaders were involved in a deliberate attempt to distort the historical record. Churchill, Roosevelt and Stalin must, according to such a theory, have come to some conspiratorial agreement still kept secret today. Yet to argue this flies in the face of all the evidence; indeed, it is worth recalling that Sir Frank Roberts has stated very firmly indeed that there were no secret deals about the division of Europe at Yalta or elsewhere.[5] He would have known if there had been.

In short, a conspiracy is not a satisfactory explanation for what happened at Yalta. In reality, it was the outcome of very different factors: neither the Americans nor the British possessed any precise understanding of what Stalin wanted in Europe in the aftermath of the war. Churchill and Eden in particular were certain that what chiefly motivated Stalin was the redrawing of borders: Russia was to achieve a net gain of territory, Poland was to lose in the east and gain in the west at Germany's expense. This might be unfortunate for the Poles (and the German expellees) but it was the necessary outcome of the war against Hitler.

Churchill and Eden were, however, mistaken; they seriously underestimated Stalin's desire for political control in Europe in 1945. He was far less concerned with the redrawing of borders than with the regimes to lie within those borders. The position of frontier-posts mattered far less to him than the establishment of Russian-dominated Communist Governments.

It may therefore be said that if Yalta is a symbol of anything it is of Western ignorance. The Yalta Conference was motivated, on the one hand, by a perfectly honourable determination on the part of Roosevelt and Churchill to reach an accommodation with Soviet Russia but, on the other, by their almost complete lack of effective intelligence about the Soviet Union which would show that this was an impossible dream.

So why were Western policy-makers so ignorant? Are we dealing here with a massive failure on the part of British Intelligence, since it was their job to unearth secret information about Russia and Communism? Some have indeed alleged the British intelligence community was totally incompetent; others have made the far graver charge of treachery. British Intelligence, they claim, did not tell the truth about Russia and Communism because it had itself been successfully subverted by the Communists. Thus, it is alleged, the penetration of British institutions and the extent of Communist subversion made Britain virtually defenceless against this concerted Soviet onslaught. But an altogether different conclusion is also possible: that Britain's policy-makers were ignorant about Soviet aims chiefly because that ignorance was in some way connected with Russia's status as Britain's ally.

There is thus a 'missing dimension' in British foreign policy both in 1945 and in the years before it. The motives of the British leadership of Churchill and Eden can hardly be faulted in terms of high policy. Yet we are still entitled to ask whether British Intelligence ever alerted the Government to the fact that it was one thing to hope the Soviets would play the game, but quite another to be certain that they would do so. Did it warn Churchill? If so, why did he fail to act? If it did not alert him, should it not be severely censured for failing to discover Stalin's most secret secrets?

If the British policy-makers had known more about Russia's aims, they might have pursued a different policy towards Stalin, and the Soviet domination of half of Europe might conceivably have been prevented or arrested. But Churchill and Eden needed to know about Stalin's secret plans *before* they had been executed, and the people whose job it was to know about secrets were, in the first instance, not Cabinet ministers or even Foreign Office officials. This task lay squarely with British Intelligence.

What has to be considered is not only whether British policy was based on a proper intelligence assessment of Stalin's true aims and whether that policy permitted British Intelligence to do its job properly, but also the extent to which the attempted subversion of British Intelligence may have contributed to the problems facing the policy-makers.

This, then, is the link which connects the laying-down of British policy in 10 Downing Street and Westminster with the officials of the Foreign Office and those of British Security; the link, ultimately, that binds the most prominent figure in Government, Winston Churchill, with one of the most obscure, Roger Hollis of MI5.

To suggest that the British policy-makers had no firm idea of Stalin's war aims does not mean that they were never suspicious of Stalin: they were. What it does mean, however, is that those suspicions were vague, often vague in the extreme, and that they certainly would not have served as the basis for any effective counter-strategy. An example of what I mean may suffice as an introduction to the problem. Two incidents are recounted by Professor Foot about Sir Fitzroy Maclean, who had expressed fears about Soviet aims in the Balkans after the war:

Mr Churchill said that as long as the whole of Western civilisation was threatened by the Nazi menace, we could not afford to let our attention be diverted from the immediate issue by considerations of long-term policy. We were as loyal to our Soviet allies as we hoped they were to us. My task was simply to help find out who was killing the most Germans ... politics must be a secondary consideration ... [6]

Foot reports that they met again in December 1943 and Maclean once again raised this issue with the British Premier:

'Do you', he asked, 'intend to make Yugoslavia your home after the war?' 'No Sir,' I replied. 'Neither do I,' he said. 'And that being so, the less you and I worry about the form of government they set up, the better. That is for them to decide. What interests us is, which of them is doing more harm to the Germans.'[7]

This is a very clear statement of Churchill's attitude towards this question, as it appeared to a serving British intelligence officer. At first sight, it seems plain enough (there was certainly no doubt as to who called the shots). On deeper reflection, there are reasons to be puzzled by Churchill's reported remarks. For one thing, we might ask why 'long-term policy' was considered a 'diversion'. Was this not something which a British Prime Minister was meant to produce?

For another, Churchill said that 'we were as loyal to our Soviet allies as we hoped they were to us'. What exactly did he mean by that? Was it enough for the British Premier to base his policy on 'hoping' the Russians were being loyal? Or was Churchill in reality suggesting the precise reverse, that both sides were deceiving each other?

Finally, Churchill said that it would be the Yugoslav people who would ultimately decide their own political fate. This implied that he thought the Red Army could be relied upon to keep out of the internal politics of the nations of Europe that it liberated. What caused him to believe this?

These are matters to which we must now turn. First we shall consider the nature of British foreign policy itself.

British policy towards the Soviet Union before 22 June 1941

Let us now seek to establish the accuracy of two key assertions. First, that the British Government was totally genuine in wanting to work closely together with Stalin in order to destroy Nazism and, second, that British policy towards Russia was grounded in a deep and disturbing ignorance about Stalin's post-war aims. It must be said at once that the wish to co-operate with Stalin emerged from a high policy requirement that Hitler be defeated; intelligence about the Soviet Union, and hence potentially subverted intelligence, appears to have had no impact on the making of this basic decision.

Yet British policy-makers were none the less often so ignorant about Russian aims that it is certainly not implausible that, had they known more about Stalin's plans for Europe, specific alterations to the fringes of high policy might have been made. Within this narrow context, then, ignorance, faulty intelligence and indeed possible subversion become factors which cannot be ruled out. Equally they should in no wise be exaggerated.

Let us first of all consider the actual policy itself. Since so much of what we are examining is contentious, it is vital to look at the documentary evidence presented by the records of the Foreign Office.[8] This evidence strongly supports the twin assertions of co-operation and ignorance. Britain was ready to give Russia a great deal in return for a joint war against Hitler; British institutions were ordered to work very closely with their Soviet counterparts. At the same time, however, despite the fact that some policy-makers expressed doubts about Russian reliability, these doubts were always overridden at the highest levels in order that co-operation should on no account be jeopardised.

The dominating factor behind Anglo-Soviet relations after the outbreak of war in September 1939 was simple. It was that without the entry of the Soviet Union into the war on the side of the Western liberal democracies, Adolf Hitler would surely win it. The British therefore decided at an early stage that it had to be a prime policy aim to bring Russia into the war.

This was, of course, no mean feat, since Russia was the loyal ally of Nazi Germany. As has often been demonstrated, Stalin took the pact between Russia and Germany very seriously indeed and was determined not to deviate from its provisions. This was in part because he feared his fellow-dictator, Adolf Hitler, and in part because the peace with the Third Reich had permitted him to extend Soviet hegemony over half of Poland and all of the Baltic States, and even to attack Finland.[9]

Right up until the German attack on Russia during the night of 21–2 June 1941 (Operation Barbarossa), Stalin continued to believe that Hitler intended to keep his side of the bargain. British attempts to convince him that he was quite wrong were apparently dismissed as 'capitalist provocation' and the Soviet dictator seems to have been obsessed with the fear that the Western democracies wished nothing more fervently than to see the two totalitarian regimes batter each other to death.

The first British move to court Stalin was a remarkably bold one. On 12 June 1940 Sir Stafford Cripps was sent to Moscow as British Ambassador.[10] Cripps was well-known as a pro-Russian; indeed, he had been thrown out of the Labour Party in June 1939 because he was one of those who believed that the British Communist Party should be allowed to merge with Labour. Cripps was not a success as Ambassador and was mistrusted by almost everyone – the Cabinet, the Foreign Office and the Russians as well, and he returned home on 14 June 1942.

What proved to be perhaps the second major initiative came about in October 1940 when Britain secretly offered to recognise the Russian annexation of the Baltic States. This was intended as an act of good will towards the Soviet Union which had illegally occupied them in accordance with the Hitler–Stalin Non-Aggression Pact of August 1939. (Somewhat paradoxically, before Churchill became Prime Minister plans had been hatched for a commando operation to be undertaken in the Baltic States in order to encourage their populations to rise up against the Soviets (see p. 279). But the plan was now forgotten.)

The final initiative taken by the British in an effort to win Stalin's co-operation has been described by Barton Whaley.[11] It was decided at the highest level to pass to the Soviet Union the various intelligence intercepts that the British had gleaned thanks to the Ultra (inter-cepted German military wireless traffic; see p. 165), which showed beyond any doubt whatsoever that Hitler intended to attack the Soviet Union, although the source was not to be disclosed in case the Russians told the Nazis that the British had broken their military codes. Yet Stalin still refused to be drawn.

The British persisted in their attempts to court the Russians. Scarcely two weeks before the unleashing of Operation Barbarossa, on 10 June 1941, the British Government officially told M. Maisky, the Soviet Ambassador, that if war broke out between Russia and Germany 'we would do all we could, for example, by air action in the West, to draw off the German air forces'. Maisky replied that:

> Russia still regards her relations with Germany as governed by the non-aggression pact of 1939 and feels no anxiety about the German concentration of troops.[12]

Thus the only real chance of success in concluding a deal with the Kremlin came after the Nazi onslaught on Russia. As Churchill has written:

> Hitler's invasion of Russia altered the values and the relationships of the war ... Up to the moment when the Soviet Government was set upon by Hitler, they seemed to care for no one but themselves ... the British Communists who had hitherto done their worst, which was not much, in our factories, and denounced 'the capitalist and imperialist war' turned again overnight and began to scrawl the slogan 'second front now' upon the walls and hoardings ...[13]

Anthony Eden recalled their excitement at the news of Hitler's attack on 21 June:

> The next morning at half past seven, the Prime Minister's valet Sawyers came into my bedroom and said, 'the PM's compliments and the German armies have invaded Russia.' Thereupon he presented me with a large cigar on a silver salver. I put on my dressing gown and went to the Prime Minister's bedroom. We savoured the relief, but not for me the cigar, and discussed what was immediately to be done. Churchill said he would speak to the nation that night and tell that we intended to treat the Russians as partners in the struggle against Hitler ...[14]

It was one thing for Churchill to state that the Russians were now Britain's ally. It was quite another to get the British people and institutions (who associated Churchill and the Conservative Party with hostility towards Russia) to accept this momentous change which would decisively alter public perceptions of British foreign policy. After all, Churchill's own earlier position was widely known. In January 1940, for example, he had spoken on the BBC about Russia in the context of the Russo-Finnish War. His words are worth considering again, because they provide such a vivid contrast with what he said in the broadcast he decided to make on 22 June 1941. This is what Churchill stated about Russia in 1940:

> Only Finland, superb nay sublime in the jaws of peril, Finland shows what free men can do. The service rendered by Finland to mankind is magnificent. They have exposed for all the world to see the military incapacity of the Red Army and of the Red Air Force. Many illusions about Soviet Russia have been dispelled in these few fierce weeks of fighting ... Everyone can see how Communism rots the soul of a nation. If at any time Britain and France were to make a shameful peace, nothing would remain for the smaller states of Europe ... but to be divided between the opposite though similar barbarisms of Nazidom and Bolshevism.[15]

Let us now consider what Churchill said about the 'dull brutish force of overwhelming numbers' and about Communism, which he had insisted 'rots the soul' and was the 'opposite though similar barbarism' to Nazidom, on the evening of 22 June 1941. His speech has, of course, often been quoted. But it is vital to mull over it with care, not least because it was, without doubt, one of the most impressive of all his wartime speeches. It was apparently made on Churchill's own initiative and without the prior approval of the Cabinet:

> No one has been a more consistent opponent of Communism than I have for the past 25 years. I will unsay no word that I have spoken about it. But all this fades away before the spectacle which is now unfolding. The past, with its crimes ... flashes away. I see the Russian soldiers standing on the threshold of their native land, guarding the fields which their fathers have tilled since time immemorial. I see them guarding their homes where mothers and wives pray – ah yes – for there are times when all pray, for the safety of their loved ones ... I see the ten thousand villages of Russia where the means of existence is wrung so hardly from the soil but where there are still primordial joys, where maidens laugh and children play. I see advancing upon all this in hideous onslaught the Nazi war machine, with its clanking, heel-clicking,

dandified Prussian officers, its crafty expert agents ... I see also the dull, drilled, docile brutish masses of the Hun soldiery ... I have to declare the decision of His Majesty's Government, and I feel it is a decision in which the Great Dominions will concur, for we must speak at once without a moment's delay. I have to make the declaration but can you doubt what our policy will be?[16]

Churchill then came to the climax of his broadcast:

We have but one aim and one single irrevocable purpose. We are resolved to destroy Hitler and every vestige of the Nazi regime. From this nothing will turn us, nothing. We will never parley, we will never negotiate with Hitler or any of his Gang. We shall fight him by land, we shall fight him by sea, we shall fight him in the air until, with God's help, we have rid the earth of his shadow and liberated its peoples from his yoke. Any man or state who fights on against Nazidom will have our aid. Any man or state who marches with Hitler is our foe. That is our policy, that is our declaration. It follows therefore that we shall give whatever help we can to Russia and the Russian people. The Russian danger is therefore our danger and the danger of the United States, just as the cause of any Russian fighting for his hearth and home is the cause of free people in every quarter of the globe ...[17]

Naturally any public speech by a British Prime Minister carries with it enormous weight. This speech had a double significance. It was not only quite clearly a landmark in the development of the war but it was also a complete reversal of what Churchill had previously chosen to say about the Soviet Union. It was a very public commitment to viewing Soviet Russia in a totally new light and, as such, it was bound to be a major determinant of British policy at all levels.

Churchill had made only one reference to 'Communism', at the very beginning of his remarks. It and the implicit notion of subversion and international Bolshevism were cast out in favour of a moving description of Mother Russia – 'the Russian soldiers standing on the threshold of their native land, guarding the fields which their fathers have tilled since time immemorial'. As Dr Gilbert puts it: Churchill's 1919 slogan 'Kill the Bolshie, Kill the Hun' had now become 'Let everyone Kill a Hun'.[18]

What Britain now realised was that a dramatic volte-face by the British Government had been executed. Good relations with Russia had become a central plank of the general war policy. At the same time, we should not forget that Churchill had secretly desired to co-operate with Russia even before 22 June 1941. For, as the Foreign Office papers show,[19] the co-operation which his public declaration presaged had, in fact, been proposed in concrete terms for many months before Operation Barbarossa. This serves to underline the crucial importance attached by the British to coming to a firm understanding with Soviet Russia; what is more, it would have been perceived as such by the Russians themselves. They knew Britain genuinely wanted to collaborate with them.

Early in June 1941, proof emerged from a highly unusual source that Eden's sincerity was well-appreciated in Moscow. A copy of an intercepted memo by D. N. Pritt, well-known as a Communist, was passed to Eden in that month by MI5's section which kept tabs on the Communists (and was led by Roger Hollis). The British Foreign Secretary must have been delighted by what he read:

> My own view of Eden, whom I scarcely know personally, is that he really does want greater confidence and co-operation ... he is only being held back by pressure from the United States ... HMG want to get help as cheap as they can and the USSR is equally right in wanting to sell it as dear as it can. [But] HMG's mistake is that a clash between Germany and the Soviet Union is quite inevitable. I believe this is terribly wrong ...[20]

Eden's readiness to co-operate with Russia had been properly appreciated by D. N. Pritt, even if the British Foreign Secretary cannot have been heartened by the final comment, which showed that the orthodox Stalinist line remained that the Soviets did not need any deal with Britain and that it was not inevitable that the Nazis and the Soviets should fall out. This point was taken up by Sir Orme Sargent, the Assistant Permanent Under-Secretary, who noted quite simply:

> We must try to establish contact with the Soviet Government as our position in the Mediterranean and the Near East deteriorates ...[21]

It is, therefore, not hard to see why, on the morning of 22 June 1941, Churchill should have offered Eden that cigar; it was indeed to be a turning point for British fortunes in the war against Hitler's Germany.

British policy towards the Soviet Union after Barbarossa: the Anglo-Soviet Alliance

Let us now consider what the Foreign Office position on Russia was after Barbarossa and what it believed was the nature of Stalinist policy, both during the war and, more critically, in the event (an event which was always taken for granted) that Hitler would be destroyed.

The foundation upon which Anglo-Soviet relations were built was the Anglo-Soviet Alliance of May 1942. Perhaps its most important clauses related to the way in which the Allies committed themselves to dealing with the nations of Europe following the defeat of the Third Reich. The treaty specifically underwrote:

The two principles of not seeking territorial aggrandisement for themselves and of non-interference in the internal affairs of the European peoples.[22]

It emphasised 'in particular' that both Britain and Russia shared the goal of:

The safeguarding and strengthening of the economic and political independence of all European countries.[23]

Those who criticise this alliance would do well to ponder upon these clauses, for it is hard to see how the apparent good faith of the Soviet Union could have been more clearly enunciated. They led directly to the perception of Russia by the British as a State whose war aims were compatible with their own, and with whom a friendly relationship could be constructed. Had it not been possible to include such clauses, British policy would deserve to be castigated for being naive or even worse. Yet with them included in a solemn and binding treaty, it is hard to see what more the British could possibly have demanded from the USSR.

It is worth recalling that Churchill's policy of friendship was not merely widely supported inside Britain but also strongly sustained by other friendly Governments. One document may serve for many. On 31 October 1941 a most secret telegram in cipher was sent to London from the New Zealand capital urging Britain to:

> Declare War on Finland, Rumania and Hungary to keep up Russian morale ... we attach the utmost importance to our taking any action within our power which might have the effect of encouraging the Soviet Government and would regard it as extremely undesirable to rebuff or discourage them when at this critical juncture they ask us to make a gesture ... particularly having regard to the fact that our inability to relieve by armed intervention the present heavily pressed Soviet army has necessarily created disappointment and indeed some misgivings both in Russia and in the British Commonwealth itself.[24]

What did the British believe at this time would be the net result of alliance with Russia? Some indications are given by the documentary evidence surrounding the negotiations concerning the drafting of the Anglo-Soviet Alliance, which proceeded rapidly and inevitably raised the question of what Britain and Russia were fighting for. Initially, the British had been quite happy to discuss their aims, but Stalin had reacted angrily, feigning suspicion about British motives and refusing to talk. So the Foreign Office produced a paper on what it believed Stalin's war aims to be. They were:

> To ensure access to warm water ports which is an old Russian ambition ... and some scheme which will ensure the preservation of Russian interests in the Baltic and Black Seas.[25]

Even more important, perhaps:

> The chief aim of Russian policy is security and if the threat to her can be conjured [sic] by some international scheme, then Russia would not necessarily have to adopt the policy which led to the partition of Poland [and] absorption of the Baltic States.[26]

In short, what the British understood to be Soviet intentions in 1941 was plain: the overriding Soviet concern after the defeat of Hitler would be to make Russia safe against any future attack; if security could not be offered by an international guarantee of some kind, then Russia would be forced into the sort of policy which had caused her to attack Poland and the Baltic States. But, the Foreign Office argued, since the British were more than ready to offer such guarantees, Russia would get the security she wanted and she would not thus feel forced to repeat her rape of Poland and the Baltic States.

There appeared to be only one real obstacle to such a guarantee: the question of the location of borders, in particular those of Poland. It is important to realise that there is no evidence that the British either thought or knew that Stalin would use Hitler's defeat in order to extend Communism westward. Borders were one thing; regimes quite another. After all, the alliance of 1942 had emphasised the Russians' commitment to 'the safeguarding and strengthening of the economic and political independence of all European countries ...' And Maisky had specifically told Whitehall that:

> Stalin had said: after the war there must be states with many different forms of Government and it was not the Russian objective to set up a Communist state in Britain ...[27]

The last bit of this was, of course, perceived as a joke, although when we consider the Communist penetration of British institutions at this time, it was rather less funny than it appeared. From the British point of view, however, this statement (whose elements were reiterated repeatedly during the war) was a firm pledge that the Soviet Union would support political pluralism in the post-war world. Today, however, it does seem most strange that the British were prepared to accept Soviet assurances at face value, not least because even at a very early stage in 1941 Maisky and Stalin demonstrated a keen interest in Britain's war aims: it was as if the Kremlin could not believe Britain was as compliant as she appeared. It was odd that the Soviet thirst for knowledge seemed unquenchable, whereas Britain's was easily slaked.

Not every diplomat, however, was prepared to scupper his doubts about the USSR. Some of them did have grave suspicions about what Stalin might do at the end of the war. But what must be made clear is that, as far as one can tell, these doubts were never supported by proper intelligence assessments of Stalin's aims (and, as we shall see, there was a good reason for this). Second, however, those doubts that did emerge were always squashed at Whitehall's most senior levels. Indeed, it was paradoxical that as the war went on and increasing evidence of Stalin's political ambitions presented itself, the squashing became more dramatic and determined.

One example of an early doubter was the ever-perceptive Roger Makins (later Lord Sherfield). On 7 May 1942 Makins had met ex-President Benes who had argued that the Anglo-Soviet Alliance ignored the real danger of a Soviet hegemony over the central and eastern part of Europe. Makins thought Benes had a point and argued that extensive guarantees to prevent this must be gained from Russia. This led to a general Foreign Office discussion. William Strang argued:

> I do not think we can counter the establishment of Russian predominance in Eastern Europe if Germany is crushed and disarmed and Russia participates in the final victory ...

While Strang did not define what he meant by 'Russian predominance', it is clear that it involved an extension of Soviet power. But Orme Sargent, the Deputy Under-Secretary, quickly put the lid on this debate, preventing any possible transfer of these doubts into actual policy changes. He wrote that there was only one logical outcome to what Makins and Strang were thinking and that was a strong and revived Germany and that he, for one, would be 'very sorry to reach such a distressing conclusion'.[28] And there the matter rested.

This pattern was often repeated, becoming ever more crass as the war neared its end. So how is this peculiar state of affairs to be explained? Despite the fact that the evidence bespeaks a fundamental ignorance about what Stalin had in mind, some prefer to attribute it to a continuation of the Foreign Office's policy of appeasement as practised initially towards Nazi Germany in the 1930s. Churchill himself has been impugned as the main architect of what might be termed the 'new appeasement'; he was said to be 'bored' by postwar plans, and the Foreign Office was imbued with pro-Russian euphoria.[29]

Such a notion is both damaging and unsound. It is also a serious misinterpretation of British policy and of Churchill's own part in all of this: he was not an appeaser, whether of Hitler or of Stalin (indeed, from his earliest days, he had always been a fighter). Yet more to the point, he did not consider Stalin and Hitler to be in the same league. The essential point about appeasement is that it attempted to buy off the aggressive Third Reich by yielding to its demands. It was a policy adopted towards a State perceived as hostile. Russia, on the other hand, was, as we have seen, not perceived as hostile but as an ally. Furthermore, the Russians continued to promise that they had no demands which were not fully compatible with British aims and interests.

If Churchill and Eden are to be castigated as appeasers, it has first to be demonstrated that they were fully aware of Stalin's deeper plans; it is only if we can prove that they knew Stalin was lying about his commitment to political independence for the nations of central and eastern Europe that the term appeasement might gain any validity. This Churchill and Eden very patently did *not* know (see pp. 32 and 251). Even if at various times they feared that Stalin might be deceiving them, these fears were always allayed. To use the word appeasement in terms of Anglo-Soviet relations during the Second World War is not merely unhistorical, but it ignores the real question that is begged by British actions: why was it that the British authorities knew so little about the real aims of Soviet Russia? What we are really dealing with is far less a failure of Britain's foreign policy than a failure of its intelligence.

Thus while there is some evidence of individual diplomats displaying an excessive enthusiasm for Stalin's Russia (see p. 282), it would be quite wrong to claim that the Foreign Office as a whole was 'euphorically pro-Russian', without pointing out that being pro-Russian was what British high policy had ordained.

The truth, then, about British high policy towards Russia is not that the British authorities never had any doubts or suspicions about Stalin's aims, but that what mattered in the final analysis was the need to co-operate with the Soviet Union and thus to disregard those doubts and suspicions. The interpretations of Soviet thinking and actions that were formative on British policy-makers all stressed the necessity of their adopting an optimistic assessment of Soviet war aims. In 1942, for example, Cripps's highly influential successor as British Ambassador, Sir Archibald Clark Kerr, sent Whitehall a report on Soviet post-war plans as they were perceived at that time:

All the thought and energy of this country [i.e. the USSR] is bent to the immediate task of winning the war. In this respect, the Soviet Government, at present in the thick of the fight against Germany, are in a different position from that of the eight exiled governments in London who . . . have more time to devote to post-war problems than has the Kremlin . . .[30]

Clark Kerr argued that the Russians were definitely not developing any secret plans for the control of the areas they might hope to liberate: while those European émigrés who were in London might plan and plot for the future, the Soviet Union was far too busy to indulge in such luxuries. Clark Kerr was, of course, not only quite mistaken about this, but he was also wrong to argue that once the war was over the Soviet Union's main concern would be the reconstruction of the devastated areas of Russia. For inasmuch as political considerations were likely to be a factor after Hitler's defeat, he continued:

> What are these political factors? In the first place territorial claims ... the Baltic States, Bessarabia ... Russia may claim an undefined protectorate over the other Slav people of Europe and a somewhat more tangible influence over the destinies of Slav-civilised Bulgaria ... One thing can be said: after the war Soviet Russia will probably be prepared to take things quietly for a considerable period of time. There will, so far as this country is concerned, be a general desire for a greater degree of comfort and happiness than was granted them before the war.[31]

One of his colleagues by the name of Rendel who acted as Ambassador to the (non-Communist) Yugoslav Government in Exile took a different view as a result of speaking to these exiles. He suggested that once the defeat of the Fascist Axis became certain, Russia would try to exercise an 'even greater mesmeric influence' over Bulgaria and establish Soviet republics in Bulgaria and Hungary. The Communists of Yugoslavia would then seek to gain power in the southern Slav countries. Rendel concluded that while there was a 'large and responsible body of opinion in England' which might like to see a 'chain of Associated Socialist and Soviet Republics in South-East Europe', he believed this to be Soviet 'imperialism' by another name, with Stalin a 'Red Peter the Great' anxious to promote the 'Sovietisation of South-Eastern Europe'.[32]

As with Makins's doubts six months earlier, however, the Foreign Office was determined that Rendel's views should not lead to any change in policy. Christopher Warner, the Head of the Northern Department which dealt with Russia, dismissed Rendel's points. Warner had previously worked for the Foreign Office's Political Intelligence Department. He argued that:

The only chance of preventing the Balkans from falling completely under Russian control will be by securing Russian agreement to Anglo-Russo-American collaboration there.[33]

Warner obviously believed not only that a post-war agreement with Russia was perfectly possible, but that it would ensure Stalin could be relied on to refrain from exercising any uncalled-for political control over the Balkans.

Rendel's suspicions of Soviet intentions were also contradicted by Sir Orme Sargent, the Deputy Under-Secretary:

I am not convinced that the Soviet Government are consciously planning to dominate the Balkans by means either of Bolshevisation or Pan-Slavism. The Soviet Government have publicly endorsed on many occasions the principle of non-intervention . . . As regards the Balkans, their territorial ambitions as disclosed in the Secretary of State's conversation with Stalin in Moscow were confined to Bessarabia and Northern Bukovina and to bases in Roumania. The present trend of Soviet policy, so far as one can judge, appears to be against unlimited expansion but of course this does not necessarily preclude the possibility that one or the other of the Balkan states (and Hungary ought also to be included in this category) may at the end of the war collapse into Communism merely as a result of the economic conditions then prevailing . . .[34]

It does not seem unreasonable to ask how Sir Orme Sargent could have been so sure of something about which he was, in fact, entirely wrong. He was plainly totally ignorant of the extent to which Soviet plans were already being developed to establish Communist regimes in post-war Europe. Why, then, was he certain that Stalin could be trusted so completely? If we accept that Stalin was in reality misleading the British (and it is impossible not to believe this), then there are really only two plausible explanations for Orme Sargent's ignorance. The first is that for reasons of constitutional propriety he simply could not bring himself to suggest that the policy being pursued by his chiefs, Eden and Churchill, was unsatisfactory. The second, however, is that Sargent's certainty was being fuelled by a false conception of what Stalin was really up to.

The doubters continued to be ruled out of court. On 4 February 1943 Eden sent Clark Kerr a fresh statement of the importance he placed on co-operation with the Kremlin. He and the Government were determined:

> On all possible occasions to treat the Soviet Government as partners and make a habit of discussing plans and views with them as a matter of course. Only in this way will it be possible to break through the crust of suspicion which results from the previous relations between the two countries and our widely differing institutions. We should not be unduly deterred by the fact that on many major questions which must arise in talks with our Allies, we have not yet reached any settled policy. Although it may often be necessary to discuss matters of policy with the United States Government before broaching them with the Soviet Government, by so doing we may risk giving offence to the latter. I propose therefore to so far as possible consult both Governments simultaneously ... it may also help to assuage the Soviet Government's susceptibilities if we on some occasions consult them first. For instance in questions relating to Eastern Europe, it may well be desirable to open discussions with the Soviet Government first.[35]

Eden's line was both consistent with high policy and absolutely clear: there was no cause to suspect that the Soviet Union had already decided upon anything which might bring it into conflict with Britain and the West. He argued that there was every reason to think that full co-operation with Russia was possible both now and in the future. Even where there were important matters upon which 'any settled policy had not yet been reached', he was convinced that if the British were to behave correctly, they and the Russians could come to an agreement.

What is even more chilling than this misjudgment is that there is evidence to show that the Russian leadership understood this to be the British position and were able to play upon it and exploit it to their best advantage. This suggests that the Soviets were fully informed about British thinking from the inside of the Foreign Office. Thus when Clark Kerr met Molotov on 20 February 1943, Molotov stated:

> In a friendly and jocular mood that in the midst of their urgent military pre-occupations, the Soviet Government had not yet got beyond the merest preliminary study [of post-war matters] ...[36]

It was as if Molotov knew not only that words like these would reassure his British allies, but also that the British were in no position to find out that they were totally misleading (see pp. 262 ff.).

A good summing-up of the British position is supplied by a paper drawn up by William Strang on 29 May 1943. The future could not be predicted by anyone, but the basic principle of British policy was clear:

> We need Russian collaboration. The conclusion of the Anglo-Soviet Treaty last year marks our decision that this must be our policy now and after the war. There is a respectable and well-informed opinion that Russia will not, either now or for some years after the war, aim at the Bolshevisation of Eastern and Central Europe or adopt an aggressive policy elsewhere. But even if fears that Russia lay a 'heavy hand' on eastern, central and south-eastern Europe are realised ... I should not like to say that this would be to our disadvantage ... It is better that Russia should dominate Eastern Europe than that Germany should dominate Western Europe. Nor would the domination of Eastern Europe by Russia be as easy as all that. However strong Russia may become, she is unlikely ever to be so grim a menace to us as Germany could again be, within a few years were her aggressive tendencies once again to revive ... The time may come when Russia will take the place of Germany as a threat to our world power or to our existence. But there are no signs that this will occur in any immediate future ...[37]

Strang's remarks are a full statement of British high policy; they could hardly be more plain. The Soviet Union in 1943 was not perceived as a threat to the security of the individual nations of the continent of Europe; there was no reason to believe that Russia would try to 'Bolshevise' its end of Europe, and even some sort of predominant Soviet influence in central and eastern Europe would be a great deal better than either a victory for Hitler or any new German aggression, a Fourth Reich. This, then, was British policy: to act counter to it was impossible. Yet at the same time, it is not unfair to repeat the question we asked of Orme Sargent above: how could he have got things so wrong?

Precisely who constituted that 'respectable and well-informed opinion' by which Strang set such store? Who was it who believed that Russia 'will not now or for some years after the war' try to subjugate Europe? Was the source in intelligence? Could it even have been a mole such as Kim Philby? Anthony Blunt? Or even the dissolute Guy Burgess? The latter was hardly respectable, but we should not forget Stephen Spender's intriguing comment: he has told us that Burgess once showed him a 'volume of Churchill's memoirs' in which Churchill had inscribed: 'To Guy S. Burgess, in agreement with his views, Winston S. Churchill.' Under this was written, 'And we were right, Anthony Eden.'[38]

Whatever the answer, it can hardly be denied that, in the very world-power terms they understood so well, the British Government failed to see that it would be the USSR and not a post-Nazi Germany which would constitute the biggest threat to the peace and security of the West. Finally, we must once again ask why, when the evidence began to come in that Stalin had indeed developed plans to 'Bolshevise' Europe, it was consistently misinterpreted until it was too late to do anything about it. Did the Foreign Office mandarins choose not to know, or did high policy itself prevent them from knowing? And what of the third alternative: that the intelligence they were receiving was faulty, even subverted?

It must be remembered that not only did high policy state that every one of Britain's political institutions which had an interest in things Russian had to uphold the principles of the Anglo-Soviet Alliance, but this obviously allowed those who wished to see Stalin, rather than Britain, prosper in the post-war world several enormous advantages. Sir William Strang implied that there were good grounds for this policy, even good intelligence grounds. Although it is difficult to know exactly what he was thinking of, we can, for reasons set out later, be fairly certain that in fact he had not meant by this secret intelligence about the Soviet Union.

It seems far more likely that the grounds to which Sir William referred were connected with the general view that any hardening of the British position *vis-à-vis* the Soviet Union might cause the Russians to try to make a separate peace with Hitler. The notion of a separate peace was often bandied about, even though the British and the Americans went out of their way to allay Russian anxieties about the West. It is by no means implausible to believe that, although Strang had not consulted MI6, he may inadvertently have been taking subverted advice on this. For the Russians often used hints of a separate peace as a device to encourage Britain and America to continue to co-operate with them.

Whether Stalin would really have attempted a re-run of the Nazi–

Soviet Non-Aggression Pact of 1939 is hard to know. Some historians believe that after the Red Army's great victory at Stalingrad, Stalin may indeed have tried to negotiate a peace deal with Hitler. Yet since Hitler was determined to destroy Bolshevism at all costs, a separate peace with Stalin seems hard to imagine. At all events, there was clearly a German dimension to the issues under consideration – hardly surprising, since Germany always constituted an area of very special significance in the wartime relationship between Russia and the West (see p. 115).[39]

We should not forget that one of Britain's intelligence officers charged with an analysis of these matters was Kim Philby, and it is by no means impossible that the views alluded to by Strang had indeed emanated from Philby in Section V of MI6, where he handled most of the intelligence concerned with Germany which came by way of neutral Spain and Portugal. It is obvious that Philby would have been under orders to play the card of separate peace whenever he could (see p. 151).

If this is what happened, we can see how Communist subversion was able to influence the making of British policy, not in the sense that a policy was embarked upon which would otherwise not have occurred, but to confirm a high policy decision which had already been taken, either by providing 'intelligence' which would lead one to act in this way or by failing to pass on information which might lead to a modification of that policy. For the power of the moles lay not merely in the sort of secrets to which they were privy, but in the influence they might exercise in policy-formulation itself.

As we have seen, Churchill himself certainly expressed no precise fears about the sort of internal political control that Stalin would impose on the lands the Red Army liberated. This does not mean that he was not at times anxious about Stalinist policies. In the summer of 1943 there was an indication, albeit a comparatively trivial one, that the Foreign Office was concerned about what it saw as Churchill's somewhat dismissive manner when dealing with the Russians.

> Churchill is the real snag ... his statement the other day about consulting the Americans and informing the Russians was no slip of the tongue. It's his deliberate policy and it's going to land us in one hell of a mess. He's been told so often enough but ... now the end of the war is in sight, my impression is that he does not care

two hoots about the Russians. If they come to tag along with us, well and good; if not, they can go and boil themselves. The pity of it is that it's the Russians themselves who are so responsible for all this. Their general bloodiness about visas ... and their general ungraciousness have made people here get the impression that it's impossible to deal with them, and as I can see this Office is the only place where it is realised that, in spite of all these things, we just have to get along with them or Europe will be a ghastly place for a long time ...[40]

It could be suggested that this bespoke a hardening of Churchill's attitude towards Russia. Yet there is no reason to believe that he had begun to suspect Soviet motives in any concrete sense by that summer, and there was certainly no change in high policy. When Geoffrey Wilson wrote to Clark Kerr that 'Churchill is the real snag' in Anglo-Soviet relations, he was not indicating any real reversal in Churchill's readiness to co-operate with Stalin.

Wilson's confidence in Soviet good faith was confirmed in October 1943 by a Soviet statement (totally cynical, as it turned out) concerning its attitude towards the future of Poland, the Danubian and Balkan States. It unequivocally reaffirmed its commitment to the 'independence and sovereignty of these nations' and guaranteed that they would be allowed to 'orientate themselves in the new [post-war situation] without being subject to any outside pressure to join this or that new grouping'.[41]

In March 1944 the Canadian Ambassador in Moscow confirmed this when he told the Foreign Office that:

A strong case can be made out for the view that it would be contrary to the interests of the Soviet Union in the post-war period to ... attempt to bring about the establishment of Communist regimes in other countries ... Stalin is said to be sincerely desirous of disproving Hitler's contention that the Soviet Union is out to bolshevise Europe ...[42]

Warner, however, was now less inclined to be over-optimistic on this issue. He believed that the Russians were bound to support their ideological partners in those nations they liberated and this distressed him. It is clear why some of his more left-wing colleagues in the Northern Department, such as Geoffrey Wilson and Christopher Hill, found him irritating.[43] Yet, and this is the important point, he saw nothing to suggest the Russians had any deliberate policy for achieving this and he certainly did not think that any change in British policy was called for.

In April 1944, the Foreign Office produced yet another major statement on its high policy towards the USSR. Its salient points show that nothing had happened to make the British reconsider the line that they had taken ever since 1941. British policy remained based on the proposition that:

Russia's major interest will be to devote her main energies for many years to come to the colossal task of post-war rehabilitation ... provided the British Commonwealth and the United States do not appear to the Soviet authorities to wish to deprive Russia of the means of eliminating the menace from Germany, Russia will welcome a prolonged period of peaceful relations with [them]. But this prediction is based on the assumption that the Russians do not suspect us of having designs hostile to her security ... should she not be so satisfied ... she will be more preoccupied with her own security ... she would then probably become an intensely disruptive force in Europe. One may predict, then, with some confidence that during a period of at least five years after the termination of the war with Germany, Russia will be preoccupied with her post-war rehabilitation and will constitute no menace to British strategic interests.[44]

This prediction was, of course, like almost all of the others, totally wrong on several counts but, interestingly, in one area its errors highlight a specific problem which has to do with a recurrent issue in this study. This concerned the political future of Germany. In the summer of 1943 the Soviet Government had set up in Moscow a so-called National Committee of Free Germany which purported to be a shadow German Government in exile (this matter is investigated again from another angle; see p. 192). On the face of it (and in reality) this could be regarded as a most ominous development because it indicated how advanced the Russians were in their planning for Germany's internal post-Nazi political life. Now, this was an area where the British were determined not to have any fixed plan until Hitler was defeated. Yet it would clearly be disastrous if a Moscow-based body could exploit this gap in Britain's policy to undertake the Sovietisation of Germany on behalf of the Kremlin. However, the Foreign Office was utterly sure that this committee was not a dangerous development and that it knew what its purpose was:

> The Free German Committee can safely be regarded as a mere propaganda weapon and its doctrines give no indication of the Soviet Government's real intentions towards Germany. It seems very improbable that Russia would welcome a Communist Germany for she might well develop into a dangerous rival. Indeed as the Soviet Union moves further from Communism [sic] the danger to her position as leader of the extreme Left in the world from a Communist Germany would clearly grow ... this consideration combined with Russia's healthy fear of German powers of organisation ... would almost certainly make Russia fear Communism in Germany ...[45]

Not only was this a very bad error but by this time it was already highly dangerous to be so wrong about Soviet policy.

As far as Poland was concerned, the Foreign Office was convinced that:

> The USSR will be in favour of a strong and independent Poland [enjoying] good relations with the Soviet Union. [As far as border adjustments are to be considered] Poland will not succeed in getting a settlement on more favourable lines ... In any case, the USSR is certainly determined not to tolerate a hostile Poland. If satisfied on this score they may well be content that Poland should retain a real independence. Russia is concerned to ensure that her forces will always be able to pass through Poland, if necessary, in order to nip a threat from Germany in the bud.[46]

Here, too, the certainty exhibited by the Foreign Office seems extremely bizarre. It still believed that the USSR had only two concerns in respect of Poland: the geographical location of its frontiers and the right to use Poland as a thoroughfare in order to let the Soviet army engage any aggressive post-war German army as quickly as possible. Yet Whitehall was inherently mistaken on both scores – Stalin had never intended that the Red Army would become simply an anti-German fire brigade. Instead, it was to be a tool to establish Communist political control throughout Europe. Communist allegations of the re-emergence of a 'German threat', made long after West Germany had become one of Europe's most stable liberal democracies, were nothing more than an unconvincing alibi for the presence of the Red Army in central and eastern Europe.

In June 1944 the Chiefs of Staff wrote that they were desperately worried that the Soviet Union's actions were no longer corresponding to the expectations of the Foreign Office but constituted a threat to Europe. Christopher Warner commented:

> The most important point in securing Russian collaboration after the war will be to convince her of our determination to go with her in holding Germany down ... instead [the Chiefs produce a paper] which barely conceals that it thinks Russia is just as likely to be an enemy as Germany ... the distance to the next step ... our building up Germany ... is a very short one, particularly for the military mind and those who suffer from the anti-Bolshevik complex ...[47]

The irony in this minute is remarkable: the alternatives that Warner posited were simply outrageous. In fact the 'military mind' had a very shrewd sense of what Stalin intended; in any case, the real choice was not between a strong and aggressive Germany and a strong and aggressive Russia, but between a liberal Western-oriented Germany and a self-contained and hopefully more liberal post-Stalinist USSR.

It must be pointed out that Warner's optimism was no longer shared by all his colleagues. Gladwyn Jebb, for example, said the Foreign Office and the Chiefs of Staff were agreed that if anyone was to be a threat after the Nazis had gone, it was going to be Russia. And Frank Roberts said unequivocally:

> I have long felt that we were adopting too negative an attitude in attempting to discourage the Chiefs of Staff from even considering the possibility of a hostile Russia ...[48]

Roberts's comments were dated 18 August 1944 and were made at the height of the Warsaw Uprising, by which time it was already clear that the Russians were not going to help the non-Communist Polish resistance escape extermination at the hands of the Germans. Thus, although there can be no question at all that Roberts was right, what is so striking about his views is how relatively mute they were and, more important, how little they appeared to be based on any adequate intelligence assessment of Soviet activities.

A further telling incident occurred in the autumn of 1944. The head of the British Military Mission in Russia, General Burrows, complained to Whitehall that he found the Russians increasingly unwilling to answer his questions. Vyshinksy decided in turn to complain about him to Clark Kerr. On 24 September Stalin himself told Clark Kerr he wanted Burrows out of Russia, and in November he was recalled back to London.[49] This ought to have alerted officials to what might have seemed a fairly obvious explanation for Soviet hostility towards the British General: that they did not want him poking his nose into Soviet affairs. What is more, this implied that such poking might indeed turn up evidence about which the Russians did not wish the British to know. Yet the Foreign Office did not pursue the point.

As the war in Europe drew to its close, the British Foreign Office was gradually forced to begin reappraising its policy towards Russia, now that there was incontrovertible evidence that Britain had been badly duped by Stalin. Yet, even so, Sargent himself, as late as April 1945, did not appear to comprehend that what Stalin sought was not simply border changes but the imposition of Communism, using the might and authority of the Red Army. Poland was now a concrete example of this.

On 2 April 1945 Orme Sargent said that with the collapse of Hitler's armies in the West, it might now be a good time to reconsider British policy:

> It was only prudent that we should in our diplomatic dealings with the Soviet Union set ourselves to propitiate our Russian Ally. On every possible occasion we tried to humour him and the Prime Minister in particular was at pains to establish a personal friend ship with Stalin. The policy was no doubt the right one at the time, though it produced no spectacular results and indeed very little response from the Soviet Government, [and] who can say that the situation would not have been very much worse if we had during this period asserted our rights on every occasion by the various means of pressure open to us such as retaliation in kind, denial of material help and isolated action in those parts of Europe where our interests and those of the Soviet Union appear to conflict?[50]

Yet this rather pessimistic, if very vague, assessment was promptly overruled three months later when, on 11 July 1945, Sargent had another crack at defining British thinking on Russia. It was, he said:

> Particularly dangerous to assume that the foreign policies of tota-

litarian governments are opportunist and fluctuating like those of liberal ones ... all totalitarian governments are able to conduct a consistent and persistent foreign policy over a longer period of time because the government is not dependent on public opinion ... Stalin [however] does not necessarily intend to obtain his security by territorial conquest as Hitler wanted. He may well prefer to obtain it by creating what might be termed ideological Lebensraum in those countries which he considers strategically important ... at the present moment, the Soviet Union has been so weakened by the war that Stalin is hardly in a position to force through his policy of ideological penetration against definite opposition ... We must of course be prepared for the Soviet Government to use every opportunity and make every effort to mould the future political institutions of Germany in order to obtain a dominating position in that country.[51]

We can see, then, that a true understanding of what the Soviet Union was up to in eastern Europe was at last beginning to dawn on British officials, but only after Soviet plans were already being executed (see p. 181).[52] There is, it should be noted, no hint as to whether this change was in any way connected to the establishment of a new section in MI6 (Section IX) whose job it was to keep a watch on the Soviet Union's intentions.

The notion of 'ideological Lebensraum' was not necessarily incorrect: what Sargent neglected to realise was that the ideological part was to be enforced by the Red Army in much the same way as Hitler had used the German Army and the SS to construct his 'ideological Lebensraum'. Yet even at this late hour not all British officials shared Sargent's muted pessimism. Clark Kerr, in one of his final dispatches from Moscow, wrote in September 1945:

The Soviet People were delighted at the reaffirmation of the unity of the Big Three at Potsdam and the consolidation of the new American administration. [There has been] a certain relaxation in the Soviet grasp over Eastern and Central Europe, the position of the Western Democracies has improved in Poland and Czechoslovakia ... It is not unnatural that we should look for the causes of the welcome change. A not unimportant one may have been the Atomic Bomb ...[53]

This was yet another one of Clark Kerr's gaffes. It was, in many ways, an absurd misreading of the evidence that now fully presented itself, actually to ascribe to the atom bomb a wholly fictional relaxation of the Soviet grasp on central and eastern Europe.

In short, a close documentary analysis of British policy towards the Soviet Union reveals that for the entire period British policy was firmly based on a perceived need to co-operate with the Kremlin and an unshakeable belief that such co-operation was totally achievable. It thereby completely underestimated the extent to which the Soviet Union was using this co-operation to advance its own aims and plans, which rested on the use of the Red Army and the Communist-led resistance to the Nazis in order to establish client Communist regimes throughout as much of Europe as possible. Consequently British policy-makers were caught unprepared and defenceless. They did not choose to ignore the true dimension of Soviet policy; all the documentary evidence suggests that they were simply unaware that a further, hidden dimension existed. British policy was, therefore, not based on the cynical appeasement of the Soviet Union, but on the honest, though ignorant, attempt to work together with it.

Before we turn to the all-important problem of why the Foreign Office was so badly misinformed, it is important once again to reflect upon the attitude of the most important policy-maker of all, the British Prime Minister.

Churchill, Eden and Stalin: who knew what about whom?

In the popular imagination, Churchill is usually seen either as totally alert at all times to the dangers posed by Russia and to its dreams of hegemony over Europe (which seems to be how he wished himself to be viewed) or, by his detractors, as someone who was secretly ready to sacrifice the Western interest in order to help Stalin achieve his aims. This issue is, of course, a difficult one (and would fill a book by itself) and it is not possible here to do more than sketch out a broad judgment.[54]

While there is no doubt that, in the specific case of Greece, Churchill did indeed act to prevent a Communist take-over, it must be said that the popular imagination seems to have exaggerated Churchill's awareness of the potential danger of Soviet expansion. For one thing, his fears about Russia, as expressed from 1940 to 1945, seem almost invariably vague. Like those in the Foreign Office, there is no indication that they were based upon any firm political intelligence about Russian post-war plans.[55] For another, there is no evidence to suggest that Churchill knew that Stalin was not acting in good faith and would not abide by his treaty obligations. Churchill himself was, it appears, in a very deep sense fundamentally ignorant about Soviet post-war plans.

Against this, it is sometimes suggested that the 'spheres of influence' agreement he reached with Stalin in Moscow in October 1944 implies that he did, in fact, know that the USSR and the West would be competing for political control over post-war Europe. This agreement did not, however, deal with all European states but only with Rumania (90 per cent USSR influence, 10 per cent the West), Yugoslavia and Hungary (50 per cent each), Greece (90 per cent Britain, 10 per cent USSR) and Bulgaria (75 per cent USSR, 25 per cent the West).[56] It was also hardly a treaty in any formal sense (it resembles an attempt at hasty improvisation) and the very fact that Churchill believed it would be possible to share 'influence' with Soviet Russia, not to mention Stalin's ultimate failure even to stick by this very limited agreement, bespeaks on Churchill's part a remarkable lack of comprehension about what the Soviet dictator had in mind. But Churchill was not conniving with Stalin, he was not appeasing him and not acting wickedly; he was, indeed, a 'victim, not a villain' in Stalin's wider schemes.

Wherever we can find examples of Churchill's fears and anxieties, we can also find evidence of their having been repressed and cast aside. His 1944 Moscow visit provides an example, in the form of the celebrated letter to Stalin:

> We are very glad that you have declared yourself against trying to change by force or Communist propaganda the established systems in the various Balkan countries. Hitler has tried to exploit the fear of an aggressive, proselytising Communist ... we feel we were right in interpreting your dissolution of the Comintern as a decision by the Soviet Government not to interfere in the internal political affairs of other countries ...[57]

This letter obviously indicates doubts about Stalin, but these were formless and clearly, in view of their date, singularly badly informed. What is more, the letter was never dispatched (largely because Churchill found the atmosphere in Moscow highly cordial; see p. 402 n.2).

Jock Colville states that on 23 January 1945 Churchill made the following remark to him as he was getting ready for bed:

> Make no mistake, all the Balkans, except Greece, are going to be
> Bolshevised; and there is nothing I can do to prevent it. There is
> nothing I can do for poor Poland either.[58]

And yet despite such fears, for which there was already firm
empirical evidence, Churchill continued to uphold his own
Government's high policy. Scarcely a month later, on 27 February
1945 (in the Yalta debate in Parliament), Churchill specifically
declared about the Kremlin, 'I know of no Government which stands
to its obligations even in its own despite more solidly than the Soviet
Government'.[59] His doom-laden forebodings were repressed:

> At Yalta we laboured for nine days and grappled with many
> problems of war and policy whilst friendships grew ... The
> Crimean Conference finds the Allies more closely united than ever
> before both in the military and the political sphere. The problem
> of Poland has been divided into two main issues, the frontiers
> of Poland and the freedom of Poland. To HMG the freedom,
> independence, integrity and sovereignty of Poland have always
> seemed more important than actual frontiers ... Most solemn
> declarations have been made by Stalin that the sovereign inde-
> pendence of Poland is to be maintained ... I decline absolutely to
> embark here on a discussion about Russian good faith. It is quite
> evident that these matters touch the whole future of mankind.
> Sombre indeed would be the fortunes of mankind if some awful
> schism arose between the Western Democracies and the Soviet
> Union ... It is a mistake to look too far ahead. Only one link in
> the chain of destiny can be handled at a time ...[60]

To be blunt, this speech can be interpreted in only two ways: either
Churchill knew full well that Stalin had not acted in good faith and
that his solemn declarations were lies, in which case Churchill himself
was deceiving Parliament. Or Churchill was telling the truth as he
believed it to be. As we have seen, the latter explanation is entirely
consistent with the evidence we have discussed so far.

A similar interpretation may be given to Eden's utterances on the
same subject. In early 1944, for example, obvious Soviet interference
in Italian affairs gave the Secretary of State cause for alarm:

I don't feel so good about Russia ... Why do they keep gate crashing in Italy? Their conduct could be explained as a calculated attempt to smash all left and all centre parties save the Communists ... I confess to growing apprehensions that Russia has vast aims and that these may include the domination of Eastern Europe and even the Mediterranean and the 'communising' of much that remains ...[61]

Yet what is striking about Eden's remarks is not that they show any great knowledge or foresight about Stalin's plans, but the complete reverse: for they demonstrate a lack of understanding which can be seen in several other pronouncements by the Foreign Secretary, most particularly perhaps on Poland. In January 1944 he wondered whether the Soviet Union might possibly intend the Polish Communists to become the backbone of a 'puppet Polish Government amenable to the Soviet Union'.[62] But we learn 'such doubts were largely set aside', and Christopher Warner added that the Russians wanted 'Left-wing regimes ... rather than Communist regimes imposed upon unwilling people'.[63]

Thus it may safely be said that both Churchill and Eden genuinely did not know the extent of Stalin's planning for the political domination of post-war Europe. Perhaps they did not want to know, although there is no reason to suggest that this is the case. It is far more likely that Churchill and Eden were quite simply ignorant about the strategies and tactics of Stalinist domination. The real question then becomes: why?

One explanation was provided by Stalin himself during a dinner in Moscow in 1942. It is obvious from what Churchill has written about this incident that he was both bemused by it and uncertain of what Stalin was actually driving at:

Stalin made a long speech proposing [the health of] the Intelligence Services, in the course of which he made a curious reference to the Dardanelles [the scene of Churchill's most disastrous military error] saying the British had won and the Germans and Turks were already retreating but that we did not know because the intelligence was faulty. This picture, though inaccurate, was evidently meant to be complimentary to me ...[64]

Not only did Stalin clearly not intend this remark to be complimentary, but what he seems to have been suggesting was that over the Dardanelles Churchill had failed because of faulty intelligence and that he was going to fail again over Europe for precisely the same reason.

The fact of the matter was that British policy towards the USSR during the Second World War was constructed upon two pillars, propped up in certain detailed areas by a third, rather shaky one. The first pillar was the absolute necessity of destroying Hitler. The second, however, was British ignorance about Stalin's real aims. For reasons we shall explore, there was almost no useful secret intelligence about Russian plans for the whole of this period.

The third pillar was that the first two factors permitted, albeit only in fringe areas, faulty and subverted intelligence to intermingle with and permeate into British foreign policy. The Grand Alliance and the need for good co-operation with the USSR made Communist subversion here both feasible and practically undetectable. In detailed areas, such as intelligence issues connected with the future of German domestic politics after Hitler, where initially the Soviet Union was able to achieve an enormous advantage, subversion may well have had an important impact.

All in all, however, subversion within the Foreign Office, by moles named or as yet unnamed, probably produced little more than the occasional piece of subverted advice and the disclosure to the Soviet authorities of what the British negotiating position was likely to be. Infinitely more damaging were the efforts of the moles within the British intelligence community itself, and it is to these that we should now turn in order to assess what sort of intelligence MI5 and MI6 ought to have provided. At the same time, however, it must be emphasised that it would be foolish in the extreme to lose sight of the overriding high policy insistence that the keynote of Britain's relationship with the USSR was co-operation and not suspicion, for this laid down the parameters within which all Communist subversion during the period must be viewed.

3

The Special Operations Executive

The heyday of Communist penetration

From the Kremlin's point of view the most serious conflict of interest between the USSR and Britain had to do with the future political shape of Europe. For this reason it seems entirely plausible to assume that Soviet subversive efforts were concentrated most vigorously upon those Government agencies which seemed to threaten their plans for the westward expansion of Communism, namely MI5, MI6 and SOE, the Special Operations Executive. From 1940 until 1942 it was SOE which appeared to present the greatest danger to them. Its purpose at this time was to promote what may be called the British way of subversion, namely the organisation and control of anti-Nazi resistance forces in occupied Europe. Success here might well give Britain, rather than the Soviet Union, the dominant role in Europe's eventual reconstruction.

Yet after 1941 SOE's concerns were altered, for reasons which even today are not entirely clear. In many cases (though not all) these changes served Russia's interests more than those of the West. Why, therefore, did they come about? Plainly, high policy must have been a factor, although in what exact sense it is hard to say. As we have seen, it was never the intention of British policy-makers that Communism should receive any advantages in post-war Europe, and Stalin's commitment to its political independence was always taken as a guarantee of his good faith. The British could thus not have transformed SOE to suit the Kremlin – first, because they did not realise how it would fit in with Soviet plans and second because it was not British policy to do so.

Equally, however, precisely because SOE, had it functioned as originally intended, would have ended up making Stalin's hold on post-war Europe substantially less secure, it is worth asking whether Communist subversion may not have played a significant part in SOE's fate. What we shall examine here has chiefly to do with the earlier part of SOE's history when it represented the biggest threat to the Kremlin and seems to have been the primary target for Soviet subversion.

We now know that at various times SOE contained some of the most important Soviet moles. Both Burgess and Philby worked for a time in Section 'D' of MI6, the forerunner of SOE. Burgess was recruited in 1938 but sacked at some point after November 1940, although he almost certainly retained both an interest in SOE and influence within it after that time.[1] Indeed, we have an official statement about Burgess's activities at this juncture from none other than Selwyn Lloyd, then British Foreign Secretary, who in 1956 told Parliament that Burgess had been in SOE, which Selwyn Lloyd described rather vaguely as an organisation 'which dealt with propaganda to neutral countries' (see p. 13). He added that Burgess also had a contact in MI5 with whom they discussed things German. Philby, on the other hand, continued to work for SOE from June 1940 until September 1941.[2]

Clearly, the moles do not have to be invented in order to account for what happened, but knowing that they were there makes our understanding of it considerably easier. Were we to assume that Communist subversion played no part at all, it would be very hard, though not impossible, to offer a satisfactory explanation for what SOE did and did not do. Furthermore, since after 1941 high policy insisted that minor obstacles to Anglo-Soviet co-operation should not be tolerated, the moles in SOE may from that time on have been pushing at an open door.

The moles were required to be most active in those areas where the Soviet Union had most to gain from the attempted subversion of British policy. And since Stalin knew, thanks to his moles and agents, how vital the British believed it to be for Britain to keep in tune with him, he also knew how far and where to press his case. In particular he understood that SOE was at the sharp end of the intelligence community; it possessed both the skills and the physical means by which the British could attempt to co-ordinate and influence the European resistance to the Germans.

The notion that this was an area where there were major differences between Britain and Russia is not one that all historians would share. The opposing view has been most clearly expressed by Hugh Trevor-Roper, now Lord Dacre; he has argued, in dismissing the notion that one of the Communist moles, Kim Philby, did much damage to Britain before 1944, that:

Until 1944 I do not believe that Philby had much opportunity or much need to do harm. His work was against the Germans in Spain where Russia was powerless and by now uninterested. Anyway, the interest of the Russians was at that time the same as ours: the defeat of Germany.[3]

This theory is, however, incorrect, since Russian interests were emphatically not identical to those of Britain. Both States shared an overriding interest in defeating Hitler; that is perfectly true. Beneath that interest, the Russians and the British had vastly different conceptions of what post-war Europe was to look like. This had been true for the period from 1939 until 1941 and it was true thereafter as well. For the Kremlin, as much of Europe as possible was to become Communist-ruled. The British, on the other hand, first firmly and then rather more vaguely, wished to promote a Europe which was established on a basis of liberal democracy.

Both for SOE from 1940 until 1942 and for Soviet Intelligence throughout the Second World War, the political control of the European resistance to Hitler was an absolutely crucial war aim. There were those both in SOE and in the Kremlin who reasoned correctly that influence in the politics of post-war Europe would be won or lost by means of the control they could exercise over the forces which would follow the Nazis. Naturally, the British authorities, from 1940 until 1942, wanted the resistance to pursue liberal democratic ends. The Russians, on the other hand, were concerned only to promote Communism.

It is sometimes suggested that SOE never possessed this political interest. Others have claimed, rather strangely, that if it did have a political interest, then it was left-wing and that therefore the Soviet Union can have had no interest in trying to subvert it. In reality, however, the facts contradict both these assertions. For a start, there was a fundamental difference between SOE as it was from 1940 until early 1942 and SOE from 1942 until the end of the war. It had two totally distinct phases and what applies to one phase does not necessarily apply to the other. In addition, those seeking to depict SOE as 'left-wing' ignore the fact that this term in fact fails to distinguish between two different and often conflicting strands, the Communist and the Social Democratic ones.

To want to support the one was not necessarily to support the other. The former was totalitarian, anti-democratic and looked to Moscow for inspiration. The latter was liberal, fully democratic and, above all, it looked to London. Thus SOE support for left-wingers who were Social Democrats was not something which the Russians could regard with any pleasure.

After 1942, however, SOE underwent a major change which robbed it of its overtly political concerns, and it was decided that it should sidestep the whole question of political support and concentrate instead on straightforward sabotage against the Nazis. Thus, as far as the Kremlin was concerned, from 1940–2 its aim was to ensure that if SOE supported any resistance groups, they should be Communist and not Social Democratic. After 1942 the Kremlin's sole requirement was that the British 'non-policy' should carry on regardless. Exceptions to it, as in the case of Yugoslavia where the British decided to support the Communist resistance, simply prove the rule. For a British 'non-policy' would end up giving the Russians a free hand. First of all, however, the Russians had to deal with the initial purpose behind SOE and the sort of policies it was set to pursue.

There is real evidence indicating that, in certain areas, the Russians had, by 1942, succeeded in neutralising SOE to their advantage. They did not in most cases manage to get the British to support Communist resistance groups exclusively, although they almost certainly did succeed in preventing Social Democrats from being treated equally, let alone preferentially as at first intended. Subsequently, they succeeded in making the non-policy stick despite much evidence that it was militating against the British interest.

So how, exactly, did the moles achieve their aims? When we deal with secret policy, and most of the policy in this study is just that, it must be assumed that some inputs are bound to be more important than others. I will later describe two sorts of policy-making processes in some detail; I have called them the formal and the informal networks by which policy was made and developed (see p. 132). It is my guess that the informal networks were the most devastating route that Communist subversion took. In the realm of secret policy, the records of these networks are hard to establish in terms of written reports and documentary evidence. In addition, by its very nature, British politics consists in large part of informal networks, advice proffered by old friends, school and university chums, exchanged at dinner or in bars and only very rarely recorded on a document, even if sometimes noted in a private diary or retained as a lively reminiscence.

For these reasons it is impossible to prove unequivocally that subversion occurred in the way in which I shall describe it. It is by its very nature not something of which documentary proof is readily available; it is always a question of probabilities and not of certainties. Some will be sceptical on this basis alone; if absolute certainty cannot be adduced, they will argue, it is unwise to assume that subversion went on at all. Others may repeat the line taken by one former Foreign Office official who was for a time concerned with intelligence issues. Claiming to have worked with Philby during the period in question, he has said that this experience led him to believe that Philby could not have acted in the ways I describe.[4]

The response to such doubts, however, is not difficult. The person who had worked with Philby presumably had no knowledge of any of his subversive activities (since Philby never informed anyone of them). That Philby did work for the Russians at this time has never been disputed. Therefore it follows that this official cannot have known what Philby was doing, and that having worked alongside him does not entitle him to pronounce on his subversive activities.

How much did this subversion matter? We should not forget that the issues that were subverted were second-division issues; they were not ones which concerned the Prime Minister, the Foreign Secretary or even the Foreign Office. British high policy was, generally speaking, a success. Britain's enemies in Europe and Asia were destroyed. It was only at the fringes of high policy that changes might have made the destruction of Hitler and Mussolini occur sooner and with less overall loss of life, and that more might have been done to promote liberalism in eastern and central Europe.

The essence of Communist subversion by the moles was the covert exploitation of perfectly legitimate policy for illegitimate ends. And there are good grounds for believing that frequently they were able to accomplish their aims. It is not impossible that the Communist moles may have managed to help engineer the change in SOE which caused it to shed its political concern with the resistance. Indeed, they may just possibly even have had a hand in disposing of the political leader who appeared to represent the biggest hazard to them.

In pursuing this matter in greater detail, a number of factors are worth bearing in mind. For one thing, some of the issues we shall look at may be described as British failures. It is important to see that most British failures cannot be explained in terms of Communist subversion.

Second, after 1941 subverted policy in SOE coincided, broadly speaking, so closely with what might appear perfectly proper high policy that it was excessively difficult to detect. Within the fake belief, in SOE and elsewhere, that British and Soviet interests were essentially the same lay both the seeds and the fruits of Communist subversion.

The British way of subversion

SOE was one of the Second World War's most secret institutional inventions. It was so secret that it is only now that its full history is beginning to be revealed, even if glimpses into some of its most dramatic exploits have been available for some time, notably due to the work of Professor M. R. D. Foot. Foot's account has recently been elaborated by the BBC series on SOE and by a fascinating new book of his which accompanies it.[5] But perhaps the most penetrating and indeed disturbing study of SOE has come from David Stafford, a former diplomat turned historian, in his masterly work on the subject.[6]

SOE was, of course, part of the British intelligence community.[7] It was one way in which secret policy, based on intelligence and intelligence considerations, could be put into practice. It scored a number of successes, but in other ways it was a failure. This was not only because of a series of devastating operational disasters, which were often inevitable, given their hazardous nature. SOE also suffered gravely in the political sphere, particularly where the future political map of Europe was at stake. What is more, errors which appeared to be simply operational can sometimes be seen to have had political implications, such as in the case of the SOE tragedy in the Netherlands, the so-called *Englandspiel* or England Game (see p. 103).

The question must therefore be posed as to why SOE failed. Was it simply the result of a variety of accidents and muddles, or was there some deeper reason why SOE's potential for success was never properly exploited, a reason which may have more than a little to do with Communist subversion?

To postulate a Communist interest in the SOE might seem rather peculiar, not least because so much of what SOE did seems to be concerned with cloak-and-dagger exploits of a one-off kind which appeared to have no political strings attached to them. In fact, despite all the daredevil cloak-and-dagger operations which came to be the hallmark of SOE, it initially had quite another side to its work. It is vitally important to realise that until 1942 SOE was explicitly concerned not simply with blowing things up but also with what was to be erected on top of the ruins.

Indeed, perhaps one of the most curious things about the history of the Special Operations Executive was why its interest in the political future of Europe was abandoned, and with disastrous results in a number of detailed instances. Communist strategies seem to have had a decisive impact in this area, yet is one justified in believing that the eventual triumph of Communism owes anything to successes scored by any of the moles? Lord Gladwyn, for example, dismisses such speculation as 'complete rubbish, absurd', adding that without Britain's readiness to co-operate with the USSR, Hitler would have won the war.[8] Broadly speaking, Lord Gladwyn's view is indeed correct: SOE's apparent failure to ensure by 1945, as far as it could, a free future for Occupied Europe, was first and foremost merely another aspect of high policy towards the Soviet Union. But, within this broad canvas, some of the more detailed brushwork must give rise to the gravest concern.

SOE grew out of the Secret Intelligence Service, MI6. Within it there was a 'Section D', commanded by Colonel Lawrence Grand (see p. 83).[9] In March 1938, before the Munich crisis and while British foreign policy was governed by the principles of appeasement, of trying to do a deal with Adolf Hitler over the aggressive territorial claims of the Third Reich, 'C' – Admiral Hugh Sinclair – the Head of MI6, had sent for Grand. 'C' had absolutely no confidence in Chamberlain's ability to secure peace and he was determined that the British Secret Intelligence Service should begin to make the necessary preparations for war. In his book, *The Black Game*, Ellic Howe vividly describes the scene:

'C' was convinced that war with Germany was inevitable and was making certain preparations. 'I want you to do sabotage,' said 'C'. 'Is anything barred?' Grand asked. 'Not a thing,' 'C' replied.[10]

Howe adds that 'By the spring of 1940 . . . Section D consisted of about 300 officers. This was Grand's estimate.' Professor Foot quotes Grand as claiming a lower number, it should be noted:

By July 1940 Grand claimed that his section had reached an officer strength of 140 (75 were actually counted on 4 August).[11]

There are two important things to note about this straight away. First, inasmuch as MI6's Section D was the forerunner of SOE, its Adam's rib, it indicates how secret SOE's role was to be. Second, there was, in wartime, to be a direct link between intelligence and action, between secret agents in the field and the use of armed force. In effect 'C' was giving Grand an extension of his own licence to kill.

Foot points out why SOE, though formed out of MI6, was in fact to be independent of it. MI6 had other things on its mind:

'C' concurred with the formation of SOE as an independent secret service over which he was to have no formal control: he had no choice. At that moment he had more than enough on his mind. Indeed, so busy was he that he had no time to spare for the affairs of Section D, and not till 4 September did he discover that by a direct deal between Halifax and Dalton, Grand's section had been taken away from SIS control altogether. By another unhappy office error, no one had remembered to tell him. Quite apart from the sound technical point that SOE's agents (once placed) were likely to create conditions too disturbed for intelligence agents (when he had any) to work with any ease, 'C' now had a personal reason for feeling aggrieved at the mere fact that the new body existed. His immediate worries were about decipher and spies. The Government Code and Cypher School ... at Bletchley had succeeded in breaking ... the Enigma machine ... and 'C' by a deft political stroke had succeeded in arranging that it was through himself that their product ... was to be handed to the Prime Minister ...[12]

'C' was also worried by his failure to set up a network of MI6 agents in Occupied Europe:

The silence from all his prearranged stay-behind agents in north-west Europe had by now become deafening. Through a series of appalling indiscretions – by the service that long derided SOE as unprofessional – the Germans had in fact cleaned up the lot.[13]

The second reason Foot advances for the separation of SOE from MI6 had its roots in domestic British Labour politics. The Labour Party, which after 1940 was to be a Government Party as well, had its own partisan interests in the secret services. Thus:

If a third secret service could be created and run by a Labour man the political difficulty could be resolved.[14]

In due course, however, following the outbreak of war, this notion of simple sabotage was refined into full-scale subversion. While most of the studies of SOE have tended to concentrate on the military and strategic aspects of subversion and on the assistance to the resistance fighters, in particular, of France, Holland and Poland, this was by no means the full story of SOE's activities.[15]

As Stafford convincingly demonstrates, there was, in fact, another dimension to them. This was its political side, a concern with what to put in the place of the Nazi occupiers once the dynamite had got rid of them. This political dimension of SOE's work has otherwise received scant attention and the main explanation for this is undoubtedly that this was one of its most secret aspects.[16]

After Hitler's invasion of France, in the period when the invasion of Britain seemed imminent, Churchill set up SOE proper. It was divided into two sections. The first, called SO 1, was concerned with propaganda; the other, SO 2, was the old Section D under another name. Both SO 1 and SO 2 were under the political control of the Ministry of Economic Warfare (MEW); SO 1's country headquarters were situated at Woburn Abbey in Bedfordshire, SO 2 in Baker Street in London, and there was a Special Duties training school at Straddishall in Suffolk. After July 1941, SO 1 was removed from sole control of the MEW and the re-formed department for propaganda to Occupied Europe was called the Political Warfare Executive, or PWE.[17]

SOE did not therefore consider subversion to be simply about explosives: propaganda was an equally vital part of its activities. In July 1940, Hugh Dalton became minister in charge of SOE and thus was also placed in charge of propaganda to the enemy. After July 1941, however, this propaganda work was controlled by a triumvirate of Dalton, Eden and Bracken (the Minister of Information).[18] Robert Bruce Lockhart, who was a former British secret agent (and a pro-Bolshevik) was asked to head it, not least to ensure that the Foreign Office interest was fully represented. Ultimately, in February 1942, Dalton was replaced as SOE's minister by the arch-Conservative, the Earl of Selborne, and Eden and Bracken took away SOE's already reduced rights over propaganda.

SOE's first political leader, Hugh Dalton, was one of the great figures of the British Labour movement. Known by his friends as

'Doctor Dynamo' (he held a doctorate from the London School of
Economics), his enemies preferred the nickname 'Doctor Dirty'. He
cut a curious and sometimes unrepresentative figure as a Socialist.
He had been educated at Eton and his father was a chaplain to the
Royal Family.[19]

In Labour's wilderness years in the 1930s, Dalton gained the
reputation of a right-winger. He frequently pilloried those on
Labour's left for their pacificism and their unilateralism, and also
for their attempt to incorporate the British Communist Party into
the Labour Party (which he called a 'piece of clotted nonsense').[20]

He represented a mining constituency in the north-east of Britain,
becoming after the war Chancellor of the Exchequer (and not
Foreign Secretary, as had been widely expected, an issue to which
we shall return later on). In the dramatic days of the Nazi attack on
the Low Countries and France, Dalton became an active participant
in the parliamentary manoeuvres which led to Chamberlain's losing
the Premiership in May 1940. He supported the candidature of
Churchill, with whom he shared a number of views.

By way of a reward for this co-operation and as a mark of
recognition for his exceptional ability and standing, Churchill invited
Dalton to join his Government as Minister of Economic Warfare
(although Dalton was not and never became a member of the inner
war Cabinet).[21] Dalton was one of only four Labour leaders, apart
from Attlee himself, of whom Churchill had decreed that: 'Their
services in high office were immediately required.'[22]

About a month after his appointment, Churchill decided to
increase Dalton's power considerably by asking him to take charge
of the new Special Operations Executive.[23] With that appointment,
Dalton was to become one of the most powerful men in the United
Kingdom. This is how Dalton himself described the appointment:

> This was to be a new instrument of war and I should be responsible
> for shaping it. Its purpose was to coordinate all action by way of
> subversion against the Enemy overseas. A new organisation was
> being created which would absorb some small elements of existing
> organisations but would be on a much greater scale, with wider
> scope and largely manned by new personnel. It would be a secret
> or underground organisation ... Subversion was a complex con-
> ception. It meant the weakening by whatever 'covert' means of
> the Enemy's will to make war and the strengthening of the will
> and power of his opponents including in particular guerilla and

resistance movements. It thus included many forms of propaganda
... I accepted the Prime Minister's suggestion with great eagerness
and satisfaction. 'And now,' he exhorted, 'set Europe ablaze.'[24]

Subversion, then, was henceforward not going to be an activity
undertaken only by Stalin (or Hitler). Britain was going to engage
in it as well. The decision to do so was to prove momentous. The
obvious sense of exhilaration with which Dalton describes his unique
appointment comes over with great clarity. He was, as he said, being
given a totally new organisation with a totally new task, which would
involve giving British arms and other help to groups of anti-Germans
who, if things turned out as planned, would help in the destruction
of the Nazi invaders and lay the foundations for the new post-war
world.

In part, of course, this new outfit was born of despair. Both
Churchill and his Chiefs of Staff knew that there was precious little
with which to try to destroy Hitler. Innovation was thus of great
urgency, and any attempt to mobilise the victims of Nazi domination
in the struggle against the Third Reich was something well worth
trying.

SOE must, then, be seen as the actively subversive wing of British
Intelligence. Indeed, Stafford goes so far as to argue that in many
ways SOE was intended to be a Western liberal alternative to the
Comintern, which was, of course, one of the main tools of Stalin's
subversive strategy. This analogy is trenchant and by no means
unfair.[25] Stafford writes that:

> SOE was an anomaly, an executive agency with its own Minister.
> The Minister, especially Hugh Dalton, claimed the right to make
> his own policy, yet simultaneously, SOE was instructed to confine
> itself to the execution of policy decisions made by others, in
> particular, the Chiefs of Staff and the Foreign Office ... Much
> about SOE will remain unknown and many of its secrets will be
> taken into the grave [for it was] a secret organisation whose
> existence was not acknowledged until after the war and when it
> had already been wound up.[26]

And he continues:

> The British were deeply involved in many aspects of European
> wartime resistance and it was Churchill and not Stalin who first

called for Europe to be 'set ablaze' with the fires of revolt.

This is a revealing point, even if its conclusion about Stalin is incorrect.

Far more inaccurate, however, is Stafford's claim that SOE must primarily be seen as a tool of repression against left-wing movements: 'an instrument for the political oppression and containment of left-wing resistance in Europe'.[27] As has been pointed out, the term 'left-wing' is really not very helpful. For although SOE did end up 'containing' Socialist resistance, it certainly did not 'contain' Communist resistance. Thus it could be argued that SOE's net, if unintended, effect was actually to promote the fortunes of Communist resistance. And, it should be added, it was a prime aim of the Communist resistance to try to destroy its Social Democratic and anti-Communist rivals along with the Nazi oppressors.

Yet Stafford also neglects the changes in policy within SOE during Dalton's tenure of office. For careful analysis of SOE's history proves that Dalton himself initially went to great lengths to try to support Social Democratic and 'bourgeois' resistance to Nazism, but that, beginning in the early summer of 1941, that line was changed. After he was replaced, SOE simply became imbued with a passivity towards political affairs which tended to favour the Communist resistance at the expense of the Social Democratic and more right-wing groups.

It should never be forgotten that most sectors of the societies of both Occupied Europe and the aggressor nations spawned resistance groups. Yet it has often been the case that historians have highlighted only one sector's resistance. In reality, it would be as wrong to discount the Social Democratic resistance to Hitler in, say, France or Germany as it would be to discount the Communist, military or aristocratic resistance in those countries. The decision to favour one group rather than another was, therefore, a political decision and one of great significance, since once the Nazis had been destroyed, those groups who were able to demonstrate that they had played an important part in the process of defeat were likely to be in a strong position to shape the post-war politics of their nations.

Stafford himself is unclear about SOE's ultimate political concerns:

Was SOE part of a wider strategy by the British war leadership to contain Communism and restore the social and political status quo in Europe?[28]

The evidence suggests it is inaccurate to argue that the tighter Conservative political control of SOE which followed Dalton's dismissal meant that SOE became anti-Communist. In fact, the reverse seems to be true.

What is more, in theory a robust Social Democrat and anti-Communist like Dalton appeared to stand a far better chance of marshalling resistance to the Nazi New Order than the Earl of Selborne who, in marked contrast to Dalton, had little understanding of continental European politics. Those sceptical of the notion that SOE had a political role will find no support in the testimonies provided by former SOE officers. One of them, Julian Amery, may serve as an example. He makes its intended political functions quite explicit. He demonstrates SOE's political concerns, particularly in respect of the Balkan theatre in which Amery worked, and he also shows up SOE's failings in this same area.[29] He notes SOE's early preoccupation with what he terms 'European Reconstruction', that is, what was to be constructed on the ruins the Nazis would leave behind.

In the Balkans, for example, SOE supported King Peter as a constitutional monarch for Yugoslavia, both as an antidote to reaction and specifically as an antidote to Communism. Amery writes:

> The purpose of our [i.e. SOE's] work was not only to liberate the Balkan countries from the Nazis but also to promote a new deal for their peoples based on co-operation and democracy ... who would liberate the Balkan countries from the Nazis? What local forces would come out on top? Nationalists and Democrats? Or Communists ... within an hour or two of Barbarossa [June 1941] all these problems were clearly formulated in our minds.[30]

Thus those working in SOE thought politically as well as explosively, even if what happened to SOE after 1942, which could be termed its political neutralisation, made its political aspects seem far less obvious even to some of its own officers.

The evidence from the field, then, proves that SOE began its life as an organisation determined to replace Nazism in Europe by liberal and Social Democratic regimes, but that it ended up assisting by default in the erection of Communist regimes, particularly in central, southern and eastern Europe. More through luck than anything else, western Europe was spared this fate although it came quite close to it. Certainly, there seems no truth in the view attributed by Stafford to Denis Healey in 1945 that SOE policy in these matters 'was designed to protect the interests of Europe's ruling class'.[31] Even the hastiest glance at Poland and elsewhere serves to show how false this was as a statement on the outcome of SOE activity.

In peacetime a body like SOE would have been impossible to justify; an intelligence service which was armed and so overtly political, designed to interfere in the domestic politics of other States, laid any democratic Government open to enormous risks. In wartime, however, where Britain was fighting for its very existence the risks were well worth taking. It was just as 'C' had told Colonel Grand in 1938:

'Is anything barred?' Grand asked. 'Not a thing,' 'C' replied.

Hugh Dalton and SOE: the politics of SOE's work

The Communists' concern with SOE reflected the two distinct phases in the history of SOE. The first may be termed the Daltonian period; it was then that SOE had an active political side which, we shall argue, was not only the object of Communist subversion, but was in principle the best way in which SOE could have been used to win the war and secure a democratic peace for Europe. The second phase deals with the post-Daltonian period when SOE was downgraded in political terms and forced to preside over an increased Communist role in the European resistance to Nazism. As we shall see, there is evidence which suggests that at least in part this change may be attributable to Communist subversion.

There are of course some who will dispute that there was any significant change at all; others will accept that there was, indeed, a change, but prefer to ascribe it either to Dalton's 'unsuitability' for office or to the wider changes in the conduct of the Second World War.

Yet even among the latter there is no unity of argument. Ben Pimlott, for example, states that Dalton's departure from SOE was provoked by the collision between the American entry into the war and Dalton's 'preference for Left-wing groups (and by implication Communist ones)',[32] an alleged preference to which we shall return. Pimlott implies that Dalton's left-wing sympathies caused friction with American Capitalist or right-wing ones. Stafford, on the other hand, suggests that after Dalton's departure SOE tended to favour the left-wing among the European resistance. One of them must be wrong.

One obvious reason for 'the confusion that prevails is that the change in SOE, though dramatic, occurred gradually, starting in the early summer of 1941 before Dalton left it. The second reason, however, is no less significant, for the Anglo-Soviet Alliance injected a new element into SOE's work.

From the beginning, SOE was dogged by persistent problems. For a start there had been the institutional wrangling over who should control SOE, whether it should be the Foreign Office, MI6, the Ministry of Information or the Ministry of Economic Warfare or a given combination of these. A further and not unrelated problem had to do with the controversial political implications of its subversive activities. For, quite plainly, SOE's work impinged upon the work of several high offices of State. Whom it chose to support in Occupied Europe would clearly concern the Foreign Office (controlled, of course, by a Conservative, Eden); the use it would make of propaganda would concern the Ministry of Information; whether it utilised British agents overseas directly touched upon MI6's activities; and its relationship to any British or Allied expeditionary force was rightly a matter for the War Office.

One of the first political problems to be grasped by SOE's new boss, Dalton, was the question of recruitment. He himself believed that special people were needed for special operations, and that it was right that he himself, a civilian, should be in charge of what were essentially paramilitary operations. As Dalton said to the Labour leader and Deputy Prime Minister Clement Attlee on one occasion:

> Regular soldiers are not men to stir up revolutions, to create social chaos or use all those ungentlemanly means of winning the war which came easily to the Nazis.[33]

But it was not simply the leaders of SOE whose politics counted. As agents, Dalton wished to use:

> Concerned trade unionists and Socialists in enemy and enemy occupied countries ... In November 1940 he was to be found telling his senior officials that if the Germans were in occupation of Great Britain and he were trying to organise a movement

against them, he would choose people like his own constituents, the Durham miners . . .[34]

He was not entirely successful in this venture, but it is certainly worth asking whether, if the intelligence services had been staffed with more miners and more trade unionists and fewer professional and academic high-flyers, its success might not have been more marked. Instead, Dalton recruited and found staff in the professions, going particularly for bankers and the like who had, by the nature of their business, good international connections which were based on mutual trust. As one of them, H. N. Sporborg, pointed out, they were all 'complete amateurs', not perhaps an entirely reassuring description, but inevitable, as trained secret agents were in short supply.

Another of Dalton's difficulties was also connected with staffing: for he had decided to sack Grand. His reasons were significant ones: Grand told Ellic Howe that Dalton had:

Asked me to get Leon Blum [the French Socialist leader], a fellow Socialist politician, out of France. I saw him a couple of days later and said I would need a submarine or a Lysander aircraft, also that he would have to go to the War Cabinet for approval. I don't suppose the Conservatives were all that interested in Blum. I said that I couldn't hazard lives and the operation could not be mounted because it was not a 'Top War Priority' affair. So Dalton sacked me.[35]

It is important to realise that Dalton wanted to get his Socialist colleagues out of Occupied Europe in order to participate in his plans for SOE, using the full resources he possessed as a minister of submarines and planes. He failed with Blum (who was captured by the Gestapo but survived a concentration camp), and he failed too in his attempt to get the non-Communist French trade union leader Leon Jouhaux to organise French workers. Jouhaux was, in the event, betrayed to the Gestapo and deported to Germany.[36] But in the case of the remnants of the German Social Democratic leadership, Dalton did succeed. He was able to bring them to England.

Dalton himself had three outstanding personal assistants – Hugh Gaitskell, Christopher Mayhew and Robin Brook – whose advice he valued very highly; Foot makes it plain that Gaitskell took an active interest in SOE work.[37] This is a point to which we must return later on (see p. 147). The first two assistants were both highly political individuals who went on to dazzling political careers. Yet (in keeping with his own apolitical interpretation of SOE), Foot concludes:

> These three energetic and intelligent young men brought Dalton plenty of news but did not at this stage seek much impact on policy. More influence was exerted at Dalton's elbow by a rising diplomat Gladwyn Jebb [who] had been Dalton's private secretary when he was under-secretary at the Foreign Office from 1929–31 ...[38]

As far as wider recruitment was concerned, Foot points out that it had to be via personal recommendation (in a comment that is as relevant to MI5 and MI6 as it is to SOE), since it was not possible to recruit to SOE by advertisement. Some recruits came from the services when SOE, from time to time, made special trawls for people with language or other skills.[39]

Foot also makes it quite clear that almost all of SOE's recruits came from a specific social background. He notes that when his first study of SOE was published in 1966, he gave ample space to the schools to which recruits had been. Some of his critics said this was 'old-world snobbery' but he quite rightly argues that:

> England in the late 30s and early 40s was run almost entirely by an educated governing class drawn from ... public schools.[40]

Like Stafford, Foot seems exceptionally anxious about the charge that SOE officials possessed a right-wing and inherently anti-Socialist bias. Perhaps they did; perhaps they did not. But the real point is that even if individual officers held Conservative views, they had virtually no impact on what SOE policy became after 1941. It was rather ironic that in terms of individual officers' politics, those who were Communists were likely to be far more satisfied with their Conservative minister, Selborne, than those who were Conservatives (in any case, as the careers of the vast majority of moles showed, one should never assume that a middle-class background meant one had middle-class values and could not be a Communist).

Dalton was, however, according to Stafford, more than a little uneasy about the staff he was himself recruiting:

> He was quick on occasion to suspect that his senior officials in

SOE, many of whom came from banking and the legal professions, were prejudiced against mobilising left-wing and labour movements in Europe.[41]

But Foot is very unimpressed by Dalton's anxieties:

Dalton could be heard grumbling about reactionary underlings from the City; most of his grumbles were LSE [London School of Economics] froth.[42]

And, of course, a lot of people were very uneasy about the recruitment of Dalton himself. In personal terms, Dalton's character left a lot to be desired. Stafford suggests that he may well have been an 'unwise choice' as SOE chief. He was often 'difficult and tactless' and he seemed to dislike Anthony Eden, whose goodwill was a vital part of SOE's success: 'wretched Eden, posing before the looking glass'.[43] He was also a bully.

Yet politically speaking, it could be argued that Dalton possessed the energy and the vision to make something of SOE. Furthermore, he also had enough experience of the aims and methods of Communist subversion to ensure that its British counterpart could give it a run for its money.

There was, of course, yet another aspect to the question of recruitment. It possessed great significance in terms of the non-British agents of SOE. SOE had to recruit personnel in the countries it wished to subvert. But what sort of people? Were they to belong to organised groups? If so, what sort of groups? Were these groups to be civilian or formed out of what had been national armies? Were they to be former members of political parties? And of which political parties? And what about practising Communists? Were they to be considered suitable SOE agents? They had the organisational skills, they were fanatically committed to their cause and they were well versed in the arts of conspiracy and secrecy. On the other hand they were, at this time, extremely dangerous. First and most important, before June 1941 the Communists were allied to the Nazis. Second, Communists could hardly be expected to fight for the ideal of liberal democracy.

As the Grand incident demonstrated, Dalton's own view of how SOE might be made operational had a firm Socialist base to it. Dalton argued that the most useful sources of resistance were going to be the labour movements of Europe which had, he believed, both the ideological commitment to fighting Fascism and first-hand organisational experience. It is as easy to appreciate the logic of this as it is to see how it might vex Conservative political leaders, who could hardly wish to see the left prosper as a result of Hitler's hoped-for defeat. But rather remarkably, perhaps, it is very important to realise that Dalton's ideas had the full support of no less an authority than the Prime Minister himself, at the beginning at any rate. For Dalton has recorded Churchill stating quite categorically in July 1940 that: 'All this [SOE's subversive work] must come from the Left.'[44]

With Churchill's clear support, Dalton's view of what SOE ought to do was, of course, the most important one since he was SOE's boss, but it was only one input into SOE at this time. It was not shared by the other dominating figure in SOE in its earlier phase, Major-General Colin Gubbins. Gubbins was not the sort to possess any great faith in Socialism; if he had any political interest it is far more likely to have been in one of the other great political ideologies of the nineteenth century, nationalism. This viewpoint was by no means less valid than that of Dalton, and it may well be that an appeal to nationalist sentiment was more likely to be successful in getting Occupied Europe to rise against Hitler and the Nazis than an appeal to Socialism. Interestingly enough, Hitler's own (anti-Communist) subversive policy in Russia was built on the encouragement of nationalist groups such as the Ukrainians; these were the people Stalin asked for and who were subsequently handed over at Yalta.[45]

What is more, nationalism had also generated its fair share of revolution both in the nineteenth and twentieth centuries and had been used as a revolutionary force, particularly in the First World War; a use symbolised especially in the Middle East, where both the Balfour Declaration and the exploits of Lawrence of Arabia were designed by the British with some skill, to encourage local revolt against the Turkish Empire.[46]

Gubbins certainly saw that there was a political side to the work he was proposing:

He was [now] applying all his efforts in trying to persuade the military authorities to take more urgent action for work in occupied territories; this needed understanding of their political background as well as their military potential.[47]

According to the BBC series on SOE, Gubbins was given two main tasks by Dalton. The first was to construct SOE's organisation along military lines, and the second was to liaise most closely with the Czechs and Poles. It was out of this task, combined with Gubbins's wish to foster nationalistic resistance, that the structure emerged which is, perhaps, most closely associated with Gubbins's name – the Secret Army.

Gubbins at any rate understood the political implications of his work. Although in public he liked to claim that:

> SOE had been given a purely military task, he was quick to claim in private ... that but for SOE's wartime work, many of the Western European countries might have been lost to NATO in the early days of the Cold War ...[48]

This was a distortion of the real position which was rather more complex.

These, then, were the issues surrounding SOE at the highest levels. But how did its junior officers view SOE? It was in the field that Dalton's ideas were to be put to the test. Let us now turn to the testimonies of people who were recruited into SOE at this time. One set of fascinating insights comes from Douglas Dodds-Parker, later a Conservative MP.

> [In 1939] in London I was asked to join the SIS. Peter Fleming [the brother of the creator of James Bond, Ian Fleming], one of the activists of those months, advised me to keep free of any definite job until war broke out; there was much to be done meantime on one's own ... I politely declined the SIS invitation, saying I wished to do something active, and not just collect intelligence. I was not told [then] about D Section ...[49]

Dodds-Parker went to get a military training (mixed with a period spent on guard duty outside Windsor Castle). He then went on a special course at Cambridge, known as 'the Gauleiters', whose aim was:

> To bring together and classify a number of officers who had specialist knowledge of foreign countries and who might be available and suitable for action rather than intelligence ... The instruc-

tion was comprehensive, from international law and economics to varieties of sabotage, physical and commercial.[50]

In due course, Dodds-Parker entered the orbit of Colonel Lawrence Grand:

Only a few men had seen the likelihood of some non-military [intelligence] action and had begun, despite financial restrictions, to prepare for it. The D Section of SIS was set up under Grand. At about the same time, a small group of farsighted and experienced Army officers, Joe Holland, Gerald Templar and Colin Gubbins, had come together in MIR, in Room 365 in the War Office. They shared many ideas, stemming from personal service in the First World War and afterwards in Russia, in the Troubles in Ireland, and later in India and Palestine. Indeed, overseas Public Security Departments were more practised than Whitehall ... sometimes the placing of these activities under the umbrella of Intelligence led to confusion ...[51]

It was an enthralling occupation for Dodds-Parker, who clearly relished not only the duties of what was to become SOE, but also the people who staffed it:

It was an immense privilege and honour to be for the next five years a junior member of the Group which formed the nucleus of Special Operations Planning and Action – Peter Fleming, Peter Wilkinson, Tommy Davies and Bickham Sweet-Escott.[52]

Another helpful account is provided by Ellic Howe.[53] Howe was a forger. His work in British secret warfare was based on his understanding of the techniques of printing. Both the printed and the spoken word were, of course, considered vitally important in the successful waging of the war, and Howe's personal motto ('If it's printed, it's true') enjoyed the widest support. Long before the RAF began to drop bombs on Nazi Germany, it dropped leaflets and, at one stage, the British authorities actually produced what must rank as an early version of *Private Eye*. Called the *Wolkiger Beobachter*, it was meant to be a spoof on the Nazi organ entitled the *Völkischer Beobachter*. It was the pride and joy of Sir Campbell Stuart, a Canadian with propaganda experience emanating from the First

World War, who was an early and not very successful propaganda chief.[54]

Howe had originally approached MI5, offering his services, but he was re-routed to Dalton's Ministry and thence to Woburn. There he came across the motley crew assembled by Dalton to wage secret propaganda war on the Third Reich. The people Howe met included several exiled Germans, including a curious man by the name of Wolfgang zu Putlitz about whom Howe discovered the following:

> The news of Ribbentrop's forthcoming journey to Moscow [in August 1939] had been leaked to London by Putlitz, a German diplomat stationed at the Hague who escaped to England just before hostilities began.[55]

He also met other German political exiles:

> Herr Spiecker (known as Mr Turner) who had been a Weimar civil servant and was a prominent member of the Deutsche Freiheitspartei, a loosely organised group of social democratic German refugees.[56]

He came across the remarkable Fritz Heine, later to become the post-war German Social Democratic Party's press chief and aide to Schumacher and Ollenhauer; Otto John, later to become head of the West German version of MI5; and General von Thoma who was captured soon after the battle of El Alamein and whose fate in British propaganda is dealt with later.[57]

The contacts that SOE officers had with foreign exiles is something to which we shall return in due course. Yet it should be noted that Ellic Howe's experience was not unique. Douglas Dodds-Parker also came across a variety of these exiles:

> [In the summer of 1939] passing through Paris, I called at a small hotel used by the Social Democrat International for Refugees ... back again in Oxford, I visited President Benes and Jan Masaryk, who had sought refuge from Prague in England ... They told me to keep in touch which was valuable when later I was a junior officer concerned with Polish and Czech affairs.[58]

In mid-September 1938 Dodds-Parker had gone to Czechoslovakia:

I had introductions to the anti-Nazi Social Democrats, in particular to those of German origin who lived in the frontier (Sudeten) areas. Storch and Wenzel Jaksch were the leaders – the latter to survive and be a colleague at the Council of Europe.[59]

The British propaganda outfit at Woburn was designed to win the war of the words, or as Howe puts it, to 'represent Great Britain against Dr Goebbels's propaganda Ministry'.[60] Life at Woburn as described by Howe and others was a mixture of high policy, organisational and institutional anarchy, and very hard work. It was also far away from the Blitz and its open country afforded the opportunity for the more skilful residents to supplement their rations with game (both in and out of season).

From time to time Hugh Dalton would arrive at Woburn. Thomas Barman, to whom we shall return at greater length, recalled in his book:

Hugh Dalton used to come down to Woburn from time to time to inspect the troops. He was a great booming bully and it used to be said of him that it was no laughing matter when Dalton cracked a joke.[61]

Yet another view of Dalton is offered by Julian Amery. He had been recruited into SOE largely as a result of having spent a Mediterranean holiday in Yugoslavia in the hot summer of 1939, during the Oxford long vacation. When war broke out, Amery decided to stay in the Balkans if he could, so that instead of trying to make his way home, he presented himself at the British Embassy in Belgrade. By virtue of his first-rate knowledge of Balkan affairs, Amery soon became a resident Embassy expert. This, in turn, led him to secret service work for D Section.

D Section, Amery reminds us, was:

Quite distinct from C section, the Secret Intelligence Service. Its object was to subvert the enemy's war effort in his own and neutral territories. By subversion was meant those operations against the enemy which lay outside the province of the armed forces and the Departments of State. It included such things as the sabotage of enemy factories and ships, the blowing up of his communications and the organisation and support of resistance in occupied territories.[62]

Amery recalls that Grand and his Balkan chief had:

Set their hearts on organising a revolt against the Italians in Albania. They believed it would tie down large numbers of Italian troops and weaken Italy's ability to wage war. The Foreign Office however took a different view. We had great interests in the Mediterranean but very limited military power. Our first object was to try to keep the Italians out of the war and not to provoke them . . .[63]

The young Amery thus found himself being asked to set up a subversive organisation in the Balkans, and was supplied with a radio and bag contact with 'D' Section in London's Baker Street where:

A modest name plate at the entrance proclaimed that this was the office of the ISRB or the Inter-Services Research Bureau which was, in fact, the HQ of D Section.[64]

Probably because he was the son of a senior Cabinet Minister, Amery also met the chief of the whole outfit, Hugh Dalton:

At our first meeting, Dalton seemed rather larger than life. He was tall and broad. His head rose to a mighty bald dome. His voice boomed and he accompanied his expansive gestures with an ominous rolling of the eyes . . . It was rumoured that he had a special chair so designed as to fall to bits at the very slightest pressure. According to the story, he would take a running kick at this when he wanted to impress a visitor with the strength of his opinion. Yet I have never known a kindlier man.[65]

Amery noticed one other thing about Dalton at this first interview. He was quizzed about his politics by Dalton:

He asked me about my political views and whether I had read certain books on economics. When I confessed to ignorance of the particular titles he mentioned, he boomed out, 'Aha! I see you are not very familiar with my works. I will send them tomorrow and then examine you upon them . . .' Then he questioned me in detail about the Balkans. He seemed at first to be arguing the Foreign Office case but this was only to take my measure. Suddenly he brought his fist down on the desk and declared, 'Of course you are right, and they are wrong. It is useless to expect any help from King Boris or Prince Patsy . . .'[66]

This was more than just idle conversation for the incident proves not only that Dalton's political interest in SOE's work was something that he made explicit, but that it did not wholly correspond to what Amery took to be the 'Foreign Office case'. The implication behind Dalton's remarks was that the Foreign Office was apparently supporting the idea that subversion be based on the governments (and monarchies) which had ruled their respective nations before the Germans invaded them, whereas in Dalton's view the people to look to were the new political movements in those nations.

There is one other extremely curious thing worth noting about Dalton's reported conversation and that is the marked similarity to an analogous point made by Kim Philby in his book. The significance of this similarity, which is too striking to be simply coincidental, is something that is discussed in detail later (see p. 143).[67]

As a member of SOE, Amery was asked to sign the Official Secrets Act and was told, rather to his amusement, to use several taxis, never one. He was also given a code name and this was always used in all correspondence and over the phone. What is more, as an agent of SOE, Amery had access to some of the most intimate secrets of the British Government:

As an Officer of SOE I saw a wide selection of Foreign Office telegrams, Intelligence Reports and other Government papers. I was on the inside of Government.[68]

SOE, then, was not established simply to blow things up. There was indeed a hard political edge to the work that it did, and even though this edge has tended to be ignored in some accounts of SOE's activities, a careful analysis of the testimony provided by SOE officers confirms the existence of a political aspect to British subversive activity.

SOE activity was the result of secret intelligence and military force, to try and achieve high policy objectives in the fight against Hitler. At the same time, it must be pointed out that it is precisely because of this that SOE must be regarded as a body in which Soviet Intelligence, both political and military, was obliged to take more than a passing interest, and a body which it would, if given the chance, attempt to subvert.

What SOE might have been: alarm bells in the Kremlin

In the last few sections, we looked at the origins of SOE as an armed intelligence organisation whose operations could, if mounted with wisdom and good sense, have helped create a post-war Europe whose political systems would have run parallel to those of Great Britain and the United States of America.

SOE was not, however, used in this way and with some important exceptions, the post-war map of Europe suited Stalin far better than it suited Churchill or Attlee, Roosevelt or Truman. This present study does not advance any single reason to explain this fact. What happens in history is almost always the outcome of a combination of factors. For one thing, Churchill was not like Stalin; and his view of subversion was not likely to be analogous to Stalin's or indeed to Hitler's. We should not forget that Hitler's subversive strategy was indeed very similar to Stalin's. As Alan Bullock has written:

> Hitler frequently became intoxicated with the prospect of a revolutionary upheaval which would destroy the entire European social order.[69]

And Goebbels, in differentiating between Mussolini, Stalin and his beloved Führer, wrote:

> The Duce ... is not a real revolutionary like the Führer or Stalin. He is so bound to his own Italian people that he lacks the broad qualities of a world-wide revolutionary and insurrectionist.[70]

For another, much – if not most – of the post-war map of Europe was the result of the military campaigns against Germany; in the final analysis Churchill, Roosevelt and Stalin all knew that Hitler could only be defeated by the military destruction of Germany using conventional armed forces – by brute force rather than insurrection.

Yet in the realm of 'might-have-beens' SOE looms very large. Had Churchill actually appreciated what Stalin would make of the map of Europe in 1945, it is not implausible to argue that he would have used SOE more fruitfully to try to scupper the plans of the Communist dictator. After all he appears to have wanted to supply the Polish Home Army in the summer of 1944, but both Selborne and the Foreign Office opposed the idea. And, of course, he refused to permit the Communists to seize power in Greece (although there seems no evidence that he saw the Greek case as part of a wider plan).[71]

So why was SOE not used in a different way? Why was it that the person most identified with such an alternative use, namely Dalton, was sacked? Finally, was one of the reasons why SOE failed in this regard that it was successfully subverted by the moles and agents of the Kremlin? Such a charge is, of course, serious and must not be made lightly. Above all, it is vital to adduce convincing evidence to support it.

Yet the first thing to note is that the evidence is neither straight forward nor overwhelming, although in my own view it is very strong indeed. We know of a number of SOE agents who were Communists and we know too that moles and agents existed within SOE (which is not necessarily the same thing). In addition, the latter were part of a conspiracy.

At the same time, many of Dalton's ideas for SOE must have failed for perfectly legitimate reasons and it is important not to make a false choice between error and conspiracy; indeed, the evidence suggests that they existed side by side, reinforcing each other in the same way as, after 1941, the aims of the moles and British high policy often merged quite happily. What we must never forget, however, is that the stakes in this secret war were not just the destruction of Nazi Germany, but the creation of a new Europe, and that the characters in those stakes were all anti-Nazis, but that some of them were Communists while others were anti-Communists.

Let us now examine in greater detail the specific aspects of Daltonian policy towards SOE which aroused Soviet interest, and seek to answer the important question of why he was thrown out of his job. If he really possessed such good ideas, why did so many of them appear to end in failure? Was it his ideas that caused his dismissal or was it their often flawed execution? And why was he replaced by someone who had no all-embracing political concept?

Hugh Dalton's memoirs have long been recognised as a vital resource for the historiography of the Second World War. Yet when it comes to SOE, Dalton's account is singularly thin. Even today, significant details about Dalton's precise plans for SOE remain locked up and unavailable to scholars, as a result of a Government decision not to release them.[72]

Dalton does provide one or two important insights into the concepts which he took to his 'black life', as he called it.[73] But he is very sparse when it comes to the details which led to his departure from it. He writes that:

> The secrets of my black life, as I called it, were surprisingly well kept and I was admirably served by my staff ... Some thought that special operations should be under the War Office but this idea found little support. I said that the W.O. had more than enough on their plate already. Branches of M.I. [military intelligence] were proliferating everywhere. What some of us had in mind was not primarily a military job at all. It concerned Trade Unionists and Socialists in enemy and enemy occupied territories, the creation of Fifth Columns, of explosions, chaos and revolution. Some said that hitherto the Foreign Office had prevented all effective action in this field ...[74]

In this passage, Dalton can be shown quite clearly to be putting forward the case for what might be termed a political role for SOE. He is, perhaps understandably, slightly elliptical about precisely what he is driving at, presumably in order not to fall foul of the Official Secrets Act. But the implication of his words is clear: SOE was not to be a War Office show and the British Foreign Office was not to be allowed to call the tune either. Finally, it was to Labour's Socialist comrades that he proposed SOE look for some of its manpower.

Dalton next added a little flesh to the bones of his concept:

> We must organise movements in enemy occupied territory, I wrote to Halifax, comparable to the Sinn Fein Movement in Ireland ... we must use many different methods, including industrial and military sabotage, labour agitation and strikes, continuous propaganda, terrorist acts against traitors and German leaders, boycotts and strikes ...[75]

As for his departure, Dalton says very, very little about this:

> There was, indeed, a suspicion that through SOE I was trying to control foreign policy or run a foreign policy on my own. Some mischief makers, I think, tried to put such ideas into Eden's head.

But my direct relations with him [presumably what he said to his face rather than behind his back] remained always friendly and easy . . .[76]

Churchill simply told Dalton he was to quit the Ministry of Economic Warfare (and SOE, of course) and was to hand it over to the Earl of Selborne who 'was said to be very close' to Churchill.[77]

On 21 February 1942 therefore, Hugh Dalton packed his bags and said goodbye to his 'black life'. But why, precisely, did he go? He provides no real clue and the scholars disagree. Had something awful happened in SOE? Had he failed to deliver the goods of subversion? Or had his plans for subversion been vetoed by his political rivals, and if so, why? And what role might the moles have played in all this? One might have expected the replacement of a left-winger like Dalton by a right-winger like Selborne to have increased friction between SOE and the Russians; but it did not, apparently, do so. Why not?

The final explanation for Dalton's departure has yet to be given. Lord Gladwyn's view that it was the result of personal enmity between Dalton and Churchill is probably the most important single reason.[78]

Dalton's recently published diaries offer a few new insights into his dismissal by Churchill. For one thing, they prove that it came as a severe shock to him. His diary entry for 21 February 1942 recorded a phone call from Churchill with the bad and unexpected news; 'this is a bit of a surprise,' Dalton told him, and it is clear from the passage that he was distressed by it.[79] Elsewhere Dalton mentions conflicts with Eden and Bracken:

Eden is being very silly and difficult again . . . afraid that I will want to control foreign policy . . . that at some moment some great movement will start in some foreign country, Italy or Germany, and I shall say it is all mine and that I therefore must run the peace conference and he be elbowed out.[80]

Although personal rivalry and animosity may have seemed, to the principals themselves, sufficient grounds for Dalton's sacking, there is some reason to doubt whether even they necessarily understood the full story. Was it really feasible that Eden's self-importance (if that is what it was) would have been sufficient to edge Dalton out, for fear that the latter might be successful in launching some 'great movement' to end the war? Or might a person or persons have encouraged Dalton, Eden and Bracken to believe their differences were personal in order to conceal the fact that the Kremlin found Dalton's plans deeply threatening on the political plane? Indeed, there is some reason to believe that – in an indirect way – subversion may indeed have played a part both in Dalton's inability to get his concept of subversion off the ground and in his eventual departure.

Like many Socialists, Dalton believed that a combination of military defeat, or even the threat of it, and a strong resistance movement supported by Britain might usefully speed the demise of the Third Reich. He was, in addition, a convinced anti-Communist and this gave his ideas on resistance an added significance. Now it is perfectly true that he supported the alliance with Russia; indeed, he believed that the British Government had failed to make full use of the Soviet Union in trying to prevent Hitler plunging the Continent into war. In a book published in 1940, he wrote:

> Oh, the chances we missed with Russia! For years, when she was there and offering to help us we did not want her; when at last we wanted her, she was no longer there ...[81]

Although Dalton argued that the 1939 Hitler–Stalin Pact owed more than a little to the British refusal to co-operate with the Soviet Union, this did not make him any the less suspicious of Soviet motives. With obvious relish he quotes the following:

> A Czech friend once said to me the Russians have very big eyes. They see many things that others don't see and some things that aren't there at all ... [But] whatever may be said of earlier stages, the Russians at the end outwitted and double-crossed us with a vengeance [which] precipitated Hitler's war.[82]

And, at the end of his book, Dalton repeated official Labour policy towards the USSR in 1940:

> Labour has always stood four-square against aggression. We had hoped that Soviet Russia would join with the democracies for the collective organisation of peace and resistance to aggression. We worked hard to that end. We condemned the clumsiness of the British Government in its earlier relations with the Soviet Union but this cannot excuse the Russian Government's Pact with the

Nazis on the eve of the war, much less its unprovoked attack on Finland in shameless imitation of the Nazi technique in foreign policy.[83]

At the same time, Dalton was clearly no mindless enemy of the USSR. In July 1932 he had visited Russia as part of a Fabian study group:

> There were about 15 of us including Graham Haldane, Margaret Cole, D. N.. Pritt, Harry Weldon [Fellow of Magdalen College, Oxford], a philosopher, and Redvers Opie, an economist who spoke and understood Russian. I returned after five weeks of talk and travel immensely stimulated. I had caught a quick but vivid glimpse of a quite new world. And this remained with me as an abiding influence.[84]

On his return from the USSR Dalton was asked to contribute to a book on his experiences. He remarked rather wryly, 'I wrote on economic planning ... neither of the Oxford dons wrote anything.'

But whatever feelings of sympathy Dalton felt towards the USSR, they do not mean he misunderstood the true nature of Communism, particularly the British Communist Party. It is of great importance that this point be fully appreciated: Dalton stood for a politically interested SOE, based on active British support for the non-Communist left. In addition, he repeatedly insisted that SOE should try to counter Communist subversion, particularly in the Balkans.

This is confirmed by Julian Amery's account. In the winter of 1941, one of Amery's jobs was to prepare a position paper which would:

> Appeal to the potential forces of resistance in the Balkans and still be consistent with British interests. The Germans and, we suspected, the Soviets, sought to dominate the Balkans ...[85]

It is important to emphasise that this is the testimony of an actual SOE officer and that considerable significance should be attached to that phrase 'consistent with British interests'. It might seem totally absurd to make this explicit, for it might be thought self-evident that Britain would always support resistance forces which were compatible with British concerns. Yet what is striking is that this is something that ultimately did not happen. And the reason for this is not, as some have alleged, because it was never British policy. Amery's testimony shows how false this idea is. Rather, it was because British policy changed.

Amery was at this stage an executor of Daltonian policy, caught up in the secret war, trying to promote British interests and counter those not just of Nazi Germany but also of its ally, the USSR. Indeed, in June 1941, Amery and a colleague were sent to Jerusalem where the King and the exiled Government of Yugoslavia had been established. The mission of the two SOE officers was clear:

> To lay the foundations of our future co-operation with King Peter. We hoped that he would play a major part in the reconstruction of the Balkans after the war. It seemed important therefore to get him to London as soon as possible to complete his studies and show him something of English life. This was easily arranged. His Ministers presented something more of a problem ... Sir Reginald Hoare, HM Ambassador to the Yugoslav Government in Exile ... suffered from acute asthma and could scarcely speak above a whisper. The Yugoslav Foreign Minister, Dr Nintchich, was stone deaf and this complicated the transaction of business ...[86]

Despite the difficulties, Amery pressed on with his task. He recalls that:

> SOE had authority to work underground in Greece, Yugoslavia and Bulgaria. We had also established a sufficient understanding between the leaders of these three countries to claim that the purpose of our work was not only to liberate the Balkan countries from the Nazis but also to promote a new deal for their peoples based on co-operation and democracy. Here was a banner under which the Balkan peoples might unite against the Germans instead of being played off by the Germans, one against the other ...[87]

It cannot therefore be denied that up until the winter of 1941, SOE's position with regard both to its broad political viewpoint and to the sources which it might tap for subversive purposes in Europe was absolutely sound. (There was in fact a curious exception to this rule (see p. 280), but it is one which confirms rather than undercuts the wider proposition being made.) SOE had a hard-baked strategy. Dalton's position was well-thought-out, and he knew how to inspire his staff (particularly his juniors). Above all, under him SOE possessed an enterprise and imagination which were attributes seemingly destined to give it a very special place in Britain's fight against Hitler and the establishment of a new Europe which would supplant him. But Dalton's SOE failed to take off.

Many of Dalton's failures occurred in the precise areas where there was a conflict of interest between the policy that Dalton proposed and the plans and strategies of the Communists. There was therefore, almost certainly, a definite Communist motive in generating SOE failures under Dalton's stewardship, and a firm and direct connection between some of those failures and the moles. The Communist strategy in respect of SOE was quite simply to ensure that the Daltonian concept was abandoned. This was a consistent aim, which began as soon as SOE was conceived and continued unabated. The only difficulty was how best to achieve it. Before the Grand Alliance one set of tactics was appropriate; after it another. In either case to show too much interest in what Dalton was doing would indicate that there was something about his plans that caused the Soviets grave alarm, and would have alerted the British authorities to the fact that Stalin had a secret blueprint for Europe. It was a thorny problem and one for which ingenious and bloody solutions were developed.

This interpretation of Dalton's SOE policies might appear to conflict with the view of the established authority on Dalton, Ben Pimlott. He supports the basic notion that Dalton had a 'preference for Left-wing [resistance] groups' but adds specifically 'and by implication Communist ones'. Furthermore, Pimlott reinforces this remark by arguing that the reason why Dalton was sacked was that the Americans disliked his left-wing concerns.[88]

In actual fact, Dr Pimlott has since clarified his position significantly. In response to a question from me, he accepts that there is no evidence at all to substantiate his inference that Dalton supported Communist resistance groups:

> I suppose that I felt that Dalton's oft-repeated urgings that SOE should try to link up with and appeal to the industrial working class of occupied countries *must* mean in practice Communists [although] in general Dalton was very anti-CP in Britain but pro-Russia. Most of his European links were with Social Democrats, not Communists, and he was most uninterested in the pre-war Communist involvement in Spain ...[89]

In the popular imagination, then, Dalton as a Labour leader might appear to have been keen on Communism. In fact, the reverse was the case. Precisely because all non-Communist left-wingers understood the nature of Communism so plainly, they were as anxious about it as those on the right (many of them had, after all, first-hand experience of it). This is something that Julian Amery's account reinforces:

> I certainly found Labour Ministers like Dalton and Ellen Wilkinson just as concerned about Soviet ambitions in Europe as their Conservative colleagues ... But outside a limited circle there was very much of a taboo in London, even after Stalingrad and El Alamein, on the public and even the private discussion of the conflicts of interest that were bound to arise after the war between Britain and the Soviet Union ... In the interests of the War Effort, the growing differences between us were cloaked in a conspiracy of silence.[90]

All the evidence suggests that Julian Amery is right about Dalton's anxieties but – significantly – wrong about the wider 'conspiracy of silence'. The Conservatives seem *not* to have been 'just as concerned' as their Labour colleagues, but rather less so. Like many others who lived through this period, Amery tends to read back into history with hindsight: the real conspiracy was not one of 'silence' but of ignorance, and for good reason.

Lord Gladwyn has added that although Dalton wished to co-operate with the Soviet Union, it would be quite ridiculous to assume that Dalton was a pro-Communist.[91] It is in any case untrue that the Americans, at this time, were anti-left. Indeed, in their own version of SOE, the OSS, they made copious use of Communists such as Jürgen Kuczynski (see p. 326).

One early problem Dalton encountered as chief of SOE was that although this Socialist outlook might be supported by Churchill ('all this,' he had said, 'must come from the Left'; see p. 81), it was opposed by a number of the people with whom he was obliged to co-operate if SOE were to be successful, including the members of the various Exile Governments in London. Many of these Governments were constitutional monarchies and many of them abhorred Socialism.

As Stafford notes, 'for most of the Governments in Exile, the prospect of Daltonian resistance was disturbing – and they rejected it'.[92] They were also upset by more immediate matters. Resistance against the Germans often triggered off the most brutal and horrifying reprisals. Stafford quotes one example where, in October 1941, in revenge for the death of one German soldier, forty-eight French hostages were murdered by the German forces at Châteaubriant.[93]

It also has to be said that Dalton's optimism about the possibilities of revolt and insurrection seemed, as the war progressed, not always very well-founded. He had forecast in 1940 that within six months 'famine, starvation and revolt [would break out] in most of the Slav lands which Germany had overrun'.[94] On the other hand, it could be argued that whether revolution occurred was one question (and a question which SOE could help to answer in the affirmative), but when this would happen was another matter altogether.

Dalton strongly approved of special facilities being granted to the Poles and Czechs, as his memoirs show. And it should not be forgotten that SOE was to promote 'apolitical' individual or group acts of subversion, such as the successful assassination of Reinhard Heydrich on 29 May 1942 (which prompted the destruction of the Czech village of Lidice by the SS in reprisal).

In this context, we should recall a spin-off from this policy. This was a political murder attempt organised by SOE, which most unfortunately failed to come to fruition. Had it been successful, the course of the whole war might have been decisively altered. The incident has been related by Julian Amery. After his meeting with Dalton, outlined above, he found himself:

> Among other things, involved in a rather farcical attempt to assassinate Hitler. As part of their contribution to the war effort, our [i.e. SOE's] Bulgarian friends had produced a Macedonian terrorist who travelled under the assumed name of Vilnar ... he suffered from cancer and had only a year to live. To die in bed in wartime seemed an ignoble end. He accordingly volunteered to try and kill Hitler ...[95]

Things did not turn out as they ought to have done. Although, much to everyone's surprise, Vilnar almost managed to dispatch the Führer, he decided to get drunk on what he assumed would be his last night alive and blurted out his story, so giving the entire game away.[96]

Yet, while Dalton still remained in the saddle, it would be quite wrong to minimise the political aspects of SOE's work. There has been a tendency to underplay this, not least because Dalton went and SOE's role was altered as a result. However, this aspect of SOE was, perhaps, its most dramatic, both in terms of the intelligence input and, because of this and its political implications, the likely input of Soviet subversion.

Three murky cases: Jewish volunteers go missing in action;
the Englandspiel; *the case of Missak Manouchian*

Before Barbarossa, if the Russians wished to scupper Dalton's plans, they obviously had to do so surreptitiously. But what of the argument that after 1941 and after the Anglo-Soviet Alliance the Russians could use their friendship with Britain to damage him?

This is most improbable. First of all, it is important to recall the reason for the Kremlin's dislike of Dalton's objectives: they challenged the prestige of Communist-led resistance groups and thus decreased their chances of power. In this way they also worsened the Soviet's chance of establishing puppet regimes based upon them. Yet this was something the Soviet leaders could not afford to make explicit, since it would demonstrate that they were determined to break their treaty obligations guaranteeing post-war Europe political independence. In short, even after 1941 the Soviets could not openly object to what SOE was doing, hence the need for subversion.

If Dalton's ideas were considered by Churchill and Eden to conflict with high policy of co-operating with Russia, this must have taken place in a very roundabout sort of way. Although Dalton himself implied that he had been sacked for the alleged crime of trying to conduct his own foreign policy, which he held to be a lie put about by unnamed 'mischief makers' (see p. 90), there was no British ruling which Dalton had actually transgressed. Thus we must assume either that someone had told Eden that Dalton's plans might one day cause a major rift with the Soviet Union, or that Dalton's obvious failures made his position untenable. Dalton's account implies the former is the more likely explanation.

Indeed, it appears that Dalton was sacked because an individual or individuals gave Eden and Churchill advice suggesting that Dalton ought to go. Furthermore, it can be argued that this advice could have been subverted. Even if this theory is not accepted, and

Dalton's departure is ascribed to his operational failures, it can still be argued that some of these failures themselves possessed a sinister aspect in no way inconsistent with the existence of Communist subversion.

For Communist moles to attempt to get rid of Dalton by direct means was a highly dangerous enterprise, since they ran the risk of alerting both British Intelligence and the political leadership to the fact that the Communists had their own ideas about the role resistance ought to play. At the same time, however, these risks should not be overestimated, since Dalton was quite clearly a controversial figure in Whitehall and the undermining of his position in SOE (if that is what it was) was not an impossible task.

Personal animosities may explain much in politics, but they do not explain why Dalton was pushed out of that particular job at that particular time. Besides, the fact that he was given the Board of Trade (by no means a junior post) implies that there was something amiss about his SOE policies which did not call into question his ability to run a domestic department. But what was it?

If we adduce Communist subversion as a contributory factor, there are three ways in which this might have been effected. The first explanation merely infers a passive role for Communist strategy. This holds that after Barbarossa high policy and co-operation with the USSR automatically made Dalton's ideas about SOE redundant. All Russia had to do in this case was intimate its displeasure and Dalton would be sacked. Yet as we have seen, the Soviets could not afford to do this, since it would have given their game away.

The second alternative was to attempt to use British moles to undermine Dalton's position within SOE itself. Since Dalton was so unpopular, there was a chance of such a strategy succeeding. The idea of direct intervention by the moles within SOE was, as a matter of fact, not quite as ridiculous as one might think. For there existed one network of moles within SOE who were ideally placed to dispatch him in this manner.

The moles could, for example, have raised doubts about Dalton's policies; they could even have attempted to ensure that his tenure in office became disastrous; for if his operations all turned to dust, the ideas which underpinned them could not be sustained. If it was the task of some of the moles to cause certain SOE operations to fail, the close co-operation between the Third Reich and the USSR before June 1941 meant this was not something that was impossible to achieve. Indeed, even after 1941, as Stalin's actions towards the

Polish Home Army showed, the Russians were not averse to getting the Germans to do their work for them.

Third, running parallel to this network within SOE, it should not be forgotten that one of the people who most wanted Dalton out was Brendan Bracken, the Minister of Information. We now know that one of Bracken's closest advisers who, as a refugee from Austria, must have had a special interest in Europe's future shape, was a secret Communist by the name of Peter Smolka-Smollett. Smolka may well have worked upon Bracken to intrigue against Dalton.

To those who balk at this theory (and they may well be right to do so) it must be stressed that to propose the existence of Communist subversion is not to offer a blanket explanation for Dalton's dismissal, but merely to suggest it was one of the strands in the decision to sack him.

Let us begin our deeper probing of these matters by examining four cases involving the anti-Nazi resistance. All were serious failures – either for Dalton himself or for his concept of what SOE ought to be doing. They all suggest that Communists may have conspired to produce failures for him and his ideas. Even though in two of the cases the failures actually occurred after Dalton had left office, they do seem to have confirmed the apparent disastrous nature of Dalton's schemes. Had they not ended in failure and had wider Daltonian policies, of which these were a part, been successful, it does not seem exaggerated to claim that a small, but perhaps not insignificant, part of Europe's post-war face might have been different.

As is commonly known, there were a whole host of incidents, all involving SOE and its interest in the future political map of Europe, which went drastically wrong both before and after Hitler's attack on the USSR. As far as we can tell, all the incidents had the same two things in common: they had to do with the creation, by means of the resistance, of potential political leadership élites in post-war Europe and they produced a situation that was bad for British interests but good, or at any rate not bad, for the Kremlin.

It is therefore entirely appropriate to argue that at this level the possibility of Communist subversion must be considered, but to what extent can the things that went wrong on this front be laid at the door of Communist subversion? And to what extent are they purely the result of errors and other perfectly harmless factors?

The first case is one based entirely on the verbal testimony of a former intelligence officer who has refused to go on the record but whose account is none the less worth serious consideration. Thanks not least to the fallibility of memory, it must be stressed that it cannot have the status of documentary evidence, yet it does seem part of a recognisable pattern; and so vivid was the recollection that, in recounting it forty years later, the former officer broke down.

This was his story:

In the early days of the war, my duties were to train native German speakers in the military arts in order that they might be dropped behind German lines. There they were to assume the status of German soldiers; to attempt to get information about German troop movements back to British agents in the Occupied countries but, more importantly, to try to infiltrate companies of German troops so as to get numbers of troops to mutiny or undertake guerrilla actions behind the lines . . .[97]

But this project was fraught with difficulties:

For one thing, it was just an experiment. For another, we knew that such native German speakers would be hard to come by and, finally, we knew that for many of these people, the most they could expect would be a brief period of active duty before their true identity would be discovered and they would have to go underground or even face death.

SOE faced one further problem: there was a major shortage of willing volunteers. The authorities therefore decided to use a group of people who had offered their services but for whom it had, so far, not been possible to find a role. These were young Jewish men, all of them from wealthy backgrounds, who had fled Nazi persecution and were living in various South American nations. Many of these recruits did not have a Jewish appearance and all of them spoke German like natives because that was what they were.

Several groups of these men were trained to fight and given a full briefing about the German army, the units they ought to try to join and, of course, a new identity. They were then taken by this officer, one by one at given intervals, to an airport near Bristol from where they were flown into Occupied Europe.

Yet an awful welcome awaited them:

The terrible thing was that none of them survived for more than one or two days. Many of them were picked up by the Gestapo within hours of landing; none of them lived to carry out the tasks for which they had been so carefully trained. At first we thought it was coincidence and we carried on sending these brave people to certain death for many weeks. Then we realised that the Gestapo or whoever really knew exactly what we were sending over and where we were dropping them. Someone was telling the Germans. But who?

As may be imagined, this entire mission was conducted under conditions of utmost secrecy. The only people who knew of the overall plan, as well as the time and place that individual Jews were to be dropped, were the British authorities.

According to this officer, MI5 carried out checks to see if there was any chance that any of the people involved might have been German double agents. In theory it was not impossible that some of the young men might in fact have been Germans merely pretending to be Jews. Against this, however, was the fact that for security reasons no man was ever told his comrades' date of departure or destination, and he learned of his own only a few hours before his parachute drop.

There were therefore only two explanations for what had happened. The first was that the undertaking was so flawed and hare-brained that it was doomed from the start. The officer believed that this might well have been the case, but it still did not explain why the young men had been picked up after a uniformly short period. There was really not much doubt in the officer's mind that the Gestapo had been waiting for the Jews.

The other answer was one which had occurred to him only many years later. This was that these young Jews had indeed been betrayed to the Germans but not by one of their own number, or indeed by any unknown pro-Nazi SOE member. For with hindsight it occurred to this officer that the Gestapo's informants could have been the Soviet intelligence authorities who had themselves been tipped off by Communist moles in SOE. For this incident had taken place before the night of 21 June 1941, at a time when the USSR and the Third Reich were close allies.

It might thus be argued that these Jews were perhaps handed over to the Gestapo as proof that the Soviets were still sincerely adhering to their pact with Hitler. Equally, however, it may have had a more sinister political cause. For in Soviet eyes, any German who was being dropped behind the German lines was, in theory at any rate, a potential German resistance leader. Since it was Communist policy to ensure that Communists dominated European resistance, potential rivals were not wanted. Young Jewish refugees from rich backgrounds were unlikely to be members of the Communist Party. Soviet policy, therefore, might dictate that they be liquidated (and serve the interests of Nazi–Soviet friendship at the same time).

Let us next examine a second case, also one more about a possibility than a probability, but one exhibiting many similar features. This was the tragic history of SOE operations in the Netherlands (about which the BBC made such an excellent and provocative documentary entitled the *Englandspiel* or England Game).

The basic elements of this case were straightforward. Dutch agents were recruited by SOE to be dropped behind the German lines in Holland in early 1942. All the Dutchmen were picked up by the Gestapo, many the moment they landed in Holland. For this there were the usual two explanations: treachery or error. As far as the former is concerned, the only treachery that has so far been seriously suggested is that there existed within SOE an as yet unknown Nazi double agent. Yet this theory seems so unlikely as to be virtually impossible. For we know that MI5's German counter-espionage division had an extraordinarily good record in discovering Nazi agents in Britain (see p. 156). It is therefore most doubtful that SOE, of all places, could have harboured a secret Nazi mole unbeknown to MI5. Treason on behalf of the Soviet Union, however, was an entirely different matter and far harder to detect and, once again, this was a case where Soviet Russia had a real interest.

The most accurate account of the details of the *Englandspiel* is contained in M. R. D. Foot's account. He claims that the *Englandspiel* was the worst of 'three cases' of German successes inside SOE.[98]

Four different army majors headed the section of SOE which dealt with the Netherlands:

> Laming till the autumn of 1941; Blunt till February 1943; Bingham till early in 1944; and Dobson. 'Blunt' was a cover name; he had no connection at all with Anthony Blunt of MI5, the art historian ... What N section got done under Laming remains almost unknown. Bad troubles began under Blunt and got no better under Bingham. The Germans' success turned on three hinges: decipher, interception, and double agency. A Dutch intelligence agent,

operating for the Dutch and MI6, called Zomer, was arrested in the late summer of 1941 with a large pile of back messages from which the Germans' cipher expert ... was able to work out MI6's cipher system ... at this time, it will be recalled SOE had not yet got its own cipher system; it depended entirely on MI6 for ciphers as for sets. With the help of a double agent, the Germans next closed in on an SOE group. They could never have had the successes they did have in Holland without the aid of these informers – Dutchmen who pretended to be resisters but in fact worked with the occupiers ...[99]

Provided with the basic knowledge needed to trap the SOE agents, the Germans then proceeded to mop them up. The British in London failed to notice that one of their agents had sent a faulty security check in one of his wireless messages, and the next agent who was duly picked up was so furious at being caught that he told the Germans various pieces of additional information which in turn allowed the Germans to be even more successful. Foot concludes:

This was, from the German point of view, a model operation. The two [German] majors who had started it up ... were allowed to carry on with it, reporting daily through Canaris and Himmler to Hitler; by teleprint, unluckily for SOE, so that there were no Bletchley intercepts to warn them how much things had gone wrong. Lauwers [an SOE agent] continued to work his set and continued to leave his security checks out; he also tried to warn home base by inserting, as often as he could, CAU and GHT among the jumbled letters with which (as a normal anti-coding precaution) every message began and ended. Unluckily for him and all his friends, those who deciphered the messages skipped these jumbled fragments, so that their eyes were not caught by these warnings; and when the deciphered texts appeared on Blunt's and Bingham's desks in Baker Street, they had been shorn of the signals apparatus of jumbled letters [although] they were each marked 'BLUFF CHECK ABSENT, TRUE CHECK ABSENT', a point N section chose to ignore.[100]

According to Foot, the total number of British agents who fell into the Gestapo's hands as a result of these grave errors was sixty-one, fifty-one from SOE, nine from MI6 and one from MI9, the military escape section. Most of them were shot by the Germans.[101] Foot notes that:

> N section's disaster was SOE's major catastrophe and it would be folly to describe it as anything else; it has become a textbook illustration, the world over, in how not to conduct clandestine work.[102]

Understandably, once the exiled Dutch in London got to hear about the *Englandspiel* many of them decided that they no longer wished to co-operate with SOE. It took the personal intervention of Prince Bernhard of the Netherlands to get them to change their minds.[103]

The official SOE explanation for this episode was that of human error. This was confirmed in a letter to *The Times* on 28 September 1984 from Christopher Woods, former SOE Adviser to the Foreign and Commonwealth Office. Woods began by stating that the FCO had offered full assistance to the BBC and that he resented their implication that German treachery was to blame for the *Englandspiel* fiasco. The full facts did not support this assertion, he stated, and added:

> No one disputes that Holland was the scene of SOE's most tragic wartime disaster nor that this was due in part to mistakes and errors of judgement by SOE. What I had hoped to see ... was some illumination of how and why SOE went wrong. Instead SOE was presented in simplistic terms as almost criminally negligent and the programme built up to a final suggestion that there was still some unrevealed mystery behind it all. There is no trace of justification for this in the SOE archive ...[104]

Woods continued:

> In early 1942 when the first crucial errors occurred, SOE was a new organisation and had not yet refined through experience the techniques on which later successes were built. For instance, security checks on which criticism hinges were still rudimentary and unreliable (mistakes in coding or transmission, atmospheric distortion, haste and stress).

What Woods is referring to here is the fact that although the

Dutch SOE agents were supplied with an apparently fail-safe device by which to inform SOE in London whether they were operating under conditions of freedom or whether they had, in fact, been captured by the Germans and were sending messages under duress, and although the agents correctly used these codes, London failed to realise they had been captured and continued to send more agents into the trap.

Woods concluded:

> When the first agent was caught he had on him the three coded messages in which he had already included his correct check. Was it really so easy for SOE to detect that he was under control?

Yet having said this, he felt constrained to accept that:

> ... It is strange that SOE's internal security investigation when suspicions were really aroused did not fasten on the early omission of security checks ...

But the explanation for this, in Mr Woods's view, is not hard to pinpoint:

> The Dutch section was a late starter – Holland was not the easiest country for SOE to operate – and zeal to get on may have impaired the section's judgement ...

Of course, Woods may be perfectly correct and the explanation, however tragic, that the *Englandspiel* was a straightforward error may well be true. But equally it must be said that his argument is a trifle thin. For one thing, as a 'late starter', SOE's Dutch section should have been expected to be more professional, not less. Its 'mistakes' were really very elementary ones, ones which no intelligence officer should have made, not even on his first day at work.

And, as Foot's account makes far clearer than Woods's, despite German successes in tracking down the SOE agents who had landed in Holland, the fact remained that at least one of those agents had consistently used the agreed procedures to warn London that he was no longer free. Serious and apparently inexplicable errors had been made in SOE headquarters in London, both in the decoding of these messages and in their analysis.

The *Englandspiel* cannot be explained simply in terms of the existence of a double agent in Holland. So were there two double agents, one in Holland and the other in SOE headquarters? And why was there no proper investigation into the affair?

There was also another aspect of the case that gave rise to the greatest concern. For the *Englandspiel* was not the only disaster involving groups of foreign nationals who could be viewed as the leadership élite of the anti-Nazi resistance, sponsored by the British Government. As a subsequent letter to *The Times* pointed out:

> The explanation given by Mr Woods would be more acceptable were it not for the fact that an almost identical disaster occurred in France involving SOE's Prosper and Scientist networks which also resulted in the arrest and execution of several hundred agents, including Miss Noor Khan, GC. Here too agents and supplies continued to arrive, despite many warnings.[105]

The author of this letter, James Rusbridger, himself apparently a former intelligence officer, argues strongly that there had been a German 'triple agent' by the name of Henri Dericourt who worked for MI6, the Germans and SOE. Rusbridger concluded with the pertinent question:

> If this is true, why was someone who had been under suspicion by MI5 from the beginning allowed to continue to maintain such an important role within SOE, even after the disaster of the Prosper network?

There are really only three possible answers to Rusbridger's question. The first is that he is right, but that there was a fatal error which permitted M. Dericourt to remain in a position where he could wreak this terrible damage. The second is that he and Foot are wrong and Dericourt was quite innocent, there being an error at other levels to explain the facts to which Rusbridger draws our attention. The third answer is, however, altogether different. It is that there was indeed treachery afoot, but that it was treachery executed in the interest not only of the Gestapo but also of Soviet Intelligence. Because of this, Soviet moles in SOE and in other parts of British Intelligence were under orders not to expose those who were betraying British agents to the German authorities.

It is perfectly feasible that any non-Communist continental European SOE agent was not simply a threat to the German domination of Occupied Europe but also to the hoped-for Soviet domination of post-war Europe which was to succeed it. Any investigation aimed at discovering German moles in SOE would thus inevitably have failed because the British authorities believed they were looking for a Nazi mole, when in reality they were looking for a Communist one.

Additional material which has recently come to light on Dericourt's activities tends to add weight to this third alternative.[106] It seems plain that Dericourt was not simply a triple agent, but that he was being protected – despite his obvious failings – by both SOE and MI6. Furthermore, his importance to MI6 was his connection with a German Abwehr officer by the name of Hans Boemelburg. It also appears that Dericourt reported personally to Colonel Claude Dansey who was, we know, often advised by Kim Philby.[107] It is possible, then, that Dericourt was not directly involved with the Nazis (indeed a French court found him innocent of this charge in June 1948) but only indirectly via Moscow, taking orders from Soviet Intelligence about which particular French resistance leaders ought to be betrayed to the Germans. What appeared to some a 'private war' against SOE (which cost 400 lives) may possibly, therefore, be better described as but another campaign in Stalin's secret war. It is certainly a possibility worth consideration.

A third equally murky case which has also recently received some attention reinforces, broadly speaking, similar points: in the early summer of 1985 French television showed a film about the Communist resistance group led by an Armenian, Missak Manouchian. A report in the *Guardian* outlined the story:

> Its members were all immigrants to France, all Communists and mostly Jewish. The group was active in 1942 and 1943 until a wave of arrests and the execution of 23 of them in early 1944. When the group sensed that the Germans were on its trail, the Communists allegedly refused to help its members withdraw [to the comparative safety] of the South. An editorial in the magazine *Nouvel Observateur* asked some hard questions: Did the Communist Party deliberately sacrifice the group to improve its own list of battle honours? (Possible.) Did it do so much more readily because it was a matter of Jews, immigrants and foreigners? (Not impossible.) Did it cold-bloodedly hand them over to the Germans? (Hard to believe.)[108]

This incident provides an intriguing parallel to the SOE incidents. It appears that even during the darkest days of the war, the Communist resistance struggled to ensure its own political supremacy; these Jewish Armenians were a threat to Soviet ambitions because, although they were Communists, they had a separate group identity as nationalists and Jews, which meant they might be disposed to challenge the authority of Moscow. If this story is true, it might have been the explanation for their destruction.

It may thus be said that although both before June 1941 and after it the Soviets wanted to see the Germans destroyed, they did not want to see anyone who was not subservient to the Communists take the place of the Germans. Naturally, they could not control every event or manipulate every circumstance. But thanks to their network of moles and agents there were some events and circumstances they could determine, and it is at least a possibility worth further examination that in these apparently mysterious 'errors' the real culprits were the Russians.

Let us now turn to an area where there is apparently firmer evidence of Communist subversion. Paradoxically, however, it may be said that although there is firmer evidence, it is at the same time far harder to estimate the precise effect of that subversion. For it seems difficult to deny that what was done in SOE, and then in PWE, occurred for a variety of reasons, of which Communist subversion was merely one.

A less murky case: German Socialists in Britain

In order to promote Daltonian subversion in Occupied Europe, it was vitally necessary to identify correctly existing and potential leaders of the resistance and then bring them into action against the Nazi forces. It was here that a group of people who play some part in this story fitted into overall British strategy and became part of British political history. These were the German Socialist exiles, the remnants of the great Social Democratic Party of Germany, and before Hitler, the largest single Social Democratic Party in the world.

The German dimension plays an important role. There are many reasons for this. First of all, as the undoubted primary source of the war, Germany's future political status was of very special concern to all the Allies. Stalin is reported to have said, 'Whoever holds

Germany, holds Europe.' It was hardly an original idea but, because
it seemed true, the treatment of things German demanded the fullest
use of the resources – most vitally, perhaps, the intelligence ones –
of Britain, of America and of Russia (and it should not be forgotten
that the British and American moles were, of course, part of the
Soviet intelligence community).

Second, however, with regard to Dalton's SOE aims, the German
dimension was especially complex and British policy seemed curiously incapable of surmounting it. As Professor James Joll has
argued, the British Government faced a difficult situation over its
treatment of anti-Nazi Germans, for 'they were confronting a
phenomenon in the case of Germany which did not exist elsewhere
in Europe'.[109]

> There is a great deal of controversy about the support given by
> Britain to various political groups within the resistance but the
> resistance as an entity in the occupied countries of Europe pre-
> sented a picture which could be fitted into an overall strategic
> plan. Now the *Widerstand* [resistance] in Germany could not be
> fitted into this. What was known about it ... produced a negative
> reaction in the British Government because again it did not fit in
> with their overall plan of unconditional surrender. What was
> rather embarrassing for the British Government in the case of
> German Social Democrats was the fact that there was in England
> a large body of indubitably anti-Nazis who were somehow not
> fitting into the overall concept of how a war was to be won ...
> During the middle years of the war ... I think very often the
> British Government made the wrong decisions and very often they
> did not support people whom they should have supported.[110]

The question that Joll's perceptive comment begs is simple. Why
did the British Government 'make the wrong decisions'? It is clear
that the Daltonian concept of resistance meant that Britain would
not want to help any old resistance groups, but only those which
would generate political regimes with which the British would themselves like to deal. Julian Amery's testimony confirms the validity of
this point which, after all, stands to reason in any case.

What is more, Dalton himself stated this view on a number of
occasions. While he did not think a revolution in Germany was
imminent, here too he had hopes for the not too-distant future:

No doubt in the earlier part of the war, the prospect of a revolution in Germany was remote. The organisation of any widespread subversive organisation there was likely to encounter great difficulties. [But] we have on our side not only the anti-Nazi elements in Germany and Austria, not only the Czechs and the Poles, but also the whole of the democratic and liberty-loving elements in Norway, Belgium, France, Holland and Italy ...[111]

There was really only one group of resistance leaders about which the British might be expected to have had grave doubts, and they were the Communist resistance leaders. There was a simple reason for this, namely, that however bravely they might fight for the destruction of Nazism, they opposed the concept of liberal democracy.

Yet not all SOE officers accepted this. According to Douglas Dodds-Parker, even when Stalin and Hitler were allies, British Communists realised that it was in their best interests to support Churchill. He states that:

Insaisissable Sabotage ... that in which it is impossible to track down the saboteurs, had been for long developed by the Communists. [Even] during the years from 1939–41 when the Soviets were in alliance with the Nazis, some British Communists were patriotic and far-sighted enough to share their skills with us.[112]

Yet to trust them implicitly was unwise. For as we saw in the case of British foreign policy, it was at the cutting edge of conflicting concerns that the real struggle between British and Soviet interests would ensue, and it was here that the Communist moles and agents would attempt to subvert British policy in Russia's interests.

For, as we have seen, one important goal the Communists were trying to achieve, at considerable cost to themselves but at even greater cost to the resistance movement as a whole, was the domination of the anti-Nazi resistance groups. They were, then, highly dangerous members of SOE.

In my book *Exile Politics During the Second World War* I examined the role played by German anti-Nazi political exiles from the Third Reich. As is commonly known, the half a million people who fled from the Nazi control of continental Europe were, for the main part, Europeans of Jewish descent or of Jewish faith. But there were some exiles who had fled, not because they had to for racial reasons, but because they were the sworn political opponents of Nazism and they wished to do all they could to defeat it.

The aspect of policy to scrutinise concerns the attitudes of the Government and SOE towards the exiled German Social Democratic Party, the SPD, whose official seat was, from 1941–5, the British capital. As I have argued elsewhere,[113] this attitude underwent a marked change in the early summer of 1941, both preceding and contemporaneously with Operation Barbarossa, the German attack on the USSR.

It is important not to overemphasise the role that Communist subversion may have played in the forming of British policy, both in regard to the wider issue of Germany and the more narrow one in respect of the SPD and SOE, and then PWE. For the latter was conditioned in large measure by the former, and the former was the result of several inputs, of which subversion might be but one marginal part.

The story of these exiled German Social Democratic Party leaders, whose official seat became London during the Second World War, was, however, a curious one: they were initially welcomed to Britain on the outbreak of war, although for various reasons they did not actually arrive until early in 1941. It had at first seemed that they would have a fruitful time in England contributing to the war effort and making preparations for the rebirth of German democracy if and when that should come to pass. Yet within twelve months of their arrival in Britain, the British attitude towards them changed drastically, to their detriment.

One main reason for this was anti-German feeling in Britain and the Churchillian policy of fixing nothing about domestic post-war German conditions until the unconditional surrender of the German forces had been achieved. Yet there were other causes as well. From the German viewpoint, these exiles represented the political leadership of the once and future German labour movement. From the British viewpoint, however, this role gave the Social Democrats, in theory at least, the status of possible resistance leaders, as a source of insurrection against the Nazis and a source of post-war political leadership on whom the British would be able to rely for two very good reasons and a third, rather partisan, reason.

The first reason was that the British authorities had saved their lives, which was bound to put these Germans under a considerable obligation towards them. These people became and remained pro-

British, sometimes embarrassingly so, when we see what happened to them after 1942.

The second reason was that these Socialists were fiercely anti-Communist. They had first-hand experience of dealing with Communists in the Weimar Republic, and they had seen how on many occasions the Communists had co-operated with the emerging Nazi Party in an attempt to destroy the Social Democrats whom Stalin had decreed were the Class Enemy No. 1 or the Social Fascists, as he liked to term them.

The third, partisan, reason why to have helped the Social Democrats and vice versa would have made sense to someone like Dalton was that, like him, they were supporters of the Socialist ideal. It was hard to see how a Conservative like Eden would take a shine to German Socialists, although it was possible that he might appreciate their anti-Communist stance. But it did seem plain that a solid Labour man like Dalton would have jumped at the chance of working alongside German Socialist exiles.

In actual fact, this is exactly what Dalton did, or, more accurately, what he began to do before he performed an almost complete about-turn for reasons which have never been fully explained. What is more, the person who had actually arranged for these exile leaders to fly to Britain in 1941 was none other than Hugh Dalton himself. Within ten months, however, he refused to have anything whatsoever to do with them, and British Intelligence ceased to make proper use of them, either as SOE agents in the field or, more fruitfully, as a major plank in the propaganda campaign to Germany on the BBC.

Those who worked within this area have sought to justify this curious fact on several grounds, all of them plausible but none of them convincing. The first is that the British public by now either disliked or actively hated the Germans, thus making it impossible for the British authorities to make use even of German Socialists (despite their having opposed the Nazis for longer than almost anyone else). Yet this argument is nonsensical, since SOE and PWE were top secret institutions about which the British public might never know anything. In any case, both MI5 and MI6 were, throughout the war, perfectly content to use Germans as agents: why should SOE have been any different? No, whatever the problem about these Socialists, it cannot have had to do with their being German. Rather, it must have been concerned with their political status. But how?

Another explanation that has been offered has to do with the high policy directive, emanating from Churchill himself, that nothing about Germany's political future should be fixed until after the war had been won. Using German Socialists, it has been suggested, might have implied the British Government was committed to Socialism in post-war Germany, which would have been a contradiction of basic policy and was thus impossible. In any case, it has been added, why should Churchill, a Conservative, wish to advance the cause of Socialists?

On closer examination this explanation seems as improbable as the first. Churchill himself had specifically sanctioned the use of Socialists in SOE (see p. 81). Furthermore, it was extremely curious that the British, for whatever reasons, were not doing something that the Russians were already deeply involved in, for after June 1941 the Russians had become very busy in the area of political propaganda to the German people, using their exiles with much profit (not least with a view to the post-war political control).

By their odd behaviour, SOE and PWE were giving the Russians a significant advantage over the British. What is more, although Churchill and Dalton may not have known this, this is something that the expert or experts within British Intelligence must have been fully aware of. Since it is ridiculous to suppose that Churchill's line was intended to encourage the Russians to do something the British were not doing, his high policy directives can have had nothing to do with SOE's and PWE's treatment of these German Socialists. For by excluding them from full participation in the propaganda war against Germany, the British were not only failing to utilise an excellent resource (which they themselves had brought to England for this very purpose) but were, in an important area, giving the Soviets *carte blanche*.

It may of course be that there is no rational reason for this failure; if one can be found, however, it seems to me to concern subversion. For it is quite clear that within perfectly legitimate high policy there existed ample scope for subversion in certain narrow and obscure areas, in such a way as to promote the interests of Russia and damage those of Britain. Might this be the true explanation for what happened?

4

Moles in the Special Operations and Political Warfare Executives

Sefton Delmer and the German dimension

There was, therefore, undoubtedly a Russian connection with the strange fate of the German Socialists in London. When we add to this the fact that we know that moles flourished within SOE, the plot begins to thicken. Indeed, it is hardly surprising that Chapman Pincher should focus in his book on these exiles and their far more successful Communist counterparts and Fellow-Travellers, whom he sees as the link between Hollis of MI5 and the KGB.[1]

Yet if Soviet concerns about the German exiles were fed into British policy, it was done in a totally surreptitious and covert way without the knowledge of most of the British policy-makers in Whitehall. For there is absolutely no record of any overt request by the Russians that the German Socialists in England be treated in any particular way.

The German dimension was bound to be an important factor in wartime policy and planning, affecting both British and Soviet Intelligence considerations in a variety of ways. There were many reasons for this, apart from the obvious one that Germany was the enemy who twice in a generation had brought the world to war thanks to its domestic political system.

Both Britain and the Soviet Union possessed a clear interest in ensuring that Germany's domestic political system would, in the future, be incapable of sustaining an aggressive war. Broadly speaking, the British believed before 1945 that this could be achieved by the physical destruction of Nazism and the punishment of Nazi leaders, while at the same time dismantling or dismembering the German national State. As for the Russians, they appeared to concur with these objectives, but added a fourth objective of their own, and a very secret one.

For, like all the other countries liberated by the Red Army, the new Germany was to become a country run by Communists taking their orders from the Soviet leadership in Moscow. The existence in London of German Socialists, strongly anti-Communist, who might be enabled to build up a following in Germany thus presented Russian planners with a very major obstacle to their bid for post-war political control and, in turn, to their overall strategy for supremacy in post-Nazi Europe.

Thus, both in its broad European context and in this German and rather narrow one, the efforts of the moles were bound to be concentrated both upon trying to make nugatory the Daltonian concept for SOE, and upon concealing the intelligence implications such a change was bound to have. It could be argued that such an interpretation, which might even include an explanation for Dalton's dismissal, cannot be correct, for the simple reason that there was no point in trying to get rid of Dalton since, by the time of his departure, he was, as far as German Socialists were concerned, prepared to change his ideas in line with perceived Russian wishes. Against this, however, speaks the fact that the German dimension was apparently a 'one-off' change of heart for him. As Lord Gladwyn has confirmed, Dalton never gave up his support for the Poles and for Polish independence, nor indeed for a Socialist (rather than a Communist) post-war world.[2] The former was reason enough to cause the Russians to hope for his transfer to a less sensitive post.

The important thing to realise is that in 1940 and 1941 Dalton had a policy and wanted it applied specifically to anti-Communist German Socialists. Yet his plans were thwarted by the activities of one or more SOE officers who, for reasons examined later, did the precise reverse of what Dalton had originally ordered.

Dalton subsequently accepted this reversal, apparently not realising that it did not serve the British interest but did serve the Soviet one. In so doing, of course, he forfeited considerable credibility. We should recall that in the case of the Foreign Office the evidence seems to indicate a fundamental ignorance of what the Russians were up to; within SOE, however, something much more sinister seems to have been going on. For SOE officers, as part of the intelligence community, were not unaware of what the Russians were doing within its area of operations, but they almost wholly failed to provide the correct interpretation of Soviet actions. This failure was to prove decisive. For the political leaders, in this case Dalton and his colleagues, could only act sensibly if they were given the proper information, properly interpreted. A person or persons within SOE and PWE could, if working for the Kremlin, ensure that its policies would, wherever possible and necessary, be undermined with relative safety. This is, I believe, exactly what happened.

The special role that anti-Nazi Germans played in the early days of SOE is amply illustrated by the testimony of Ellic Howe in his book *The Black Game*. He goes to great lengths to provide chapter and verse of this role and he quite rightly draws our attention to the activities of one SOE officer in particular, working in the field of subversive political warfare at Woburn Abbey. This man was Denis Sefton Delmer.[3]

Delmer was the major contact the exiled Social Democrats had within SOE, and he was destined to play a key part in the tangled interrelationship between the British secret services and things German, and not simply before and during the war but after it as well (see p. 234). Delmer's interests – indeed, his entire career in this field – were, to put it at its mildest, distinctly curious; inasmuch as he was prepared to work seriously with German exiles during the war, he has been viewed as a 'pro-German' British figure. Such a view is inaccurate. Delmer was not pro-German, either during the war or after it and, despite being extremely knowledgeable both about Germany and about propaganda, he produced exceptionally poor propaganda during the war. What is more, once it had been won, he demonstrated an uncanny and unfailing ability to reflect the Soviet propaganda line against the new democratic West German State. Delmer was one of those intelligence officers with sufficient understanding to utilise effectively the German Socialists. Yet he seems to have been instrumental in ruining them; subsequently, he did his best to do post-war German democracy down.

There are additional reasons for expressing doubts about Delmer's true allegiance. For a start, it is significant that Putlitz and John, two of his closest collaborators in PWE, later defected to the East (see p. 226), and Delmer continued to maintain very close links with them after their defection. By making this explicit, it should be emphasised, one is not trying to imply 'guilt by association'. Delmer, like anyone else, was entitled to choose his own friends at will. Yet such friendships were scarcely compatible with alleged right-wing political beliefs. In addition, after 1945 it became Delmer's mission to keep alive the notion that the German people had remained inherently Nazi sympathisers. With the enthusiastic support of Lord Beaverbrook, Delmer used the *Daily Express* to go to absurd lengths in order to try to substantiate this. What is more, his typically wild and exaggerated allegations were made in the full knowledge that they constituted a vital part of Soviet post-war propaganda, which was that a resurrected West German Nazi Reich would attack eastern Europe as soon as it was able. Finally, Delmer's behaviour over the Otto John case (see p. 233) seemed to some observers to prove that he possessed obvious Communist sympathies and to throw a new and distinctly suspicious light upon his activities at Woburn.

One of the few people to have hinted at this openly was Richard Crossman, who also worked for SOE (and, of course, later became a senior Labour Cabinet minister), when he attacked Delmer for supporting Otto John. Ellic Howe has dismissed Crossman's critique of Delmer as motivated by 'jealousy' but this is unfair. Crossman was right to point out that:

> It was a result of proving his reliability on Delmer's staff that Otto John was later recommended by HMG with disastrous consequences to be the first head of counter-espionage in the German Federal Republic.[4]

In this connection we should not forget that Dalton had a high opinion of Crossman:

> He had originally been recommended by Quintin Hogg [Lord Hailsham]. Not everyone liked him or trusted his judgement ... But I regarded him as one of our best propagandists to Germany ... On the whole he did not disappoint me. And after I moved on, he became our outstanding propagandist to the Germans working under Eisenhower.[5]

There is, then, a considerable amount of evidence to suggest that Delmer himself was almost certainly suspiciously sympathetic towards those in British Intelligence who subsequently defected, and also towards the Soviet propaganda line both during the war and after. It thus becomes by no means unreasonable to consider carefully whether Delmer himself may not have been a mole, able to direct several major subversive coups both during the war and in the post-war period. After all, like others with suspicious aspects to their careers, Delmer had tried very hard indeed to get into MI5 on the outbreak of war; like Blunt he proved initially unsuccessful. One rejection from MI5 did not, however, preclude another attempt to get into it. Howe writes:

In those days, MI5's right hand did not invariably know what its left one was doing ... Delmer was [offered a job in MI5] but told that its vetting process might take a long time ... finally [it was] hinted that MI5 had again rejected him ...[6]

Delmer then decided to apply for SOE. Here he was successful and, by virtue of his pre-war journalistic experience in Berlin and his ability to speak German, he was soon considered SOE's chief German expert.

In May 1941 Sefton Delmer and Richard Crossman took over the BBC's German Service which had served both the BBC and SO 1 (which in July 1940 had merged into SOE). The BBC had sole responsibility for what was called 'white' propaganda; SOE took charge of 'black' propaganda.[7] The distinction was an important one for the British because it implied there was a difference between 'the truth', for which the BBC possessed a brilliant reputation, and 'propaganda', which was not something normally associated with British broadcasting but was an indispensable tool of warfare.

Delmer set to his new work with a will, and it might be supposed that the German Social Democrats in exile were going to be prime source material for what he had in mind. Yet although, as individuals in an apolitical setting, some of them were used by him, they were never utilised as a political group, and for reasons which are a great deal more peculiar than they at first appear, reasons which go right to the heart of SOE's work and the almost certain subversion of it by Communists.

Hugh Dalton and Germany's future

As has been described elsewhere,[8] the leadership of the German Social Democratic Party in exile had first moved to Prague after 1933 and then, in 1938, to Paris which became its official headquarters. Following Hitler's attack on the Low Countries and France in 1940, several leading German Socialists, including Hans Vogel, Erich Ollenhauer, Curt Geyer and Fritz Heine, made their way through Spain to Portugal, and in 1940 and early 1941 the SPD's leaders were flown out of neutral Portugal to England by the RAF. There exists, in the Public Record Office, the document which provided them with the necessary paperwork to get out of continental Europe.

On 17 December 1940, the Foreign Office was instructed to telegraph visas to Lisbon to these exiles because:

> The Ministry for Economic Warfare [i.e. SOE] are keen to get these men to the UK ... as they are needed for a special purpose.[9]

The 'special purpose' was Daltonian: the exiles were to be used to assist in the subversive war against the Third Reich. We should recall that these were precisely the sort of people Dalton had wanted to recruit for SOE from Europe: 'concerned trade unionists and Socialists in enemy and enemy-occupied countries ...'[10] Their role was to be political; the British authorities intended to exploit them as a political grouping, as the leadership of an anti-Nazi political party with an international reputation and a proud history. Dalton himself put a special premium on this group because they were Socialists, with the added attraction of being anti-Communist.

Dalton's memoirs show not only that he had a special concern for German affairs but also that German Socialists were considered by him to be the political allies of British Labour.[11] Furthermore, in 1940 Dalton had published a little book entitled *Hitler's War*, in which he had gone out of his way to show that he was not anti-German.[12] The war, he said, was caused by Hitler and the Nazis, rather than by the people of Germany.

Dalton was not uncritical of what he saw as the failings of German Socialists but he did accept that:

> Weimar Germany [which was created by the SPD] did have some achievements to its credit ... many of the German young tasted freedom for the first and last time under what the Nazis called the sow Republic ... It is to the discredit of Britain and France that they did not go out of their way openly to make friends with the democratic leaders of Weimar Germany and help increase the prestige of these leaders in their own country. This was a grave mistake.[13]

While it would be wrong to portray Dalton as a 'fan' of the SPD, it would be equally wrong to ignore the fact that not only had he brought the SPD's leadership to freedom, but he had a constructive attitude towards it.

Both this constructive approach to things German and a wish to incorporate such an approach in British policy were the opposite stance to the more celebrated one, whose best-known exponent was Lord Vansittart. It is worth recalling that Vansittart, who had of course been a very senior figure in the Foreign Office and retained a reputation as a German expert, forcefully put across the line that Germans were little more than congenital criminals, and that the corollary of this was that Germany needed to be destroyed since the entire German people were: 'A race of bone-headed aggressors ... the scum of the earth'.

Needless to say, in propaganda terms Vansittartism was little short of disastrous. His obsessional anti-German diatribes helped cement the German people to Hitler when all British efforts should have been devoted to driving a wedge between Volk and Führer. In this context, Dr Goebbels's comment on Vansittart should not be forgotten:

> We ought to be paying him for his propaganda. After the war we ought to build a memorial to him, inscribed 'To the Briton who did most for the German Cause'.[14]

Dalton was more circumspect, arguing that once Hitler had been defeated, it would be possible to co-operate with Germany. What is more, he saw the political and propaganda advantages of such a stance. In his book, Dalton argued that as soon as Hitler had gone, the British should at once:

> Negotiate with a new German Government ... I do not wonder that some thoughtful people [believe] the only way to get security is to get Germany down and then sit on her head ... [But] my own view is that such a course is short-sighted ... As Britain and France, both aggressors in their time, have outgrown this bad habit, so may Germany too.

Thus Dalton concluded that:

> We should say even now while the war continues, 'we are opposed to any attempt to break up Germany from outside. We do not seek the humiliation or dismemberment of your country. We desire to welcome you without delay into the peaceful collaboration of civilised nations ... we must seek, however great the difficulties, to win the co-operation as an equal partner of a Germany governed

by a political system whose aims and needs run parallel with ours ...[15]

In short, Dalton wanted to pursue a constructive line towards Germany, which had important implications for British propaganda. Furthermore, Dalton's ideas, despite apparent inconsistencies with Churchill's public stance towards Germany, were not in conflict with his directives in terms of the secret war. As far as SOE proper was concerned, this emerges clearly from a Foreign Office document dated 27 June 1940:

It is part of our present military plan to create, at an appropriate stage, widespread revolt in the territories ruled by the enemy. [German] political refugees could play a considerable role in this. Their first aim would be to formulate a policy to counter-act the influence of MI5 who are tainted with the Nazi propaganda claim that the refugees are fifth columnists.[16]

As for propaganda, we know that Churchill appears to have said nothing which might have ruled Dalton's plans out of court. He had other things to do than pronounce on details of this kind. As PWE's director, Robert Bruce Lockhart, has written:

If only the Prime Minister had been interested in political warfare. Unfortunately for us, this great man, himself our greatest war propagandist, attached at best a secondary importance to all forms of propaganda.[17]

How, then, was this revolt in occupied Europe to be instigated? One way was by dropping agents behind enemy lines; the other, more subtle but possibly more effective, was by radio waves.[18] It was precisely in this area that the German Socialists had such a key role to play: the presence of the SPD leaders, broadcasting from London to the Reich, provided Britain with a unique opportunity to marshal Germans (particularly Socialists and trade unionists) inside Germany. The idea was that German listeners would hear people, whose status and names they would recognise, telling them to resist the Nazis and thus earn the right to be treated fairly after Hitler's defeat. Even if most of them would not have accepted this, there were undoubtedly some who would have responded to such a message of hope.

The BBC and anti-Nazi Germans

The person in PWE with special responsibilities in this area was, of course, Sefton Delmer. We should now look a little more closely at the sort of war that he was having; it was distinctly curious.

In October or November 1940 (before Dalton had brought the German Socialists to England) Delmer had hit upon the idea of a clandestine radio station, called the 'European Revolutionary Radio Station', which was to broadcast political propaganda to Germany, with the aim of getting the German working class to resist the Nazis. Its staff were to be:

> Revolutionary Socialists whose theme should be specifically directed towards the German industrial workers ... It was to be ... a proposed Communist station.[19]

Once the Social Democrats had arrived on the scene, it was decided by two of Dalton's Labour colleagues, Patrick Gordon Walker (later Foreign Secretary) and Richard Crossman, that they should be included in this venture.[20] Yet Delmer seems to have been severely discomforted by this suggestion. All of a sudden, he decided to change his radio station in a very significant way. On 8 June 1941 he informed Ellic Howe that his plan now was:

> To spread disruptive and disturbing news among the Germans which will induce them to distrust their government, but making no attempt to build up a political following in Germany.[21]

Delmer had thereby abandoned his scheme for a 'Communist' radio station with an overtly political message, in favour of 'disruptive and disturbing news' with no party political overtones. Within a few days the German Socialists were told they would not be permitted to broadcast as German Socialists, but merely as unnamed German speakers. Delmer was thus robbing them of the very attribute which would make a propaganda impact (it was, after all, the reason they had been flown to Britain in the first place) and was negating perhaps the only sensible antidote to Radio Moscow's German broadcasts. In due course British radio propaganda to Germany ceased to be subversive in the true meaning of the word. Not surprisingly, the German Socialists could not understand what was going on, and they went to see Ivone Kirkpatrick at the Foreign Office on 8 July 1941 – but to no avail.[22] Although some Socialists, such as Richard Lœwenthal and Waldemar von Knœringen, continued to broadcast anonymously on the BBC for another year, the SPD in exile was now silent.

It was not, it should be noted, simply the German Socialists who found Delmer's actions hard to understand. Bruce Lockhart himself seemed puzzled – not least when he was visited by the Soviet Ambassador, M. Maisky, who had told him:

> How bad Britain's left-wing propaganda was and how much better the Russians could perform this task ... the implication was that we should appeal to the German right and the German officer class and leave the left and the ordinary soldier to the Russians.[23]

In the event, this 'deal' never took off since, thanks to Delmer, the British abandoned all of these groups to the Russians.

Crossman, too, found it hard to understand or support what Delmer had done and, later, castigated him for supporting 'Stalinists, Trotskyists, International Brigadists and SS men' but, clearly, not German Social Democrats.[24]

Precisely what, we may well ask, was Delmer up to? How could the very person with special responsibilities and specialist knowledge end up doing something which went against obvious British interests? It seems to me that there can be only one explanation for his actions. He was being told to behave in this way by the Russians. For from the Russian viewpoint, a Communist radio station in Britain was an enormous advantage to them – not least because, in the autumn of 1940, Russia and Germany were still allies and the Soviet Union could therefore not broadcast subversive anti-Nazi propaganda. After 1941, however, what the Russians wanted changed: they themselves could now openly try to incite the German workers to rise up against the Nazis and get German Communists and others to make this case for them. What the Russians could not tolerate, however, would be German Socialists stealing a march on them by speaking on the BBC from London. Thus, when Dalton produced the German Socialists, alarm bells rang in the Kremlin. The SPD was bound to interfere with Delmer's quaint plan, and so the Kremlin soon decided his Communist station had to be wound up. It was better for the Soviets to have no radio propaganda than radio propaganda showing that German Socialists were helping the British to fight Hitler. After

Barbarossa, the same thing applied even more. There can be no other satisfactory explanation for Delmer's actions. There was, as Bruce Lockhart makes plain, no specific high policy directive which might have applied and, as for pleading the Anglo-Soviet Alliance as a reason, what Delmer had been required to do had predated Barbarossa itself, let alone the Alliance. In any case, the Alliance did not instruct the British to leave political propaganda to the Russians. I suspect the political leaders never even knew that Delmer was taking their name in vain. For if British political propaganda was claimed to contravene high policy, Soviet political propaganda did so too and, had Churchill and his colleagues known this, they might have altered this policy to take account of it.

What makes Delmer's volte-face all the more sinister is not merely that (after it had been executed) it was perceived by his colleagues as something that would please the Russians (although no one seems to have asked why), but also that his changed tactics were echoed by the Foreign Office. On 18 June 1941 (three days before Barbarossa) the Foreign Office declared that German political exiles were no longer to be seen as constituting a useful weapon in Britain's secret war. Germans would regard them as 'traitors in enemy pay', and by using them the British would be 'forced to advance the political fortunes' of Germans who had 'little or no following in Germany' and who had 'earned the active distrust of the population'.[25]

Yet even if the Foreign Office did not fully comprehend the detailed and highly complex issues that lay behind Delmer's plan, he himself cannot have been blind to the help he was giving to the Soviets, at a time when more generally SOE was working hard to sustain the non-Communist resistance movements in Europe.[26] Moreover, Delmer seems, in some way, to have managed to get Dalton himself to forsake his own policy towards the German Socialists.

There is hard evidence of this: when an exiled SPD leader from America, called Friedrich Stampfer, made the perilous wartime journey to England in an attempt to discover why nothing had come of Dalton's subversive plans, he was totally cold-shouldered. Although Dalton agreed to speak to him, the interview was so unproductive that both Stampfer and Dalton chose to forget it when they wrote their memoirs. Stampfer specifically asked Dalton to use the SPD as a political weapon in the PWE propaganda war, on the lines of de Gaulle's talks to the French people. Dalton said no:

Personal talks [talks where the speaker's political identity would be revealed] had been considered, but subject to certain exceptions [such as de Gaulle] we are against them.[27]

Stampfer (who was no chicken) pointed out that the OSS, the American counterpart to SOE, was making good use of German Socialists in America, and that one of them had regular meetings with Colonel Donovan, the OSS chief. Dalton seemed unimpressed.

It is important to emphasise that this changed policy, which continued to govern Britain's political warfare, struck even some of those involved in it as distinctly curious. One of them was no less a figure than Robert Bruce Lockhart; yet he was not a German specialist and his anxieties remained unresolved:

> In our propaganda to Germany we were handicapped by a problem which we never solved. This was the vexatious question of what we called a 'hope clause' for Germany. For a long time there was no official policy about the future of Germany [so] we were not allowed to make any promises in our propaganda ... Were there sufficient so-called good Germans to justify a promise of a reasonable peace, provided that they turned against Hitler before the end of the war? We propagandists favoured the hope clause ... its absence was a severe handicap to our propaganda.[28]

As Bruce Lockhart makes plain, there was no specific policy on this matter, and yet someone was able to restrain PWE from doing what, on the face of it, even its director believed made good sense. PWE's predicament is confirmed by the testimony of Bruce Lockhart's deputy, Thomas Barman (who after the war became the BBC's chief diplomatic correspondent). He dealt with the particular matter of Bruce Lockhart's plan to engage the services of Bishop Bell of Chichester, a leading advocate of 'hope' policies towards the German people (and a personal friend of several leading anti-Nazi Germans including Dietrich Bonhœffer). Barman wrote:

> If Bell had taken a hand in our propaganda, our appeal to the so-called good Germans might have been rather stronger than it was. The events of the 1944 plot [when Hitler was almost assassinated] might have taken a different and more effective turn. On the other hand, given the Government's policy of unconditional surrender ... it was just as well that George Bell did not get involved with

us. He would almost certainly have collided head-on with the Prime Minister, and his association with our work would have made the Russians even more suspicious of British good faith than they were . . .[29]

It is important to be quite clear about what Barman is saying. It is that if British propaganda to Germany had been different, the German opposition to Hitler might have been more successful and might even have managed to overthrow the Nazis altogether but that, had PWE taken such a line, the Russians would have been 'even more suspicious' than they were.

From what both Bruce Lockhart and Barman state, it is plain that someone with a detailed knowledge of the German dimension was working hard to neuter British propaganda to Germany; further-more, that someone was extremely clever, because he was able to justify what he was doing in high policy, either towards Germany or the USSR, and with considerable authority too. At the same time, his actions did not serve British interests but did serve those of the Soviet Union (which was itself doing the very thing that Bruce Lockhart and Barman wished PWE to do), while quelling any British doubts by playing on possible problems with the Russians if any alteration were to be made. It seems to me that only Delmer could have done all this (although Philby may also have played a part; see p. 143). Furthermore, there has been a suggestion that Delmer's war work was later seen within intelligence as lying under some sort of cloud.[30]

If, as I believe, this is subversion in action, the beauty of its execution was such as to make it virtually undetectable. Who, looking back on this extraordinarily complicated matter, could have spotted a mole at work? Who was there sufficiently knowledgeable and brilliant to unravel this muddle of motive and alibi? Yet beneath this tissue of complexity, there was the clear outline of the subversion of British policy by Soviet Russia, although no one even suspected this.

After Barbarossa, the Foreign Office was very anxious not to upset the Russians although, once again, this did not mean they were prepared to give the Russians advantages. They had no qualms at all about preventing a non-Communist German from broadcasting to Germany and their reasons were highly significant. Ellic Howe recalled that General von Thoma, who was captured soon after El Alamein, was mooted as a broadcaster:

What probably killed the plan was Bruce Lockhart's statement quoting von Thoma that 'he looks to us to protect Germany from Communism'. Sir A. Cadogan minuted (as if apprehensively), 'He wouldn't put this out, I suppose?' The Russians already had von Paulus ... and it is likely that the last thing that Sir Alec wanted was suspicious enquiries from our Soviet Allies ...[31]

There seems little reason to doubt that the Russians did not want to see German Socialists, and indeed others, being bolstered by the British authorities, and thus ordered their moles and agents within SOE to try to prevent this.

At any rate, this is what a number of those involved in the political resistance to Hitler, such as Fritz Heine, believed. They argued that British policy tended to ignore them, so ultimately favouring Soviet plans. For them the issue was a straightforward one. Once Hitler had been defeated a new Europe would emerge. Those who had opposed the Nazis would be bound to play a major part in the creation of that new Europe. The important thing, or so they argued, was to ensure that it had a liberal and democratic basis and this meant that the new Europe must not be dominated by Soviet Communism. The Russians were actively promoting the Communist and Communist-led opposition to the Nazis. By failing to assist the non-Communist German resistance, they went on, the British were *de facto* helping the Russians.

The Russians certainly were working hard in this area. While it has now been reasonably well established that Russia did not expect to be attacked on the night of 21 June 1941, there is evidence to show that the Russian policy of trying to undermine the Nazi regime from within, and ensuring that the opposition to Nazism was led and controlled by German Communists, was well under way before 1941.

The Soviets seem to have believed, both for ideological and more practical reasons, that it was possible to construct a German opposition to the Nazis' Third Reich. It was to be based on the remnants of the German Communist Party, the KPD, for whom over five million people had voted before its dissolution as a result of the Reichstag fire of March 1933.[32] Even in the heyday of the Hitler–Stalin Pact, it was, apparently, Communist policy to try to reactivate the basic unit of the German Communist Party inside Germany, the cell.

One of the German Communist leaders, Herbert Wehner (who later left the Communists and became a Social Democratic Cabinet minister under Willy Brandt), was sent by the Kremlin to Sweden to co-ordinate the Communist renaissance in Germany. It should not be forgotten that the German Communist Party had over 350,000 members, of whom a large number were well versed in the tactics of clandestine political activity. Many of them showed the greatest bravery in facing up to the barbaric methods of the Gestapo, who were determined to try to destroy German Marxism for ever. Although Wehner was arrested in 1942 by the Swedish police on a charge of subversion and sentenced to prison, his efforts bore some fruit.

The Kremlin's aim was that these cells should form the nucleus of the new, post-Nazi German labour movement which would be led by a resurrected KPD. The main obstacle to this was, of course, the existence in exile of a German Social Democratic Party, and this is why the arrival of the SPD in London in 1941 presented Moscow with a difficult and thorny problem, but one for which subversion by its moles could provide a solution. It seems certain they met with success.

Whether this subversion was of great significance is, of course, a difficult question to answer. It obviously mattered to the Socialist exiles, but it was hardly a disaster for them. In addition, it can be argued that even if Churchill and Eden had known that Stalin's policy towards 'his' German exiles was different, they might still not have altered their policy to 'their' exiles in London. On the other hand, there is no way of testing this and thus the question must remain open. One should not put it more strongly than this. Once the problem of the SPD had been settled, Delmer concentrated on a political radio goonery which was both ineffective and puerile, as far as the British war effort was concerned. It has received a far better press than it deserved, not least thanks to the efforts of Delmer himself. For the real political history of British radio propaganda is nothing but a dismal chronicle of wasted opportunities.

Delmer's hatchet job on the German Socialists suggests that it is not ludicrous to believe that, in one small but crucial area, a mole was able to disrupt Dalton's entire propaganda policy. This in turn may have been one reason why Dalton was almost a complete failure as SOE chief. The Kremlin, on the other hand, not only produced a propaganda policy which suited its own secret objectives, but it was also able to execute that policy without any interference from Britain. This must, if nothing else, rank as yet another of the Kremlin's masterstrokes in the secret intelligence war.

There is one final piece of evidence to consider in this context. It is provided by Michael Tracey in his biography of Sir Hugh Carleton Greene. Greene worked for the BBC's German Service and in July 1944, when he learned of the Generals' Plot against Hitler, he prefaced a news item about it with the headline 'Civil war has broken out in Germany', and got into terrible trouble about it as a result.

This headline was, of course, not to prove correct (possibly, it may be argued, because of the failure of British propaganda to Germany). But the reasons for Greene's difficulties went far further than simple exaggeration.

Greene's specific job was:

> To see that the news beamed at Germany was as near to the truth as he could get it, given the limitations and needs of the war effort. His self-appointed task was to resist as many outside pressures as was possible to establish as much autonomy ... as was feasible ... Marius Goring observed that he 'had just as many pressures from the BBC to follow certain lines which he did not want to follow as he had from the Government through PWE' ...[33]

In any case, German émigrés continued to be kept away from the air, a decision which flowed from the move away from Dalton's original precepts:

> Émigrés were kept at some distance not only from editorial decisions since this was to be a manifestly British station but also as far as possible from the microphone ... One of Greene's most persistent problems was how his service should view the German people and how these people should be encouraged to see their future. Unconditional Surrender meant no negotiation with any part of German society, yet should not a distinction be made between ordinary German people and Nazis?[34]

It was while exploring the ramifications of this policy that Greene decided to exploit the July Plot to see if the Germans might be encouraged to rebel against the Nazi leadership, to sow a little subversion, so to speak.

But his headline absolutely enraged the Foreign Office:

> The Foreign Office was utterly furious because the Government line was still one of unconditional surrender and they thought that

any idea of Germans fighting Germans would arouse Russian suspicions.[35]

What, we may ask, was the point about all this? Surely the Russians would have been delighted if civil war had broken out in Germany? On reflection, it will be seen that the answer is 'no', they would not have been delighted, and for a reason which underlines the case we have been trying to establish.

By 1944, any suggestion that the British were taking too close an interest in German oppositional groups was thought, by the Foreign Office, to be dangerous. What the Foreign Office did not appreciate was the fact that the Russians did not want to see civil war in Germany promoted by anyone other than themselves and their underlings, the German Communists. They were clearly not going to be keen to see aristocratic Prussian officers take over the German Government, since this would conflict with their aims for post-war Germany.

An alert British intelligence organisation ought to have asked itself what was going on, and British propaganda policy could then have been adjusted accordingly. It was not unreasonable to suggest that it was neither in Britain's nor in Russia's interest for the German army to avoid being defeated on the battlefield. But it was not a question of using the opposition as an alternative to military defeat (in any case, it failed to dispatch Hitler), but as a useful corollary to it. However, just as in the case of Rudolf Hess, the British authorities decided to sit tight and do nothing spectacular. Was this really in the British interest? Or had a net been drawn over British propaganda policy which, ever since 1941, had a subverted strand to it?

To conclude, then, the high policy explanation for SOE's obvious shortcomings is forceful; it explains a lot and, if we postulate that we are dealing with people who were not very bright, it might indeed explain everything; as it was, they were the 'best and the brightest' and they were, of course, intelligence officers.

Two things are remarkable about the abandonment of Daltonian ideas of subversion. The first is that the reasons hitherto advanced are often surprisingly superficial; there is no evidence that deeper probes were set in motion as to precisely why the Russians adopted a particular line and projected it so forcefully. The second is that this was, indeed, an area in which Russia had vital interests and therefore an area into which the Kremlin's agents would clearly have been ordered to infiltrate.

How the moles operated within SOE and PWE:
informal and formal networks

It seems there were two main ways in which Communists might be expected to be able to subvert British policy, using its spies (to pass on secrets) and its moles (to do both this and help in the actual formulation of policy). The first lay through the use of what may be termed formal networks, the official routes used by employees of SOE and of the wider intelligence community to guide and advise the authorities (both politicians and civil servants) who possessed the final decisions on what was done. The second lay through the use of informal networks, the utilisation of friendships and unofficial contacts between colleagues. The latter were particularly well-suited to the British Establishment, and were sometimes, indeed often, based on homosexual relationships (not incorrectly referred to as the 'Homintern'). The British political class was small and usually led by a select group of people who were in large part composed of well-educated graduates from Oxford and Cambridge. This élite was particularly successful in maintaining its members' influence in the corridors of power, not least by its ability to exclude rival groups, such as trade unions, from positions of importance and authority.

Both sorts of network might, in theory, be utilised to pass on information or misinformation, or to fail to pass on information, or to instil into the minds of decision-makers ideas which would assist Communist strategies. Formal networks might be expected to generate written records of subversion (whose existence might, in time, filter into the public domain). Informal ones would be highly unlikely to do so: people rarely make a record of chats over the telephone or pieces of advice proffered in pubs or at cocktail parties.

Informal networks, then, are the most sinister source of subversion since they are the hardest to track down. It might be supposed that to gain access to someone in authority via an informal network would have presented the Kremlin with an insurmountable problem and, for many countries, this may have been true. But in the particular case of Britain the opposite was the case. It was precisely because the British political class was so small, and so heavily dependent on a few select public schools and Oxbridge, that to penetrate it was so relatively easy and effective. Once a mole or an agent had managed to infiltrate into the groups from which the élite replenished itself, subsequent subversion was fairly simple to achieve. Had pre-war Britain been less class-bound and Oxbridge-obsessed and more widely meritocratic, it would have been a great deal harder to subvert.

The bases of these informal networks were friendships and the loyalties that went with friendship. It is a truism that whom one knows can often be at least as important as what one knows, and it is a truism that applies as much to moles as to doctors or politicians. No one, perhaps, realised this more clearly than the Kremlin's rising star, Kim Philby. For his early membership of the pro-Nazi organisation, the Anglo-German Fellowship, was designed specifically to ensure that if Britain went Nazi, he would have as many friends in high places under Adolf Hitler as he had under Winston Churchill (see pp. 205 and 343).

Andrew Boyle has argued that there was something specific about Cambridge élitism in the 1920s and 1930s which made the moles as influential as they were.[36] This is only partially true: a Cambridge education was not the chief reason why subversion was successful. The real 'climate of treason' was generated by the Anglo-Soviet Alliance which (for legitimate reasons) was the climate in Whitehall in the 1940s, not Cambridge in the 1930s.

Even though formal networks are bound to leave more traces than the informal ones, by its very nature concrete proof of subversion was and is unlikely to be discovered. As we have seen, the scenario of subversion was, for obvious reasons, obscure and complex, made even harder to pin down by virtue of the brilliance of the moles: they were clever people who knew how to hide their tracks. This is, of course, a problem historians share with the mole-hunters from MI5; the importance of gaining confessions out of people like Blunt or Philby emanates from the stark truth that there was absolutely no conclusive documentary evidence with which to convict them.

On the other hand, thanks to the vast number of leaks emanating from former officers of the intelligence community, as well as the exposure of Anthony Blunt by Andrew Boyle, that of Leo Long by Nigel West, and Mrs Thatcher's important statement in Parliament on 15 November 1979, as well as a variety of admissions by other people, we probably now know as much about the extent and composition of both formal and informal networks as we are ever likely to know. For this reason, then, it is not only the formal networks that may be analysed; the informal ones may be scrutinised as well.

For the historian of politics, the undergraduate friendships, whether homosexual or not, are of importance only because they became the seed-bed of countless numbers of informal networks within the Government services, which would proliferate and flourish. This is why the élite was significant; it could support a Communist network whose role could possess political influence out of all proportion to its size, let alone to its wider popular support. Further more, it would be very hard for British Security to penetrate these friendships, especially where they were cemented by common erotic experiences which at that time constituted grave criminal offences.

It is indeed remarkable that the group of traitors which included Blunt, Philby, Maclean, Burgess, Long and the alleged traitor Goronwy Rees was based firmly on friendships forged at Cambridge from 1926 (when Blunt became an undergraduate at Trinity) to 1937 (when he finally left for London). During this period, Blunt collaborated with all these people and possibly with Ormond Uren as well.[37]

It is also not without paradox that an élitism which was developed to safeguard the position of the bourgeoisie and semi-aristocratic groups was to constitute such an excellent means of undermining them. It is also worth recalling that the number of middle-class traitors was relatively large, while the number of working-class ones relatively small, although this may be simply another indication of the fact that the British political system tended to exclude working-class men and women.[38]

It is, however, important to state that there is no comfort in this kind of study for those who seek guilt by association. With the exception of Sefton Delmer and Otto John, all of those analysed here in terms of Communist subversion have admitted to being moles.

Moles, of course, did not simply pass on British secrets to the Russians; they also managed to influence the very process of policy-making. As we shall see, there was no shortage of candidates for the job.

As far as formal SOE networks were involved, what immediately strikes one is the large number of potential moles working within its ranks. We have already noted Dodds-Parker's view that the Communists in SOE readily 'shared their skills' with the British.[39] Any Communist, secret or otherwise, would have been morally and ideologically obliged to work for Stalin, although this did not mean that he or she did not also work for Churchill.

In another part of his testimony, Dodds-Parker talks about his own attitude towards Communists in SOE:

In those three years from the summer of 1940 to 1943 ... Communists played a considerable part at first, being almost the only groups trained and ready in 1939. Any attempt to ascribe credit or blame to those who resisted ... would be sterile ... traditional Russian imperialism, although masked in the guise of economically ineffective Marxism, by its behaviour was being revealed as a greater and more immediate threat to Eastern European freedoms than to the Anglo-Saxons ...[40]

Ellic Howe, in his testimony, offers further insights into the Communists who worked for SOE and explains that Philby actually got into MI6 via Section D:

Philby joined Section 'D' in July 1940, a few weeks before Grand himself was sacked and what was left of the section became SOE; he was instructed to report to none other than Guy Burgess.[41]

Furthermore, Howe states that Philby was charged with the training of SOE propaganda agents:

The training of SO 2, the later SOE, propaganda agents [was to be] done in conjunction with Mr Philby. Kim Philby's transfer from SOE to the SIS did not take place until September 1941.[42]

It has to be said that Howe does not believe that Philby did much harm while in SOE (a view I believe is unsupported by the evidence). But Howe's testimony does prove Philby's deep involvement in the matters here under consideration. Howe concludes:

During his Section 'D' and SO 2/SOE period (June 1940–September 1941) he was of no great use to his Russian friends. Whereas once in the SIS, he was ideally placed to carry on his traitor's activities on their behalf. According to a friend who had some knowledge of the much later inquest, Philby clearly did more damage during the 1941–45 period than has commonly been accepted ... Amongst other things, he attempted to sabotage SIS operations and did his best to undermine (for the benefit of the Russians) the usefulness of SIS agents abroad. He did this by exposing them to the capture of the Nazis ...[43]

Evidence of the extent to which the Soviet Union and its British helpers were interested in the activities of SOE is provided from other sources as well. Julian Amery, for example – hardly someone celebrated either then or now for his sympathy with the Communist cause – specifically sought Communists for his Balkan exploits in 1941:

> One of our problems in SOE was to recruit liaison officers for the Balkans who knew something of irregular warfare and if possible something about Communism. It occurred to me that there might be Englishmen who had fought in the International Brigade in Spain who would possess both qualifications. The Home Office and the Security Services seemed to have no lists of the individuals involved ... I therefore consulted Ellen Wilkinson, the Under Secretary of State for Education who had been a leading supporter of the Spanish Republic ... She had spent all her life on the Left wing of the Labour movement and knew the British Communist Party and its fringes well. Having worked with it and against it, she had no illusions about it, or its Soviet masters. She was, indeed, one of the first members of the Government of any Party to recognise the threat which the Soviet Union would present to Europe after the war ...[44]

M. R. D. Foot also deals with this matter. In one sense he seems to accept that the Communist subversion of SOE constitutes a matter which is worthy of some, albeit limited, investigation. On the other hand, however, what may be called his gung-ho attitude to it indicates that he does not believe this to be an area where Communist subversion played any truly significant role (a view he shares with Lord Gladwyn):

> What harm, at that moment [not precisely specified in the text] was any of [the moles and agents] doing to the allied war effort against the axis? 'Our gallant Soviet ally', that phrase, reiterated from countless platforms and in countless broadcasts in 1942–43, was a great deal more than a phrase. It was only this solidly tyrannous lifebelt that kept the grand alliance of free peoples afloat through those two terrible years. Stalin's and Beria's iniquities [sic] have now become journalists' commonplaces and were iniquitous indeed; yet hindsight, though it sometimes clarifies, can also distort. Had it not been for Stalin and Beria and their iron grip on the Soviet Empire, no British reader of this book aged under

35 would (in all probability) have been born at all because his or her father would have been deported to work in a Nazi labour camp in eastern Europe with no chance to beget a child. Without Russian help Great Britain would have lost the war against Nazi Germany ...[45]

While supporting the general thrust of Foot's argument, it has to be said that, although from the British viewpoint, Soviet and British interests appeared to be the same, from the Soviet viewpoint this was patently not the case. Since the moles operated from the latter position, it is certainly not implausible to believe that harm was indeed done by them in specific areas, even if Foot is correct to argue that at the end of the day, if Communist subversion had not existed, things might, broadly speaking, not have been very different.

Foot goes on to mention six moles and one Communist who at one time or another worked for SOE or had a particular interest in it (Philby, Burgess, Springhall, Uren, Klugmann in Cairo, John Eyre in Bari and Frank Thompson). Of the first, Foot says:

Philby was in SOE for a year, in the training section ... his father was a famous man, a cousin of B. L. Montgomery who was best man at his wedding; far to the right, and his schooling had been impeccable. He drank heavily at the time; so did many others, and on a major's pay, tax free, he could afford it (No one in SOE paid British income tax). As Yvon Morandot testified, he was extremely good at his job; his colleagues at Beaulieu found him reserved but likeable and were sorry to see him go. Presumably he reported to his Russian masters what he knew about SOE which was quite a lot; it would certainly have included Dalton's ... identity and those of several other senior personalities such as Gubbins and some firm news of the areas in which SOE was planning to operate. He was in no other way a liability to SOE. On the contrary, for the year he was in it, he was an asset.[46]

Foot's verdict here, namely that for Philby to pass on the names of SOE chiefs and the addresses of their operations was not particularly damaging, might appear a trifle bizarre. What is more, the implication that such actions were the only actions that men such as Philby took totally ignores both the urgent needs of the Russians and the potential possessed by formal and informal networks for the execution of subversive activity.

There is in addition very clear evidence that the moles worked hard within the German dimension. Burgess, for example, was officially stated in Parliament by the then Foreign Secretary, Selwyn Lloyd, to have used his connections with MI5 in this area:

The only connection which Burgess had with MI5 [during the war] had been [that] whilst working for the BBC he had from time to time reported to an informant information about Germany received by him from a contact.[47]

This could and probably was taken to mean that Burgess was supplying information about the Nazis. This is implausible, for what interested Burgess about Germany was primarily its future political shape (the informant, incidentally, was probably Wolfgang zu Putlitz; see p. 227).

Indeed, Burgess is on record as having had:

A plan [in 1940] for going to Moscow to negotiate with the Russians an agreement about support of anti-Nazi resistance movements in Europe. Sabotage and resistance were concerns of Burgess's Department ... The deal would be that the British would support Communist resistances in Western Europe if the Russians would promise to support non-Communist as well as Communist resistances in the East. Even though Burgess proposed to take his considerably more respectable friend Isaiah Berlin, a fluent Russian speaker, the idea did not meet with favour.[48]

This shows quite clearly how Burgess's mind was working for, as a mole, he would have known that it was the first half of this deal that the Russians were interested in and not the second. It also underlines SOE's importance to the Russians and demonstrates why both Blunt and Philby, as well as Burgess, were ordered to take a direct interest both in SOE's general concerns with the resistance in Europe and in the German dimension to its activities.

Of Burgess, Foot notes chiefly that Gubbins got rid of him; not, he adds, 'for political reasons', but because he was a heavy drinker and a homosexual and therefore a security risk (Foot presumably means a security risk as far as Nazi espionage was concerned, although this is not clear).[49] Foot continues:

There was one other known Soviet sympathiser in SOE in England.

In April 1943 MI5 discovered that this man was in touch with Douglas Springhall, the national organiser of the Communist Party of Great Britain, and was starting [sic] to explain to him what he knew about SOE (which was a great deal less than Philby did). Springhall was arrested and sentenced to seven years for quite another matter: receiving secrets from a woman in the Air Ministry. His acquaintance in SOE, Ormond Uren, a captain in the Highland Light Infantry who was a junior staff officer in SOE's Hungarian Section, was a recent convert to communism and was also sent down for seven years ...[50]

Foot's account could be held to imply that what was important about this matter was not that SOE was the subject of Soviet subversion but that Springhall had passed on RAF secrets to the Russians (involving, according to some commentators, the secret of the jet engine).

Stafford gives a slightly different interpretation of the Uren case, despite pointing out that 'evidence on Uren's offence is lacking'.[51] Furthermore, Stafford argues that Uren's conviction was a failure for the Russians, since it alerted SOE to the possibility that it was the subject of Soviet penetration. Stafford writes:

It should be noted [for 1943] that German penetration of SOE was not the only worry expressed about its security. As concerns about the post-war world and future relations with the USSR increasingly dominated the minds of those responsible for strategic, diplomatic and intelligence matters, fears arose about the Communist penetration of SOE ... while evidence on Uren's offence is lacking, it is possible that he passed on to Springhall information about peace feelers received by SOE from Hungary. But whatever it was, the fact of Communist interest in the inner working of SOE served to fuel the flames of SIS and Foreign Office anxiety and contributed to the attacks against SOE ... it also foreshadowed the growing importance which concerns over Soviet objectives in Europe were to play in SOE operations during and after the liberation and presaged the purge [sic] of all known Communists from Britain's secret organisations.[52]

The implication behind Stafford's claims is that Soviet penetration was, at any rate by 1943, perceived as a threat to British Intelligence by the intelligence community itself. The astounding thing is not only that he fails to provide a source for such a sweeping assertion, but that this assertion is simply not supported by the documentary evidence, or indeed by the verbal testimony provided by former officers such as Julian Amery or Douglas Dodds-Parker.

Indeed, as we have seen (and it is a point which Foot *mutatis mutandis* supports), the very reverse was the case. Once Barbarossa was under way, SOE ceased to fret about Communist subversion because the Soviets were deemed to be on the same side as Britain. In part, of course, they were; but as we have seen, there was very much more to it than this.

As to the precise nature of Uren's offence, correspondence in the *Listener* in the winter of 1981–2[53] produced a most interesting letter from Uren. In it, Uren stated that he did not pass any important policy decisions to Springhall, although he admits that if he had possessed access to them, he would have done so. What Springhall had asked for was simply:

An outline of the work I was doing for SOE which I gave him. This naturally involved describing the work of the department in which I was employed and the functions of SOE as a whole. The very existence of SOE was highly secret at the time and in terms of the Official Secrets Act, the offence was a serious one but it was hardly of a nature to change the map of Europe. My feeling is that at that stage Springhall was not so much interested in information qua information but as a means of establishing my bona fides and, as is now painfully obvious, as a means of black-mail ... The evidence on which I was convicted came entirely from my own statement. On this score, I think I am entitled to consider my debt paid.[54]

It is of course quite natural that Uren should make these points and it would be wrong to re-examine the Uren case, were there not one aspect of this rather squalid story which appears so far to have escaped attention. This is that Uren has, in the *Listener*, publicly admitted that the Soviet Union was interested in SOE's subversive work although he has denied that he had access to policy decisions or that his offence was likely to 'change the map of Europe'.

The charge of changing the map of Europe is, however, not quite what it seems. For the point is not whether by himself Uren managed to execute such a change but that, more broadly, this was something in which SOE had been involved and that it was this aspect of its activities that had been of such interest to the USSR. However, it has to be stated that Uren, who joined SOE in 1942 at the age of twenty-four, is in any case not wholly responsible for what the Kremlin managed to extract from the situation. He was merely a minor cog, punished by MI5 to prevent others from following his example. On the other hand, it cannot be disputed that the information that he passed to the Soviets was bound to be extremely useful. Although any information was important to the KGB and the GRU, in Uren's case the information would be of the greatest value, because it would allow the USSR to see whether the information about SOE which they were being passed via official channels was, in fact, full and frank (see p. 269).

About Klugmann and Eyre, Foot makes the briefest of comments: Klugmann in Cairo achieved 'high rank in charge of operations in the Balkans', Eyre was the 'intelligence officer of the Albanian section in Bari'.[55] Yet, Foot says (and there is no reason to think he is being ironic in any way), 'like Philby in MI6 they worked tremendously hard'. Thompson, by all accounts a very brave man, also worked in the Balkan area where he was executed in May 1944.[56]

Foot's argument, then, is that there were indeed moles and agents in SOE itself, but that this did not make much difference to what SOE was trying to undertake. As Foot explains:

All through its short life SOE stuck to one primordial rule: it was anti-Nazi. Therefore it opposed the Nazis' friends and allies ... A corollary to this doctrine of opposing the Nazis' friends is sometimes overlooked: in the early days, while the Nazi–Soviet pact operated, SOE and its predecessors were anti-Russian or at least anti-Soviet. [But] agile as a seasoned Marxist hard-liner, SOE reversed its line overnight, on 22–23 June 1941, to conform with the Prime Minister's memorable evening broadcast; anyone the Nazis attacked was SOE's friend as well as Churchill's. There were never any SOE missions into occupied Soviet home territory behind the German lines; all the partisans there were supposed to be under strict party control from Moscow.[57]

The issue facing SOE, however, was not whether Britain ought to have wanted to co-operate on an equal footing with the USSR, but why it failed to achieve this. For the fact was that the Soviet Union first stymied British subversive policy and then managed to impose its own subversive policy on wide areas of Europe, including those where formally SOE had clearly-established interests.

What is more, Foot accepts that no one was more skilled in subversion than the Communists, and he specifically singles out Stalin as evidence. For Stalin himself had spread subversive propaganda and fought in a revolution.[58] How could SOE have been so sure, how can Foot be so sure, that the Communists in SOE were behaving as the British expected them to behave and not as the Kremlin might order them to?

As far as the formal networks in SOE are concerned, the answer must be that they were so well infiltrated by Communists and their sympathisers that they were not only able to conceal Soviet subversive interests but also ensure that anyone who appeared to challenge those interests was effectively neutralised.

Every Communist and secret Communist who was an SOE officer occupied a position in a formal SOE network; every one of them must have been instructed exactly how to use his or her position, in order to enable Communism rather than liberalism to triumph at the end of the war. Many Communists, like Christopher Hill, may have refused to take orders from any Soviet controller, although it must have been hard to reconcile their membership of the CPGB with such a refusal, for the moles themselves certainly worked hard on the Communist sympathies of all those whose names they were given. This is something that Blunt himself conceded.[59] Even those who balked at the idea of actually promoting Communism in Britain probably had no qualms about advancing it when it came to the continent of Europe.

At the same time, however, it should not be assumed that, for the high policy reasons repeatedly mentioned, to work for Russia in this way caused deep moral problems. What is more, again for high policy reasons, they could be fairly sure that their activities were virtually undetectable, because what they did and what British high policy demanded merged into each other almost without conflict.

We should, of course, not underrate the importance of the informal networks. Any employee of an organisation knows that there are certain people in that organisation who are able to exercise an influence which is out of proportion to their position in it. Such people are often characterised as 'high-flyers', people of whom great things may be expected in the future.

Even if men such as Burgess or Philby were only formally in SOE for a short period, they were seen as high-flyers and were thus in a position to retain influence in SOE, thanks to the informal networks by which they could maintain access to it after their departure. This was subversion on the cheap. It was one thing to smuggle documents out of a ministry, to meet up with a Soviet controller in Hyde Park: such things were fraught with danger. But to have a quiet word with a good friend in another Government position, to intimate that a particular action was likely to upset 'our gallant Soviet ally' and should therefore be dropped: these were other matters altogether.

Kim Philby on active service; the Putlitz Papers part one; Peter Smolka-Smollett

Perhaps the most important networks were based on Philby. He was in SOE at a very critical period, from the early summer of 1940 until September 1941, a period, as we have seen, when SOE underwent a decisive change. We know today that Philby understood precisely the nature of subversive activity – indeed, that he was a past master at it – and we know, too, that he fully comprehended the relationship between covert resistance during the war and the political geography of the European continent after it. We know this, it should be added, because he has told us so:

> Worry about the future shape of Europe was my chief preoccupation. On the side of political subversion, the difficulties [facing SOE] were even more serious because they involved fundamental aspects of British policy. By and large, the British Government had accustomed itself to supporting the monarchs and oligarchs of Europe. Such men were strongly averse to any form of subversion.[60]

And Philby continued, in a highly significant passage:

> In reality the only people likely to put up any sort of resistance to Hitler were the Left-wing movements, the Social Democrats and the Communists ... yet they were extremely unlikely to stir for the sake of a British Government which insisted on playing footsies with the King Carols and Prince Pauls who had persecuted them between the wars ... small wonder that when the crunch came, the resistance movements leant so heavily on the Soviet Union ...[61]

There are clearly a number of things to be said about these words which emanate, of course, from the horse's mouth. For a start (largely, I suspect, to embarrass the British authorities), they give a totally accurate indication of the problems which were of concern to Philby (and to the Kremlin) during the war. They prove that for the Soviet Union subversion had an overtly political aspect, as we have already alleged, and that this political aspect was targeted not at the present but at the 'future shape of Europe'.

These issues were subjects about which Philby was paid by British Intelligence to have a view during the war. They were issues upon which he had to formulate solutions which would satisfy his masters. At the same time, however, these solutions would also have to satisfy the longer-term aims of the Kremlin. In this passage, then, Philby summarises the areas in which he operated: British policy towards the resistance to the Nazis, alleged (but unfounded) British sympathies for conservative and reactionary regimes, as well as the inevitable struggle between Communism and Social Democracy for leadership of the working-class movement which he rightly foresaw would be a major theme in post-war European politics.

What is more, Philby also provides an intimation of the solutions that he proposed, as well as offering, by virtue of his own professional position, an indication of the ways in which they were to be implemented. For Philby's avowed aim was to ensure that the British line was one which would drive the resisters of Europe away from Britain and into the hands of the Communists.

From 1940–1 Philby was in a formal position, within SOE, to promote this aim; from 1941–4 when he was in the Iberian section of MI6 he retained his authority to influence the activities of his colleagues and friends, but only in an informal way, except where German issues were involved. In addition, both Blunt and Philby attended meetings of the Joint Intelligence Committee, the body set up to co-ordinate intelligence for the Chiefs of Staff; this has been 'officially' admitted by the Duke of Portland who also came into contact with Burgess.[62] That Blunt and Philby came occasionally to JIC meetings should not be taken to imply they in any way helped with the making of high policy for, in any case, if Howarth's line is to be followed, the JIC was not very influential in the formulation of high policy. Rather, it was an indication of the prestige and authority these men enjoyed within their own services. This undoubtedly would have helped them to develop 'low' policy, policy on the

detailed and minor issues with which Cabinet ministers did not want
to be bothered.

Clifton Child, who was working in PWE at this time and took a
close interest in the German dimension to its work, has written that
in his view there was no doubt that Philby worked to undermine the
anti-Communist opposition to Hitler from Section V of MI6 (Child
knew that Section V was involved; he knew that Philby had headed
it only after the war; see p. 203).

Philby was convinced that post-war Europe would be in the grip
of a 'revolutionary mood. It would sweep away the Europe of the
1920s and 1930s.' But he knew that such a mood would have to be
both encouraged and then exploited by the USSR if it was to have
any chance of dominating Europe after Hitler. In his book, he argues
that this was less difficult than it might have been:

> Attlee, Bevin, Dalton and other Socialists [did not have] a post-
> war policy which would be an attractive alternative ... the lack of
> a suitable political alternative dogged us throughout the war.[63]

What Philby forgets to mention is that the above statement is true
only for the period after the early summer of 1941. In fact, it is quite
incorrect for the period from 1940 until 1941 for, as we have seen,
under Dalton's aegis SOE had a very different policy. Indeed, it is
quite remarkable that Philby should skip over the extent to which
Dalton's policy ideas matched his own (although Dalton, of course,
was determined to counter Communism and promote Social
Democracy). We should not forget that conversation between Julian
Amery and Dalton, when the SOE chief specifically advanced his
own pro-left policy:

> Then at last Dalton questioned me in detail about the Balkans.
> He seemed at first to be arguing the Foreign Office case but this
> was only to take my measure. Suddenly he brought his fist down
> on the desk and declared: 'Of course, you are right and they are
> wrong. It is useless to expect any help from King Boris or Prince
> Patsy.'[64]

What is so striking is that Philby's reasons for opposing British
policy were almost identical with those Amery reports, in direct
speech, as being Dalton's reasons supporting the very same idea. It
is almost as if Dalton had been speaking to Philby on this very

subject. It may, of course, be the case that this is just a fluke; perhaps Julian Amery had read Philby's account about a British Government which 'insisted on playing footsies with the King Carols and Prince Pauls' and the phrase stuck in his mind. But even if this verbal compatibility is mere coincidence, its fundamental significance remains untouched. Both Dalton and Philby wanted the left to prosper, except that for Philby the left meant the Communists.

Philby was, of course, a junior officer. In addition, as in all intelligence organisations, SOE was meant to observe a distinction between the policy-makers and the intelligence-gatherers (though this was probably rarely maintained). Yet even if Philby's job in SOE made it quite impossible that he himself could have had any influence whatsoever on Dalton, we should note that his job was an important one and had access to others in the policy-making process. For let us recall the testimony of that other SOE member, Julian Amery, who stated quite categorically that:

> As an officer of SOE I saw a wide selection of Foreign Office telegrams, Intelligence Reports and other Government papers. I was on the inside of Government.[65]

Philby himself declares that:

> [I travelled from Woburn Abbey to London] virtually at will. This was valuable for developing contacts with other SIS contacts and with MI5 and other Government Departments interested in our work ... Most of my work with MI5 concerned the so-called B Division, the place where intelligence was received and assessed and where subsequent action was usually determined ... In 1943 I cultivated MI5 assiduously ... My opposite number in MI5 was Roger Hollis, the head of the section investigating Soviet and Communist affairs ... we got on well and were soon exchanging information without reserve on either side.[66]

The obvious irony implicit in Philby's remarks about MI5 and Roger Hollis, whose job it was to prevent people like Philby from subverting British policy, is something that we shall consider again at greater length (see p. 176). Here it should suffice for us to realise that Philby's place within SOE and SOE's place within the wider British intelligence community gave him a commanding position from which to attempt the subversion of detailed areas of British policy, and it would be quite idiotic to suppose that it was not one of Philby's major aims to get Dalton and SOE to abandon its policy of aiding Social Democrats in general, and German Social Democratic exiles in particular.

Yet we must not forget that Philby was not merely part of a formal structure which permitted him access to secret policy and gave him opportunities to subvert it, he was also a key member of an informal network which linked him directly to Dalton. His contact was, of course, none other than Hugh Gaitskell, later to become leader of the British Labour Party. It is, it must be stressed, certainly not being suggested here that Gaitskell realised that he was part of such an informal network, or that he ever suspected that the advice proffered by Philby was tainted.

Gaitskell was one of Dalton's protégés and became Dalton's Chef de Cabinet in the Ministry of Economic Warfare.[67] Dalton told Gaitskell that he would share his 'black life' to the full. 'I promised Gaitskell that I should have no secrets from him.'[68] What is more, Gaitskell had a particular concern for German affairs. As his official biographer reports:

> Gaitskell's wartime role had been settled early for German speaking economists were few and in demand ... his best language was German but Noel Hall was in charge of German intelligence [in the Ministry of Economic Warfare] and Gaitskell was attached to the neutral countries section ... In December 1939 Gaitskell took Hall's job as Director of Intelligence with enemy countries.[69]

And Gaitskell and Philby were very old friends who shared an interest in things German:

> Gaitskell's old Vienna acquaintance Kim Philby used to consult him over sausages and mash in a Berkeley Square pub about the political content of their propaganda; Philby felt that Gaitskell and Dalton would have liked to have been more revolutionary but were constrained by the Foreign Office.[70]

Philby's networks, however, were not the only Communist networks within SOE. Another one involved no less a personage than Lord Vansittart. Indeed this was, perhaps, the most paradoxical network of all, because it proved that people could end up doing one thing in the mistaken belief that they were actually doing something completely different. This particular network was a mixture of formal and informal structures. It came about in the appointment of Lord Vansittart to Dalton's staff. As Dalton wrote:

> The Prime Minister proposed to me that I should have Vansittart who had at last resigned from the bogus post of Chief Diplomatic Advisor to the Government, as my Chief Advisor in SOE. I welcomed this idea ... Vansittart and I worked closely together ...[71]

What neither Dalton nor Vansittart realised was that one of Vansittart's most important sources of information about Germany (and Vansittart liked to consider himself the supreme expert on Germany) was himself a secret Communist called Wolfgang Gans, Edler Herr zu Putlitz.

Putlitz's case is dealt with in greater detail later, since he was essentially concerned with providing secret intelligence and thus also entered into MI6's sphere of operations (see p. 220). He gave accurate information to MI6 about German plans which formed the basis of Churchill's pre-war attacks on Britain's defence policy. He then escaped to Britain in 1940 and was set to work at SOE, where Ellic Howe encountered him:

> Putlitz was a former German diplomat who had supplied Lord Vansittart with information before the war ... He spent a period in the USA, then returned to [Woburn Abbey] ... On his return 'C' [the Head of MI6] put him on to Delmer ... After the war he was given a British Passport and proceeded to defect to the German Democratic Republic ...[72]

In his book, Putlitz provides a chilling list of his contacts.[73] He knew Lord Vansittart and also a 'Mr Anthony Blunt whose kindness and understanding I will never forget'.[74]

In the case of Lord Vansittart, however, there is documentary evidence which proves beyond all doubt that Putlitz was, indeed, a close friend of his (see p. 225). Putlitz, as a secret Communist, would, like Philby, have made it his business to try to prevent the Social Democrats from gaining recognition in the fight against Hitler. It is not insignificant that Vansittart was one of the leading detractors of the German Social Democrats in Britain and attacked them repeatedly in the press and in Parliament.

Yet Putlitz himself was also part of a third network; a wholly informal one. For Putlitz was a raving homosexual (his man-servant Willi was the cause of much mirth in London). Needless to say, Putlitz's sexual tendencies, combined with his aristocratic ante cedents, his concern for things German and his post in British Intelligence, soon brought him into contact with Guy Burgess who had himself worked in Section D of SIS. Guy Burgess was during this entire period the boyfriend of none other than Harold Nicolson who, until July 1941, was the Parliamentary Secretary at the Ministry of Information and a very highly respected member of the British Establishment.

Somewhat curiously, perhaps, one of the few things that Nicolson chooses to record about his relationship with Burgess was the latter's keen interest in the sort of regime the Russians tried to install in Warsaw in 1944.[75]

Finally, and most remarkable of all, there was another network which has hitherto gained little attention although it may, in part at any rate, go some way to explaining in greater detail the mystery surrounding Dalton's departure from SOE. Broadly speaking, I have argued that the most important single reason for Dalton's departure was not that he was disliked, but that the ideas for which he stood were seen as being in some way in contradiction to the dictates of the Anglo-Soviet Alliance. I have suggested that this was an impression the moles did their best to cultivate.

All the moles would have had to have done was to fail to explain that Russian and British interests were incompatible, and hint that the Russians would not like Dalton's ideas, although they never spelt out precisely why this was so. Since after 1941–2 high policy demanded that SOE co-operate with the Soviets wherever feasible, they therefore had an exceedingly easy ride (even if they ought not to have done). While Dalton changed his views in some respects, as we have witnessed, in other areas (particularly his support for Socialism rather than Communism, and for the Polish exiles) he remained a real threat to Stalin's plans. It may thus be surmised that the Communists may have attempted a far more audacious move against Dalton.

I suspect the moles always exaggerated the extent to which the Russians were going to be difficult and the extent to which any resistance to Soviet aims might cause the Russians to pull out of the war. Furthermore, because the Russians knew they could manipulate the British fears on this score, they were always ready to turn on the taps when required. Their moles would also be able to inform them beforehand of the base line of British policy so that they would never go too far.

In Dalton's case, however, there is one clue that could be taken to suggest the moles tried direct means to scupper him. It is provided by Dr Pimlott in his study of Hugh Dalton (see p. 76). In adducing the basic reason for Dalton's dismissal in 1942, Pimlott concludes that he was 'almost certainly shifted because Bracken [the Minister of Information] and Eden asked the Prime Minister to get him out'.[76] In a letter to me, Dr Pimlott repeats this point:

> I think that there is fairly strong, though not absolutely conclusive, evidence that he was shifted, in a general government shake-up, because of pressure from Bracken and Eden which was motivated by frustration, anger, ambition etc. over the quarrel between Dalton and Bracken in the propaganda field.[77]

We have seen how what may be termed propaganda matters were, in fact, central to the main thrust of Dalton's SOE policy, and we have also seen how, apparently for quite legitimate reasons, Eden's own field was being impinged upon by Dalton's concepts. What has to be explored, however, are Bracken's motives. These are of particular significance for there is now overwhelming evidence to suggest that one of Bracken's most trusted advisers, Peter Smolka-Smollett, was a Communist mole.

Smolka was chief of the Ministry of Information's Russian section and his advice was frequently sought by Bracken whose full confidence he obviously possessed. After the war, Smolka returned to his native Austria, where in due course it emerged that he had been a secret Communist throughout his period in Britain. Smolka was also a friend of Kim Philby's first wife, Litzi. Finally, although Christopher Hill did not know of Smolka's true allegiance, Smolka was the man who organised the publication of Hill's 1945 eulogy on Stalin's Russia, discussed later (see p. 285).

Official Government records show both how influential Smolka was and also how he operated. One document in particular provides a fascinating insight into Smolka's tactics and may well serve as an example for the workings of formal Communist networks.

The moles did not simply say, 'we must do whatever the USSR wants', for the obvious reason that this would arouse British suspicions. Rather, they appear to have said, 'what Russia wants in this specific case is absurd and should be rejected; as a quid pro quo, however, we must make sure that Russia gets what it wants in other areas'.

On 4 November 1941 M. Gusev, at that time head of the Western Department in the Peoples' Commissariat for Foreign Affairs, complained to the Foreign Office about certain anti-Soviet articles which had appeared in the British press. Smolka was asked for a view on this. He responded:

> In no circumstances do we think that the Russians can maintain that these articles go beyond the justified expression of political views which they, no doubt, realise is the privilege that the press in this country enjoys. Generally speaking in cases of this sort, I believe our job on the one hand will be to educate the Russians as far as we can to a proper appreciation of the meaning of the 'freedom of the press' and the limitations of the Government's powers of interference under the Defence Regulations and on the other hand we shall just have to try to persuade newspapers how very touchy the Russians are.[78]

Smolka's mode of operating can be clearly discerned; by refusing to give in to an exaggerated Soviet demand, he avoided appearing pro-Soviet, yet at the same time that exaggerated demand was used to justify pro-Soviet intervention in other cases – 'we shall just have to try to persuade newspapers how very touchy the Russians are'.

This apparently minor incident demonstrates both the power of Communist subversion and the difficulties either of estimating its overall significance or of detecting it at the time. It was perfectly reasonable for the Ministry of Information to warn other Government institutions or the British press that the Russians were touchy. This was, presumably, meant to imply that the Russians would, in the final analysis, pull out of the war against Hitler unless they were well treated by the British, and would be a very effective argument in a whole host of different cases. In the hands of legitimate officials this was an important tool to possess.

Yet in the hands of a mole, such an argument could wreak havoc. The mole would have been told precisely what issues were mere subterfuges, about which the Russians really cared little or nothing, and where vital Soviet interests were at stake, so that he or she would know which ones could safely be yielded in order to gain goodwill from the British and which ones had to be pressed very hard indeed.

Furthermore, by being able to refer back to the Kremlin via their controllers, they would be able to reinforce their influence on British affairs by getting the Russians to react as they had predicted.

It is plain that any civil servant, whether in SOE, in the Foreign Office, in MI5 or MI6, who warned a British authority to steer clear of arousing Soviet antipathy by, for example, asking too many questions, was acting acceptably only if he or she were not a Communist sympathiser. If a mole were to do this, however, the Soviets were being given an enormous boost from within the bowels of Whitehall which would enable them to achieve important successes. In addition, unless a man like Smolka was actually overheard getting orders from his Soviet controller, there was absolutely no way of knowing that his apparently legitimate stance was, in fact, a subverted one. It is vital to realise this, for in his official capacity as chief of the Ministry of Information's Russian section, Smolka was required to have regular contact with the Russians. In other words, merely seeing Smolka talking to a Russian would in no way indicate that there was anything suspect about him or his policies.

It therefore seems perfectly fair to say that the issue was indeed not whether subversion took place, nor indeed whether it stood a good chance of being successful but, rather, why it was not more successful and on more occasions. The formal and informal networks promoting subversion were so powerful, and they extended so widely within SOE, that they must have presented an almost insurmountable obstacle to a man such as Dalton and to policies such as the ones he was advancing.

Now it has to be stated firmly that, having said all of this, the direction in which the Communist moles and agents moved mirrored very closely the direction that British policy was taking in any case. Had these moles and agents not existed, it is doubtful whether, on balance, anything more than a detail here and there would have been different – but we will never know.

The essence of the subversion that I have described consisted in forming views and guiding policy preferences along predetermined routes. Putlitz would have a word with Vansittart, Philby with Gaitskell; Gaitskell would then ask Vansittart's advice and, finally, Dalton would be approached by Gaitskell. In public life information is a vital resource. Anyone who can offer important information must be listened to.

Finally, it must be stressed once again that what these moles and agents did was not simply pass secrets to the Russians: they did far more damage than this. By 1942, their work in SOE had largely been completed. With the abandonment of Daltonian precepts, subversion within SOE became little more than a matter of fine tuning. The real challenge for the Kremlin now lay in other areas of intelligence activity: in MI6 and MI5, which held in their hands the key to secret intelligence-gathering, counter-espionage and the atom secret. Partly because of this and partly because of what appeared to be chance personnel movements, the Communist caravan moved on.

5

MI5 and MI6 on the Outbreak of War

The development of MI5 and MI6, 1909–45

As we have seen, there is considerable evidence of Communist subversion within the United Kingdom and overseas on the continent
of Europe, about which British Intelligence clearly ought to have
been more alert than in reality it was. In order to discover why it
dropped its guard, we must now turn to an analysis of the activities
of the institutions charged with the protection of British security at
home and with the provision of secret intelligence from overseas,
namely MI5 and MI6.

It is important to stress that although in absolute terms both of
them certainly ought to have known far more about the dangers of
Communism, their failure was by no means appalling and it has been
grossly exaggerated. Indeed, it can be demonstrated that when we
take into account the specific difficulties that MI5 faced from 1941
until 1945, its record in particular was, with some exceptions, not
bad.

Before we turn to their general level of failure, however, we must
first attempt to define the precise duties that MI5 and MI6 were
supposed to discharge. Broadly speaking, for the period under
review, MI5 was required to protect Britain's security, to act against
spies from abroad operating in Great Britain and its colonies, and
to counter home-based subversion. To do so it had to gather its own
intelligence as well as gaining intelligence from other friendly agencies
and from MI6.

MI6, on the other hand, was charged with providing secret intelligence from overseas. There has been some debate as to whether
MI6 also had its own counter-intelligence role, which somewhat
crudely expressed, means the elimination of hostile agents. There
seems no doubt that at certain times and in exceptional cases MI6
did possess a 'licence to kill'.

It must, however, be added that it is impossible to know when and how often MI6 exercised this licence. Although in the public imagination James Bond is the archetypal MI6 officer, the work that Bond did was hardly what might be called routine intelligence-gathering (indeed, his forte was plainly counter-espionage). The fictional characters of Smiley and Sean Lemas[1] appear to some an accurate representation of the sort of people who worked for MI6, although John le Carré himself has emphasised that his works are fictional and not intended to mirror the secret world of which he was, at one time, a part. Generally speaking, those British intelligence officers I have been able to interview seem more of a cross between academics and army officers than the cut-throat drinkers and wom-anisers of fiction (all of them, however, greatly relishing their double identities).

Those who have been close to both services have often alleged that MI6, despite the awful responsibilities for life and death entailed in its work, provided an easier and more sharply defined area of activity for those who worked within it than did MI5.

As far as MI6 is concerned, its activities in respect of Communist subversion were divided by an important caesura, namely the decision taken in the summer of 1944 to establish within MI6 a new section, Section IX, to deal specifically with the potential threat to British security which the Soviet Union might pose following the defeat of the Third Reich.

While it is true that the duties of both services were to be confined almost exclusively to fighting the Fascist powers and their helpers, British Intelligence continued throughout the war to have pro-fessional duties with regard to things Russian. The precise nature of these duties – which may seem, particularly in the case of MI6, rather remarkable – is dealt with in detail later (see p. 262). MI5, of course, was required to protect Britain from Communism and hostile Soviet policies. Bearing in mind, then, that from 1939 until 1945 the Soviet Union waged an intense and successful espionage campaign against Britain, serious questions must be raised about the apparent lack of response to this campaign by British Intelligence.

Enormous damage has been done to the reputation of the British intelligence community (and thereby more widely to British morale in general) by the repeated allegation that Britain's inability to counter Stalin's secret plans for Europe, and its failure to prevent the penetration of British Intelligence and other high offices of State, can be simply and solely attributed to the widespread subversion by Communists of British Intelligence itself. Such a charge cannot be dismissed out of hand: there obviously was subversion (even if its scale should not be exaggerated) and the Soviet Union plainly derived considerable benefits from it. But does this actually validate the allegation?

In the opinion of one of Britain's most experienced defence journalists, Chapman Pincher, the answer would appear to be 'yes'. He has written:

> During the Second World War the performance of MI5 and MI6 against German, Italian and Japanese enemies was outstandingly brilliant ... Since [then] however, the reputation of both services has plummetted not only in Britain but abroad and particularly in the USA as well as, one would imagine, in the Soviet Union following a succession of disgraceful spy scandals. What is the reason for this apparently sudden change in performance? The basic answer is straightforward: the Germans were totally unable to penetrate the British secret services. Against the Soviets, [however] ... performance has been pathetic because both MI5 and MI6 ... have been deeply penetrated by Soviet agents ...[2]

However, this is not only a gross oversimplification of a very complicated problem, but also desperately unhistorical. For it assumes that the desire to counter Communism had the same status in Britain from 1939 until 1945 as the fight for survival against the Nazi Third Reich. The truth is that it did not. At the same time, Britain did attempt to act against Communist subversion at home and MI6 did have a presence in the Soviet Union and an interest in Soviet affairs, particularly after 1944. Yet things Russian were never on a par with things German. In short, the full historical context in which intelligence had to operate must always be borne in mind.

Furthermore, there can be no monocausal explanation for MI6's failures both before and after 1944. Some of them can be attributed to British high policy (see p. 262). Some were the result of straightforward errors in political judgment. But in others it cannot be doubted that subversion played an important role. What is more, most of those failures involving subversion that we know about can be directly or indirectly attributed to the personal role played by Kim Philby; if, particularly after 1944, MI6 was *hors de combat* in the Soviet theatre, it was almost certainly thanks chiefly to him.

It must, however, be pointed out that by arriving at this verdict on MI6, we are giving the other branch of the secret service, MI5, an even more decisive role in our story. For with MI6 incapable of sustained action against Russian-inspired subversion, it was MI5 who had to shoulder the chief responsibility of dealing with things Soviet. What this meant is crystal clear: at the end of the day, thanks to Philby's personal treachery and his own considerable authority within MI6, a very heavy burden indeed was bound to fall upon his opposite number in MI5, Roger Hollis.

A number of full accounts have been given of the origins of both MI5 and MI6, or the Secret Intelligence Service, as the latter is sometimes known.[3] Although all these accounts claim to be authoritative (and thus correct), they differ in certain important respects. Christopher Andrew's book *The Secret Service* is the most scholarly, although the period dealing with the Second World War is dispatched in under one hundred pages, compared with four times that number for the period from 1909 until 1939.

All the accounts, however, seem agreed that in 1909 it was decided to set up a British intelligence body distinct from the purely military intelligence body which had existed ever since the late 1880s. It was this new intelligence body which was subsequently split into two parts, the forerunners of MI5 and MI6. Andrew states that in 1909 a Secret Service Bureau was set up, initially divided into a military and a naval section. However:

> Within a year these had given way to a home department responsible for counter-espionage (the ancestor of MI5) and a foreign Department in charge of espionage (the forerunner of SIS or MI6).[4]

Nigel West, armed with a mass of detail, states in his book *MI6 1909–1945* that what can be seen as the original MI6 was set up in 1909 as the 'Foreign Section of the Secret Service Bureau'. On 1 October a navy man, Commander Mansfield Smith-Cumming, was made its chief and installed at its headquarters at 54 Broadway, near St James's Park. The domestic side of the secret service which became MI5 was set up at the same time and placed under the command of an army man, Vernon Kell.[5] B. Page *et al.*, however, claim in *The Philby Conspiracy* that MI6's forerunner was not set up until 1916. It was not known as MI6 until the 1930s.[6] There is also a debate as to why the head of MI6 was known as 'C': some argue that it was because he was the Chief, others because the first head of MI6 was called Smith-Cumming, and still others suggest that it corresponds to some secret Whitehall code.[7]

There is, however, no disagreement that to this day every head of MI6 is known, even to fellow-colleagues in Whitehall, as 'C' and that his identity has always been a closely guarded secret, subject to a Government 'D' notice forbidding its publication.[8]

Many civil servants, particularly in the field of foreign affairs, may well have met a 'C' during their careers, either formally or informally, without being aware of this. One former diplomat recalled with a shudder a party at which it was whispered that the tall thin balding man with the piercing blue eyes was none other than 'C' himself, head of the 'funnies' or 'funny people'. Such secrecy has without doubt become counter-productive in recent times, for if the main object of secrecy was to enable MI5 and MI6 to do their work efficiently, it has now proved a stumbling block: it is, after all, human nature to wish to uncover secrets when one is confronted with them. Furthermore, where secrecy prevails, the imagination can run riot; something that is secret, though legitimate and obvious, may seem to those kept in the dark to be of major importance and deeply sinister. If people now exaggerate the significance of the secret services and see evil plots and conspiracies where none exist, that is in large part the fault of the secret services themselves. It should, of course, be added that some secrecy is vitally important and it would be foolish to contradict the view put forward by some former intelligence officers, that lives and the national interest often depended upon the maintenance of secrecy.

The historian is, of course, presented with very special difficulties here. While there is no shortage of secret service officers who are prepared to answer questions, most of them continue to refuse either to permit their names to be used as sources or to receive acknowledgment for the help they have given (considerable help in the case of the present study). Inevitably this, too, is counter-productive. The scurrilous writer can claim 'inside' authority with as much credibility as the serious one; and it is all too easy to invent a fictitious source to 'confirm' some pet theory.

It is certainly arguable that the great damage done to British interests and morale by the fictitious 'exposure' of Roger Hollis could have been prevented by a timely and open official history of the questions I have dealt with in this study (and one must hope that more intelligence papers will find their way into the Public Record Office).

In 1924 Smith-Cumming was succeeded by Admiral Hugh ('Quex') Sinclair. It was during Sinclair's time that it was decided to fund MI6 via a secret Foreign Office vote. Page *et al.* offer some figures for the amount MI6 received in the late 1930s: the sum for 1936–7, for example, was £350,000. By 1940 the figure had grown to £1.5 million, to which must be added secret monies. During Sinclair's tenure of office:

> MI6 worked in a relatively leisurely manner, sending young men, usually with City or Service connections, out to cover European countries.[9]

By 1919 MI6 had hit upon an ingenious disguise for MI6 agents abroad: they were given the cover of 'Passport officers' attached to various key British Embassies.[10]

The head of MI5, known as the Director General, or DG, from 1909 until 1940 was Major General Sir Vernon Kell. In 1940 he was succeeded by Sir David Petrie. Their deputies were Sir Eric Holt-Wilson and Brigadier A. 'Jasper' Harker respectively.[11] For a short period following Kell's dismissal by Churchill, Harker became Acting DG.[12]

The chiefs of MI5 and MI6 were in close touch with each other; indeed West claims that a secret telephone exchange connected 'C' with the DG of MI5, the Foreign Office, the Ministry of Defence and the Metropolitan Police Commissioner.[13] There is no doubt that MI5 enjoyed the closest relations with Scotland Yard; all MI5's arrests were undertaken on its behalf by the Special Branch of the police force, which also tapped telephones for MI5.

MI6's headquarters were, in the 1930s, 55 Broadway Buildings in Victoria. MI5 was based first of all in the Cromwell Road; it then moved to the Thames Road and Horseferry Road; on the outbreak of war, it moved yet again, to Wormwood Scrubs. During the Blitz in 1940, part of MI5 moved out to Blenheim Palace, using Keble College, Oxford, as an annexe. This part was the division which dealt with MI5's intelligence-gathering rather than with its counter-espionage work. It is also where Roger Hollis worked on gathering intelligence about Communist subversion. One former MI5 officer believed that it was .possible that Hollis might have had his own small Communist counter-espionage unit.

Counter-espionage, 'B' Division, led by Guy Liddell and Dick White, stayed in London where intelligence about Germany was collected and evaluated.[14] It was this work that was considered MI5's most significant function. A former officer has said that almost 100 per cent of MI5 work after 1941 was concerned with Germany; Hollis's duties, therefore, were something of a back-water.

There are no reliable figures for the numbers employed in MI6 after the outbreak of the Second World War; Anthony Verrier states that before the war it had 'not more than 30' staff members at its HQ.[15] It has been estimated that between 1935 and 1940 MI5's staff tripled from thirty to about 100 full-time officers.[16] One former officer recalled an establishment of twenty-nine officers in MI5 in early 1939. Precise figures are still a closely guarded secret.

As far as the period before the outbreak of the Second World War is concerned, it seems to be generally agreed that while the service provided by MI5 was more than adequate, that offered by MI6 during the 1930s was poor. There were several reasons for this. There was no real 'overlord' of intelligence, and responsibility was divided between the Prime Minister of the day and the Joint Intelligence Committee of the Cabinet. MI5 had an input into and direct access to the Home Office and Home Secretary, whereas MI6 had equivalent input and access to the Foreign Office and Foreign Secretary and the War Office and War Minister.[17]

The issue of who, if anyone, was to have overall control of intelligence-gathering and analysis was an apparently insoluble problem. It is a token of the importance of secret intelligence operations that so many different groups wished to have a decisive say over them. It raises, in addition, important constitutional and political questions: it is precisely because the role of intelligence is so vital that it seems undesirable to vest overall control in the hands of any one person, whether a civil servant or an elected representative in the form of a senior Cabinet minister.

It could be argued that a Civil Service mandarin is an unelected official and that the political power which emanates from control of the security services should not be given to someone who is not fully bound by democratic or parliamentary constraints. On the other hand, an elected minister might abuse that power for party political ends or have conflicting departmental loyalties to contend with. Thus a Foreign Secretary might well find incompatibilities between the Secret Intelligence Service, on the one hand, and the Foreign and Commonwealth Office, on the other, impossible to resolve impartially. Recently, the disclosures concerning MI5 vetting at the BBC caused the then Home Secretary, who has political responsibility for both MI5 and the BBC, considerable difficulties.

Critics of British Intelligence have often overlooked the fact that in a liberal democracy a certain amount of laxness, which may appear to be inefficiency, is a necessary side-effect of a democratically sensitive secret service. In a totalitarian State, such as the Soviet Union or Nazi Germany, it is easier for a secret service both to appear and actually, be highly efficient. But a KGB and a Gestapo are rightly unacceptable to a liberal democracy; indeed, the very power possessed by a secret police is an indication of the extent to which the perverted use of secret intelligence has become one of the chief features of the totalitarian State.

It should be stressed that the keynote of MI5's work at this time was not to lock subversives up in order to safeguard British security, but to ensure that such people were kept away from areas where they might do damage.

It is not without irony that those who claim to want a more liberal security service, pointing to MI5's failure over the years, in fact end up inadvertently supporting those who argue for a far more insidious form of countering subversion. It is not hard to construct a more effective or efficient security service, but the price would be far less liberty, not more.

This principle of operating an intelligence service in a liberal democratic State which freely permits people to seek to change the minds of their fellows and thus to win political power is something which has been explicitly associated with both Sir Dick White and Sir Roger Hollis by a number of people who worked for them (see p. 319).

Another reason for MI6's shortcomings at this time was intense departmental rivalry within the service, so that different departments pulled in different directions. Richard Deacon states that in the 1930s, for example, MI6 was overconcerned with the Bolshevik threat, underestimating the growing menace posed by the Third Reich:

> Consequently, Sinclair was never able to provide sufficient factual evidence to back up reports of the extent of German rearmament. When Winston Churchill was campaigning against the National Government on this very subject in the 1930s, he relied mainly on his own private intelligence service.[18]

There was possibly yet another explanation for MI6's lack-lustre performance in the 1930s, although it deserves to be treated with considerable scepticism. Page *et al.* draw our attention to the sort of people who worked for the Secret Intelligence Service at this time: they were, on the whole, not very imaginative ex-Indian police officers or rather flamboyant ex-officers from HM Services.[19]

The kind of people the intelligence services recruit must have a direct bearing on the kind of intelligence they produce. Like any other profession, intelligence undoubtedly requires all its good practitioners to have a flair for the job, and to combine an imaginative streak for culling information with a careful analytical mind in order to evaluate it coolly and with objectivity.

It could be argued that these qualities are not ones automatically associated with ex-Indian policemen or retired forces personnel and that, as a result, if the intelligence services were going to provide first-rate information they needed high-calibre people to do it for them.

During the late 1930s and particularly once war had broken out, there was indeed growing support for the idea that British Intelligence needed a transfusion of young talent. Former officers in both MI5 and MI6 have mentioned their delight at the influx of bright young graduates during the early days of the war; they had all been overworked and it seemed that relief, of an imaginative and creative kind, was now at hand.[20]

Interestingly, MI5 had shown far more concern here than MI6. Guy Liddell, who had come to MI5 from Scotland Yard, seems to have possessed a special gift for recruiting clever young men. West writes:

> One of Liddell's assets was to spot talented young staff and encourage them. He trained Tar Robertson and Dick White ... [the former] a friend of Kell's son John. Dick White was first introduced to Guy Liddell by Malcolm Cumming [an MI5 officer]. At the time White, a young school teacher, was conducting a party of boys to Australia and Cumming was on the same liner on his way to an army exercise. The two men struck up a friendship and as a result White was appointed Liddell's assistant.[21]

White had been an undergraduate at Christ Church, Oxford, and had done postgraduate work at the University of California. He then went into school teaching and worked for the BBC, including a period spent as an assistant editor of the *Listener*.

It appears that Sir Dick was specifically engaged to do German work in MI5. He entered MI5 in 1936 and was sent to Germany as a 'student' in order to gain first-hand knowledge of the politics of Nazi Germany. Another young recruit into MI5 at this time was Roger Hollis (see p. 392).[22]

It was only the outbreak of war that made MI6 think about this matter more carefully. Soon it, too, had its share of new talent: Stuart (later Sir Stuart) Hampshire and Gilbert Ryle, the Oxford philosophers; Charles Stuart, the Oxford historian; Hugh Trevor-Roper (later Lord Dacre), another historian; and, of course, Kim Philby. With the exception of Philby, these people all came into MI6 via the radio security service.[23]

One former MI6 officer has told me that the significance of the conflict between the 'old buffers' and the brilliant young could hardly be minimised. The 'old buffers' were seen as laughable and inefficient, obsessed by the 'Bolshevik Bogey' and failing to realise that the contemporary world was far more threatened by Hitler than by Stalin (see p. 204).[24]

With hindsight, however, the view that the 'best and the brightest' would rescue British Intelligence from the doldrums was more than a little misguided. There was an argument in favour of recruiting 'high-flyers' if they could provide some proof of practical ability and achievement. However it was a severe indictment of the principle of selecting unqualified 'high-flyers' that a not inconsiderable pro-portion of them has proved unreliable.[25] One source of good recruits quite shamefully under-utilised was, of course, the British Labour movement.

As far as the recruitment of high-flyers in 1939 and 1940 is concerned, there is considerable irony in reading the comments made by Page and his colleagues (eleven years before Blunt's public admission) in respect of MI5's apparent good fortune *vis-à-vis* MI6's lack of it:

Some remarkably talented men worked for Petrie during the war: Victor Rothschild, Herbert Hart, Anthony Blunt [and others].[26]

In 1939 Sinclair left MI6 and died shortly afterwards. But in any case a new wind was blowing through the Secret Intelligence Service, partly because of the outbreak of war, and partly because in November 1939 MI6 suffered one of the most serious setbacks in its entire history. Two relatively senior officers, Payne Best and Stevens, were lured across the Dutch-German border at Venlo in the belief that they would be making contact with anti-Nazi German generals. In fact, they were awaited by German counter-intelligence.

Both men were arrested and divulged considerable information; after the war (which they spent in Sachsenhausen and Dachau concentration camps), they were apparently treated with contempt by their former employer.[27] Thanks to information the two supplied, the Germans were able to compile a full list of the leading members of the British secret service. This was perhaps the first time, but not the last, that the names of British intelligence agents were communicated to this country's enemies while remaining a closed book in Britain itself.

Sinclair was succeeded by Stewart (later Sir Stewart) Menzies. He was:

> Then forty-nine years old. He had been educated at Eton where he had won the Consort's prize for French and German ... when he left Eton, he had been commissioned into the Grenadier Guards.[28]

He had shown the greatest bravery in savage fighting in the First World War. In 1915 Menzies had moved into military intelligence and he was to remain in the intelligence field for the rest of his life.

Menzies had two immediate problems. The first was to think of a way of minimising the disaster of Venlo. The second was to co-operate with the major review under Maurice (later Lord) Hankey of Britain's intelligence services. This review had been ordered by Neville Chamberlain, but it was during Churchill's Premiership that it was executed.[29]

MI6 by now consisted of ten sections in London and its stations overseas. The London sections included a political one whose co-director was David Footman, an expert on Soviet Russia who went on to become a Fellow of St Antony's College, Oxford; sections dealing with army, navy and air intelligence; a counter-espionage section, known as Section V, headed by Colonel Valentine Vivian, an ex-Indian policeman, until January 1941, and thereafter by Felix Cowgill; and sections which dealt with finances and various aspects of communications.

Winston Churchill and wireless intelligence:
MI6 and the Ultra secret

Section V was, perhaps, the most celebrated of all MI6's domestic
sections since it processed the results of Ultra – the material emanating from the secret Enigma machines.[30] Without any doubt its
control of the Ultra material was MI6's biggest success during the
whole of the war. Until 1974 no open reference was permitted to be
made to the fact that during the war the British had been able to
read many of the German military codes. Since then, this story has
often been told, most fascinatingly perhaps by Ronald Lewin, R. V.
Jones and David Kahn.[31]

In 1939, in a remarkable feat of co-operation and forward-
planning, the British, French and Polish secret services collaborated
in order to spirit out of Warsaw an encoding machine of the type
used by the German armed forces, called Enigma. This was then
shipped to London, largely due to the diplomatic skills of an 'Oxford
professor' who was, in fact, Menzies himself in disguise.[32]

The Enigma machine was then established at the Government
Code and Cipher School at Bletchley Park, whose director was 'C'.
In order to break the codes the Germans were using, MI6 had to
sponsor the recruitment of a team of highly gifted mathematicians
(for there were over 6,000 million million possible permutations of
the cipher).[33] One of the most colourful members of the team was
Professor Turing, a genuine Oxford professor, of whom it was said
that on the outbreak of war he converted all his assets into cash and
then buried it in a field near Bletchley as a reserve against 'disaster'.
Sadly, he forgot the location of his hoard and it was never recov-
ered. Turing worked closely with Gordon Welchman at Bletchley.

The importance of the Ultra material (West states that it was given
this code name because it was 'ultra secret'[34]) cannot be underestimated, for it allowed the British to read some (though not all)
German military wireless traffic. 'C' made full use of his stewardship
of the Bletchley material to reinforce his right of access to the very
top of British Government, Winston Churchill himself. Dr Martin
Gilbert writes:

> The ability to read these German messages in the exact form in
> which they were sent out and for the most part with little delay,
> was a major intelligence victory. The work of decyphering these

messages was so complex that it involved by 1942 nearly a thousand men and women at Bletchley Park ... In the summer of 1940 a pattern soon emerged whereby Churchill was to be able to make the maximum possible use of this most secret source. As soon as a set of messages was decyphered at Bletchley, they were sent to the headquarters of MI6 at Broadway, London, only five minutes from Downing Street, a selection was then made, and immediately sent by messenger, locked in a special buff-coloured box, to Churchill. Churchill alone had the key to the box. To protect the source of these messages, the code name Boniface was used in the hope ... of suggesting that the material came from an individual agent ...[35]

In due course, the Boniface front was dropped (West says because the service chiefs had had enough of MI6's agents). Ultra was then referred to as CX and later, after 1942, as MSS (most secret source). Churchill continued to call the material Boniface, however, and referred to the staff at Bletchley as 'the geese who laid the golden eggs and never cackled'. Other wireless intelligence was called Signals Intelligence or Sigint.[36] Gilbert estimates that only about thirty of the most senior policy-makers had access to Ultra material.

By the end of September 1940 Churchill decided to institutionalise the arrangements for his receipt of Ultra:

Boxes were to come every day from 'C' marked 'only to be opened by the Prime Minister in person' ... Sometimes, 'C' himself would bring a box across from MI6 headquarters ... sending a note to the Private Secretaries to say that he was on his way.[37]

Churchill was quite clearly deeply impressed by Ultra, as well he might be, for it did not simply mean that strategic policies could be most skilfully contrived, but also that fewer British lives would be lost. This was particularly true once it proved possible to break the German U-boat codes in July 1941.[38] He showed great encouragement to those analysing Ultra material, particularly R. V. Jones.

It is, however, the case that Ultra was military intelligence, and the great reliance which Churchill placed upon it seemed to signify that a premium was being put on military intelligence to the detriment of political intelligence. If this was so (and it is by no means inconsistent with Churchill's thinking in other areas) then this had certain disadvantages.

The first of these was that military intelligence was just that; one knew what the enemies' armed forces were up to and how to counter them. Yet sometimes it would have been more useful to have political intelligence, since the actual use of the military was a political affair. Indeed, good political intelligence may obviate the necessity for military action. One contemporary example of this was seen during 1983. Military intelligence told the British Cabinet that the Argentine forces were on the verge of attacking the Falklands. This took them by surprise and the attack was successful. Good political intelligence, on the other hand, could have enabled the military aggression to have been predicted and could have encouraged the British Government to take suitable political precautions against the Argentine authorities.

Churchill seems to have had a natural antipathy towards political intelligence, possibly because of the Venlo fiasco, possibly because someone in the intelligence community was encouraging him to be sceptical about it: after all, it was easier to come by military intelligence (a fact still true today).

One view expressed both by MI5 and MI6 officers was that political intelligence was rather a dubious commodity, not least because its significance could change so rapidly. Political decision-makers can easily alter their minds about issues, whereas the facts and figures about military hardware, and how and when it might be used, change far less frequently.

On the other hand, what appears to be pure military intelligence can also have political implications, and where such intelligence consistently points towards a particular piece of high policy, it can obviously lead to its uncovering. Stalin's secret plans are but one example of the failure by the British to realise that a consistent military strategy was bound to have far-reaching political repercussions. Churchill's own lack of interest in Stalin's secrets is all the more peculiar in the light of his own well-documented concern with secret intelligence about Russia before the Second World War.[39]

According to Anthony Verrier, much of Churchill's political intelligence was provided by an aide called Desmond Morton:

> A greyer eminence than Menzies [who] was not only very close to Churchill and SIS, he also arbitrated many SOE issues. Morton was certainly no friend of the Left; he was deeply concerned with the spectre of post-war European Communism.[40]

Morton may have been a member of the Joint Intelligence Committee.[41] William Cavendish Bentinck, a chairman of the JIC, has reported that he was told to provide Morton with intelligence for Churchill.[42] Martin Gilbert cites one occasion when Morton warned Churchill's private secretary Jock Colville about the Comintern,[43] and another which proves that Morton knew about Enigma and 'C' 's role concerning it.[44] According to Colville, Morton was frequently involved in discussions on intelligence matters with Churchill. Colville also states that Morton became the Prime Minister's contact with the Allied Governments in London and 'some branches' of the secret service, 'but Churchill made less and less use of his services'.[45]

A former MI6 officer has recalled that Morton had been an MI6 agent for a time and was far closer to MI6 than MI5; his interests being mainly intelligence rather than counter-espionage. On the whole, he has been viewed as someone full of good ideas of little practical value, which were never taken seriously. By way of a comment upon Colville's claims, this officer stressed that Churchill had only one official intelligence adviser, and that was 'C' himself. Indeed, it was Churchill who set the precedent, since followed by every British Prime Minister, that 'C' is the personal intelligence adviser to the Premier.[46]

Although Verrier may be correct in ascribing to Morton a perceptiveness about Soviet intentions for the post-war world, Morton was not a serving MI6 officer. Furthermore, his influence declined just when the intelligence requirements about Russia were hotting up. Finally, even if Morton was still close to MI6, he would have known only what MI6 knew which, as we shall see, was not a great deal (see p. 213). For the point is that whatever Verrier alleges, there is no evidence that Churchill was in any way influenced by Morton's possible perception of Stalin's secret war aims.

A further problem was that there existed the real danger that at any time the Germans might discover their secret wireless traffic was read by the British. It is interesting to speculate why they did not, in the event, ever tumble to this. One explanation has been given by David Kahn, who has pointed out that German Intelligence was very badly co-ordinated, with various agencies all competing against each other.[47] Another explanation is that the German military and political leadership was simply too arrogant about its own management of the war to consider it a possibility.

Curiously, it does seem that the German Post Office managed to unscramble the special telephone link used by Churchill to communicate with Roosevelt in Washington.[48] There has, however, not been any estimate of the extent to which this caused damage.

One final reason why Ultra remained a secret was, of course, that MI5 was remarkably successful in keeping it so. As Lewin rightly points out:

> The key concept was that of security ... this whole operation trembled on a razor edge for if the Germans had come to believe that their most important ciphers were being broken the disaster for the British would have been ... final ...[49]

A critical area which it was feared might lead to a leak emerged out of Churchill's order that Ultra, suitably disguised, should be passed to the Soviet Union. The fear was either that Stalin would transmit the information to Hitler in order to curry favour, or that the invading German armies would fall upon some document or other making it clear that Enigma had been broken.

Martin Gilbert states that as early as 24 June 1941:

> Churchill instructed 'C' to divulge certain Enigma intelligence to the Russians 'provided no risks are run'. Subsequently, in scrutinising the contents of his buff box, Churchill was often to ask 'C' whether a particular decrypt had been sent or why it had been withheld ... 'C' was able to assure Churchill that the essential details 'were being sent to Moscow' [yet] even a year later, on reading his daily box of decrypts, he minuted to 'C': 'has any of this been passed to Joe?'[50]

There has been some suggestion that either Blunt or Philby passed on the real secret of Ultra to the Russians but, if this is true, there is no evidence of it having had any adverse effect.[51]

As we have seen, 'C' made copious use of his right of access to the Prime Minister, a right which ensured for MI6 a very special position in the making of policy. There is no doubt that a number of senior ministers used intelligence material – most significantly, perhaps, the Foreign Secretary Anthony Eden, who always showed great interest in intelligence matters and who had ministerial rights over MI6.

It is also worth trying to discover who else was a customer of secret intelligence. For one thing, it gives us some indication of the areas where intelligence inputs may have played a critical role; for another it was one major link which might connect intelligence with policy-making.

Some authors either downplay the extent to which intelligence is to be seen as an input into policy-making, or discount it altogether (for this view see Trevor-Roper's opinion mentioned on p. 207). Verrier, admittedly talking about the post-war period, claims that:

> The British Secret Services do not make recommendations to their political masters, let alone make policy. The services' main task is to acquire and distribute intelligence about Britain's enemies and friends on the basis of specific directives from the Prime Minister or the Foreign Secretary ... when [one or the other] decides on a certain course of action which will involve SIS, the word is passed verbally, rarely in writing, to the Cabinet Secretary. He ... passes the requirement to the Joint Intelligence Committee whose Foreign Office Chairman, armed forces, security service and treasury representatives then discuss it with the Director General [sic] of SIS and his colleagues ... the JIC writes assessments, it does not make recommendations.[52]

Yet, writing of an earlier period immediately prior to the outbreak of the Second World War, David Dilks claims:

> We do not know how frequently the head of SIS or some other officer of that Service saw the Foreign Secretary or the Prime Minister or how much material derived from secret sources was placed before Ministers; nor can we tell whether it was heavily filtered and interpreted by intelligence officers or by the Foreign Office itself ... the probability on the present evidence is that 'C' saw Ministers very rarely but the Permanent Under Secretary at the Foreign Office commonly, especially in times of crisis ... MI5 also had direct connections to the Foreign Office and would sometimes provide timely intelligence about subjects in which, on the face of it, SIS had a greater interest ...[53]

As Dilks points out, it is plain that useful secret intelligence would go right to the heart of the policy-making process, even if via Civil Service channels through the Permanent Under-Secretaries, rather than to ministers direct.

Thus although certain ministers may have taken steps to ensure that they were removed from the world of espionage and counter-espionage, those who had to make and execute policy looked upon intelligence as a most useful resource.

Lord Sherfield, who may serve as an excellent example of a very senior civil servant, has stated that he always regarded both MI5 and MI6 as a service to be utilised as and when required. He himself had not required it for lengthy periods during the war itself, not least because he had been overseas after 1943. But even then, while based in various Embassies, he knew that certain of his colleagues there were MI6 officers and after the war, in Washington, he was regularly briefed by the resident MI6 officer. He did not, of course, make any direct contribution to the work of either service: he had his 'own job to do – there was a division of labour'.

After the war Lord Sherfield recalled interviews with both Sir Dick White (after 1947) and, less frequently, with Roger Hollis. They would come to see him if they had material they thought he ought to know about; and Jim Skardon, MI5's leading interrogator, had informed him in person about the atom spies Klaus Fuchs and Bruno Pontecorvo. He relied greatly upon the knowledge that the secret services would see him whenever they thought it appropriate. Sherfield stressed that he always studied intelligence intercepts and reports most carefully (or 'read the mail' as he put it), although, when it came to exercising his judgment on policy, he did not give it undue attention, for the significant reason that he himself could never know how good or how bad specific pieces of intelligence were.[54]

In short, there can be little doubt that secret intelligence was an important and sometimes vital resource for policy-makers in areas where intelligence had a role to play. Full use was made of both MI5 and MI6 as a policy-making service, either in the form of reports made by the relevant departments and sent direct to clients, or via the Joint Intelligence Committee or the Anglo-American Joint Intelligence Staff into which there was an important British input.[55]

One further indication of how important secret intelligence was considered to be is provided in an unreferenced remark made by Lord Bethell, who claims that in November 1949 it was decided to inform the heir to the British throne, Princess Elizabeth, about an MI6 operation that was being directed by David Smiley from Malta: the Princess was visiting her husband on the island at the time and it was felt that she ought to be informed. Interestingly, although she was told about the operation (which was, incidentally, betrayed to the Russians by Kim Philby), the Governor of Malta, who was a Labour Party supporter, was not told.[56]

Equally, however, Lord Sherfield seems to be making a more general point when he states that the intelligence services were expected to do their own work and to do it as well as they could; what they offered was accepted at face value and not excessively analysed or criticised. It was not the Foreign Office's job to generate secret intelligence or counter-intelligence.

It is clear that such considerations had the effect of adding to the importance of the reports that MI5 and MI6 produced; they had a monopoly over secret intelligence and, in the crisis of war, what they produced possessed considerable authority which would hardly ever be challenged. They could work with confidence, since they knew that few questions would be asked about either the quality or the scope of what they were offering.

As has already been mentioned, a major watershed was reached in the development of MI6 in 1944 when it was decided to reorganise it in order to pay greater attention to the perceived potential threat posed by the Soviet Union. West writes:

> It was in the summer of 1944 that Menzies, consulting with his Vice-Chief [sic] Valentine Vivian ... gave his approval to the creation of a new section, Section IX, to deal with Soviet espionage and subversion ... [this] marked a significant turning point for SIS. It was also a recognition that after the liberation of western Europe there might well be a prolonged struggle for the liberation of countries occupied by Soviet forces.[57]

This reorganisation was significant for two reasons. First, it suggests that British Intelligence, albeit rather late in the day, was waking up to the fact that Stalin might possibly have his own secret plans for Europe and that it was vital to start making preparations for counter-measures. Second, the creation of a new Section IX was significant because of the choice of the person to head it. For it was another of the master-strokes of Communist subversion during the Second World War that the MI6 officer placed in charge of Section IX was none other than Kim Philby.

MI5 and Communism on the eve of Barbarossa: the duties of Roger Hollis

As far as MI5 was concerned, its major reorganisation occurred in May 1940 when Kell was sacked by Churchill.[58] Two main reasons for Kell's enforced departure are commonly given: the sinking of the *Royal Oak* in Scapa Flow in October 1939, which was held to be the work of German spies and therefore caused by lax security which showed MI5 in a poor light; and the confusion which reigned at Wormwood Scrubs as a result of German bombing, in particular the loss of many of its files. West adduces a third major reason, namely a poor personal relationship between Kell and Churchill.[59] They had argued about the overall control of the intelligence services. But it is quite possible that there was another, as yet unknown, reason why Kell was dismissed.

West adds that after Kell's departure, the control that the DG was able to exercise over MI5 was considerably reduced. It was Lord Swinton's committee, the Security Executive, which took over. The Executive had a number of powerful members, including Sir Joseph Ball, a former head of Conservative Central Office. Its secretaries were William Armstrong (later Lord Armstrong) and Kenneth Diplock (later Lord Diplock).[60] It was, West states, Swinton's committee which decided that the Acting DG, Harker, should not be made DG but that the post should go to David Petrie.

Petrie was an ex-Indian police officer who had also been involved in intelligence work; he had then gone to Palestine. West writes that one of Petrie's first actions was to employ a business consultant to provide an efficiency analysis. His major conclusion was that there should be changes in the method of recruitment to MI5.[61] Until 1940 entry into MI5 was confined to people who were personally known to serving officers (see p. 392).

MI5 by this time consisted of a number of Divisions. The two which have attracted most attention are, first, 'B' Division, the counter-intelligence department and, second, 'C' Division whose task it was to carry out 'vetting'. The main thrust of 'B' 's work was to act against subversion from Nazi Germany; 'C' 's duties lay in the weeding out of extremists from both left and right. When war broke out, MI5 was confronted with two major tasks. The first was the neutralisation of German subversion; the second, which was not unconnected with the first, was the execution of the order to intern all enemy aliens.

Before the outbreak of war, MI5 had been instructed to arrest all suspect enemy aliens; those who were not classified as suspect were to be interrogated by special tribunals. There were well over 50,000 'enemy aliens' in the United Kingdom in 1939, although the vast majority of them were in no sense 'enemies'.[62] During the first few months of the war, 73,000 Germans and Austrians were screened by 112 tribunals.[63]

It must be stressed that many MI5 officers hated the policy of internment, and that a number of them have since spoken about the episode with deep distaste. First of all, they argue that in practical terms the policy was a failure, since it removed from British life thousands of people who had a real contribution to make to the British war effort – people who were almost certainly not Nazi sympathisers or fifth columnists (the vast majority of internees being Jews). In addition, and perhaps more important in the long term, as a method of dealing with people who were suspected of being subversive, it conflicted with, and indeed contradicted, the principles of a democratically sensitive secret service.

The main conclusion drawn by these officers was that internment had been justified only by the panic the political leadership felt at the worst moment in Britain's recent history, when the Germans seemed about to invade, and that it should never again be seen as a valid means of dealing with possible subversion. They insisted that thereafter MI5's role should be secretly to keep possible subversives from getting themselves into a position where they could do harm, by making the areas where damage could be done fully secure. It should never again mean making the people secure by interning them.

Even with hindsight, none of these officers believed that the fact that MI5 did not succeed in their efforts against most Communist moles invalidated the basic principle here at stake.

As far as this present study is concerned, however, the Division of MI5 which is of most interest is the one charged with the monitoring of Communist subversion – and the position of Roger Hollis within it. Interestingly, there is no agreement among authors as to which particular Division dealt with this during the war.

'B' Division dealt with counter-espionage and was headed by Harker and then, after 1940, by Guy Liddell until 1947.[64] In his first book on MI5, West states that in 1940 both Dick White and Roger Hollis were in 'B' Division and that Dick White, together with T. A. ('Tar') Robertson, dealt with German counter-intelligence, while Hollis dealt with Communist subversion. Yet in his tables West places Hollis in 'F' Division at an unspecified date, but describes his duties as being responsible for 'Communists', working together with Roger Fulford and a Kemball Johnston, and with Graham Mitchell who had responsibilities for 'Fascists'.[65] By 1941, 'B' Division also contained Anthony Blunt, previously in 'D' Division, Herbert Hart and Victor Rothschild in a unit headed by Helenus Milmo.[66]

West suggests that Hollis was then transferred from 'F' Division to 'B' Division where he worked alongside 'B' 's anti-Communist expert, Maxwell Knight (later to become a popular BBC presenter); previously Liddell had been the anti-Communist expert, but his brilliance required that he be asked to deal with the German threat. It is impossible, however, to be absolutely certain from West's text where Hollis was based and whether he had sole, chief, or indeed any responsibility for anti-Soviet intelligence action. The uncertainty is compounded in West's MI5 sequel,[67] where he implies that Hollis did not have sole authority in this area but more general responsibilities:

> After two years studying the Communist Party of Great Britain and the Comintern, he had been promoted to Assistant Director rank. He had also joined Lord Swinton's wartime sub-committee monitoring the growing Soviet activity in London . . .[68]

This could even be read to suggest that by the time he became an Assistant Director, Hollis had ceased to be concerned with the CPGB or the Comintern. It might well be thought that the confusion that exists about the precise nature of Hollis's duties from 1939 to 1945 is in part intentional. The secret services believe that precise information about who did what and when could be of enormous interest to hostile powers in their attempts to circumvent British counter-intelligence, and former officers will either not give precise details or supply the wrong ones. (It is not without irony that, thanks to Blunt and Philby, the Russians have known for over forty years the precise nature of Hollis's duties, even if until comparatively recently the British public had never heard of him.)

As far as one can tell then, Hollis worked initially from 1938 until 1940 in 'A' Division, that is to say, MI5's administration.[69] Thereafter he moved into 'F' Division, sometimes called Branch or Section, which was transferred to Blenheim, and he remained there until 1946. 'F' Division is, therefore, the critical one from our point of view. It only remains to discover precisely what it did.

Some light is shed on the matter by none other than Kim Philby. For in his (occasionally erratic) memoirs, he writes:

> [After my appointment to Section IX] it was necessary for me to

continue the good work [in liaising with MI5] and place our relations on a new and friendly basis. My opposite number in MI5 was Roger Hollis, the head of its section investigating the Soviet and Communist affairs. He was a likeable person, of cautious bent, who had joined MI5 from the improbable quarter of the British-American Tobacco Company ... Although he lacked the strain of irresponsibility which I think essential (in moderation) to the rounded human being, we got on well together and were soon exchanging information without reserve on either side. We both served on the Joint Intelligence Sub-Committee which dealt with Communist affairs, and never failed to work out an agreed approach to present to the less well-informed representatives of the service departments and the Foreign Office. Although Hollis had achieved little in respect of Soviet activity, he had been successful in obtaining an intimate picture of the British Communist Party by the simple expedient of having microphones installed in its King Street Headquarters. The result was a delicious paradox. The evidence of the microphones showed consistently that the Party was throwing its full weight behind the war effort ...[70]

It is interesting to note that Philby, doubtless intentionally, puts his finger on one of the major questions concerning Hollis's failure to uncover the Communist moles: quite rightly he suggests that the Headquarters of the Communist Party of Great Britain was not the right place to uncover the secret moles. In fact Hollis knew this; whether, as some allege, he deliberately chose to look where nothing could be found is a matter discussed later on (see p. 335).

Philby's remarks, which undoubtedly must have upset Hollis considerably, tally with Anthony Blunt's statement to *The Times* made in November 1979:

Q.: Was MI5 at the time [1940] concerned about Soviet activity in Britain? A. (i.e. Blunt): Theoretically, yes, but of course it was a very minor issue. Everything was focussed on the German problem and there was a section technically looking after Soviet activities but it was very small and very inaccurate as one can imagine.[71]

Both Blunt and Philby locate MI5's anti-Soviet activities firmly in a small department separate from 'B' Division; which Philby says was led by Roger Hollis. It is, of course, conceivable that both these people, for their own ideological reasons, may have wished to focus attention upon Hollis, at a time when Hollis's name as a possible mole was not known in public. This surmise is discussed in greater depth later, for it has wide implications in connecting the campaign against Hollis with a wider Soviet-inspired strategy (see p. 395).

There remains, however, the more detailed description of Hollis's job. Chapman Pincher and Philby have put him in charge of MI5's activities against Communist subversion. We must ask whether Hollis's brief really extended so widely. West, for example, provides him with a far narrower one:

> Studying the Communist Party of Great Britain and the Comintern ...[72] Coincidental with the move to Blenheim ... Hollis retained his brief for monitoring the CPGB ...[73] Max Knight [in 1941] continued his penetration of the Communist Party in King Street, whilst Hollis concentrated on the covert links between the NKVD detachment now established in Bush House, the Soviet Embassy and the CPGB.[74]

The matter is, of course, of the greatest significance, for if Pincher is right then Hollis's position was one of extraordinary importance in the fight against Communist subversion, since he was working virtually alone. If, on the other hand, what West seems to be saying is correct, then Hollis may have had other duties and only limited authority in anti-Communist work, and any attempt to pin upon him alone MI5's undisputed failings in this area would be grossly inaccurate and unfair. Furthermore, we need to know whether Hollis was ordered simply to monitor the CPGB or Communism *qua* Communism.

We have seen that the real thrust of Communist subversion in the UK was not through the Communist Party of Great Britain but through the use of secret Communists and members of the Comintern as moles and agents. This point has been repeatedly confirmed, not least by the moles themselves (see p. 20).[75] It must thus follow that, if Hollis's job was to watch the CPGB, rather than monitor Communism, he can hardly be blamed for having missed the moles who were not CPGB members. However, if his job was the surveillance of all Communist activities, this neat solution might not be so appropriate.

In actual fact, former MI5 colleagues have now stated unequivocally that Hollis's job was indeed the monitoring of Communism in Britain in all its forms, and any MI5 officer with this brief would have been bound to take the secret and hidden element into account; MI5 understood that mere monitoring of the CPGB would supply incomplete information as far as subversion was concerned.[76]

Thus in order to do his job properly, Hollis needed to analyse carefully Comintern activities, work closely with the Foreign Office in order to assess Soviet foreign policy aims, and keep watch upon Communist sympathisers who might prove to be secret members of the CPGB, as well as upon the CPGB itself. Evidence of Hollis's interest in foreign policy comes from Hollis himself, albeit some years later when he was Director General of MI5: as we can see from his letter to Sir Patrick Reilly, MI5 had a close and obvious concern in the Russian work done by the Foreign Office (see p. 373). Of course, what Hollis needed to do and what he was able to do are possibly two quite different things.

If Hollis himself is to be seen as the main reason why Communist subversion in Britain was so successful, a direct connection must be made between Hollis's duties and MI5's successes and failures. If others had similar or even greater responsibilities, then they too must be included into the equation which Hollis's detractors have constructed.

The evidence suggests that Maxwell Knight himself was relatively unimportant. Chapman Pincher has written authoritatively:

> To people like West who have only superficial knowledge of what went on, characters like Maxwell Knight pose a problem when in fact their position was straightforward. Maxwell Knight was an agent-runner, whose job it was to recruit and run agents and submit their reports to the relevant desk officer, Hollis being the one for Soviet and Communist affairs. Agent-runners operate separately for security reasons and rarely visit HQ. Knight operated from a flat in Dolphin Square and though he had big ideas about himself he was, officially, junior to Hollis. Knight was concentrating on the Communist Party of Great Britain, through agents like Driberg [Tom Driberg, leading member of the Labour Party] whom he recruited. His reports were passed to Hollis for action (or inaction) and he kept the identities of his agents to himself on the routine need-to-know basis.

Pincher concluded:

> Liddell was Director of B Branch during the war and while avail-

able to Hollis for advice, was not his boss. Hollis would have been invited to attend some of the Directors' meetings, though having no right to do so, and could then have received advice all round. Actually, I am told, the concentration on Germany was so intense that Hollis was rarely bothered and had a clear, independent field for operation (or inoperation).[77]

Yet there is no doubt that Knight worked very closely indeed with Roger Hollis (indeed Hollis's son recalls being taken to the zoo by Knight!). The issue then becomes whether Hollis was his own master in his own house, or whether Guy Liddell kept a close watch upon what he did.

Perhaps the most authoritative statement about the precise nature of Hollis's job during the Second World War period comes from Sir Dick White's entry for Hollis in the *Dictionary of National Biography* published in the autumn of 1986 (although some might suspect the information for obvious reasons):

Hollis started as a student of international Communism, a field in which he was later to become an acknowledged authority. During the war, when the bulk of the Service's talents and resources were committed to German, Italian and Japanese counter-intelligence, he managed with small resources to ensure that the dangers of Russian-directed Communism were not neglected. Consequently, when the war was over and the Security Service turned to face the problems of the Cold War, he had already become one of its key figures ...

Other former colleagues have confirmed this account. We may therefore safely conclude that Hollis's brief was, for most of the war period, the monitoring of Communism in Britain in all its aspects. He had chief responsibility for understanding what Communist aims were in respect of the United Kingdom and he therefore plays an absolutely central part in this study. How, and with what success, he fulfilled his task can, however, only be examined after an analysis of further Communist subversion, about which Hollis and MI5 ought to have been alert but were clearly ignorant. This subversion did not take place only in terms of covert Soviet policy; rather more frighteningly, it also occurred within MI6 itself.

6

MI6 as the Object of Communist Subversion, 1941–5

Six cases where MI6 failed

There are very strong grounds for believing that from 1939 until 1951 there were at least six major instances of Communist subversion about which MI6, rather than MI5, ought to have informed the British authorities but failed to do so. Five of these cases lay in the field of secret intelligence from the Kremlin concerning the continent of Europe. To these five must be added one further case of Communist subversion. Indeed, the sixth was perhaps the most chilling of all. This was the actual subversion of part of the Secret Intelligence Service itself. Yet this was by definition not just a matter for MI6, but also for MI5, whose duties included vetting and, of course, counter-espionage, known as CE work.

The five cases were all connected with the level of ignorance among Britain's foreign policy-makers about the dangers implicit in the Grand Alliance with the Soviets (see Chapter 2). The first, a general one, had to do with the fact that Britain's policy-makers simply did not know that, beneath the demands Stalin openly made during the war, he and his advisers had concealed a second set of secret policies designed to extend Soviet power as far westward into Europe as possible. This was a prima-facie case of Soviet subversion (in direct breach of Russia's treaty commitments) and it can therefore quite safely be argued that MI6 ought to have alerted the policy-makers to the existence of this second, hidden agenda.

The next case has to do with Moscow's sponsoring of so-called National Committees and their analogues. These were the nuclei of central and eastern Europe's post-war puppet regimes in exile, whose job was to facilitate (and conceal) the Sovietisation of this area by the Red Army after Hitler's defeat. To this we must add those cases with a 'German dimension', connected with the existence of a German opposition to Hitler. They had a bearing not only on the future shape of Germany, but also upon the means by which the war against the Third Reich was to be completed. Here the activities of Otto John and Wolfgang zu Putlitz are crucial. Finally, we must turn to the Volkov affair and the Albanian fiasco.

It is perhaps worth pointing out straight away that a great many of these cases are directly or indirectly connected with the rise of Kim Philby to a position of prominence within the Secret Intelligence Service. Philby was plainly a man of exceptional ability. He was clever and he worked hard. Earlier than most of his colleagues, he grasped the possibilities that a mole working in intelligence might exploit. He saw how information could be suppressed and how it could be used to gain influence over others. He also knew how to cover his tracks so well that even those who worked with him for long periods had not the slightest idea that he was a mole. He understood how to utilise the various networks peculiar to Britain and British government. Finally, he was undoubtedly a killer.

There are Philbys in every totalitarian secret service, although there should ideally be no place for such people in a democratic one. Philby, however, managed to penetrate MI6 and his obvious attributes singled him out for promotion, even for the post of 'C' itself. It is frightening to realise that if Hitler had invaded Britain in 1940, Philby would undoubtedly have occupied as high a place in the 'British' Gestapo or Abwehr as he would have done in a 'British' KGB, had Britain, by some strange fate, become a Communist state.

The Kremlin and the anti-Nazi resistance in Europe: National Committees and secret blueprints

It has been a consistent theme of this study that Stalin and his helpers possessed a secret plan for the domination of post-war Europe and that almost certainly this plan became, after July 1941, the underlying basis both of Soviet strategies and of individual Soviet actions – particularly, of course, in the diplomatic sphere. It is, furthermore, quite possible to argue that this plan had been in the minds of Soviet policy-makers ever since the first months of 1939 or even before, for was it not implicit in the Hitler–Stalin Pact of 1939 and the incorporation of the Baltic States in 1940? Of course we do not know, and we probably never will, whether it was merely a collection of directives bound together by one grand strategy or whether it constituted a single secret command.

At least two former MI6 officers have said to me that they now accept that such a plan or plans existed and, furthermore, that British political leaders ought to have received intelligence from MI6 on this. One of them, however, argued that Churchill and Eden had indeed known that Stalin possessed a hidden agenda, but that, like the Foreign Office as a whole, they had simply been 'powerless to act against it'.[1]

Yet, if such knowledge truly existed, it is hard to see why there is such a complete dearth of evidence proving its existence. For neither the documents, let alone the policies, reflect such knowledge.

What makes this all the more poignant is that Stalin's blueprint plainly had a number of paragraphs concerned exclusively with Britain, and enacted well before 1941: hence his mole strategy. For the Soviet dictator and his advisers seem to have concluded that Britain would never become a Communist State by means of a general election victory by the CPGB. Consequently, the Russians' best strategy was to hope that a Communist Britain might develop gradually, while in the shorter term trying to ensure that British policy would not conflict with Soviet aims. The means adopted consisted of the laying-down of moles whose labours would increasingly bear fruit over the years ahead, by their gaining access to the leadership élites of British society in the political parties, the high offices of State, the press, the BBC, and above all the secret services. Clearly, this policy was not without its successes, and is first-hand proof of Stalin's subversive intentions.

As far as continental Europe was concerned, Stalin and his advisers clearly believed that an additional strategy could be followed. They appear to have assumed that because of the political devastation caused by the Nazis and Fascists, the States they had controlled would, on liberation, experience a vacuum in their political life. It was vital therefore to ensure that the Russians and Communists were enabled to exploit it by gaining control of the new, post-Nazi political class. Their position, as is commonly known, was to be bolstered by the use of the Red Army in order to add force to political persuasion.

In order to triumph, therefore, Stalin needed to ensure that the Communist-dominated national resistance leadership was totally 'co-ordinated' with the policy of the Kremlin, and strong enough to crush bourgeois democratic opposition once liberation had been achieved. The means chosen by him, and subsequently utilised by his successors, whether in Cuba, in Vietnam or Afghanistan, was the 'National Committee' an executive Politburo-in-waiting, which the

USSR would recognise in official political terms and fund, and which would claim to represent all anti-Fascists, by most craftily (and successfully) combining Communism with patriotism and nationalism.

The debate concerning the policy of National Committees is not about whether or not they existed or about their immediate purpose. Rather, it has to do with the extent to which they may fairly be described as part of a blueprint developed well before the end of the war and, consequently, with whether British and American Intelligence ought to have detected such a blueprint and advised their respective Governments accordingly.

For those who, like myself, argue that they were indeed the constituent parts of a blueprint, there remains only the question of why British and American Intelligence failed to perceive this, particularly since there were so many repeated examples of such bodies. But before we address this point, we must deal with the fact that this interpretation is strongly contested by a number of experts who claim that what with hindsight may appear to be a blueprint was, in fact, simply a series of unconnected pragmatic decisions.

They argue that what seems to be Stalin's plan (and would thus have been capable of detection by a good intelligence analysis) was, in reality, nothing more than the outcome of his risk-taking and sheer good luck. Consequently, it was quite impossible to know what Stalin was up to until after he had actually done it. (What is more, when British Intelligence, in the form of MI6, did see this, it acted at once by setting up Section IX to deal with it).

The most celebrated, and certainly the most forthright, of those who deny the existence of Stalin's blueprint is Vojtech Mastny.[2] Mastny's fundamental position, which he states with such frequency and force that it soon gains a momentum all of its own (one which it seems almost heretical to question), is clearly expressed in the following passage:

The point at issue is Moscow's presumed 'Grand Strategy' in 1941–45, that is, the selection and pursuit of long-term objectives during and immediately after the war against Germany. What was the vision of the post-war world that inspired Soviet actions at that time? What were the Russian aims in east central Europe especially where both world wars and also the Cold War originated? How were the Russian aims related to the historic Russian interests there? And how did the results measure up to the expectations? A few standard assumptions have been common among western authors, both the traditional and the revisionist variety [that is, those who blame America rather than Russia for the Cold War]: Stalin's determination to regain the territorial acquisitions he had achieved during his pact with Hitler, his quest for a division of Europe into spheres of influence, his desire to establish dependent regimes in neighbouring countries. Yet such readings of Stalin's aspirations, though not necessarily wrong, may be misleading. Whilst plausible with the benefit of hindsight, they do not always conform to the contemporary evidence without important qualifications ...

Mastny then declares:

Stalin's goals should be considered as evolving, rather than a design firmly fixed and singlemindedly pursued ... The striving for the optimum presupposed at all times an effort to match the feasible with the desirable and a continuous reassessment of both from the dictator's particular perspective.[3]

Mastny is, of course, right to argue that the National Committee issue has been dealt with many times and that there is no longer any real chance of striking new evidence. Yet he is wrong to appear scornful of subjecting existing evidence to renewed analysis, not least because, as he himself shows, the same pieces of evidence can be taken by different authors to imply different motives. Furthermore, Mastny obliges one to re-examine the facts because he himself in one crucial passage has (obviously inadvertently) altered their meaning.

It must be said that the view expressed by Mastny that Stalin's goals should be seen as 'evolving ... rather than [being] firmly fixed' is one which fully echoes the documentary account provided by the British Government records. Indeed, it is easy to understand why Mastny advances this particular theory when we realise that his analysis is based largely on an examination of those records. Since they continually imply a British assumption that Stalin had no sinister plans, Mastny wrongly assumes that it is self-evident that none existed.

What Mastny's theorising ignores, however, is that in this particular case there is empirical evidence both of an interlocking set of individual tactical decisions and of an overall plan, and thus the burden of evidence militates strongly towards the logical conclusion that a plan did exist.

In part, Stalin may have been motivated by the traditional aims of Russian foreign policy, which may be summarised as the need for security from attack by any western European power, as well as the desire to share in the riches with which nature had endowed the western end of Europe, especially the Ruhr.

In addition we must not forget that Stalin was a true revolutionary, both in terms of his personal background and because the source of his political power was inherently revolutionary. He and his advisers were all motivated by an ideological desire to promote a revolutionary foreign policy whose aim was the ultimate victory of world Communism. Of course, like Hitler, Stalin had from time to time to trim his sails (as, for example, during the mid and late 1930s when he appeared ready to co-operate with Social Democrats). But the millennial goals of revolutionary policy could never be eschewed. To have done so would have been to undermine the whole position of the Communist Party and, even more, Stalin's own position within it. Stalin could no more pass up his chance to spread Communism westward after Hitler's defeat than he could afford to move Lenin out of the Red Square mausoleum or express doubts about Marxist theory.

Stalin's strategy, certainly after the summer of 1941 and probably as early as 1939, was clear-cut; it had two pillars – the Red Army and the establishment of National Committees. It may, of course, seem amazing that such a plan was developed at the very period when the existence of the Soviet Union seemed most in doubt. However, there are at least three reasons why it is less surprising than may at first appear. For one thing, none of the belligerent nations ever appears to have permitted the assumption that they might lose the war to become the basis of policy-making. This was certainly true of Britain in 1939 and 1940. Even when Churchill and his ministers seriously considered the prospect of hand-to-hand fighting in Whitehall (in which Dalton and Churchill wanted to take part), British policy continued to operate on the assumption that Hitler would be defeated. Why should Stalin and his colleagues have been any different? Second, it is precisely at a time of maximum danger that we might expect the Soviet leadership to put most faith in the ultimate victory of Communism. Finally, Hitler's aggressiveness made the European situation fluid, and fluidity would give Stalin his best opportunity of pushing westward.

The Kremlin intended these National Committees to be the basis for its puppet Governments (subsequently set up in the period 1945–8). Thus the German National Committee, which included bourgeois and military elements but was securely in Communist hands, mirrored closely the subsequent East German regime, based on an 'understanding' between Communists and other groups and led by a 'coalition' of Social Democrats and Communists to form a 'Socialist Unity Party', which was, in reality, run by hardline Communists.[4]

In order to ensure that the graft of a 'National Committee' would take, the Red Army and the KGB were to be used to make it secure and to fasten the regimes on to the people they claimed to represent (see Djilas's account of this on p. 256).

Indeed, even Mastny – quoting from Khrushchev's alleged memoirs – is obliged to concede that Stalin had 'hoped to annexe Finland with the help of the puppet government of Otto Kuusinen',[5] although he does not accept that this indicates the existence of any deeper strategy.

Yet Mastny skates on very thin ice when he discounts the significance of the next major example of Stalin's ruthless drive to extend the power of Communism, namely the massacre of Katyn in the spring of 1940. It seems hard to dispute that Stalin's aim in trying to exterminate the core of the Polish officer class was to ensure that when the time came to impose a Government on all of Poland using the Red Army, there could be no opposition from the one force capable of producing effective resistance, namely the Polish army. Mastny, however, alleges that:

> The most atrocious as well as the most puzzling Soviet misdeed in the spring of 1940 was the massacre of several thousand interned Polish army officers at Katyn. So crude a mass murder was not typical of Stalin's style of disposing of his opponents, an aspect suggesting that it may have been committed by overzealous subordinates who misinterpreted his wishes.[6]

But Mastny is quite wrong. Far from being atypical of Stalin's political style, Katyn fits firmly into a well-proven pattern.

As far as Poland is concerned, we may recall Stalin's refusal to come to the aid of the remnants of the Polish Home Army in 1944, which gave the SS free rein in massacring it (see p. 55). Interestingly, Mastny accepts that Stalin's actions were deliberately designed to allow the Germans to get rid of the Home Army.[7] Yet even here,

Mastny objects to the notion of any plan on Stalin's part:

> A straight road seemed to have led from Katyn to Lublin [the setting up of the Polish National Committee in Poland at the end of 1944] ... [but] this seemingly neat design does not necessarily mean that Stalin had planned it that way or welcomed the outcome.[8]

Instead, Mastny claims that it was only in July 1944 that 'Soviet behaviour took a decidedly sinister turn' (thereby implying that Stalin had suddenly decided to move in a new direction). Katyn and the Warsaw massacre are, quite plainly, not perfect parallels, but it seems very hard indeed to deny the existence of the same underlying intention on Stalin's part in both cases. In addition, of course, the concept of mass extermination (even of an entire class of individuals) in order to destroy potential opposition was very much in evidence in two other major revolutionary campaigns waged by Stalin: the extermination of the kulaks and the mass purges in the mid and late 1930s, in which many thousands thought to be likely to oppose Stalinist Communism were wiped from the face of the earth.

Finally, we have Stalin's own testimony on this matter, as reported on at least two occasions by Churchill and his retinue. At Teheran in 1943, for example, Stalin argued – much to Churchill's and Roosevelt's discomfort – that 50,000 or more German army officers ought to be shot once Hitler had been defeated, in order to end for ever the threat of German aggression.[9] At the same conference he also told Churchill that:

> When he [Stalin] asked German prisoners who came from the labouring classes [such is the record, but he probably meant Communist Party] why they had fought for Hitler, and they replied they were carrying out orders, he shot such prisoners.[10]

It seems, therefore, very difficult indeed to sustain the argument that the mass-shooting of groups for political reasons was not a definite and relatively well-documented feature of Stalinist policy, and that what all these groups had in common was that they could be seen as constituting a potential threat to longer-term aims which involved the domination of their nations by the various Communist Parties.

By physically eliminating opposition to Communist rule, Stalin was naturally increasing the chances of survival for the various National Committees, and the British refusal to fix anything about post-war Europe helped rather than hindered him (see p. 56). This was something which Stalin would fully have understood as early as the autumn of 1941, when Russia and Britain were discussing this issue against the background of the making of the Anglo-Soviet Alliance in negotiations which were often conducted from the Soviet side by a senior military intelligence officer. Thus when Mastny finds it 'surprising' that Stalin should accept a treaty without any precise 'territorial clauses', it is, in fact, not in the least surprising.[11]

Let us turn next to the second aspect of Stalin's blueprint for Europe, the National Committees. We know that the first time the British heard of this notion was early in July 1941 when the Russians gave an explanation of them to Anthony Eden himself. This is clearly an important event so we must analyse it in some detail. We have already put forward a theory as to how the National Committees were meant to fit into Stalin's overall design. We shall see that they were something to which the British Foreign Office attached absolutely no special significance. Finally, we have asserted that they were an excellent indication that Stalin had something secret up his sleeve, a full analysis of which might have led directly to the discovery of his blueprint.

For Mastny, however, the National Committees possess no wider significance; what is more, he argues that his verdict upon them is confirmed by the fact that the British Foreign Office did not regard them as important! Finally, Mastny states that they cannot be deemed part of any secret plan because otherwise the Russians would not have told the British of their intention to establish them.

If Mastny is right, the idea of a Stalinist blueprint suffers a heavy, though not fatal, blow: it is hard to see how the committees can be considered part of a secret plan if the Soviets had actually asked Eden for British approval in establishing them. As Mastny writes:

> This offer aroused apprehension and retrospectively has been viewed as a ploy to set up puppet regimes. This was hardly Moscow's intention at the time; if it had been, the proposals would not have been addressed to the governments to be replaced nor would Maisky have consulted with the British Government beforehand as he did.[12]

If this account is accurate, the case against Stalin must become much harder to sustain. Most remarkably, however, Mastny is not accurate. Indeed, in several important respects he has misinterpreted the evidence to support his theory. For if we turn to the source given by Mastny,[13] we discover that the facts are really very different from those he alleges. Certainly there was a meeting between Eden and Maisky on 4 July 1941 to discuss the planned Russian National Committees, but Maisky did not come to make any 'offer' of consultation to Eden concerned with a prospective policy, but rather to present him with a *fait accompli*. The document in question (which is Eden's official note of the meeting) makes this entirely clear:

> The Soviet Ambassador asked to see me ... when he said that he had brought me a message from his Government. They had been considering their relations with Poland, Czechoslovakia and Yugoslavia. They had taken the decision to give facilities to all three states to form National Committees in the USSR which would have facilities to form national military forces ... The Soviet Government undertook to supply arms and equipment to these forces ... All Polish POWs in Russian hands would be handed over to the Polish National Committee. With regard to Poland, Soviet policy was to favour the establishment of an independent Polish National State ... the form of internal government to be set up in Poland was, in the view of the Soviet Government, entirely a matter for the Poles themselves.[14]

It is thus quite plain that Maisky did not consult Eden 'beforehand' (as Mastny claims), but that he told the British *after* the decision had been taken. Furthermore, in order to allay any doubts or suspicions, Maisky added that the USSR wanted an independent Poland (a claim, as we have seen, that it repeated continually). Yet the very fact that Maisky should add this qualifying rider to a statement about the National Committee for Poland shows, to the suspicious mind at any rate, that there was a direct connection between the concept of the National Committee and the sort of regime the Russians wanted in Poland.

Eden plainly sensed trouble (albeit of a raw and undefined nature):

> I asked the Ambassador whether his Government proposed to make public his important declaration, for clearly it would have considerable effects both on the nationals of the states concerned and also on American public opinion ... Maisky supposed this

was contemplated since the decision to recognise the National Committees had already been taken.[15]

There are a number of things to be said about this incident. The first is to remark upon its date: 4 July 1941. If it is accepted that the National Committees strategy was an integral piece of Stalin's blueprint, his plan had been developed very early on, either immediately following the Nazi onslaught (which began on the night of 21–22 June 1941) or some time before that date.[16] In view of the conditions of near panic that are said to have existed in the Kremlin after 22 June 1941, it seems more likely that the blueprint was drawn up well before that time, to be put into effect when the first opportunity for a reorganisation of Europe presented itself.

Yet whichever date is the correct one, it is important to note that Stalin's blueprint preceded the development of the Tube Alloys project, thus lending the lie to the notion that Stalin's intention to colonise as much of Europe as possible was merely a counter-measure to the Anglo-American decision to develop nuclear weapons. For although research on nuclear fission had been going on even before the outbreak of war, it was not until the late autumn of 1941 that the making of a nuclear bomb became a hard policy option, and not until June 1942 that the Tube Alloys project got properly under way.[17]

It must also be emphasised that the Soviets' declaration was not presented as a 'proposal' to the 'governments to be replaced', as Mastny asserts, but as a decision already taken. Indeed, it is plain that Sikorski, the head of the Polish Government in Exile, was extremely agitated about what he saw as a move by Russia to spread 'red Panslavism', and that Eden agreed with him that Moscow's action was 'not correct', although he did nothing about it.[18]

Thus a central pillar of Mastny's argument can be safely discounted: the concept of National Committees did occupy a very important role in Stalin's plans and it was a measure the Soviets forced through at a very early stage against the wishes of the 'governments to be replaced' and with a marked lack of enthusiasm on the part of the British.

In short, the evidence that Stalin did have a secret set of war aims for the Communist domination of Europe is truly overwhelming.

Yet if this is in fact true, why did Stalin reveal anything about them at all? The answer is a simple one. Stalin knew they constituted the visible tip of the iceberg, but the risks involved in not disclosing them to the West were obvious. Sooner or later they were bound to become apparent (because they had an open political purpose). Perhaps even more important was the consideration that the exiled 'governments to be replaced' would sooner or later have discovered their existence. This would then have been communicated to the British, who would have realised that Stalin had deceived them in a key area. So on balance it seemed wiser to disclose their existence while at the same time denying, in tones of injured innocence, that they had any long-term purpose. This is precisely what the Russians did.

All of which suggests that the most important question is not whether or not Stalin had a blueprint, but why the British failed to tumble to it. There was plainly no shortage of evidence which pointed towards the existence of a plan. And although that evidence was contorted and complex, an alert intelligence service charged with providing intelligence from overseas sources ought to have collected and analysed it and come up with its true interpretation.

The point is that Britain had an intelligence service for domestic and overseas use, namely MI6, but it was obviously failing to do what an intelligence service ought to have done. It was not that the British policy-makers understood but did nothing: they simply did not understand. The failure, therefore, lay not in the Foreign Office or in Downing Street, but in intelligence.

The ignorance of MI6

Why did the British Foreign Office not appreciate that there was a consistent red thread running through Soviet policy? Why did Eden take at face value Maisky's assurance about Russia's long-term wish to see a free and independent Poland? Was he stupid? Was he remarkably naive? Did he not think of asking MI6 for advice? Or was a trusted source of intelligence telling him that things were perfectly all right?

To ask the questions is easy enough; it is the answers that cause the difficulty. Although there are many who have questioned Eden's skills, particularly after he became Prime Minister in 1955, on balance the evidence suggests that Eden was certainly not naive. Furthermore, he was the last person to eschew secret intelligence. On the contrary, there is ample evidence that Eden repeatedly took intelligence advice on issues of this kind.

It has to be said that there is no documentary proof of any intelligence input into Eden's passivity on this matter in 1941. This does not, of course, mean that there was no intelligence input; it might simply be the case that the advice was removed or never even recorded. There is, however, documentary evidence relating to a rerun of this issue in 1943, albeit in terms of a National Committee for Germany rather than for Poland or elsewhere. And this documentary material does contain advice emanating from British Intelligence.

In April 1943 John (later Sir John) Wheeler-Bennett, who was at that time a Foreign Office representative in Washington specialising in political intelligence, warned Whitehall that left-wing German political exiles in America who were members of the Social Democratic Party and the Communist Party were apparently making plans to merge into a united Socialist Party. To Wheeler-Bennett this smelt like something the Foreign Office ought to check out.[19] He did not think, however, that this had anything to do with the Soviet Union.

The reaction of the Foreign Office was significant. It immediately asked MI5 to investigate the German left-wing exiles in London to see if any similar moves could be discerned. MI5 produced an accurate report which saw a possible Russian dimension and confirmed that similar moves had indeed been made in Britain, and it stressed specifically that the moves had taken place 'under the direction of the Communists' and that British interests were likely to be endangered by such moves.[20]

British policy-makers became even more anxious about Soviet intentions in July. On 25 July 1943 the British Embassy in Moscow duly reported to the Foreign Office that a 'Free German Committee' had been formed in Moscow. We know from the British documents that this announcement took the British totally by surprise. 'What does all this mean?' Eden demanded, and he ordered Clark Kerr, the Ambassador, to 'ask Molotov'. On 27 July Clark Kerr telegraphed the war Cabinet in London with 'particular secrecy'. He pleaded his 'complete surprise' at these events and said that the US Ambassador had been 'baffled' as well.

It is interesting to see that there is no indication in these documents that any connection at all was being made by the Foreign Office between the events of July 1943 and those of July 1941, although they both had to do with National Committees in Moscow. Two other things also need to be noted carefully. First of all, it is important to see that Eden's reaction was to turn to his Ambassador in Moscow for advice rather than ask MI6, which would have appeared the appropriate action. Second, Eden did not hesitate to ask MI5 to deal with the domestic aspects of this matter, namely the German political exiles in London.

Sceptics who might argue that the 'real' intelligence world was not troubled with such trifles can be effectively floored by pointing out that no less an authority than a former senior MI6 officer, Stephen de Mowbray, has decided to break cover and publish an article on this very issue (discussed at length later). Although, as we shall see, his conclusions are quite wrong, the very fact that he writes about this matter proves that it is a vital core piece of evidence.

De Mowbray, as a former MI6 officer, does not in fact address himself to the question of why MI6 failed in this area. Instead he tries, for very doubtful motives, to implicate MI5. His allegations are serious and need careful analysis, but while pursuing them we should not forget that the fundamental issue of MI6's silence must not be allowed to slip away.

First of all, however, let us examine the facts as reflected in the documents.[21] They show that the fear that the German National Committee might be another term for a puppet Communist regime in exile was very quickly abandoned. Frank Roberts, usually the shrewdest of observers, suggested that the German National Committee was simply a:

> Most effective propaganda move. Unfortunately neither we nor the Americans can safely indulge in this sort of political warfare since it is likely to confuse our own public ... the most important aspect of it is its encouragement given to the appeasers of Germany and to the anti-Russian school in the USA.[22]

By 1 August 1943 the Foreign Office officially accepted the idea that the Committee was simply a propaganda move, although Frank Roberts now warned that Britain should not forget the Bismarckian precept of an alliance between Germany and Russia which might be realised at some future date in order to make a compromise peace between the two nations.

However, at the very same time as the Foreign Office reached its conclusion on this matter, the question was reopened by a letter from the Bishop of Chichester, George Bell. Bell said that he believed that the National Committee might be part of a secret plan on Stalin's part to foist upon the German people a Soviet-dominated Communist

Government after Hitler had been defeated. Bell stated:

> The Communists control the National Committee of Free
> Germans even though its programme is liberal and this is a far
> better way of Communist penetration than the way of force [Bell
> was referring to the German Revolution of 1918–19] tried after
> the last war.[23]

There was of course a considerable amount of objective evidence
which suggests that Bell had got it completely right. Post-war events
confirmed this, for the leaders of the Free German Movement were
Walter Ulbricht and Wilhelm Pieck, later to become the leaders of
the East German puppet regime.[24] Yet Bell's theory was dismissed.

Eden wrote in his customary red ink on the top of Bell's letter,
'more from this pestilent priest but I fear I must reply'. Clark Kerr
stated that one thing was absolutely certain about the Committee,
and that was that it was not a shadow German Government in exile.
William Strang, the Assistant Under-Secretary of State, wrote that
Bell could be considered a 'German Bishop' and he concluded that
all Bell was doing was:

> Raising the Communist bogey ... he and his like will lead us into
> a new war in half a generation if they have their way.[25]

As I have remarked elsewhere,[26] the choice of the word 'bogey' is
highly suggestive. If Strang had said, 'Bell is right but there is not a
damn thing we can do to stop the Russians trying to take over in
Germany after Hitler' or even, 'a good dose of Communism will do
those German so-and-so's good', it would at least have shown that
Strang knew how the German National Committee tied directly in
with all the other Soviet-inspired National Committees.

Instead, one of the most senior policy-makers in Britain dismissed
a totally correct judgment as 'raising the Communist bogey' and a
malicious fiction. In this way, the Soviet Union could get on with its
plans for post-war Germany with not so much as a mild protest out
of London.

There is, however, yet another vitally important angle to this story.
Bell's letter had required an answer (he was, as a member of the
House of Lords, in a position to make trouble if he did not get one).
Eden and his close advisers felt that they ought to ask MI5 to do
another check on the German political exiles in London to see

whether there had been any movement which might support the Bell thesis.

MI5's report, for which Hollis was personally responsible, was not inaccurate about the dangers posed by the existence in London of Communist exiles (although it was none too clear about the German Social Democratic ones) and it quite properly warned the Foreign Office that it ought not to underestimate the Communist move. In other words, it is perfectly clear that MI5 did draw the attention of the Foreign Office to the Communists' bid for power over the exiles in London, with the implication that once they all returned to Germany this might place the Communists in rather a strong position (see p. 128).

If we now turn to Stephen de Mowbray's testimony, we can see how important this whole issue is.[27] De Mowbray served in MI6 for many years before being given, in November 1964, one of the most sensitive posts in the history of British Intelligence. He was one of seven intelligence officers asked to join the 'Fluency Committee' which was set up to investigate the extent of Soviet penetration into Britain's secret service, and he was a colleague of Peter Wright, whose allegations about Sir Roger Hollis inspired Chapman Pincher's critique of Hollis.[28]

Indeed, it was de Mowbray who in 1974 demanded to see the then Prime Minister Harold Wilson in order to put to him the proposition that Hollis had been a Soviet mole. De Mowbray claimed he had a sudden revelation about Soviet penetration; for years he had been struggling with the difficult evidence and then, all at once, the explanation became blindingly clear: the reason the Soviets had been so successful was that the person charged to act against them for so many years, namely Hollis, had been one of them. De Mowbray refused to accept the findings of the Trend Enquiry which cleared Hollis (see p. 396) and supported the allegations made by his former colleague, Peter Wright.

Yet, as we shall see, de Mowbray is guilty of an offence which no serious historian ought to make; he has failed to point out that a crucial piece of the evidence in this jigsaw, one which shows that MI5 wished to alert the Foreign Office to the dangers of subversion, emanated personally from Roger Hollis. It may be that he overlooked this; or did the evidence severely undercut his theories about Hollis? Had Hollis been a mole, the last thing he would have done is pass on this sort of information to people who did not particularly wish to receive it.

De Mowbray's analysis begins with a discussion of the extent to which the Soviet Union practised deliberate misinformation during the war in an attempt to conceal its true intentions from the British and Americans. By the end of 1943, de Mowbray claims:

> Under the influence of lies deliberately propagated by Stalin and supported by his henchmen and his intelligence services, [British policy-makers] had begun not merely to hope but actually to believe that a period of co-operation with the Soviet Union would be possible after the end of the war: the wartime Anglo-Soviet Alliance began to be referred to as the cornerstone of British post-war policy in Europe.[29]

As we have seen, the evidence supports this particular view, however dramatic it might appear. De Mowbray focuses on one specific reason for the success of Soviet aims:

> The Western failure to understand and take into account Soviet deception techniques.

Although he does not spell out the implications of this statement, it seems obvious that this 'failure' was a failure of intelligence, either on the part of the Foreign Office itself, whom de Mowbray criticises very strongly, or on the part of the intelligence services, about whom de Mowbray is relatively silent, doubtless fearing prosecution under the Official Secrets Act.

It is at this stage that de Mowbray mentions the MI5 report sent to the Foreign Office in an attempt to enlighten it, but fails to state that this report was sent by Roger Hollis.

De Mowbray then describes several Soviet propaganda ploys, including the dissolution of the Comintern (the Kremlin's co-ordinating body for international Communist parties), and notes how gullible British officials were about them all:

> Knowing what we now know of Stalin and his post-war policy, it is hard to believe that Stalin ever had the slightest genuine interest in post-war co-operation with the West. Calculating that the war would provide opportunities for Communist expansion, he used deception to mask his determination to exploit those opportunities. His use of deception conformed with the normal definition of its purpose which is to create favourable conditions for the

success of a military or political initiative by weakening, under-mining or diverting resistance to it.[30]

In short, what de Mowbray is arguing, from the vantage point of a career in British Intelligence, is that Stalin got away with his secret plans by successfully mixing subversion and misinformation, and that this led directly to the British pursuing a faulty foreign policy. He then reduces his analysis to some cases in point, of which the most weighty is undoubtedly the establishment of the German National Committee.

He notes in this connection that in May 1943 Stalin told the Reuter's correspondent in Moscow that the reason he had abandoned the Comintern was that this would:

Expose the Hitlerite lie that Moscow intended to intervene in the internal affairs of other nations and 'Bolshevise' them ... it also exposed the old calumny that Communist parties in various countries acted not in the interests of their own peoples but on orders from outside.[31]

Thus when, on 21 July 1943, *Pravda* published the manifesto of the National Committee of Free Germany, it is to be seen not just as an important stepping-stone in Stalin's blueprint, but also as a successful example of Soviet deception (see p. 53).

One individual singled out for special mention by de Mowbray in this context is none other than Peter Smolka-Smollett, the head of the Soviet Relations Division of the Ministry of Information. On 25 February 1943 Smolka had produced a paper on 'countering the German campaign on the Bogey of Bolshevism', in which he urged the British authorities to notice three things: first, that in the post-war period Russia was going to be too busy to do anything other than reconstruct itself; second, that they would need to rely on Anglo-American help for years to come; and third, that their main aim, to gain security, could only be achieved in alliance with the Western democracies.

De Mowbray draws attention to Chapman Pincher's assertion that Smolka was a Soviet agent (see p. 150), which is hardly surprising since de Mowbray was, perhaps, the informant on this matter. Finally, he states that the reaction of the Foreign Office was to dismiss the entire enterprise as a mere propaganda stunt which Soviet

Russia could carry out because it did not have to pay any attention to public opinion. De Mowbray writes:

> Looking back at it now, it is clear that the formation of the National Committee of Free Germany was indeed a real political initiative on the part of the Soviets. It could not have fulfilled its long-term political function if it had been set up in secrecy. On the other hand to have declared its real aims openly would have caused a major rift in the wartime Alliance with the West and would have jeopardised the attainment of its ultimate objectives.[32]

De Mowbray's conclusions are a curious mixture of powerful pointers and rather confused and confusing retractions:

> What the Foreign Office papers show is that Communists, near-Communists and Soviet agents whose affiliations were in some cases known or partly known at the time, were able to influence British official thinking about, and therefore policy towards, the Soviet Union, primarily because of a weakness, common to Russophiles and Russophobes alike, in the Foreign Office's assessment of information on the Soviet Union ... information from one Communist source was accepted as independent confirmation of information from another Communist source. None of the officials showed any awareness of Soviet political deception technique.[33]

Yet despite the strength of this conclusion, which points both to the possibility of subversion within the Foreign Office and to an apparently astounding failure by de Mowbray's own former colleagues, he also states that his conclusions:

> Provide no basis for arguing that British war-time foreign policy was influenced by crypto-Communists or hitherto unidentified Soviet agents in the upper reaches of the Foreign Office hierarchy.[34]

In short, de Mowbray's testimony is well worth examination, first because it confirms that these matters are legitimate objects of secret intelligence work and, second, because of the Hollis connection (to which we shall return later on).

It is, perhaps, instructive to compare de Mowbray's testimony with that of another commentator, about whom it has been claimed that he too was at some stage a British intelligence officer, namely

Anthony Verrier.[35] Verrier's assertions on the self-same issues (unsupported, it must be emphasised, by serious documentary evidence) would have us believe a quite different story. In Verrier's view:

> Between 1942 and 1944, the traditional hostility of British Governments towards Russia was revived by Stalin's patent determination to dominate Eastern Europe and exercise influence or exert pressure on the continent as a whole.[36]

Verrier's opinion simply cannot be sustained. In this respect de Mowbray's views are sounder than Verrier's. Even so, it is peculiar that what de Mowbray appears to give with the one hand, he then proceeds to take away with the other (secret Communists did influence British policy and then again they did not).

De Mowbray implies that MI5, which had vetting as well as other intelligence responsibilities, must be held answerable for the British failure to perceive Stalin's blueprint. Yet as we have seen and will see again, while it is true that MI5 did not 'spot' Smolka, it is untrue that MI5 did not warn the Foreign Office about the true purpose of the National Committee. There is no doubt that, on this latter score, MI5 discharged its duties (something, incidentally, de Mowbray could have revealed, because the evidence is publicly available and he would therefore not face prosecution). The real doubts must be about de Mowbray's own branch of the secret service, namely MI6. Here, we might think, is a classic example of a case where correct secret intelligence from overseas might have alerted the British authorities to an integral part of Stalin's blueprint.

Once again, then, we must persist with the questions, still unanswered even by de Mowbray. Why was MI6 silent about Stalin's National Committee policy? Why did it fail to offer an interpretation of the National Committee of Free Germany? Was the intelligence MI6 was supplying faulty or inaccurate? Was it actually supplying any intelligence about the Kremlin at all?

The German opposition to Hitler

Detailed examination of the National Committees issue demonstrates that if Western policy-makers had been alerted to it, they
might have stumbled upon Stalin's secret plan for the Sovietisation
of Europe. Furthermore, we can see that in the specific case of a
National Committee for Germany, there is documentary evidence
to prove both that it was at heart an intelligence matter and also,
paradoxically, that it was apparently not a matter upon which MI6
provided Whitehall with much-needed information.

Indeed, if we probe even further into the intelligence aspects of
what might be called the German dimension, it soon becomes plain
that the problem is even more sinister than it seems. For there are
unmistakable signs of the deliberate and consistent suppression of
intelligence over an extended period, any piece of which might have
altered British and American policy in this detailed area.

The intelligence issue has to do with MI6's advice to the British
Government on the internal German opposition to the Nazis. We
have already seen how German political exiles in England failed to
make any real mark in the propaganda war. Here, however, we need
to consider Britain's refusal to offer aid to those Germans inside
Germany who wished to rise up against the Nazis. The crux of the
matter is simply that the British Government underestimated the
significance of the existence of anti-Nazi Germans inside the Reich.

This is curious, because MI6 was supposed to be carefully monitoring them and had, in the enigmatic person of Otto John, a prime
agent working for it. Yet when we realise that the person with main
responsibilities in this area was Kim Philby, much of the mystery
disappears. Philby's purpose was to conceal evidence about these
Germans in order to prevent any change in British policy which
might have damaged Russian plans. It is not being suggested that
the British Government ought necessarily to have behaved differently
towards these people (some of whom were simply war criminals),[37]
although it can be argued that greater support for them might
have ended the war more quickly and prevented the Soviets from
penetrating as far west as they did. Rather, the issue at stake is, once
again, British ignorance both about these Germans and about the
implications of its refusal to support them, which indirectly assisted
the Soviet Union's plans for post-war Germany.

Whether post-Nazi Germany was to be controlled by the West or by the East was certainly not the only trophy of war but it was one of the most important. It was also a trophy the Russians almost walked off with.

'Germany' had a double meaning for MI5 and MI6. Where 'Germany' implied the Third Reich and Nazism, British Intelligence in its domestic format, namely MI5, demonstrated the greatest success, particularly in the running of German double agents (see p. 369). Where 'Germany' implied the future political shape of Germany and the dangers of Communist success, what evidence there is shows that Hollis himself was fully alive to the dangers posed by Communism in Germany even if SOE's moles apparently escaped his attention.

The record of MI6, on the other hand, on both these scores was really rather poor. MI6 does appear to have run a number of agents inside Nazi Germany, including, of course, Otto John, who was working for MI6 by 1944, and possibly even earlier.[38] Indeed, it has sometimes been claimed that Admiral Canaris, head of the Abwehr or military intelligence, was an MI6 agent or informant himself.

Curiously, the John case may provide a link between MI5's and MI6's interest in things German. One former MI6 officer has stated that he had been led to believe that after 1945 Otto John became an MI5 agent, run by Roger Hollis, who took him over from MI6 and Kim Philby.[39]

There was a pronounced difference between the policies of the Soviet Union and the United Kingdom concerning Germany's future political format. The British decided at an early stage that Germany was to be defeated almost exclusively by military means, and that there was to be no major political offensive in order to try to overthrow the Nazi regime from within. The Russians, on the other hand, appeared to take a quite different line, stressing in public that after Hitler's defeat life would go on for the German people, and that they ought to get rid of him as soon as they could because there was something to look forward to afterwards. In addition to this policy, however, the Russians produced another, secret one. For it was their aim to legitimise in Moscow a German National Committee which could serve as the basis for a Communist German puppet Government.

Of these two approaches, the truly significant one was the second (and it was, of course, the one they had to conceal). Indeed, it was more than likely that the Russians did not in fact want the German opposition within Germany to overthrow Hitler and the Nazis, for an obvious reason: an internally led putsch by the German army might have produced a peace and a new German Government which would have been able to reject the authority of Stalin's National Committee in Moscow.

Thus Churchill wanted Germany to be flattened before thinking precisely about what sort of Government was to be constructed, while Stalin needed Germany to be flattened, precisely because he had such a clear idea about the Government it should have.

As the war entered its final phase, particularly after the successful Normandy landings, the political control of post-Nazi Germany became an ever more critical issue. It was intensified by the British obsession with the apparent Soviet fear that the German opposition to Hitler might try to overthrow the German Führer and do a deal with the West. This, in turn, might prevent the Red Army from executing Stalinist policy in that portion of Germany which it was agreed should be occupied by the USSR.

Once Hitler's defeat became a matter of months and then weeks, the Russians knew they would have to move quickly to establish a Communist regime in their zone, which could serve as the bridgehead for a Communist advance throughout the whole of what had been the German Reich. The longer the Western Allies had to observe Russian actions, the more they would be determined to prevent them from achieving complete success.

There was only one major obstacle to Russian aims. This was the emergence in July 1944 of an armed German opposition to Hitler in the form of the Generals' Plot: were it to succeed in overthrowing the Führer and making peace, it might have made it far harder for the Kremlin's plans to be realised. Yet both Roosevelt and Churchill had been determined not to deal with the German resistance to Hitler. From Russia's point of view, it was vital to ensure they did not change their minds. In order to achieve this, it was therefore important to keep from the West intelligence about the opposition which might produce such a change.

This was an area where Kim Philby in Section V of MI6 was, until the summer of 1944, in a key position not merely to inform Stalin about how little the British understood about his secret plans, but actually to do something positive to ensure that British policy did not interfere with Soviet ambitions. For he led the MI6 section which gleaned intelligence about Germany from neutral Spain and Portugal.[40] In this instance, Philby was able not only to pass secrets to the Russians, but also to help shape British policy by means of the intelligence he possessed. For he was, it seems, the chief MI6 expert on the German opposition to Hitler.

It is important to point out that this hypothesis is more than an artefact of the historian's imagination. Clifton Child, a distinguished and highly respected former Foreign Office official who worked in intelligence during the war, has confirmed the accuracy of the questions here being asked. Mr Child states:

> What a mistake we made and how many lives we lost in the gas chambers, in the London Blitz and elsewhere, by not fighting with a German opposition on our side as we fought with a French, Danish, Yugoslav, Polish and other European oppositions on our side. To me, Dr Otto John has always stood as an alternative to what has happened in East Europe and indeed in Eastern Germany itself, as the result of the machinations of the Philby gang and of their Stalinist associates ...[41]

Clifton Child was, of course, at the time observing Stalin's policies from within the British intelligence community. It was quite plain to him, if to no one else, that Philby was working hard at this time to discredit the German opposition to Hitler to the extent of actually endangering the lives of its members (although he did not learn of Philby's actual identity until later):

> There was a quite obviously deliberate disregard of the basic canons and practices of security in the handling of reported moves by the German opposition, which reports, as I knew at the time, were the responsibility of the MI6 service dealing with the affairs of the Iberian Peninsula. I only learned later that the section in question was Section V of MI6.[42]

Kim Philby in MI6

The extremely influential position that Philby gained for himself during the war has been widely noted. Lord Sherfield is but one example of a number of senior diplomats who have no doubt whatever that, of all the moles, Philby caused the greatest damage.[43] In addition to his formal role, which was one of considerable responsibility, Philby was one of those people who also enjoyed enormous informal authority. One former colleague has described to me how Philby's brilliance allowed him to be consulted informally by a whole medley of figures in the wider government of Britain.

This former colleague, who chose not to be named, continued that:

> Philby seemed so bright and so dynamic that by 1942 he was generally seen as a future 'C'. The 'old buffers', the pre-war ex-Indian police officers who formed the core of MI6, were simply not a match for him; he was able to ridicule the 'Indian Policemen' with a whole host of Cowgill and Vivian jokes [his superiors Felix Cowgill and Valentine Vivian], obsessed with Communists and drinking cups of tea. His position was tremendously powerful; similar to Blunt's in MI5 although Kim was more in the heart of things. Like Blunt, too, Philby was simply a very clever man, far above the level of most of the other officers. The fact was that by 1942 Philby was very, very important.[44]

This source pointed out that Philby was able to exploit a feeling shared by many of the young recruits into MI6 that it had previously concentrated so much on the Bolshevik menace that it had neglected the threat from the Third Reich; they were determined not to fall into the same trap. They knew that the Soviet Union was England's only hope of defeating Hitler, and people persuaded themselves that Russia had changed.

Such people, the former MI6 officer claimed, felt they had been deceived about Russia's role by people 'like the deposed King and Mrs Simpson', who argued that the Nazis were a bulwark against Communism and that another war against Germany would lead to the end of civilisation. After 1941 they realised how much they needed Russia. That did not mean that MI6 had no secrets from Russia, this former officer added; a team of people was specially charged with drawing up bundles of intelligence for Russia, marked 'OK for Russians', which excluded certain details (such as Ultra's source). Naturally, they had no idea that thanks to Philby the Russians were probably getting it all in any case (see p. 169). The former officer added:

> Chapman Pincher is quite wrong to see Oxbridge intellectuals as responsible for this sort of view. The *Daily Mirror* and Cassandra were far more significant: it was an anti-upper class populism

that made us so pro-Russian. Everybody who was intelligent and powerful underestimated Soviet long-term plans in the intelligence sphere. People had different illusions about Russia and its future; they underestimated its intelligence operations and their range. They knew that one day Russia might be our main target, but for the moment it was the Germans who were the bad ones.

Interestingly, this person had been reminded many years later (when investigations into Philby's career were being undertaken by Sir Dick White, then in MI5) that he had, during the war, expressed doubts about Philby's loyalty to Britain to one of his friends who had later reported them. This former officer recalled how Philby had insisted that his youthful Marxist leanings had been fully extinguished by his Spanish exploits. Proof of this, according to Philby, was the celebrated medal he had received from Franco, as well as his membership of the pro-Nazi Anglo-German Fellowship. Yet to this former colleague, Philby's conversion to right-wing politics had always seemed phoney (see p. 133).

Philby was not, of course, in charge of providing the Government with intelligence directly about the USSR before the formation of Section IX in the summer of 1944 (see p. 216). However, not only is it fair to suppose that he was being consulted on issues which technically exceeded his brief, but there was at least one area where his brief came directly into contact with questions of Soviet policy and Stalin's blueprint (or 'long-term plans', as this former MI6 officer described them).

Such an indictment of Philby differs from previous ones since it seeks to locate Philby's treachery in the wider framework of Stalin's secret war aims. Philby thus comes to occupy a highly important position because he was one of the very few people (for reasons explored later; see p. 247) in a position both to see evidence of Stalin's blueprint and to decide what should become of that evidence. This assessment, it should be added, thus directly contradicts the verdict given by Hugh Trevor-Roper, who has minimised Philby's overall importance here (while admitting that Philby did damage). As we shall see, he is wrong to do so and indeed this was something for which this former MI6 colleague criticised him strongly.

Trevor-Roper himself wrote in 1968 that Philby had in fact personally intervened, albeit on only two occasions, suppressing evidence which tended to suggest that the German opposition to Hitler was a political force to be reckoned with, since it was actively about to initiate an uprising against him.[45]

Clifton Child, however, has argued that what Philby did went rather beyond straightforward suppression of intelligence: he was actually trying to destroy the opposition itself.

This is what Trevor-Roper wrote about Philby's suppression of intelligence:

> Late in 1942 my office had come to certain conclusions which time proved to be correct about the struggle between the Nazi Party and the German General Staff as it was being fought out in the field of secret intelligence. The German Secret Service (the Abwehr) and its leader Admiral Canaris were suspected by the Party not only of inefficiency but of disloyalty and attempts were being made by Himmler to oust the Admiral and to take over his whole organisation. Canaris himself at that time was making repeated journeys to Spain and indicated a willingness to treat with us: he would even welcome a meeting with his opposite number 'C'. These conclusions were duly formulated and the final document was submitted for security clearance to Philby. Philby absolutely forbade its circulation, insisting it was 'mere speculation'. He afterwards similarly suppressed as 'unreliable' a report from an important German defector Otto John who informed us in Lisbon that a conspiracy was being hatched against Hitler. This also was perfectly true. The conspiracy was the Plot of 20 July 1944 and Canaris, for his contribution to it, suffered a traitor's death in Germany. At the time we were baffled by Philby's intransigence which would yield to no argument and no argument was used to defend. From some members of Section V mere mindless blocking of intelligence was to be expected. But Philby, we said to ourselves, was an intelligent man: how could he behave thus in a matter so important? Had he too yielded to the genius of the place?[46]

Trevor-Roper apparently failed to report Philby's transgression. As an intelligence officer this inaction was perhaps remarkable; however, he deserves considerable praise for his frankness in pointing out that Philby did suppress evidence on those two occasions. His account has, of course, often been quoted and requoted.[47] Yet several things about it have not been made as explicit as they ought. The first is the obvious connection between this whole issue and Stalin's blueprint. Trevor-Roper argues that Philby acted suspiciously on only two occasions in respect of this matter. It is, however, hard to imagine that if Philby acted in this way on two occasions, he would not have done his best to influence British policy-makers on every similar case that came his way.

Trevor-Roper claims that Philby did little damage at this time, for he believes that Philby did not have the opportunity:

> To do [us] much harm. His work was against the Germans in Spain where Russia was powerless and uninterested. Anyway the interests of the Russians were at that time the same as ours: the defeat of Germany.[48]

This view is very flawed. For reasons (not of Philby's making) which are explored in detail later, it seems fair to suppose that most of the intelligence which could have smoked Stalin out did in fact come into Philby's bailiwick, via the Iberian peninsula.

As for the claim that British and Russian interests were the same at that time, this has already been dealt with. Yet at least one former MI6 colleague has stated unequivocally that he himself always knew that, apart from defeating Hitler, the interests of the two were incompatible. What he was not able to do was to prove this, because of a shortage of evidence. When, in 1945, that evidence presented itself, it was too late to do anything about it.[49]

Thus it seems quite plausible to believe that Philby did intervene both formally and informally wherever he could, doing great damage in MI6, in SOE (see Chapter 3) and in the Foreign Office (see Chapter 4).

Trenchant evidence, however, of the esteem in which Philby was held in Whitehall by March 1944 emerges from many quarters, including the celebrated private letter sent to the Editor of *The Times*, who had asked to have Philby on his staff:

> Philby is not on the Foreign Office Establishment ... but his work is well known to the Foreign Office and is of particular interest to us and I am afraid that I must tell you that if ever we were consulted about [his release] we should be bound to recommend most strongly against his removal from his present post ... his present work is so important and he performs it with such exceptional ability that I am afraid his departure would be a real loss to us.[50]

This sort of statement has led some authors to believe that Philby did in fact do some good work for MI6 while also working flat out for the Russians.[51]

The early days of Otto John

Anyone investigating the deplorable lack of political intelligence in relation to Soviet plans for Germany would soon find him or herself considering the curious, contorted case of Dr Otto John.[52]

The evidence concerning John falls into two parts. The first has to do with the period from 1944 until 1950 when John was an MI6 agent (and possibly an MI5 agent as well). The second deals with the period from 1950 until 1954 when John led the West German equivalent of MI5, the BfV (Bundesamt für Verfassungsschutz) or Federal Office for the Protection of the Constitution (see p. 229).

John's story seems to begin in 1944 (although Trevor-Roper has indicated that John had been an MI6 agent ever since 1942, which John denies).[53] He was held in such high esteem by British Intelligence that his 1950 post was in large part the result of British support for him (John denies this as well, despite the evidence to the contrary; see p. 230).

John was born in 1909 in Marburg. In 1937 he joined the legal department of Lufthansa's Berlin office, a job which allowed him to make excellent and influential contacts since his boss was Dr Klaus Bonhoeffer, brother of Dietrich; both Bonhoeffers were courageous leaders of the German resistance to Hitler. Another colleague was Prince Louis Ferdinand of Prussia, the second son of the heir to the Hohenzollern dynasty. He also got to know other important anti-Nazis including Jakob Kaiser, Wilhelm Leuschner, Julius Leber, Hans Oster (who worked for Canaris) and zu Putlitz. It is curious that despite John's relatively humble position, he was not called up for military service, even at a time when old men and boys were being enlisted. He was, perhaps, being protected from war service, but by whom and for what purpose cannot be said.

On 22 July 1944 the anti-Nazi opposition attempted to assassinate Hitler, but the plot failed and on 24 July John flew to Madrid on a scheduled Lufthansa flight.[54] Once there he set about trying to get to London, in order, as he has claimed, to inform the BBC about what was really going on in Germany and repeat in public what he

1 *Above:* Hugh Dalton (*right*) with SOE officers Gladwyn Jebb (*left*) and Colin Gubbins (*centre*), c. 1941

2 *Below:* Julian Amery, former SOE officer (*second from left*), with Randolph Churchill and the Prime Minister in the run-up to the 1945 election

3 Fritz Heine (*second from right*), leading German Social Democrat – and former British Intelligence officer – visits the House of Commons with his boss Kurt Schumacher (*second from left*), post-war SPD leader, in 1946

4 Fritz Heine's identity card, made out by the American authorities – note the false name and his description as 'Technical Adviser'

5 Klaus Fuchs leaving London airport for East Berlin on his release from prison

6 Denis Sefton Delmer: one of the most ambiguous figures in secret political warfare

7 Otto John (*centre*) being deported from Britain in February 1959 after being declared an undesirable alien

8 *Above:* Philby (*right*) gives a press conference after being cleared by Harold Macmillan of being the 'third man'

9 *Below:* Anthony Blunt, Surveyor of the Queen's Pictures, with Princess Margaret at the Courtauld Institute in 1958

10 *Above, left to right:* Sir Patrick Reilly, by now British Ambassador in Moscow, in the Kremlin in February 1959 with Selwyn Lloyd, Prime Minister Harold Macmillan, Soviet leader Nikita Khrushchev, and Andrei Gromyko

11 *Below left:* Sir Dick White in 1945, while engaged upon the secret hunt for Hitler

12 *Below right:* Sir Roger Makins, later Lord Sherfield, at the Foreign Office at the time of the defection of Burgess and Maclean

13 *Right:* Sir Roger Hollis, Director General of MI5 from 1956 to 1965

14 *Below left:* Sir Roger playing golf with Lee Kuan Yew, Singapore's Prime Minister, in May 1965

15 *Below right:* grandfather and granddaughter – Sir Roger in retirement

SECRET

Telephone No.:
OXFORD 48411-6.

Telegraphic Address:
SNUFFBOX, LONDON.

420/Germany/F.2.b/MJEB.

BOX No. 500,

G.P.O.,

OXFORD.

10th September, 1945.

Dear Bromley,

Although it was compiled before the Potsdam Conference, you may care to see the attached copy of a report regarding Russia's European Policy as reflected by the German Communist groups in Great Britain. This reached us from a source in this country which has proved reliable on other occasions.

The information given is not up-to-date in every respect, for instance the statement in the first paragraph that German and Austrian Communists in this country realise that the Russians apparently do not need them and are not at all keen on recalling them for the present. According to the "Daily Telegraph" of the 4th September 1945, Wilhelm KOENEN, one of the most prominent German Communists now living in this country, has been included in the Berlin Shadow Cabinet set up by the Russians. We have had confirmation of this report from another source.

Yours sincerely,

R. H. Hollis.

T. E. Bromley, Esq.,
Foreign Office.

MJEB/MRA.   Enclosure.

16 Documentary evidence of Roger Hollis in action keeping tabs on
German Communists

had been telling MI6 for some time: that the opposition was a force to be reckoned with and the plot was more than a palace revolution, as the British believed.[55]

Otto John has stated that in 1944 he told the British:

> They simply could not allow the Russians into Europe and so make the world-wide antagonisms between Britain and the Soviets insoluble for all time.[56]

Yet the British would not listen because of their 'steadfast loyalty to their treaties with the Russians'.[57]

John did not succeed in changing British policy but was soon employed by British Intelligence and the BBC, where he worked under Hugh Carleton Greene (see p. 130). The real question, however, is why John did not succeed. For no one could doubt that he was close to a number of the leaders of the German opposition and that his views counted for something. What John *claims* he said was that the British refusal to support the opposition would give the Russians considerable advantages in Europe (a view which was undoubtedly correct, and not one that the Russians would have wanted the British to listen to seriously).

No less an authority than the late Sir Maurice Oldfield, 'C' from 1973–8, argued that British policy had been wrong on this very score and associated John himself (whom he believed to have been loyal to the West) with this issue. As Oldfield's self-appointed biographer Richard Deacon has written:

> [The fact that Philby had dealt with John's case] was enough to cause Oldfield to take a keen interest in Dr John's case. But it also enabled him to see how many chances were lost of finishing off World War Two much earlier by neglect of the aid proferred by the German resistance. He had seen how in the Middle East the use of German double agents had been enormously effective.[58]

Although Oldfield did not know John until after the war and is now dead and unable to corroborate Deacon's account, there is supporting evidence for it from a former MI6 officer, Miss Jean Alington, who was asked by Oldfield to research the John case (interestingly, Oldfield also believed that Sefton Delmer had been shabbily treated for his work in intelligence).[59] There is, curiously, a final twist in the Oldfield–John saga. Deacon claims that it was

Delmer who first introduced John to Oldfield some time after 1958; yet on the next page he quotes Phillip Whitehead as saying that Oldfield had been John's contact in MI6 after 1945.[60]

Let us therefore suppose John's words had not fallen on deaf ears; the British might have changed their propaganda line to one of 'hope' towards the German people and, at the same time, have begun to re-examine detailed areas of their policy towards the Soviet Union. In addition, of course, John's account would have suggested strongly that there was something odd about Philby's negative attitude towards the German opposition and might well have prompted a more precise examination of his activities.

Was it, therefore, Philby who advised that John be ignored? He had a duty to the Russians, which would have demanded that he try to undermine John's reports. Furthermore, John himself has alleged that Philby was the source of all his misfortunes in this regard. Let us suppose, therefore, that this was the case. Philby's argument would have been based on the theory that John's views were unsound, because they reflected the Nazi line that Britain and America were fighting Russia's war. There is evidence to show that this was, indeed, used against those in intelligence who were anxious about British policy.

Michael Balfour has written:

The thesis that Bolshevism was the real enemy, that the British and Americans were backing the wrong horse and betraying the traditions of Europe was Goebbels's stock in trade. His motives in harping on this theme were obvious. Therefore it became a matter of honour not to believe him.[61]

Julian Amery's analogous suspicions about Russian motives were quelled in this precise way. 'Have another drink,' his superior told him, 'anyone would think you'd been listening to Goebbels.'[62]

Having said this, however, there are three important reasons for believing that Philby did not do this, but that something very different had gone on. The first is that by impugning John as one of Goebbels's lackies or a stooge of the German army, Philby would have been forced to disown John and discount the intelligence he had been providing. Yet Philby quite obviously did not do so, since John continued to be highly valued by British Intelligence. Second, if John had been seen as a German nationalist who had tried to mislead MI6 in the interests of the German army, he would not have been asked by the British, as he subsequently was, to interrogate German generals with a view to preparing their prosecution. Nor, for that matter, would he after 1950 have been nominated by the British as West Germany's security chief. Finally, of course, John's action in defecting in 1954 means one is obliged to wonder whether John really did try to draw Britain's attentions to Soviet plans.

It is not implausible, therefore, to believe that Otto John did not contradict Philby's intelligence assessments but that he confirmed them. After all, after the war John argued that in reality the German opposition did not represent majority feeling in Germany, but had simply been a small group of courageous people fighting for Germany's honour. Indeed, Trevor-Roper himself provides support for this theory when he states that John:

> Despises the docility, the vacillation, the blind stupidity of those classes who in Germany held power – power to rule and make war ... He is particularly impatient of the wartime generals who were such bold conspirators in talk, so pusillanimous in action. He has little respect for the German people or their comfortable myths. He does not allow that it was the demand for 'unconditional surrender' that prolonged the war; the war, he insists, was prolonged by the faults of the Germans, by their stupidity and their lack of civil courage.[63]

And although Trevor-Roper confirms that John did bring news of the opposition to London, it seems to have been unfavourable:

> He had hoped to tell the Allies of the 'other Germany' which by then was even more distracted and impotent.[64]

If John himself has misled us on this critical point and the doubts about him here can be substantiated, then the damage that Philby did would have been even greater and the policy of ignoring the German opposition even less open to reconsideration. At any rate, it is more than curious that there should be such a remarkable contradiction between Trevor-Roper's recollection of John's comments and John's own record, and that it should occur precisely at the critical conjunction of secret intelligence, British policy – and the interests of the Soviet Union.

Whatever the final verdict on John will prove to be, one thing is absolutely certain: that his is a case about British Intelligence and

Communist subversion. Those who consider him an innocent, if misguided, individual argue that what they see as a private tragedy was caused by the subversive strategies of the Soviet secret services (and in particular by Kim Philby). Those (like myself) who find his own and his friends' accounts of his career overfull of inconsistencies and peculiarities may choose to consider another view of John: that, at some stage in his career, John may have become a Russian agent or even a mole. Were this theory to be substantiated, then John would be seen not as a victim of subversion but as one of its tools.

It must be emphasised that final proof either way is lacking (although I believe the evidence is weighted against John, not least because of his failure to answer properly the case against him). In 1986 the West German President granted John a state pension, suggesting that he believed John had been hard done by. British Intelligence seems divided on the John case; and one former MI5 officer told me that although he himself believed John to be innocent, despite the facts that spoke against him, he had known of no one in the service who had been certain or believed the truth would ever be known.[65]

7

MI6 and Britain's Ignorance about Soviet Intentions, 1944–54

Kim Philby as a future 'C'

One of the Kremlin's most brilliant victories in the subversive intelligence war against the West was the appointment in 1944 of one of their very best people, Kim Philby, as head of a new anti-Soviet counter-espionage unit, Section IX.

Philby's rise to prominence within the Secret Intelligence Service is significant for a whole host of reasons. The first is that by the summer of 1944, MI6 appears to have decided that its intelligence and counter-intelligence work in respect of Soviet subversion was inadequate. It seems reasonable to ask why. Why, precisely, did MI6 decide at that particular juncture to revitalise its anti-Soviet output and, unintentionally, put a Communist mole in charge of its efforts?

The answer is of enormous significance. For if the explanation were that MI6 had suddenly tumbled to the fact that Stalin had a secret set of war aims about which it knew nothing, it would, albeit very late in the day, ameliorate the harsh judgment otherwise passed upon MI6's record. Such an explanation, furthermore, is not on the face of it implausible. By the summer of 1944, information about Stalin's aims, particularly in respect of Poland, may have suggested that MI6 had not been doing its job properly.

However, another quite different answer can also be posited. This would suggest that following the establishment of a Western Allied bridgehead in Normandy after 6 June 1944, the end of the war was in sight. This being so, it would follow logically that with Hitler's disappearance there would now be only one conceivable source for any major threat to Western security, namely the Soviet Union, and that the time had come to prepare for this. If this is the correct explanation, as seems the case, then as late as the summer of 1944 MI6 was still failing to put together the various pieces of the jigsaw which suggested that Stalin had aimed at Sovietisation of as much of Europe as he could get his hands on.[1]

Prior to 1944, Soviet matters were the responsibility of different parts of MI6: David Footman's desk in Section I, which dealt with running operations through agents (of whom more later; see p. 264), and a radio unit of Section V which was based at Bletchley. This unit and the work that it did is of the greatest interest and we shall return to it in detail later (see p. 249).

Robert Cecil, a former diplomat and academic, who claims to have been in a position to know, has stated that MI6 had only one person technically supposed to do anti-Soviet work and this was Felix Cowgill. He, however, had been put to work on German material on the outbreak of war:

> The only harbinger of the future anti-Communist section (section IX) was a small records unit.[2]

As we shall see, however, this statement is inaccurate, for within MI6 David Footman worked on Russia and there were other individuals with an interest in Soviet Communism (see p. 263). In addition, it seems more than likely that the 'records unit' to which Cecil refers was the MI6 section at Bletchley which recorded Soviet wireless traffic.

Cecil is, however, quite right to describe Philby's promotion as a 'masterstroke in the history of espionage'. And he provides some helpful information about Philby's own plans at this time which, in retrospect, must be regarded as his second masterstroke. For Philby, it seems, was now the most vociferous of those expressing anxiety about future Anglo-Soviet discord. He thereby managed to seem more holy than holy in declaiming against Communist subversion, which many people, including Cecil himself, had not been disposed to take seriously. Cecil, it must be said, failed to realise that Philby was a mole. Cecil was, of course, a diplomat and not an intelligence officer, and despite disagreeing with my own view of Philby's strategy, he does confirm the general thesis outlined above, that ignorance was the keynote to British understanding of Soviet secret intentions at the time (see p. 32):

> In late February or early March 1945 there arrived on my desk the document that Philby describes in his book as the 'charter of Section IX'. It included a substantial number of overseas stations to be held by officers under diplomatic cover who would be directly responsible to the Head of IX. With hindsight it is easy to see ...

why Philby aimed to create his own empire within SIS. Quite apart
from his covert aims, it is also clear that he foresaw more plainly
than I the Cold War ... I sent the memorandum back to Philby
suggesting that he might scale down his demands. Within hours
Vivian and Philby had descended upon me, upholding their
requirements and insisting that these be transmitted to the FO ...
I gave way ...[3]

All authors are agreed that Philby worked very hard indeed to
ensure that he became chief of the new section. Indeed, it is just
possible that the person who first developed the idea of a new Section
IX was Philby himself. It certainly bespeaks his great personal influence in MI6 that he was able to outmanoeuvre other possible
contenders, in particular Felix Cowgill.[4]

While Philby's prominence in MI6 after 1944 might seem surprising in the light of the suppression of information about the
German resistance to Hitler, he had gained a reputation for good
and accurate intelligence about things German, sheer hard work,
and an ability to know how institutions select people for jobs.
Cowgill's failure to get the post precipitated his resignation from
MI6 altogether, and today he lives silently in retirement in Ireland.
Ironically, of course, he might well have uncovered Philby had he
remained in office. As it was, victory went to the 'best and the
brightest' in MI6 – the 'old buffers', the 'Indian policemen' were on
their way out. At any rate, Philby's new post gave him a whole set
of opportunities and undreamt-of scope for further subversion. First
of all, as head of Section IX, he was able to assemble his own
staff, although there is some disagreement as to whom he actually
recruited. West says that he offered posts to R. W. Carew-Hunt, the
academic specialist on Communism, and Jane Archer (who had
helped with the interrogation of Krivitsky in 1939), both of whom
were part of MI5's anti-Soviet forces under Roger Hollis.[5] Boyle, on
the other hand, states that one of Philby's first actions was to get rid
of Jane Archer.[6]

There is an analogous disagreement among the specialists as to
the precise duties of Section IX. Page *et al.* are in two minds about
this: its chief purpose was either to act as an intelligence-gathering
organisation or as a counter-intelligence one; that is, either to set up
networks to generate information or to devise ways of acting against
the Russians' agents in Europe and beyond.[7]

In fact, Section IX probably did both these things. Philby, who seems to have had a staff of about 100 (which is a lot) subsumed the section that had previously been concerned with gleaning intelligence about Russia and, since CE work had not been done for some years, it seems fair to assume that IX both gathered intelligence about Soviet Communism and acted covertly against it. It clearly fulfilled this latter function in Albania (see p. 219). Cecil adds that Philby was required both to establish networks of British MI6 officers throughout the world and to deal with defectors such as Konstantin Volkov and Igor Gouzenko which might require counter-intelligence measures to be taken.[8]

There is no doubt that Philby had created for himself and his Soviet masters an organisation within MI6 that could and did do great damage to the interests of the West. In some ways, however, he may have been able to do less damage as Head of Section IX than he could working as the up-and-coming brilliant young man in Section V. The essence of his success lay in the existence of the Anglo-Soviet Alliance of 1942 and his skilful exploitation of the various networks which exist at the top of British public life to give advice and express an opinion.

As Head of Section IX, however, the formal division between those who gather intelligence and those who make policy may well have become far harder to breach, if only because Philby would have been obliged to be far more careful that obviously inappropriate advice did not lead to doubts among colleagues and others about his loyalty. Formal responsibility carried with it its own restraints. More important, however, was the fact that by 1945 the scene had been set for Stalin's take-over of eastern and central Europe and his hitherto secret plans had now become explicit, so that by 1947 the whole of British and American policy had altered as a result. Any attempt by Philby to minimise the significance of Soviet actions after late 1945 or 1946 would immediately have caused him to be suspect, and thus his potential to influence policy decisions in the interests of the Soviet Union would have declined.

Yet despite all of this, Philby does appear to have been widely consulted both formally and informally about the USSR, both then and even after 1952 when, technically speaking, he was not on the payroll of MI6. And although Philby could not prevent MI6 or the policy-makers from taking military action to try to push the Communists from power in the states of eastern Europe, he still possessed the resources to ensure that such attempts proved dismal failures.

In addition, Philby could continue to do great harm in personnel matters; he could both promote and encourage like-minded individuals and, to a limited extent, prevent those who threatened his position from being listened to.

Two opportunities for damaging the West presented themselves to Philby in August and September 1945. For these were the dates when two major Soviet defectors, Igor Gouzenko and Konstantin Volkov, offered themselves, in different parts of the world, to Western intelligence. It was a coincidence that Philby in MI6 proved unable to attend to the Gouzenko case himself: it did, in fact, come under the aegis of Section IX, rather than MI5's Roger Hollis who ended up dealing with it.[9] As it was, Gouzenko's defection led to the first major indication since Krivitsky that moles had penetrated deep into the most vital areas of British life.

Gouzenko's testimony was almost certainly taken as seriously as it ought to have been (see p. 310). It formed the first rung on the ladder which led gradually to the exposure of a whole series of moles. Furthermore, Gouzenko's testimony proved not only that the moles played a very important role in Soviet strategy, but that for the Russians, at any rate, Soviet and British interests had ceased to be compatible long before 1945 (see p. 181). Volkov's defection, on the other hand, which could have produced far more important results, never properly got off the ground, due, of course, entirely to Philby himself.

The Volkov story has been told many times and it should merely be outlined here.[10] Volkov, a KGB representative at the Soviet Consulate in Istanbul, had defected bringing with him, according to Andrew Boyle and others, the names of three Soviet moles, two in the Foreign Office and one in intelligence. In actual fact, former MI5 and MI6 officers have implied that Volkov did not have a list of names, but a list of where Soviet agents and moles worked.[11] It also seems that the list contained more than three locations (and hence any number of candidates). Philby was able to ensure that the Russian secret service was alerted and Volkov was hauled back to Russia with the identities of the moles still secret.

Yet what Philby had done was enormously risky and, in due course, almost bound to reflect badly upon him. The question is, therefore, why he took such a risk. Both he and his Russian controllers knew that he was in line for the post of 'C' itself, yet this cloak-and-dagger exploit might well have scuppered his chances of the job. Did the Russians believe Philby was unassailable and could

therefore take any risk? Did they believe that Volkov was so dangerous that any risk was justified? Did they think that Philby's chances
of becoming 'C' had declined? Or did MI6 by this time contain
a whole new generation of up-and-coming moles, making Philby
expendable? We shall, of course, never know the answer, although
on balance the first two explanations seem most likely.

Philby does appear, however, to have had one last fling at influencing high policy and so, before we turn to his two final cases (which
involve people rather than nations), we should briefly consider the
Albanian fiasco. This has been frequently 'revealed' (most recently
and most fully by Lord Bethell).[12] What is most interesting about
the débâcle from the point of view of the present analysis is that its
ingredients are so very similar to those of the cases of Communist
subversion executed during the war itself and already described in
detail. The essence of the Albanian concept was the use of political
exiles from Albania, mostly dwelling in Italy. Indeed, Julian Amery
(who had worked with the Albanian anti-Communist leader Abas
Kupi for a time during the war) was sent to Rome in 1949 to organise
an Albanian Government in Exile which was to become the seedbed
of an anti-Communist puppet Government supported by the West.[13]

The Albanian adventure was a conscious attempt by British Intelligence to learn from the examples provided by the Soviet Union
during the Second World War – the very things, it should be added,
which British Intelligence had failed to comprehend while the Soviet
Union was actually carrying them out. 'Giving Stalin a taste of his
own medicine' was how Julian Amery described it at the time and,
from Lord Bethell's well-researched account, it is clear that Amery's
interpretation was the correct one.

In 1948 the Foreign Office had established a 'Russian Committee'
headed, in 1948 and 1949, by Gladwyn Jebb (now Lord Gladwyn).
Members of it were Ivone Kirkpatrick (later British High Commissioner in Germany and Permanent Under-Secretary at the
Foreign Office), William Hayter and Frank Roberts (both later
Ambassadors in Moscow) and Roger Makins (Lord Sherfield). The
chief aim of the Russia Committee was to attempt to learn from past
failures connected with British ignorance of Soviet aims and, if
possible, to try to undo some of the damage that ignorance had
caused.

The Committee itself declared:

Our aim should certainly be to liberate the countries within the

Soviet orbit by any means short of war ... [of which one example might be] to detach Albania from the Soviet orbit ...[14]

It was decided to dispatch a mission to Albania to execute this in the autumn of 1949, to be led by David Smiley based at Malta. Bethell says of Smiley and his colleagues, Amery and Fitzroy Maclean:

They did not share the general British wartime reverence of Stalin and the Great Soviet Ally. [In 1943] most British and American people saw Stalin as the hero and this was the prevailing mood at their base, SOE HQ in Cairo ... it seemed to many, not only of left-wing persuasion, that Communism was the way of the future and that Communist resistance movements were the most effective and that Britain should therefore give them the bulk of her support. Some of the SOE officers like the writer James Klugman were Communist Party members. Others were of the political left ... and opposed the line taken by Maclean and Amery ...[15]

As we have seen, the documentary evidence simply does not support these sweeping assertions. Bethell confuses the lack of a policy towards these matters after 1942 with a pro-Communist policy on the part of SOE. (The fact that the net result of this lack of a policy was the success of Communist policy does not mean that SOE was pro-Communist.)

At any rate, Philby got to know all about the plans for Albania, which by now involved the CIA. In October 1949 Philby had gone to Washington as the representative of British Intelligence in the United States, with links with both the FBI and the CIA (where his contact was the celebrated James Angleton). Bethell states:

He was also SIS's link with the Office for Policy Coordination (OPC) set up in June 1948 to carry out anti-Soviet covert operations.[16]

As always, Philby's influence was enormous. Bethell continues:

George Jellicoe ... remembers frequent meetings with Philby at the SIS Office in the Washington Embassy ... 'Kim was the one who made all the operational decisions. I was just there to give political guidance ... He was intelligent, professional and hardworking. How on earth he found the time to do a job for the Russians, I just don't know.'[17]

The Americans mirrored the British interest in the political exiles from Stalin's Europe, albeit on a far grander scale for they established a 'Committee for Free Europe':

> It was, according to the State Department, a private organisation with Committee members well-known in American society, among them Allen Dulles [later head of the CIA and brother of the Secretary of State, John Foster Dulles] and Dwight D. Eisenhower. Its aim was to collect émigrés from all Eastern Europe into a political body and together cause the destruction of the Soviet orbit.[18]

Finally, there was one other parallel with the operations of the Second World War. The BBC was to be used to broadcast messages and disinformation in an attempt to conceal the attempted coup against the Communists.

In the event, the entire operation proved a terrible and costly disaster, and Lord Bethell is in no doubt that the major responsibility for this must lie with Philby, although he accepts that other factors also contributed to the failure of the mission. It had many repercussions, of which the most important was that the West never again (as far as we know) tried to use Stalinist tactics to get rid of a Communist regime in mainland Europe (although the Americans have tried this tactic elsewhere). Nevertheless, the Albanian fiasco illustrates one thing if nothing else. After 1945 both the British and the Americans believed they had a lot to learn from Stalin's secret blueprint for Europe.

The Putlitz Papers part two

Dr Otto John may well have been the most intriguing German in British Intelligence, but he was by no means the only one. The activities of Wolfgang Gans, Edler Herr zu Putlitz (for which an adequate English translation might be 'noble lord of the manor of Putlitz') in SOE and PWE have already been discussed (see p. 148).

On balance, it seems hard to dispute that Putlitz was a secret Communist throughout the 1930s and 1940s.

Putlitz's final performance on the political stage came in January 1952 when he decided to cross the Iron Curtain, although whether he 'defected' or whether he simply 'went' depends on what one believes about him. If we assume that Putlitz defected, however, it means that he is to be seen as yet another classic example of a Communist mole managing to penetrate into the British intelligence community and very nearly achieving a high office in the fledgling West German State to boot. Putlitz, as a German, would have been instructed to return to Germany as soon as he could in order to attempt to gain a position in the British Government of occupation after 1945 and thence act for Russia. In the event, the West German State refused to have him. He died in September 1975 at the age of seventy-six.

If Putlitz was a mole and if Otto John was one too, they both represented the 'tip' of the Stalinist policy iceberg. What is more, both of them failed to be properly investigated by MI6 and by MI5. Even if Putlitz had been thoroughly checked out and found totally innocent, he would still have been an important signpost pointing at Stalin's secret blueprint and at many of the British moles working within the British intelligence community. At least two of them might well have been caught as a result. Certainly, the very circumstances surrounding his case were so suspicious that, on the face of it, a major investigation of Putlitz and his circle ought to have been undertaken. What prevented this from happening may have been incompetence (or worse) within British Intelligence. Equally, however, Putlitz was well-connected, and this may have protected him. In addition, we should not forget that during the 1930s, whatever Putlitz's true political persuasion, he provided first-rate secret intelligence about the Third Reich to the British authorities, particularly about German rearmament.

Putlitz's career contains many parallels to John's. It begs at least four important questions. First of all, was he really a mole or was he merely a romantic, if misguided, German? Second, if he was a mole (or at least appeared likely to have been one), why did British counter-intelligence not deal with him? Its failure to spot and neutralise him would constitute yet another failure for MI5, with Putlitz joining the band of moles and agents who slipped through the net during the war (an issue dealt with later in the section on MI5). The third major question is why, when his memoirs were published in

1957, were his British associates not interrogated? This, too, is an MI5 matter. And, fourth, what ought the Putlitz saga to have told MI6 about the German dimension to secret political intelligence?

It has to be said at the outset that it is not the facts of Putlitz's case that are in dispute but their interpretation.[19] Putlitz, in his early days, had been a keen supporter of the German revolution of 1918–19 and was known as 'das rote Puttchen' or the little red chicken. While his support for the German revolution in no way proves that he was a Communist sympathiser (for the revolution was supported by the German Socialists as well as the Communists), Putlitz did admit to Communist sympathies at this time and refused to use arms, as ordered, in putting down a Communist insurrection in Munich in 1919.

Yet subsequently, on the eve of Hitler's accession to power in 1933, Putlitz claimed:

> There could only be catastrophe ... there were only two great powers among the people which could revolutionise Germany, the Nazis and the Communists. Of the Communists I knew nothing ...[20]

Putlitz's plea that he was ignorant about Communism was rather peculiar. For not only, on his own admission, had he gained first-hand experience of it, but he also states that a close friend was a Communist.

Putlitz became a career diplomat and appeared to accept the Nazi take-over in 1933. Secretly, however, he began to supply British Intelligence with excellent information about German rearmament (some of this information actually reached Winston Churchill) and when, in 1939, Putlitz realised that war would shortly break out, it was MI6 in the person of the hapless Captain Stevens who arranged for him to leave Holland (see p. 164).

Once in England, Putlitz wrote that he renewed his friendship with a 'British intelligence officer'. In his memoirs, Putlitz gives him a pseudonym ('Tom Allen').[21] According to Chapman Pincher, Allen was none other than Anthony Blunt, who put him up in the famous flat near the British Museum belonging to fellow-MI5 officer Lord Rothschild. It seems hard to dispute this interpretation, for the text matches what we know about Blunt at this time. There is also a further reason to believe that Allen was Blunt. Putlitz's book was dedicated to:

Lord and Lady Vansittart, Sir Colville Barclay, Colonel Graham Christie and Mr Anthony Blunt whose kindness and understanding I will never forget ...[22]

Putlitz believed very firmly that the German Socialists were to be castigated as 'appeasers' of Hitler, and he was determined to help those who took the same view (a curious coalition, as it happened, running from the extreme left through to people such as Lord Vansittart).[23] Indeed, it was for this reason that Putlitz began to supply material to Vansittart personally. At this point Putlitz's actions begin to take on sinister overtones. For as we have seen, the German Communists were determined to oust the German Socialists as the chief spokesmen of the German working class. And the German Socialists soon proved to bear the brunt of Vansittart's ill-conceived diatribes against the wickedness of the German race. Putlitz claims that he enjoyed a close relationship with Vansittart and he clearly shared Vansittart's views about the German Socialists. Thus, and this is what is so remarkable, Vansittart quite unwittingly, but most effectively, supported the Communists in their fight against Social Democracy (something that helped the Communists in East Germany after 1945).

Of course none of this means that Putlitz definitely was a secret Communist (even if he was taking the Communist line). After all, Lord Vansittart was of the same opinion but he was plainly no Communist. What is far more incriminating is that as early as 1939 Putlitz was on record as having urged the British Government to set up a Free German Committee in London, 'to discuss the mobilisation of resistance inside Germany'. Since these Free Committees were simply front organisations for the Communists (analogous to National Committees in Moscow), this strongly suggests that Putlitz was, by the outbreak of war, on the receiving end of instructions from Moscow; by now he was almost certainly either a Communist or a Fellow-Traveller.

His friendship with Blunt may thus have been based on this shared faith in Communism. But the 'little red chicken' had another interest in common with Anthony Blunt; both were homosexuals. Indeed, Putlitz had managed to get the British to grant a passport to his 'servant' Willi at the same time as one was prepared for him.

Yet Putlitz soon decided to quit Britain. Thanks to his close friendship with Vansittart, he knew the British Government had absolutely no intention of forming a Free German Committee, and

Putlitz may well have decided that his friendship with Vansittart was more useful than trying to plug something which would not happen and which might well destroy that friendship. Putlitz (and Willi) set off for America where they did participate in various Free German enterprises. Indeed, Putlitz admits that:

One day I heard on the wireless from Moscow [!!] that a National Committee of Free Germany was to be formed. The very next day I got going. I wrote in German greetings messages to the German Committee and sent it with a letter to the Soviet Consul in New York ... shortly afterwards, I found myself in his study ... I felt he not only understood my point of view but was in sympathy with it. He told me simply, 'We shall utterly defeat the Nazis and after we have done that we shall help to build up a new Germany. But that task must really be undertaken by the German people ... so we shall be glad to help every sincere anti-Nazi German ...[24]

For reasons that are not entirely clear, Putlitz soon returned to England. If he was a secret Communist, it may be assumed that he did so on orders from Moscow. Once there, we know that Blunt installed him at Woburn Abbey under the tutelage of Sefton Delmer (see p. 148). They seem to have had a rare old time – 'all day long the news came rolling in to us from the British Intelligence Service' – but sadly 'Tom Allen' had been transferred to SHAEF.

Why did Putlitz reveal all of this if it was truly as incriminating as it seems? The simple answer appears to be that once his double life for the Russians was over, he was, like Philby (and others), ordered by the Russians to fulfil one further useful mission. By publishing an account of his career, he could cause severe embarrassment to British Intelligence, by pointing out that he, a defector to the East (and probably a covert Communist), had been repeatedly helped by their officers. This theory is supported by the fact that Putlitz published an English version of his book, which he was under no obligation to do as he had, apparently, severed all links with Britain almost ten years earlier.

As we can readily see, if Putlitz was, as I believe, a secret Communist, his case bears many of the hallmarks of Communist subversion: the National Committee ploy, the faithful rendering of the Soviet line on Germany and Europe and, most startling of all, the fact that whether Communist or not, someone who was politically unreliable (on account of his homosexuality if nothing else) had gained admission into the British intelligence community. Finally, there seems to be an intimation that, like Otto John, Putlitz was being encouraged by a person or persons within intelligence to return to Germany and continue to act ostensibly for MI6 but in reality for the KGB.

Thus it was that in 1946 Putlitz set off for Germany (sharing his Harwich–Hoek berth with Albert Pierpont, the British Government hangman who was also en route to Germany for a rather different purpose).[25] Putlitz was employed as a translator for the British and, after an attempt to find a post as a diplomat in Berlin, he met Blunt, who seems to have encouraged him to persevere with his attempts to get into the German administration, and so Putlitz set off for Bonn.

There is one important bit of documentary evidence about this stage of Putlitz's life that is worth pondering on. Although a number of people have been intrigued by the Putlitz saga, their accounts have been largely based on his own memoirs. Since these may have been written for evil purposes, there is no reason to believe all they say (although in my own view their purpose was to embarrass British Intelligence by being entirely truthful about the things chosen for revelation). But in the Foreign Office papers there is clear proof not only of Putlitz's status but also that he was indeed both a good friend of Vansittart and held in high esteem by the Foreign Office. However, the evidence also suggests that someone was trying to block Putlitz's plans for high office, and it is by no means implausible to believe that that someone was Roger Hollis, who was one of the few British Intelligence officers aware of the dangers implicit in the Free Committees concept which Putlitz had so keenly supported.

On 1 August 1946 Putlitz wrote to Vansittart from an address in Kiel:

> My Dear Van: I wonder whether Saville received my letter where I told her about the dreadful misfortune which made me a total beggar overnight. It seems quite certain that my entire luggage has been stolen and will never be found again. It handicaps my official standing as my compatriots are all apt to say, 'What is being dumped here? Probably they are glad to be rid of him?' I only mention this because I want to make something clear which is fundamentally more important: things are drifting into a state which will be fatal not only to me but also to you ... For the British I am a German and therefore not trustworthy as a matter

of principle. For the Germans I am a traitor, at least a Junker with a title and therefore suspicious. The fact that I stood up against the Nazis means nothing – in many ways it is even a handicap . . . With all my love, Wolfgang.[26]

At any rate Putlitz soon decided that:

In the eyes of some of the British, if I was not a Nazi then I must be a Communist. I began to feel I should take the plunge and turn . . . to the East.[27]

In the summer of 1950 Putlitz stated that he contacted the Soviet Consul in New York and that after an interview he decided to 'go to the East'. Yet it was to be two years before he finally took the plunge.

It is possible that Putlitz was entirely innocent of the charge of Communism. In its obituary of him, *Der Spiegel*, the German news magazine, argued that Putlitz had returned to his hereditary home village of Putlitz, in Potsdam, not because he was the 'Red Baron', but because he was given a job in the National Council of the National Front (the organisation which regulated party affairs in the German Democratic Republic). Furthermore, *Der Spiegel* concluded somewhat obscurely, his brother had died in 1948 and, since geese had lived in Putlitz for 800 years, a Putlitz had to live there too (*Gans* is the German word for goose).[28] Yet even *Der Spiegel* realised that this explanation was a trifle thin. For it pointed out that it was peculiar that he had gone to the Communist puppet state of East Germany, where his brother had died in prison and from where anyone with any sense was trying to escape.

There is, on the other hand, much circumstantial evidence to link Putlitz with the cause of secret Communism. Several of Putlitz's contacts in post-war Germany believed he had been 'serving two masters at once', though he had never been pinned down.[29]

According to Michael Graf Soltikow, Putlitz had been blackmailed into working for the Communists while in London, on account of his homosexuality. Communist agents had somehow discovered that his servant Willi was in fact a surrogate wife and threatened that he would be denounced to the British police unless he co-operated.[30]

There is one additional piece of circumstantial evidence. Putlitz was certainly in contact with known Communist moles. He mentions in his memoirs, for example, that in London in the summer of 1950:

I ran once again into Guy Burgess, one of the most controversial characters of modern England. I had known him on and off for 25 years. We had first met in 1932 at a party in Cambridge. I was, I remember, immediately fascinated by him because he was one of the first Englishmen of good family I had ever met who seemed really to have made a study of Marxism [that 'really' implies that Putlitz too had made a study of Marxism] ... He never revealed to me the true depth of his political opinions ...[31]

Putlitz then met Burgess again during the 1930s and in 1940 when Burgess was working, so Putlitz thought, both for British Intelligence and the BBC. Burgess invited Putlitz to spend the weekend with him on several occasions at Rothschild's house in Regent's Park.

Putlitz adds:

The last time I saw him was in 1949 or 1950 ... at his farewell party ... [at which] Hector McNeil, the Minister of State for Foreign Affairs, as well as several other high officials of the Foreign Office and members of the Intelligence services [were also present]. It was a very gay party.[32]

Hans Frederik states that Putlitz was also introduced to Otto John at this time and became very friendly with him.[33] Otto John has confirmed his friendship with Putlitz and adds that Putlitz had been extremely cross 'not to have been given a permanent post in the British secret service'.[34] John did not want him in his own secret service either, ostensibly because Putlitz had an 'English passport'. It is more likely, however, that John realised that he would himself be seen to be acting oddly in giving a British reject a post. Indeed, in March 1954 when Putlitz was on one of his visits to the West, John claims he warned 'the chief of English security', presumably Dick White, that Putlitz had re-surfaced in Bonn. Much to John's surprise, he was told that it was of no interest to British Intelligence. Of course, had Putlitz been interrogated, he might have revealed Blunt's identity and thus the nature of Blunt's own work for the Communists. If MI5 truly was not interested in Putlitz, this was indeed a slip-up.

It is obviously important to stress that guilt by association is not a reliable method of proceeding in intelligence matters. After all, any self-respecting mole was bound to have as many important friends as he could, none of whom were meant to realise that he was a mole and none of whom may have been sympathetic towards him. Yet Putlitz's circle of friends was an unusual one and MI5 ought to have taken a closer look at it.

Leo Long in Germany

Another curious case has been revealed by Michael Thomas, who was a German political exile who returned to Germany in 1945 to help rebuild his country. His line was that the Germans ought to be encouraged to see the British as their friends. His work was not easy and one of the major obstacles to it was a lieutenant working in British Security by the name of Leo Long. Long's superior, incidentally, was said by Thomas to be a 'Brigadier Williams'. In fact, we now know that this was none other than Dick White, on secondment to military intelligence at this time and engaged in the secret hunt for Hitler (see p. 288). Long was, of course, publicly indicted by Nigel West in November 1981 of having been a Soviet agent, a charge that Long admitted.

Long, Thomas wrote, was a brilliant man who hated him and what he stood for.[35] Long repeatedly told Thomas the Germans would have to reckon with decades of being ruled by the British, and he made it his personal business to make life difficult for Thomas whenever he could. Thomas concludes that Long did not wish to promote the fortunes of Germans who wanted the West to be seen as an ally.

The Long story is also an integral part of the German dimension to British Intelligence. Long had worked in a division of MI5 which had dealt with German troop movements, and had then been seconded to British Intelligence in Germany. He had been recruited by Blunt in the 1930s (Blunt had supervised his French studies at Cambridge), and either Straight or Blunt or both, it appears, had exposed him to MI5 in 1964. During the war, Long may well have passed individual pieces of Ultra information to the Russians. Blunt met him regularly throughout this period. It has even been suggested that Blunt tried to persuade Long to seek a permanent post within MI5 to ensure that the Kremlin would continue to possess a mole there after Blunt's return to the art world. Long's ability and ruthlessness would certainly have made him a senior officer in due course.

Unlike Blunt, Long appears to have tried to get back into MI5 but to have been rejected.[36]

The Otto John saga: the post-war years; high noon for Otto John; the case against Otto John

If Otto John is to be believed, his case is a terrible example of the way in which guilt by association can have the most appalling consequences in the 'wilderness of mirrors' which makes up the secret intelligence world. For John ascribes most of his problems directly to his relationship with Kim Philby. The irony of this is that John claims that he only discovered that he had had a relationship with Philby in the late 1960s when British journalists explained that the man who had handled his material during the war was none other than the most important of all the Soviet moles.

After the end of the war, John worked in various capacities for the British.[37] It has been said that he was given a job thanks to vigorous lobbying by Sir John Wheeler-Bennett, for whom Otto John had done first-rate research work (particularly in connection with his masterly study on the German Army, *The Nemesis of Power*).

John went to Germany in the guise of a war reporter, but he seems to have been engaged to spy on the future German political class. His knack for getting to know important people was doubtless a useful asset. He then returned to England where he came into contact once again with Hugh Greene of the BBC. He was subsequently sent back to Germany where he assisted with the trials of German war criminals, including von Manstein, von Brauchitsch and von Rundstedt.[38] John had been able to prove that von Manstein had known about the extermination of the Jews, by careful attention to a detailed entry in his war diary. However, John also helped defend people: he tried to help Ernst von Weizsaecker (the father of the subsequent West German President, on trial for having helped the SS with the extermination of the Jews, for which he was found guilty).[39]

In 1950 John's career once again took a dramatic, if somewhat murky, turn. For rather suddenly he became head of the West German version of MI5, the BfV, and by virtue of this one of the most senior figures in Western Intelligence, working at the heart of its operations against Communist subversion.

John's version of his appointment[40] was that it emerged out of a friendship with Theodor Heuss, the first West German President. Heuss was a friend of a woman by the name of Lucie Manen, who was later to become John's wife. Heuss told John (according to John himself) that he had taken a liking to him and wished to promote his fortunes. Then, in October 1950, John went to meet Heuss once again in order to introduce John Wheeler-Bennett to him. The previous day, John had discussed a possible post with Jakob Kaiser, the leader of the Berlin Christian Democrats, the CDU. The CDU was, of course, also the party of Konrad Adenauer, but Kaiser was a political enemy of his (and John too thought Adenauer hated him).

Kaiser recommended John to apply for the job of head of the BfV, and indeed wrote supporting his application to the Federal Minister for the Interior, Robert Lehr. John was also, perhaps not surprisingly, able to enlist the support of the Federal President. There can be no doubt that Kaiser did press John's claims, as has been confirmed by Kaiser's then private secretary, Ludwig Freiherr von Hammerstein-Equord.[41]

By this time, West Germany was in the process of receiving full domestic sovereignty, which meant that it would also have to be responsible for its own domestic security and counter-espionage work. Now John has claimed (and the point is important) that *despite* the efforts of British Intelligence to destroy his reputation, he managed to be given the job.[42] About twelve other candidates had already been interviewed and rejected: the thirteenth, John, was successful.

John's brief was very similar to that given to the Director General of MI5, upon which the BfV was modelled.[43] As BfV chief, John's conduct became increasingly bizarre. This is something that even his friends admit, ascribing it to excessive drinking due to his feeling that he was simply not up to the job. Those who find this explanation unconvincing point to the fact that John's competence before 1950, as far as secret intelligence was concerned, was obviously very highly regarded by the British. As for his drinking, this may well have had something to do with strains of a very different nature, for by this time John was himself under surveillance by the CIA.

From his own evidence, John concentrated on the perceived neo-Nazi threat to the Bonn Republic. What happened next is a matter of fierce debate, and real and threatened libel actions. According to one of the many powerful British supporters of John's position, Hugh Trevor-Roper, John had been 'in touch' with British Intelligence ever since 1942, warning of the various plots against Hitler. Now, in the early 1950s, John saw it as his patriotic duty to warn the British about what he saw as the growing threat of a Nazi revival in Germany, which Trevor-Roper claims was being condoned by none other than the Chancellor, Konrad Adenauer.

John, Trevor-Roper suggests, had blotted his copy-book in Aden-auer's terms by helping the British prosecute Nazi war criminals:

> Naturally, these activities did not commend him to those whose ideas about Nazism were more tolerant than his and of whom Dr Adenauer would be more tolerant than he.[44]

When it came to setting up the BfV:

> The old opponents of Nazism were naturally anxious to ensure that this appointment should not fall into sinister hands and who ... could be more appropriate than one of the few survivors of the active opposition against Hitler. Adenauer did not relish the appointment but he had to accept it ... It was particularly dis-tasteful to the most famous and successful of the survivors of the old Nazis and pro-Nazis, Reinhard Gehlen, who was now seeking American support to become the head of a new German secret service and who would not scruple to incorporate into it old associates in the Nazi party and SS ...[45]

Trevor-Roper thus paints a picture which is based on the theory that John represented anti-Nazi virtue against what amounts to a conspiracy led by Adenauer to give prominent positions of power in the new German state to former and pro-Nazis. If nothing else, this was a novel variant upon the mole theme; in this case, John was a virtuous mole, trying to undermine a wicked West German Govern-ment led by Adenauer. To attack Adenauer in this way was a serious travesty of the facts. However, the fear of a neo-Nazi revival, which was something of a canard, was one particularly popular in Britain where people such as Lord Beaverbrook and Sefton Delmer made easy money out of it (see p. 234).

For Otto John, matters came to a head in July 1954. We shall begin with Trevor-Roper's version: after attending a celebration for the tenth anniversary of the Generals Plot against Hitler:

> John left his hotel in West Berlin and did not return. The Bonn

Government was alarmed: both defections and kidnappings had happened lately in that still unwalled city. The disappearance of an important Federal Official, the head of its internal secret service, was therefore very sinister. Only one official could devise any satisfaction from it. That happy officer was General Gehlen. Asked for an opinion about John, Gehlen spoke clearly, 'once a traitor, always a traitor'. A few days later Gehlen's happiness was increased when John held a press conference in East Berlin at which he made statements satisfactory to the Russians. From that moment on, John was written off as a defector . . .[46]

John's supporters argue that he had been kidnapped by the East Germans. He was taken to East Berlin and then obliged to play along with the Communists in order to avoid execution.

John's explanation for his 'kidnapping' is that for a period of years he had been under medical surveillance by a Dr Wohlgemuth who had also prescribed him certain pills, allegedly to test his resistance to them. On 20 July 1954, John went to see Wohlgemuth (who lived in East Berlin but had an office in the West) to get a medical certificate for a third party; John was then drugged and taken unconscious across the Iron Curtain. He did not know why he had been abducted, but soon realised that unless he was to play the game the East German Communists would kill him. He made a series of public statements, including one on the radio when he claimed that Adenauer was a neo-Nazi revanchist, which John later alleged was 'a really big lie' designed to show people in the West that he was acting under duress.

Yet according to Trevor-Roper and many others, John actually believed the things he was saying in East Berlin. Thus if John was telling the truth in his book, he must have lied to Trevor-Roper about this same matter. If, on the other hand, John was not telling the truth in his book, then what he said in East Berlin was a frank account of what he truly thought about Adenauer.

John always asserted that what he had said in the East was not meant to be taken seriously, that it was common practice for Western intelligence services to tell their agents that if they were kidnapped they were to follow the Soviet line and not do anything of a daredevil nature. Clifton Child, who worked for many years in the Foreign Office (and who is convinced of John's complete innocence; see p. 243), has written:

It was a cardinal principle of Western intelligence at the time that if ever caught by the Soviets, you did not scream defiance, which would have been useless, but strung along with them as much as possible, and, above all, mouthed their clichés against the West if they ever gave you a chance of airing your views in the press or on the radio. I well remember teaching myself to refer to American friends almost instinctively as 'trans-Atlantic cannibals'. By the careful use of such jargon, you could at least let your friends know that you would be back at the first opportunity.[47]

From this it would follow that John was an admirer of Adenauer and that his repeated calls for German unity from East Berlin (echoing the Communist policy on this) were intended to imply support for a divided Germany. Since, however, John despised Adenauer and wanted a reunified Germany, his East Berlin words were quite genuine.

John's shakiness on the whole question of his supposed abduction has clearly embarrassed other supporters. Phillip Whitehead, for example, who has made a careful study of the John case and is convinced that John is innocent, nevertheless argues that he was not initially abducted but went of his own free will.[48] Yet Whitehead deems him to have been *de facto* abducted, because he was not allowed back. This is not and never has been John's version, so it is plain that even Whitehead assumes that John is capable of lying. In fact, there seems to be watertight proof that John was not abducted to East Berlin (see p. 237).

An interesting additional piece of evidence on this aspect of the case has come from Sefton Delmer. For he was one of two Western journalists invited to East Berlin to hear John's press conference and afterwards have a private lunch with him. Later he stated quite categorically that John was *compos mentis* and not acting under duress.

However, the following year, when John returned to the West Delmer decided to change his testimony. He now said that he had been quite wrong, and it was clear that John had not been a free agent but acting out of fear for his life.

There are two highly suspicious points about Delmer's volte-face. The first is that what John stated in East Berlin, about Adenauer and West Germany being the prelude to a Fourth neo-Nazi Reich, corresponded very closely to what we know was Delmer's own viewpoint, as expressed repeatedly in the columns of the *Daily*

Express. Furthermore, Delmer was often briefed by John before 1954 and John was the source of many of his articles. Thus Delmer's verdict of '*compos mentis*' was hardly surprising, since if what John had said was proof of his being coerced by the Communists, then Delmer's own articles became highly suspect. Indeed, the British Foreign Office noted that:

> Delmer is a popular contributor to the East German press ... there is a marked similarity between Delmer's articles and John's press statements in East Berlin ... they are both pursuing the same ends ...[49]

Delmer's entire role in this affair is capable of an even graver interpretation than a desire to substantiate his ridiculous reports. For if we posit that John was a mole, and indeed that Delmer was one also, then Delmer's line in 1954 and his line after 1955 (which contradicted each other) were actually connected by one common thread: the need on the part of the Communists to give credibility to John's statements. In 1954 Delmer would have been instructed to ensure that maximum credibility was accorded to John's East Berlin statements, because to call them into question would naturally have destroyed their considerable propaganda impact.

Equally, on John's return, to have argued that John had been *compos mentis* would have destroyed John's defence and all his subsequent attempts at misinformation. It is worth noting that many of Delmer's own dispatches from Germany fitted in neatly with the general Soviet propaganda line on West Germany: that it was a revanchist neo-Nazi State with hostile ambitions (thus obliging the USSR to keep a large army in its European satellite countries). It is therefore not implausible to argue that the Delmer of PWE and the Delmer of the 1950s are part of the same phenomenon: Delmer the mole.

Let us now turn to the evidence that can be adduced against John himself. If it should prove convincing, it not only depicts John in an unfavourable light, but also raises very serious questions about MI6's support for him. It is vitally important to realise that in order to 'start a spy case' against someone, one needs clear evidence both of subversion and of a motive. In addition, in this case one has to be able to demonstrate a direct link between John and Communist intelligence.

This formulation, it should be added, is not the historian's but the actual formulation used by former MI5 and MI6 officers. There is indeed clear evidence of all three elements: John seems to have defected to the East, his motive was self-stated, namely the destruction of Adenauer's policy of resisting the Soviet plan for German reunification and for binding the Federal Republic to the West, and there was a direct link between John and Communist intelligence – certainly in John's close friendship with Wohlgemuth and, in my own view, equally certainly with Putlitz.

During the early 1950s, it could be asserted, the strain of living a double life began to take its toll and John started drinking. We know that American Intelligence (though, significantly, not MI6) had noticed this drinking and also the fact that John had suspicious friendships. Furthermore, Adenauer and his Interior Minister Gerhard Schröder had already indicated that they wished to dismiss John, because of his 'unreliability', once West Germany achieved full sovereignty (hoped-for in 1953–4, but after the failure of the European Defence Treaty not achieved until 1955). John certainly chose to defect at a most critical time, at the precise moment the French Parliament was about to ratify this treaty, which would have permitted West Germans to rearm. By defecting when he did Otto John achieved two things: he assisted the Communist propaganda offensive which alleged that the West Germans should not be allowed to rearm (so contributing to the French decision not to ratify the treaty) and, second, his defection seriously undermined the standing of the BfV and of British Intelligence, leading to further difficulties between Britain and America on this score.

Yet such an explanation begs one vital question. Why did Otto John come back? For one of the riddles of the John case has always been that he returned from the East in the December of 1955, on the very day the Bundestag enquiry into his disappearance was due to start. His return led to his arrest and John was sentenced on 22 December 1956 to four years' gaol (two more than the prosecution had asked for).

Further light on the case against Otto John has been shed by the release of British records relating to the summer of 1954.[50] In effect, the British and the West German Government collaborated in what some would call a damage-limiting exercise and others a cover-up. What seems to have happened is that, on learning of John's defection, Adenauer almost at once decided to argue that he had been abducted in order to spare the British authorities any embarrassment. For Adenauer knew that John had been pushed into the post of BfV boss, not least (and perhaps most importantly) because he was the nominee of British Intelligence. To state publicly that John had defected would suggest that British Intelligence had injected a Communist mole into the West German security service and raise other questions as well. Both the British and West Germans would appear in a very poor light: the British for forcing Adenauer to accept someone who was a Communist mole, and Adenauer for being so willing to please the British that he took someone he did not really trust. In this way, to claim that John had been abducted made considerable sense.

Yet having come out with this story both Bonn and London found themselves obliged to stick to it, despite the fact that John gave every indication that he was a defector out to damage West Germany in public, and thus even more gravely in private, by telling the Communists all they wanted to know about British and West German Intelligence and counter-intelligence.

At the same time, however, it seems plausible to believe that the Western cover-up (which was a sign of its vulnerability) gave the KGB a marvellous, if daring, brainwave. Had John been termed a defector by the West at once, his propaganda value in the East would have been minimal. However, the claim of abduction gave the KGB two almost incredible opportunities. For one thing, it would mean that John could be used for propaganda purposes after all (if the West said he had been abducted, all the East Germans had to do was to prove that he was a free agent). Second, when the time seemed ripe, John could return to the West.

This in turn would allow the KGB to continue to use John in the West to undermine the standing of Western Intelligence by the spreading of deliberate misinformation. For we should not forget that no one has a greater interest in the weakening of morale and the public standing of MI5 and MI6 than the KGB, and that 'revelations' about the incompetence of Western Intelligence, particularly through 'autobiographical' accounts, are an excellent device for achieving this. This is shown by the works of Philby and almost certainly by those of Putlitz and perhaps John himself, not to mention other, more recent 'revelations'.

There was another advantage, too. This was that John's return to the West might forestall a major investigation by the West into the intelligence and security services, which would (if done properly) identify a number of moles, of whom the most important was of course Kim Philby himself, who had been associated with John since the war. Naturally, the KGB could not have foreseen a trial, although it has to be emphasised that John's trial was not actually a trial for treason, so the KGB did get that bit of it right.

This story can be traced through documentary evidence from the Public Record Office. The British originally thought that John had been kidnapped but, almost immediately this view was sent to London, another version was wired by the British High Commissioner, Sir Frederick Hoyer Millar (now Lord Inchyra). This version said that it had now been established that before John had left for East Berlin he had visited a man called Wohlgemuth, 'a man of known Communist tendencies', although the British still assumed the visit had been unpremeditated. However, it was clear that John had not been drugged – 'he walked normally and of his own volition. Although there is a probability that he was drugged, it looks most probable that he went of his own accord.'

Yet a third telegram on the same day introduced a new element into the story: the interests of the German Government. Professor Walter Hallstein, Adenauer's close adviser, came to see Hoyer Millar:

Hallstein, with whom we have discussed this at length, thinks it preferable to take the line with the Press that he was abducted. You will, I hope, also follow this line. [Furthermore] it seems desirable that we should as far as possible play down John's contacts with the Western Allies although certain facts will of course come out . . .[51]

There are two things to note about all of this. First, the British were putting out a story (and continued to put out a story) which they knew to be a lie. John had not been drugged and abducted but had gone of his own free will. Some days later, the West Berlin border police informed the British Government that they recalled John and Wohlgemuth's car passing the checkpoint and that the two men were smiling cheerfully as they were waved past.

This latter finding was confirmed in 1959 with the publication of the memoirs of Peter Deriabin, a Soviet defector.[52] Deriabin had been one of the case officers dealing with Germany who had access to John's file. He defected to the West in February 1954 and stated categorically that John had not been kidnapped but defected because the KGB had material about him purporting to show that he had been a Nazi agent.[53]

The second thing to note is the British Government's anxiety about 'John's contacts with the Western Allies' and 'certain facts'. This factor continued to play its part in British thinking. Although in due course the British were able to say (in private) that:

As we have throughout feared, [John's broadcast] suggests John has defected ...

they still wanted to claim that:

It seems desirable to play down as much as possible John's defection both from a political and technical point of view.

They still insisted on stating that John had been abducted:

Despite the fact that the latest evidence suggests quite the contrary ... West German customs officials checked the progress of the two men and described them as 'normal, indeed cheerful'.[54]

The question is thus raised what these 'certain facts' were. As we have already indicated, they were straightforward and had to do with John's appointment. As the documents reveal, although the West Germans were allowed to put forward names, they all had to be approved by the Allied Directors of Intelligence:

This procedure was followed in the case of Otto John. The German Government put forward about a dozen names for the Head of the Agency, to all of whom there were objections. They then put forward John's name and no Allied objection was raised.[55]

As this document shows, this was an MI6 issue. Since John had worked for MI6, the only Allied intelligence organisation which could possibly take a view on John was MI6. As the most senior MI6 officer to have dealt with John, it seems plain that the person who would have been asked for the 'Office view' upon him would have been Kim Philby, and it would therefore follow logically that the British attitude towards the head of the BfV would have been formulated largely by Philby himself. In addition, John's claim that British Intelligence tried to prevent his appointment can be seen as a fabrication (see p. 230).

The KGB's idea (if it existed) of pushing John back into the West to forestall any investigation of MI6's support for John was clearly a desperate move. For MI6, and indeed MI5, had already by this time begun to entertain serious doubts about Philby. In 1950, when John was appointed, Philby was still the heir-apparent, the first 'C' to be coming from within the Service. By 1954, however, former MI5 and MI6 officers have stated that both Dick White and Roger Hollis in MI5 believed that Philby was an agent of the KGB. But they had been unable to provide any proof or to undermine Philby's position. He had, of course, been forced to resign from MI6. Yet he still enjoyed the full support of Sinclair, the 'C' of MI6, who even found a part-time salary for him.

Although Philby was safe as long as the 'C' was Sinclair, when, in 1955, Dick White became 'C', John's return to the West may once again have postponed Philby's day of reckoning.

If John was a mole or agent, he was almost certainly recruited by Philby in 1944 or spotted as a likely Communist sympathiser far earlier. He was then carefully built up in order to become a nominee for a sensitive post in the fledgling Republic. Against this harsh verdict, we must of course put the whole host of theories (some more obscure than others) which have been put forward to explain John's actions in a light favourable to him. They range from the discovery of new suspects[56] to the fact that John took no papers with him. It is true that John left his personal papers in his hotel room, but if he had been stopped by the Allied authorities with his pockets full of secret material he would have been arrested at once. In any case, if he were a mole, there would not be any need to take his notes with him, for the Russians would have them already.

Others have said that John's real purpose was to achieve German reunification. He fled when he did, they allege, because he was genuinely worried that Adenauer's policy of Western alignment would prevent it. It is certainly true that while in East Germany, John went to visit Field Marshall von Paulus (who had been captured by the Russians at Stalingrad) in an attempt to make a joint plea for German unity, and that John's insistence that his major concern was a reunified Germany was something he repeatedly emphasised.

Indeed, one former MI6 officer, who confessed to still being uncertain about John, made the point that a German going to East Berlin was not totally the same as a German going to Moscow. He thought it feasible that John had really wanted to prevent the division of Germany.[57]

Yet while it is true that the German issue is a complicated one, there is a certain naivety about this proposition. Although before the uprising of 1953, East Germany could just possibly have been regarded as a 'Socialist German State', after its bloody repression it was impossible to dispute that it was, in fact, a Soviet puppet State using Russian tanks to stay in power. No one ought to have known this better than the head of West Germany's security service. The Russians controlled political life in every way, not least by virtue of the National Front organisation for which Putlitz worked (see p. 226). What is more, John must also have known his call from East Berlin for reunification implied reunification on Soviet terms, which was that Germany could only be reunited if it renounced its political links with the Western liberal democracies. Indeed, in detailed terms, John's proposals quite consciously echoed the German National Committee concept, something John himself underlined by going to von Paulus while in East Germany. Von Paulus had been one of the original supporters of the National Committee for Free Germany set up in Moscow in 1943 (see p. 192).

The stark truth is that the 'misguided patriot' thesis does not stand up, either in terms of sheer common sense or in terms of John's own story. Not only were there many other places where John could have gone in order to plead the cause of German unity more effectively than East Berlin, but also any genuine patriot anxious to promote his cause would know that a base in East Berlin would cast doubt on such a patriot's true motives, for it was hardly an appropriate place to launch a campaign to unite the nation.

Indeed, the British archives provide evidence concerning John's view of East Germany which itself raises the most serious doubts about John's allegiance to the West. For in the papers of the Foreign Office, there are reports from John about the East German uprising in 1953 which appear, on the face of it, to be deliberate distortions of the truth. Furthermore, these distortions all tended to throw the Soviet Union in a favourable light and thus downgrade the significance of those brave East Germans who tried to stage a revolt against the Soviet control of their country.[58]

Finally, when the appearance of Soviet tanks on the streets of East Berlin made it clear that John had offered the British a 'misreading' of the situation, John appears simply to have said nothing.[59]

As far as John himself is concerned, the detailed evidence tends to confirm the view that he was a Communist mole. Yet it has been contested. Fritz Tobias, for example, whose work on the Reichstag fire has been widely praised and who knew John well, was also a BfV officer, based in Lower Saxony. In a note prepared for me, Tobias states unequivocally that in his view John was not a Communist agent but simply an 'idiot'. He had personally worked together with John and he had been 'ashamed about him because his behaviour was quite inconsistent with his high office'. Other colleagues in the BfV with whom Tobias discussed this had noted the same thing: John was often drunk, indeed so drunk that he would fall asleep at crucial meetings and in court. He was also consistently badly informed and obviously uninterested in what was going on.[60]

Tobias accounts for John's state by claiming that John never wanted to be BfV Chief but was forced to take the job 'because Heuss and the British insisted. Their motive was probably that co-operation with John would not cause any problems!'

Tobias further relates that at the gathering on 20 July 1954 before he went to East Berlin, John had openly wept, partly because he grieved for his dead brother, partly because he knew that Schröder was after his blood. These two factors, Tobias argues, forced the 'labile and possibly bi-sexual John' to accept Wohlgemuth's 'crack-pot scheme' (*Schnappsidee*) to go to East Berlin. Tobias adds that at this time many drunken West Germans tottered across the border. Furthermore, thanks to the Communist agent Heinz Felfe (who was sentenced to a long prison sentence) John was of no use to the East Germans in any case.

John, Tobias concludes, was not unintelligent and did not lack ability but he would have preferred a post with Lufthansa, and thus sought solace in alcohol. Yet as we have seen, the drinking might have been an indication of the stresses of a double life: Burgess, Maclean, Philby, even Michael Bettaney exhibited extreme drunkenness. Indeed, John's subsequent BfV colleague and co-defector, Hans Joachim Tiedge, got so drunk that his driving licence was revoked.

As for the point that the Communists already had an agent and therefore did not need another, the fact is that Heinz Felfe was in the BND, the German secret intelligence service, while John was in the BfV. The two services, like MI5 and MI6, had the closest links but quite different duties. Felfe was convicted in 1963 and exchanged in 1969. He then became, somewhat ironically, a professor of criminal law in East Germany and has recently published his 'autobiography'.[61] Rather interestingly, Felfe praises John as a 'democrat' but speaks of his 'mindless defection to East Berlin'. Bearing in mind that the KGB itself doubtless chose these phrases it is clear that the Russians wish to imply that John was both an idiot and a patriot: reason enough for treating both these views with suspicion.

As for John's dealings with Dr Wohlgemuth, they too suggest more than a mere friendship. At any rate, that was the view of the CIA (indeed the officer trailing John, Captain W. Hoefer, killed himself on 23 July 1954, presumably because he assumed his failure to arrest John following his visit to Wohlgemuth's office had been blameworthy). Besides, spy chiefs and security bosses are simply not ordinary citizens and cannot have Communist friends. If Sir Dick White or Sir Roger Hollis, for example, had been friendly with known Communists, this would have caused great damage to their authority and reputations.

It is of course just possible to argue, as John's supporters do, that John was a helpless pawn caught up in something he could not comprehend or control. Many people, such as Fritz Heine, who knew John reasonably well, while not knowing whether he was a mole, have argued that they could never understand what qualifications he possessed for his post.

Yet if we assume that John was totally unsuitable, not because he was a mole, but because he did not have the qualities a security service boss needs to possess, that in itself raises very awkward questions. For if John really was such a useless individual, why should the British reject twelve candidates for the BfV post in order to appoint him? The appointment of an incompetent but well-meaning fool to a sensitive post can mean only one thing: that someone or some people wished such a person to be head of the BfV. Since those people were clearly not German, they must have been English. And if they were English, who were they?

That there was a Philby dimension to John's case cannot be disputed. After all, John himself adduces the reason for his alleged abduction as a Soviet desire to discover whether Philby had remained true to the Soviet Union in 1944. For John claimed that, while in East Berlin, he was taken to Russia and interrogated about MI6 and its attitude towards the German opposition.[62] By confirming that MI6 had not accepted the John version of the status to be accorded to the German opposition, Moscow was able to confirm that Philby had done his duty and remained loyal to the KGB. It was, John says, only after a British journalist pointed out to him in 1967 that Philby had been the officer dealing with his case, that John appreciated the fact that the questions put to him in Moscow had all been concerned to test Philby's reliability. Until 1967 he had had no idea of Philby's identity.

This theory has been supported by Trevor-Roper.[63] However, it presupposes a number of contentious matters. First of all, it seems hard to believe that either at the time or later John did not know about Philby's interest in him or that Philby had been in charge of the Iberian section of MI6. For when John became BfV chief he had, by virtue of this post, become one of the most important figures in Western intelligence.

Clifton Child, however, has no doubt that the Philby alibi is true. Indeed, he himself believes that Philby played a most evil role in his own history. Child first met John in 1944 when he was taken to PWE at Woburn to work with Delmer. He has written:

Delmer did not have to warn me that John was in the greatest danger ... from an element within our own intelligence, section V of MI6. The latter was, as we now know, dominated by Philby and before the events of 20 July 1944 had been actively involved in trying to betray the main 'conspirators' to the Nazis. In John's case, they had invariably named him openly and consistently as the source of their supposedly secret reports from Spain and Portugal and in doing this, they knew full well that the contents of the reports would fall into the hands of the Gestapo ... it was because of this great danger to John and of the need to keep his presence amongst us as secret as possible [he was in fact given the cover name of Oskar Jürgens] that Delmer and I used all our influence to prevent John from openly broadcasting to the Germans an appeal in his own name ... I must say that my then chief Sefton Delmer behaved most honourably in all this, as he did in all matters relating to Dr John after the latter's post-war return to Germany. Delmer, a dedicated Tory, stood nobly by me, a life-long Socialist, whenever I came under attack from the Philby faction of MI6. I was put on a Soviet black list in my student days, when I was Secretary of the Socialist club at Birmingham University ...[64]

Yet if Child's broad approach is fair enough, his details are rather loose. For a start, while we would accept that any self-respecting mole would have betrayed John to the Germans, had John been what he said, no mole would have dreamt of betraying John had he been a Communist or a Communist sympathiser. The fact was that

John had not been betrayed and that Philby had been, if Trevor-Roper is right, in a position to do so ever since 1942. The merest whisper to the Gestapo would have sufficed to seal John's fate. There clearly was none.

Second, John would not have been allowed to broadcast under his own name in any case, as we have already examined. Third, it was not very likely that a mole in MI6 could have made life difficult for Child (or indeed John). It is far more likely that Child's troubles emanated from MI5, particularly, perhaps, from Anthony Blunt who we know was a respected visitor to Woburn. Indeed, it was Blunt who managed to get Delmer to take on Putlitz (see p. 224).

Finally, John did not have a bad time until 1954; he had an extremely good time as far as his contacts with British Intelligence were concerned, as we see from his appointment to one of the top intelligence posts in the Western world.

The Otto John saga has not been fully explained, either here or anywhere else. It probably never will be. It is clear that the case against John is extremely strong. But like so many spy cases, it is based on circumstantial evidence and not on hard proof. Furthermore, if he was a mole, that is to say, if he actually helped make and execute policy rather than just pass secrets to the Soviets, his own position would have allowed him to conceal important evidence which might subsequently have helped to incriminate him. Perhaps, of course, John was just a monumental idiot, although in that case one must continue to wonder why British Intelligence thought so highly of him.

Even if John was quite innocent his case still demonstrates that British Intelligence slipped up badly in the struggle against Communist subversion in general, and in the German dimension and the Kremlin's plans for Europe in particular.

Working together with the Russians: MI6 and the USSR

We have seen that, despite some real successes, particularly in terms of intercepted German wireless traffic, MI6 failed to alert British policy-makers to the specific dangers implicit in co-operating with Stalin in order to defeat Hitler's Third Reich. These dangers have been characterised as Stalin's secret blueprint for the extension of Soviet power westward, using the Red Army and the KGB to establish and maintain puppet regimes in the various nations of central and eastern Europe, regimes which had in many cases started life as 'National Committees' set up by the Kremlin in Moscow. It does not seem unfair to call this policy a subversive one, because it was executed in secret and without the knowledge of Russia's Allies, Great Britain and the United States of America. Like the injection of moles into the high offices of the British State, this policy was part and parcel of Communist subversion.

Furthermore, there is clear evidence of another form of Communist subversion, this time within MI6 itself, where the certain existence of at least one major long-term penetration agent, Kim Philby, and the probable existence of a number of others gave the Russian leaders enormous advantages in the secret campaigns of the Second World War.

There are, therefore, two vitally important questions which must now be addressed. First, why, precisely, did MI6 fail to provide British policy-makers with secret intelligence about Russia's plans? And, second, why was British Intelligence not aware of the fact that within its own ranks it concealed the agents of the Soviet Union?

To be sure, one answer has already been provided. For the subversion of MI6 in part explains why MI6 failed. Yet, as we have already noted, this is indeed only a very partial answer. Although Kim Philby, for example, was able to suppress information which, had it been passed on, might have alerted Whitehall to Stalin's aims, the information that came across Philby's desk was merely the tip of the iceberg, the ramifications of a central strategy as perceived from various oblique angles. Why, we must ask, did MI6 not provide secret intelligence whose direct source was Soviet Russia itself?

Today we know that there was no single explanation for this; it was a mixture of factors, ranging from the existence of subversion and errors of political judgment right through to British high policy, which dictated that the Soviet Union was to be treated as the full ally of Great Britain, with all that this entailed.

While good secret political intelligence might have strengthened the hand of those who urged a tougher line against Russia, and might have prompted Churchill, who clearly possessed his own rather vague suspicions, to be firmer over issues like a Western landing in the Balkans, the changed political climate which Churchill himself had managed to bring about in 1941 would have made such firmness very difficult, if not impossible, to achieve.

Nor should it be assumed that it was simply Anglo-Soviet relations which determined Britain's policy: the American input was also of supreme importance and it is too often forgotten that the American wartime Government of Franklin D. Roosevelt was adamant that the American demands for a good working relationship with the Soviet Union should not be challenged.

One view expressed by a number of former intelligence officers who worked together with Americans during the war was that their American colleagues often accused them of harbouring old-fashioned 'imperialist' attitudes towards Europe and Russia which, in order to co-operate closely with them, the British felt they had to be very careful to discard. As we shall see, American secret service co-operation with the USSR was taken as seriously by the Americans as by the British.

Simply because the climate of politics changed yet again after 1946, for perfectly justifiable reasons, it would be quite unhistorical on the British or the American part to deny that another climate had ever existed. Nevertheless, the fact remains that the biggest single reason why Stalin won the subversive war against the West from 1941 until 1945 was that he was able to exploit the British and American desire to treat him as a full ally.

Those believing that few changes would have been possible to British policy are supported by the existence of some very strong domestic factors. The first was that British policy was Winston Churchill's policy, and that it was developed for a whole host of reasons, of which the need to procure accurate intelligence about the Soviet Union was not one. Furthermore, the Anglo-Soviet Alliance was popular and it commanded the support of the vast majority of Britons. It is very hard indeed to believe that a tougher policy towards the Soviet Union before 1945 could ever have been justified to the British public.

The argument that policy based on intelligence was secret, and that it therefore could quite happily have contradicted public policy, is something that, while technically feasible, would not, in the view of the officers I spoke to, have been tolerated by British Intelligence chiefs. It was also highly dangerous, since if the Russians had discovered it, they might have withdrawn from the joint front against Hitler (although it has to be pointed out that Russia's discovery that she was being excluded from the nuclear project did not have this result).

Thus it must be stressed, and it has been accepted by leading figures in the British intelligence community, that Britain 'dropped its guard' (as did the USA) and that British ignorance about Stalin's true intentions could in theory have been avoided by a more thoughtful and aware programme of intelligence activity.

Without doubt the biggest single reason for British ignorance of Soviet motives was self-imposed and not the outcome of subversion. It was self-imposed in two major ways. First, on 22 June 1941 the decision was taken to stop decoding Soviet wireless traffic. Second, orders were given that, far from trying surreptitiously to get to the bottom of Soviet policy, British secret intelligence ought to ensure that it co-operated closely with its Soviet counterparts.

Both decisions have received far less scrutiny than they deserve. As far as the first is concerned, there are indeed those who do not believe it to be true, arguing that this has been stated merely to cover up British incompetence. Others have suggested that even if the first decision was implemented, it was in itself the outcome of subversion.[65] Both these theories seem untenable. The fact is that developments in modern technology, in particular the wireless – the most important potential source of intelligence – had, by the 1920s, created the ability to listen in on the radio messages of one's enemies. Indeed, it could be said that wireless traffic, consisting of military orders, of messages from agents to their controllers overseas, and of political intelligence from an Embassy to its Ministry at home, became the most important single object of all intelligence-gathering operations.

The advantages of such intelligence are obvious: agents do not have to be sent out in the field; it is possible to get far higher grade intelligence from, say, an Embassy's messages to a foreign affairs Ministry than from most agents. Indeed, in the particular case of the Soviet Union, its political leaders have always maintained such a tight cordon that it has, apparently, always proved impossible for the West to penetrate it in the same way that Communist moles and agents were able to penetrate British offices of State. Radio traffic was therefore an important new intelligence resource for the West: one to be exploited fully, since a scientifically advanced society could hardly be expected to rely on methods of espionage which dated back to prehistory.

There was only one obstacle which had first to be surmounted if the resource was to be utilised, and it should not be minimised: wireless traffic had to be deciphered, since by the early 1920s governments had discovered how to send secret orders and messages in code.[66] Yet this obstacle, though grave, could be surmounted. Over

and above this, however, whatever the theoretical reasons for listening to wireless traffic or signals intelligence, there was a good
practical one why British Intelligence or MI6 needed to concentrate
on this particular resource. This was that Winston Churchill held
such intelligence in high regard. Ever one to utilise scientific discoveries and advances, he attached the greatest importance to the
notion of first-rate intelligence being produced by modern science.

Churchill's interest in signals intelligence, most recently confirmed
by Sir Jock Colville,[67] and his interest in intelligence about the USSR,
also recently confirmed by Christopher Andrew,[68] make it all the
more curious that on 22 June 1941 it was decided that Russian
wireless traffic was no longer to be used as an intelligence resource.
Why?

The first intimation of this momentous historical fact came with
the publication of Professor F. H. Hinsley's massive official history
of British Intelligence during the Second World War, albeit as a
footnote.[69]

In order to ensure that this information was indeed correct, I
wrote to Professor Hinsley asking him to confirm that the footnote
meant what it said it meant and to give a view on who had given
this order. Furthermore, I asked him specifically whether it was his
opinion that from 1941 until 1945 intercepts of Russian wireless
traffic were not being decoded by British Intelligence.

Professor Hinsley replied:

> I have no evidence as to who made the decision. Presumably it
> was taken by Y Board [see p. 251]. There is no Russian material
> in the voluminous intelligence files for the remainder of the war
> and considerable lack of information about Soviet matters from
> any source except the Axis ciphers.[70]

This decision did not mean that Russian wireless traffic was not
recorded, it should be pointed out, merely that it could no longer be
subject to decoding and that therefore it was not an intelligence
resource.

How much intelligence this unit would have been able to generate
is hard to assess. Indeed, there still appears to be some dispute about
this within British Intelligence. There are those who argue that
this decision effectively sabotaged MI6's work against Communism;
others, however, have said that MI6 was not ordered to stop listening
to Russian messages, but that its efforts were useless in any case.

One former MI6 officer, for example, has stated that throughout the war a unit continued to listen in to Soviet wireless traffic, but that he had been led to understand that it had never made any headway for the simple reason that the intercepts could not be decoded. No one, he believed, had ever actually ordered the monitoring to stop; the problem had been the Russian codes:

The Russian ciphers were inviolable. We couldn't understand them.[71]

The same individual added that this work was done together with one of MI5's Russian experts, Colonel Alexander. Christopher Andrew offers corroborative evidence for the above statement (although he might have got it from the same source):

Between 1927 and the Second World War GC&CS [Government Code and Cipher School] was able to decrypt almost no high-grade Soviet communications (although it continued to have some success with Comintern messages).[72]

Yet the record shows that this former officer erred in assuming that Russian wireless traffic could not be decoded by MI6. A more senior former MI6 officer has stated firmly that this was not the case: the ciphers *were* very difficult to decode but the technological advances made at Bletchley during the war would have made them readable. In any case, the Comintern's messages (which would have yielded excellent intelligence concerning Stalin's plans for Europe) could have been tapped with benefit, at any rate until May 1943 when, presumably, with the dissolution of the Comintern the codes also ceased to be used (see p. 255). In this person's view (a view which was confirmed by another colleague), Hinsley was right to state that a specific decision had been taken to stop working on Soviet traffic. The question was: who had taken it?[73]

Clearly, if there really was no secret intelligence about Russia from 1941 until 1945, much of the mystery surrounding British ignorance of Stalin's aims and plans might be explained. On the other hand, if there truly was such a decision, not only was it a very remarkable one to take, bearing in mind the USSR's reputation for subversion, but whoever took it was thereby imposing the gravest restraints on MI6.

Sir Patrick Reilly, who was the personal assistant to 'C' in MI6

from April 1942 until October 1943, has stated unequivocally that
at no time could he recall ever having seen any Soviet intercept in
the MI6 office. He added that he believed that Soviet coding and
ciphering were executed with a very high level of proficiency and
that they were very difficult to break (though the Comintern codes
were apparently a different matter). It may therefore be inferred
from what Sir Patrick has said that, even if Soviet traffic had been
properly monitored, it would still have revealed very little. And, Sir
Patrick adds, when, after 1945, it did become an intelligence resource,
it could only be decoded in part, and it proved possible to read only
a few difficult fragments. On the other hand, Sir Patrick believed
that it could hardly be denied that successfully decoded signals
intelligence might have alerted Britain's policy-makers to Stalin's
post-war strategy.[74]

Sir Patrick's recollections are confirmed by a recent account of the
Joint Intelligence Committee's wartime work.[75] With regard to its
intelligence forecasts about the USSR, the JIC stated in January
1944 that they must be:

Subject to a wide margin of error because we have so little intelligence about Russia's strength and intentions and no information,
official or unofficial, from Moscow other than its communiqués.

It therefore seems impossible to doubt that from 1939 until 1947
or thereabouts there were, in reality, no Soviet decrypts upon which
to work, because an order was given to cease trying to decode them.
The argument advanced by Chapman Pincher that this decision
applied to 'legal' traffic and that Roger Hollis failed to decode 'illegal'
wireless traffic (traffic not emanating from the Soviet Embassy in
London) and treated decoded intercepts in the same way as Philby
treated German intercepts is, however, quite untrue. Although 'illegal' traffic could be easily discovered, it was virtually impossible to
decode. Pincher errs in one other vital detail. It was not Hollis's job
to attempt to decode Soviet traffic, whether legal or illegal.[76]

As we shall see, the fact that there was a record of at least some
Soviet wireless traffic was to play a significant part in the post-war
story of Communist subversion. For it was this material – known,
it seems, either as Venona material or U-Traffic – which had such a
bearing upon the career and reputation of Roger Hollis (see p. 306).

There remains the question of who took the decision to stop
decoding and trying to decode Soviet wireless traffic on 22 June

1941. Is Professor Hinsley correct to assume that it was taken by committee? And if it was a committee, was it one upon which a mole might have sat? We know that both Philby and Blunt occasionally sat on the Joint Intelligence Committee. Might they have made the original recommendation to cease using Soviet signals intelligence? While this is not totally implausible, the facts appear to present a very different picture. For at least three very senior figures in British public life, one a former intelligence officer and the others former leading diplomats, have stated that an order of this importance can only have been taken at the very highest level, namely at 10 Downing Street.[77] All of them agree that the decision must have been taken by the Prime Minister himself, perhaps, though not necessarily, with the approval of either the Cabinet or the Joint Intelligence Committee and after consultation with 'C'.

The former intelligence officer believes that Churchill almost certainly took the decision entirely of his own initiative and then announced it to the appropriate channel; he said he could visualise Churchill saying, 'Now there must be none of this spying business on the Russians; they would not like it.'[78]

Sir Patrick Reilly has said that he does not believe a decision of this nature would have been taken anywhere except at the highest ministerial level. While Anthony Eden might have taken it on his own authority as the minister in charge of MI6, Sir Patrick thought this was highly unlikely. 'Y' Board, he believed, was really just concerned with technical matters. As to the suggestion that Philby or Hollis might in some way have been involved in this decision, Sir Patrick states that this is utterly inconceivable.[79]

One of the most senior figures in British diplomacy, Lord Sherfield, has said that in his opinion such a decision could not have been taken by a committee but only by the Prime Minister himself, perhaps, though not necessarily, together with 'C' and the Cabinet.[80]

Another former intelligence officer has confirmed Sherfield's view, although he has suggested that the decision would have been taken only after the full approval of the Joint Intelligence Committee had been given. This, however, may have been given *post hoc*, since this officer argues that this would have been entirely consistent with Churchill's method of making policy. He too was able to conceive of a sudden decision being made off Churchill's own bat and being put into effect immediately. There seems to be no record of any intelligence officer expressing any disquiet about this decision, it should be added, with the possible exception of one person to whom we shall turn later.[81] That person was Roger Hollis (see p. 330).

It must, however, be emphasised that not all British surveillance of Communist activities ceased on 22 June 1941 and that MI6, SOE and PWE continued to have Russian connections, but at what level and with what purpose is a complex question into which we must delve with precision (see p. 263).

At any rate, the decision affecting wireless traffic was bound to have momentous consequences, of which the most critical was that the best source for discovering Soviet secret plans during the war and, indeed, for unmasking Soviet subversion as a whole was denied to British Intelligence. It was a decision which was, of course, the corollary of Churchill's high policy towards the Soviet Union in other respects (see Chapter 2). But was it a foolish decision?

Lord Sherfield (who was not in any way personally involved in the decision) has stated that it is a cardinal feature of good relations between allied powers that no espionage is undertaken between them. As he put it: 'You do not spy on your friends.' Sherfield's point is patently true. The fact remains that British Intelligence's single most vital resource, which would almost certainly have revealed the presence of all the moles we know about today, was confiscated by a high policy decision.

There is a curious paradox, an irony about this decision. Churchill took it in order to prove that 'my enemy's enemy is my friend'. What would have happened had he not taken this decision but merely said that he had taken it? Churchill, we might theorise, might have rejected such a course on the grounds that, sooner or later, a mole would have told Stalin that he was being double-crossed; this might perhaps have caused Stalin to pull out of the war. Of course, this sequence implies that Churchill knew that British Intelligence might not be watertight. It might even suggest that Churchill knew the Russians were spying on Britain but that he thought it best not to return the compliment since ignorance was sometimes preferable to knowledge. Such a theory could have much to commend it; Churchill was certainly very shrewd, he was interested in signals intelligence and he might, one could argue, have suspected MI5, MI6 or SOE of being leaky.[82]

So did Churchill suspect British Intelligence might contain moles and think that plans should be made accordingly? On balance, this theory can be safely rejected because we know that he thought Britain's secrets, for example over Ultra and Tube Alloys, continued to be kept, and he took a close personal interest in their security.

The utter irony, of course, is that the nuclear secret was itself betrayed to the Russians, principally by Klaus Fuchs and Alan Nunn May, and Churchill clearly had no idea that this was so. It therefore seems wholly unlikely that Churchill suspected British Intelligence might itself either be leaky or incapable of providing absolute security. It seems equally improbable that Churchill ascribed much significance to the possibility that Soviet moles lurked hidden within British institutions (although he would have known their presence was suspected; see p. 326). What this means is that Churchill's order must be seen as an important corollary of his demand that Britain treat the Soviet Union as it would treat any other ally. The subsidiary order that intelligence should genuinely seek to co-operate with its new ally must be seen as an inevitable consequence of the same decision.

There is no doubt that vitally important pieces of intelligence about Soviet aims and intentions could have been accessible to British policy-makers if they had been both permitted and able to read Soviet wireless traffic. They would, for example, have picked up intelligence about the role of the Red Army in post-Nazi Europe, about the base-line Soviet diplomats would adopt in negotiations. Finally, they would also have discovered important military secrets, not least the fact that Klaus Fuchs was leaking the 'Tube Alloys' project.

Although military intelligence and strategic secrets were the most prized forms of intelligence which wireless traffic could have provided, two other forms of intelligence were also worth having – information about subversion itself and wider political intelligence. Both of these would almost certainly have been provided by wireless intercepts, which would also have revealed the existence of Blunt, Philby, Burgess, Maclean and all the other moles. These names could also, of course, have been provided by other means, namely by surveillance, by domestic intelligence-gathering and good counter-intelligence or counter-espionage. Yet this was likely to be a very much more difficult operation. We should not, however, forget that such work continued to be undertaken throughout the war by the division led by Roger Hollis.

Yet the net intelligence product was undoubtedly meagre: it could hardly be otherwise when we consider it, as we must, within the historical context of the period.

Thus, when these factors are added to the Soviet strategy of the subversion of British Intelligence and other policy-making institutions, it is not hard to see why British policy-makers were so ill-informed and why the role played by subversion achieves such a special significance. For inadequate British efforts at monitoring Soviet plans coincided with the very period when so many Soviet moles and agents were able to penetrate the British political establishment.

So it was that high policy decisions, inadequate intelligence resources and moles all came together: they were, in fact, the secrets of the secret services.

The failure to realise that although Winston Churchill was perfectly happy to treat the USSR as a full ally, the USSR was not going to return the compliment was, indeed, a desperately serious intelligence error. Although the Soviet Union knew both overtly and covertly (from its moles) that Britain had ceased all spying on it by MI6, it continued to subject Britain to an intensive espionage campaign. It was also able to develop its plans without fear of obstruction from the West.

Yet, as we have seen, the British decision not to spy upon the Soviet Union, momentous though it was, does not mean that between 22 June 1941 and the summer of 1944 there were no secret intelligence officers taking an interest in Russian matters. There were such officers, both in the field, so to speak, and at home. Before we address the question of what these officers did, if they were not spying on Russia, and why they did what they did, we ought first to consider exactly what sort of secret intelligence MI6 could have gained from overseas, and whether it would actually either have helped alter British policy or at least caused its assumptions to be more widely questioned.

We are fortunate in that we have two important examples of the sort of intelligence that could have been gathered by MI6 officers in Moscow during the Second World War but was plainly not so gathered. Both these examples would have provided clear evidence of Stalin's secret intentions towards the various nations of Europe. Both are an ample illustration of the usefulness of what there was to discover and, specifically, of the extent of Stalin's secret planning.

The first example comes from the well-known account of Stalin's wartime planning by the Yugoslav Communist leader Milovan Djilas.[83] Let us suppose, for the sake of argument, that on one of his Moscow trips Djilas had been persuaded by an MI6 officer to tell MI6 all that he knew. He would, so to speak, have become a Blunt or Philby in reverse. Whether he would, like Blunt or Philby, have been able actually to assist in the formulation of policy seems rather doubtful because of the nature of Soviet Government although in the field of international Communism a man like Djilas clearly did give Stalin policy advice.

Djilas would have told MI6 that the Soviets possessed a perpetual fear, which dominated all their thinking, that:

The Western Allies, primarily Great Britain, might resent [sic] its taking advantage of the misfortunes of war in the occupied countries to spread Revolution and its Communist influence.[84]

Already here there was something which would have caused British minds to spin, for Britain would indeed have resented any such moves, had they but known of them in time to counter them.

In March 1944 Djilas flew to Moscow to set up a Yugoslav mission to Stalin. It was, however, the secret purpose of this mission to develop plans for the 'co-ordination' of the future Yugoslav Government with that of the Soviet Union. One of Djilas's prime contacts was Dimitrov, the legendary Comintern leader, who at the Reichstag fire trial in 1934 had so brilliantly managed to put Goering on the defensive. After 1943 Dimitrov, together with D. Z. Manuilsky, headed the directive of the section of the Soviet Central Committee for the Foreign Communist Parties.[85] Djilas would further have recounted that although the Comintern's work continued to be done, the actual organisation had been dissolved:

The Comintern really had been dissolved and Dimitrov's only job now was to gather information about Communist parties and to give advice to the Soviet Government and the Party. Dimitrov told me how the idea of dissolving the Comintern first arose. It was at the time when the Baltic States had been annexed by the Soviet Union and all forces had therefore to gather around it. The dissolution itself had been postponed because of the international situation to avoid giving the impression that it was being done under pressure from the Germans with whom relations were not bad at the time ...[86]

Yet the purpose of the dissolution of the Comintern was not that its work should not continue to be done, but that its work should be done by others, most importantly the Red Army. For the outbreak of the Second World War meant that the most vital agent of subversion was no longer going to be the individual Communist Parties of the nations of Europe which the Comintern had co-ordinated, but Stalin's military might.

Djilas added one important, if sinister, detail: the representatives of the Communist Parties of the various nations of Europe (which he called 'Foreign Units') were:

> Under the supervision of the NKVD General Zhukov. Pale, thin, fair-haired, still young and very resourceful, Zhukov was not without humour and a refined cynicism.[87]

Here, too, we have a statement that would have been of the greatest interest both to MI6 and the British Government. It would also have illustrated the deep irony of the fact that the British secret service, in terms of SOE, was doing its level best not to let 'its' resistance groups think about post-war political struggles at the very time that the Soviet version of the same body was busy co-ordinating and schooling its 'Foreign Units'.

It was a double irony that this should be so because SOE, in the eyes of its first minister, ought to have done some concrete planning for the post-war world (see p. 90). Of course, the Russians used their 'units' quite differently from the way in which SOE would have used its political groups. Djilas, as a Communist (if not a Stalinist), would not have wished to make this explicit. Although the NKVD (the KGB's forerunner) was the opposite number of MI5, MI6 and SOE, it operated entirely differently, since it gave its units careful training in how to exercise political control over the people it would govern and how they were to make sure that their domestic policies ran parallel to the interests of the Soviet Union. Their states were to be Russian protectorates, and they were the modern equivalent of the client kings of Rome.

SOE, on the other hand, was interested in the liberation of captive nations. This was but one distinction between the way in which a totalitarian regime might use its intelligence services to be a secret police, and the limitations placed upon a democratic Government which was bound to the notion of a secret service.

In due course, Djilas was taken to meet Stalin. In order to preserve secrecy, Djilas did not know exactly when this meeting was to take place until he was in the car speeding him towards the Kremlin. He was ushered into the dictator's presence past guards wearing the blue caps of the NKVD. There was an enormous globe in Stalin's office and the first person of consequence whom Djilas met was Molotov – 'stocky and pale in a perfect dark suit'. And then Djilas saw Stalin:

> Stalin was in a Marshal's uniform and soft boots without any medals, except a gold star, the order of the Hero of the Soviet Union on the left side of his breast. In his stance there was nothing artificial or posturing ... he was not quiet for a moment. He toyed with his pipe which bore the white dot of the English firm Dunhill ... I was also surprised at something else. He was of very small stature, and ungainly build. His torso was short and narrow whilst his legs and arms were too long. His left arm and shoulder seemed quite stiff. He had quite a large paunch and his hair was sparse though his scalp was not completely bald. His face was white with ruddy cheeks. Later I learned that this colouration so characteristic of those who sit long in offices was known as the 'Kremlin complexion' in high Soviet circles. [He had the head] of the common people, the peasants, the father of a great family with those yellow eyes and mixture of sternness and mischief.[88]

Of rather more critical importance than Stalin's general health and attitude (although this was of political significance) were the talks that Stalin and Djilas then engaged upon. Djilas stated that he needed US $200,000; Stalin replied that this was a 'trifle' and surely not enough; they could have it straight away. Djilas then said that it would all be repaid after liberation:

> Stalin became genuinely angry. 'You insult me. You are shedding your blood and you expect me to charge you for the weapons! We are not merchants. We are fighting for the same cause.'[89]

In short, Stalin was only too happy to finance the military efforts of the Communist partisans and he saw their cause and his own as the same.

Stalin then invited Djilas to see him again. Djilas wrote:

> I remember exactly when it happened: on the eve of the Allied landings in Normandy. [Stalin had been keen to drop supplies to partisans but could not get Russian pilots to risk it; they were 'cowards' according to Stalin.] ... The substance of Stalin's suggestions was that we ought not to 'frighten' the English, by which he meant that we ought to avoid anything that might alarm them

into thinking a revolution was going on in Yugoslavia or an attempt at Communist control ... 'What do you want with Red Stars on your caps? The form is not important but what is gained ... by God, there is no need for Red Stars' ...

And Stalin continued:

'Perhaps you think that just because we are the Allies of the English we have forgotten who they are and who Churchill is. There is nothing they like better than to trick their Allies. During the First World War they constantly tricked the Russians and the French. And Churchill? He is the kind of person who will pick your pocket for a kopeck! By God, a kopeck! And Roosevelt? He is not like that. He dips in his hand only for bigger coins.' He kept stressing that we ought to be aware of the [British] intelligence service and of English duplicity especially with regard to Tito's life. 'They are the ones who killed General Sikorski in a plane and then neatly shot down the plane – no proof, no witnesses' ...[90]

This passage is significant for all sorts of reasons. By far the most important one is Stalin's assertion that he did not believe the British were truly treating the Soviet Union as an ally in intelligence terms. Broadly speaking, this was of course untrue and Stalin knew this, both from his moles and from official sources. Yet he may have believed that despite what he was being told, the British could not be as naive as they appeared, or he may have been implying that he knew that both the Ultra and the Tube Alloys secrets were being withheld from him. At any rate, Stalin's suspicions implied that he would be taking steps to ensure that Russian secret intelligence about British plans continued to flow and this, in turn, would almost certainly have alerted the British intelligence community to the possibility that Britain's most secret secrets might be being leaked.

Even if one were to assume that Stalin was simply being his usual suspicious self, it would certainly have merited further investigation to see whether his suspicions were related to anything specific.

Stalin's reference to Sikorski's death is interesting not as a theory of why the Polish Prime Minister in exile died, but because he should happen to choose this as an example of British perfidiousness. (It is noteworthy that a whole succession of writers, from Rolf Hochuth to John le Carré, have argued that MI6 did blow up Sikorski's plane, but, as far as le Carré is concerned, it is further evidence of

Communist subversion in MI6, since he holds Philby responsible for it.)

Djilas then went off for a splendid meal with Stalin, who ate and drank prodigious quantities of food and drink (Stalin liked to mix red wine and vodka in little glasses). It was at this dinner that Stalin said a few more things about intelligence and the Western powers. 'They steal our dispatches. We steal theirs.'[91] As we have seen, this was not so: it was only the Russians who did the stealing.

Djilas met Stalin once more, in the final days of the war, but when relations between the Soviet Union and the western Allies 'were still in the wartime honeymoon'.[92] Djilas also met Stalin's secret police chief, Beria, 'rather a short man, plump, greenish and pale, with soft, damp hands'. It was at this meeting that Stalin delivered his well-known philosophy:

> Today Socialism is even possible under the English monarchy. Revolution is no longer necessary everywhere ... This war is not as in the past; whoever occupies a territory, also imposes his own social system. Everyone imposes his own system as far as his Army has power to do so. It cannot be otherwise.[93]

This statement, too, would have been of the greatest interest to British intelligence; it not only showed that the Russian concern for spreading Communism was alive, despite the death of the Comintern, but it also made Stalin's secret policy towards Europe crystal clear. It was not, of course, true that the British or the Americans possessed similar secret plans to impose their own liberal democratic regimes upon the states that they liberated from the German army; 'their' part of Europe was not to become the vassal of either Britain or America.

Djilas ended his dinner at Stalin's being told an anecdote by Molotov. Had MI6 got to hear of it, it would have caused considerable amusement, since it elaborated on a little matter that we know had niggled Churchill (see p. 61). It will be recalled that rather to the Prime Minister's surprise, Stalin had proposed a toast to secret agents and the secret service.[94] Molotov told Djilas that the point of his toast had been to remind Churchill of the failure of the Gallipoli venture and to imply that Churchill had lost it because of faulty intelligence (Churchill himself, however, assumed Stalin was 'evidently being complimentary ... by saying the British had won').

There was a clear intimation in Stalin's rather crude allusion that if Churchill had been fooled once by poor secret intelligence, he might be being fooled again. He was.

Djilas did in fact get to see Stalin one last time but it would appear nothing remarkable was said. Stalin expressed his awe and respect for the atom bomb: 'That is a powerful thing, pow-er-ful.'[95] He also told Djilas that Germany would now remain divided: the West would make western Germany its own. 'We shall turn Eastern Germany into our State.'[96] Neither of these pieces of information about Germany was very startling, it should be pointed out, for by now empirical observation by the West suggested that Stalin was intent on the Sovietisation of eastern Germany.

A second person from whom British secret intelligence could have gained much of importance was Wolfgang Leonhard.[97] Leonhard did in fact defect to the West in November 1950 (going first to Yugoslavia in 1949), and was presumably extensively questioned by MI6 after that time. He had fled as a child with his mother to Moscow in the 1930s. His mother had been an Austrian Communist and Leonhard was identified, while still a schoolboy, as useful talent for the German dimension of Stalin's plans.

After completing his university course, Leonhard was sent to an 'agricultural college', in reality the Comintern's training school. There were over twenty different nationalities represented in it. All recruits had their own 'Party name' and were not allowed to reveal their true identity. They were given instruction in political and military subversion and, above all, in the theory and practice of Marxist-Leninism. They learned that science proved that the Western capitalist system was doomed, and they received detailed instruction in the strategy and, above all, the tactics of political action.

They attended courses on political action, on whom to work with, whom to struggle against, and how to adapt by offering pacts to different groups within society, to the Social Democrats and even to the Conservatives. Their fundamental preoccupation was to mobilise the majority when Communists were still a minority, in order to create a classless society.

These were all ideas which Leonhard could accept with ease. He was even prepared to accept that the purges had been necessary, although he had been horrified by them. Over 7 million people had been arrested in the period 1936–8, 10,000 each day. The main difficulty that Leonhard felt about the process he was going through stemmed from his growing awareness that political terror and intimidation were part of Stalin's plan for Europe and had not simply been a phenomenon adopted because of the need to adapt Marxism to a backward country like Russia.

Nevertheless, Leonhard was picked to join the first group of German Communists leaving Moscow for Berlin after the German capitulation; in fact, he accompanied Walter Ulbricht, the Communists' boss, on the very first planeload of German Communists to land in Berlin. He had come with a carefully developed plan for the Sovietisation of Germany in his pocket. It had been decided that the Communists were not to make an immediate open bid for power, but to attempt to use the power of the Red Army to establish their position secretly. In public they would not seek the leading posts in local Government, but give these to representatives of other parties. In return the Communists were to insist that their people were put in charge of the apparently less important jobs of personnel, education and the police.

As early as May 1945 Leonhard and his colleagues were busy trying to identify Communist sympathisers among the German population. Leading posts, of course, were reserved for those who had been in exile in Moscow. Within a few weeks the Communists had been so successful in creating a power base for themselves that Ulbricht ordered them to ensure all important positions would be held by Communists 'whether it looks democratic or not. We must have everything in our own hands.'

Leonhard estimated that it took but fourteen days to complete the effective Communist control of the Russian zone of Germany. This may be an exaggeration, and negotiations with other parties, particularly the Social Democrats, continued for many months (although the dominant and dominating position of the Communists was obvious from the start to all but the most naive). Yet the fact is that the British and the Americans were taken by complete surprise at the actions of the Communists and the speed with which they were set in motion. It was to take the British over six months to permit 'their' Social Democratic exiles to return, despite the fact that these men were staunch anti-Communists and supporters of liberal parliamentary democracy.

Had either Djilas or Leonhard been secret British agents before 1945, it is clear that MI6 would have been able to supply information to Whitehall which would have alerted it to the dangers posed by Stalin's secret plans. It is perfectly true to say that the intelligence they would have offered was primarily political intelligence and that the premium, as we have seen, was on military intelligence. On the other hand, in this particular instance good military intelligence needed reinforcement by good political intelligence, since in Stalin's scheme military and political modes of control were closely inter-connected.

Britain, however, did not have the benefit of either political or military intelligence about Russia: MI6 did not produce information of this kind for the education of British policy-makers in Whitehall. Yet there were British intelligence officers concerned with Soviet Russia both in Moscow and in London, and scattered in different parts of the intelligence community. It is thus not illegitimate to wonder why this sort of political intelligence was not provided.

It has to be said, of course, that in 1944 MI6 did, in fact, decide to set up its Section IX and to reactivate its interests in the Soviet Union (see p. 155). In practice, though, even after 1944, MI6 does not appear to have got hold of Djilas-type political intelligence.

What, then, were the reasons for this, in addition to the actual subversion of MI6 dealt with earlier? The underlying explanation at any rate is perfectly clear. The Soviet Union was regarded as a friendly nation and not as a hostile one. The keynote of British secret intelligence policy was therefore that all intelligence-gathering in respect of Soviet Russia was to be conducted on the basis of a mutual exchange of information rather than covertly and with potentially hostile motives. Furthermore, those people and sections whose job before 1941 had been to spy on Russia were now ordered to spy with Russia against Germany.

This principle applied as firmly to political intelligence as it did to military intelligence, often to the chagrin of those who worked in intelligence, particularly to the military establishment who, as we shall see, were more uncomfortable about the intelligence impli-cations of high policy than almost anyone else. The minutes of the Joint Intelligence Committee show that the Chiefs of Staff were frequently highly doubtful about such policies as unconditional sur-render, the view that the Russians and Germans would not make a separate peace, and anxiety over Soviet post-war intentions; their doubts, however, were invariably quashed by the Foreign Office, apparently on the basis of intelligence assessments as far as the first two themes were concerned.[98]

Thus British high policy did not mean that individual intelligence officers or even groups of them did not have grave misgivings about what they saw as Stalin's true intentions *vis-à-vis* central and eastern Europe; some of them did. But even among these people there was no hint that they were ready to take a stand against the British high policy, even if, after the war was over, some of them feigned amazement that a Conservative Prime Minister and a Conservative Foreign Secretary could have presided over such a pro-Russian platform.

There were, it would appear, about half a dozen leading figures in British Intelligence concerned with Russian affairs. The most senior was probably Robert Bruce Lockhart (whom we have already looked at; see p. 122), who had the rank of a Deputy Under-Secretary of State at the Foreign Office and was Director General of the Political Warfare Executive from Dalton's departure in 1942 until February 1944, when he became Ambassador to the Czechoslovak Exile Government. But he remained a policy adviser to the Foreign Secretary on PWE and a member of it until the end of the war.[99] Next in importance, perhaps, came Brigadier George 'Pop' Hill, a veteran British agent who had been sent to Moscow in 1941.

The third important intelligence officer concerned with Soviet affairs was Thomas Barman. Barman had been PWE's Denmark specialist and a Deputy Director to Rex Leeper at Woburn. When, in January 1943, PWE was reorganised, Barman resigned and went to Moscow where he worked on PWE issues.

Fourth, if Nigel West is correct, was one George Berry who arrived in Moscow in June 1943, with an assistant, Cecil Barclay.[100] Barclay's father, it will be recalled, was a close friend and associate of Wolfgang zu Putlitz (see p. 223). Sir Patrick Reilly, personal assistant to 'C' from 1942 until 1943, recalled that Barclay had been a Naval Attaché. After the war he went to Greece, where he still lives as a painter.[101]

A further British expert on Soviet Communism was Brigadier E. O. Skaife, an adviser to the Foreign Office on Russian military affairs who had been a liaison officer with the old Tsarist army.[102] Skaife, who headed the Foreign Office Research Department, was by all accounts a most charming man. He had been the only person in June 1941 to predict that the Red Army would not be defeated by Hitler.[103] To Skaife must be added the heads of the British Military Mission in Moscow, at various times – Generals Martell and, after early 1944, Burrows. Martell, whom Eden described as 'something of a calamity' for Anglo-Soviet relations, was recalled for political reasons: it was felt he was too hostile towards the Soviets.[104]

In addition to these major figures, there were of course others who counted as experts on Soviet matters and on Communism. In theory one of the most influential ought to have been David Footman of MI6's Political Section and an expert on Russia. In practice, however, Footman did very little in terms of advising Whitehall about Stalin's policies.

It was the duty of this MI6 section to liaise both with clients of MI6 and its agents, and to distribute the intelligence gained. The operative sections, of course, ran the actual agents. Footman and his staff then processed the intelligence and passed it to their clients, while passing clients' requests to the agents. Footman (who after his retirement from MI6 became a Fellow of St Antony's College, Oxford) was not a highly imaginative officer. Sir Patrick Reilly has described him as competent but unexciting. He knew a lot about Russia, but 'he was emphatically not the man to commission any study of Stalinist policies'. Footman, the son of a parson, had been at the consular service before entering MI6.[105]

Thus it seems entirely fair to argue that since no wireless intercepts from Russia came to 'C''s desk, and since MI6's political section did not commission political intelligence about Stalin's plans, the state of British knowledge about Russian intentions was, of necessity, so limited as to be virtually non-existent.

What this meant was that by plain default as much as for any other reason, where Soviet Communism was concerned, one of the most important British intelligence officers – if not *the* most important – was Roger Hollis in MI5.

It is hard to state with absolute certainty precisely which of these experts was responsible for what. Of those in Moscow – Barman, Hill, Berry and Barclay – all were charged with duties which could be called secret intelligence work. Barman, who, as we have seen, had worked for PWE in England, appeared to represent PWE as the personal assistant to the British Ambassador, Sir Archibald Clark Kerr. Hill was said to be both the SOE and the MI6 representative.[106]

The most significant thing to note about the British intelligence officers in Moscow is, however, straightforward: their task was not to spy on the Soviets but to work with them in the intelligence offensive against the Germans, representing their respective organisations.

It is of course true that by co-operating with the Russians, these people would also gain a certain amount of political intelligence about Russian plans. Indeed, Thomas Barman is on record as having used his meetings with Soviet officials to form judgments upon their intentions (for an example of one, see p. 274). Yet because they were not charged with spying on their opposite numbers they were basically limited to discovering what the Russians were prepared to tell them about Soviet thinking, which was not a great deal. In fact, for reasons which seemed to escape them at the time but now seem quite plain, the Russians refused, whenever they could, to exploit the British (and American) offers of co-operation. For thanks to their moles in British Intelligence, they knew it all already, and the greater the distance between the Western and Soviet intelligence officers, the more secure the Russians would be. (Nowhere did this cause greater consternation than in the Military Missions.)

Professor Bradley Smith expresses considerable surprise at the extent to which there was secret service co-operation between Britain and the Soviet Union:

> Until Hitler's attack on Russia in June 1941 tossed Britain and the Soviet Union into each other's arms, SOE officers had never dreamt of co-operating directly with the NKVD. In fact, SOE had developed plans to sabotage Russia on the grounds [that] ... it had a non-aggression pact with Germany and was supplying Hitler with war material ... But taking a cue from Churchill's declaration that 'anyone who marches against Hitler is our friend' and realising that Britain was so desperately weak ... that it could not be choosy, Dalton and the SOE chiefs immediately decided to add one of their men to the Cripps mission ...[107]

Yet such surprise seems remarkable only if the historical context of the Grand Alliance is ignored. While Smith may be right that the extent of that co-operation, particularly in respect of NKVD co-operation with the British intelligence community in London, may have been something about which some post-war British Governments felt uncomfortable, this has never been a secret.[108] Robert Bruce Lockhart's memoirs, published in 1947, and more recently both Thomas Barman's book and indeed the Public Records provide ample evidence of the practical effects on intelligence gathering of the Anglo-Soviet Treaty.

Furthermore, co-operation with Soviet intelligence agencies was also enthusiastically pursued by the American Secret Service, in particular by Colonel 'Wild Bill' Donovan of the OSS. Smith quotes a letter from Donovan to General P. M. Fitin, Chief External Intelligence Division NKVD, dated 10 October 1944, in which Donovan wanted to:

> Express my appreciation for the spirit of friendly co-operation you have shown us. We have tried to reciprocate. I think the degree of success we have had so far in our joint enterprises shows what allies may do together.[109]

Smith states that the guiding principle for this co-operation on the part of the American Secret Service right until 1945 was the fact that:

> Franklin Roosevelt, the Joint Chiefs of Staff and the State Department were staking their whole policy on maintaining the best possible relations with the Russians ...[110]

Such a statement can hardly surprise any student of British intelligence policy during this period, for we can see how fully the American official line mirrored that taken by the British. It also seems fair to suggest that because the United States was so much stronger both militarily and economically than Great Britain, if there had been any attempt by the British to adopt a less helpful stance towards the Soviet Union in this field, American fury would have been considerable.

It is interesting to realise that the main challenge to Donovan's instructions to co-operate with the USSR's secret service came in 1943 with the creation of the National Committee of Free Germany. This important event appears to have also aroused the interest of PWE and MI5 though, significantly, not MI6, as Michael Balfour has recalled (see p. 273). Smith writes:

> Men like Grafton Rogers, Dermitt Poole and John Wiley had no doubt that the Soviet Union intended to capitalise on its military triumphs over the Nazis to establish dictatorial control of much of Europe and Asia. When Moscow began to make extensive propaganda use of captured German officers like Field Marshall von Paulus ... these OSS men showed signs of increased nervousness. Then in July 1943, the Soviets announced the creation of a Free German Committee ... and Poole, Wiley, Rogers and the other OSS rightists fell into a near panic. They saw the creation of Freies Deutschland [sic] not as merely a Soviet psychological

propaganda warfare weapon to undermine the Nazis but as the first step in a long-range Soviet plan to weaken Germany in preparation for a Communist takeover ... in September Dulles asserted 'while we and the British have been devoting ourselves to the military sphere with the slogan 'unconditional surrender' as the sole political programme, the Russians have been active and effective in the political sphere ...'[111]

Yet despite the fears of this group of 'rightists' US policy, like British policy, was not altered as a result of what proved to be passing fears about the German National Committee. What this suggests is that if the evidence contradicted the policy, it was the evidence that was ignored and not the policy.

Thus an old spying hand like George 'Pop' Hill must have found his time largely wasted. Hill had enormous personal experience of Russia.[112] His father had been a general merchant with a business that 'stretched over Russia across Siberia and down into Persia' and as a child he travelled from London to Hamburg, Riga, St Petersburg, Moscow, to the 'World's Fair at Nijni Novgorod, down the Volga to the Caspian Sea'.[113]

During the First World War Hill, like Bruce Lockhart, had argued that 'co-operation with the Bolsheviks was the best means of serving the Allied cause against the Germans in Russia' and he was in fact sent to establish contact with Trotsky.[114] He got on so well with the Bolsheviks that he was asked to 'organise a Bolshevik Counter-Espionage section to spy on the German Secret Service.[115] Together with Arthur Ransome, the novelist and journalist, Hill also made contact with the legendary Comintern leader, Karl Radek – 'a queer-looking being with a straggly beard which grew all round the side of his face ... it made me think of him as a sunflower.'[116]

Hill was rather scornful of his notorious colleague Sidney Reilly; in particular he disliked Reilly's plan to arrest the Bolshevik leaders and march them through the streets of Moscow 'bereft of their lower garments in order to kill them by ridicule'. Yet Hill was a realist. He understood the power of Bolshevism when, following an assassination attempt on Lenin by one Dora Kaplan, the Bolsheviks executed 500 White Russians as a reprisal and he knew that:

The Bolsheviks together with the Third International have built up a new and powerful secret service organisation which plays a prominent part in international intrigues and which calls for the most brilliant counter-espionage work on the part of the countries they attack ...[117]

According to Thomas Barman, Hill's duties consisted solely of co-operating with the Russian secret police, the NKVD. Hill's name was put forward in 1941 and passed to Molotov, who agreed to put his name to the Kremlin. When Molotov next met the then Ambassador, Sir Stafford Cripps, he said:

'We know all about Hill.' He raised his arm, 'We have dossiers that size about him.' In due course, Hill came to Moscow. He wore his Tsarist decorations with his DSO and MC and no one took it amiss.[118]

Barman recounts how, on one occasion, Hill decided to invite two NKVD men to the British Embassy for dinner:

They acted their part to perfection; that is to say they behaved as I had always expected secret service people to behave ... They parked their car some hundred yards or so away from the Embassy, well out of sight, and arrived on foot trying to look like men without a care in the world, out for an evening stroll.[119]

When Barman saw them enter the Embassy he became alarmed and told the Ambassador that:

'There are two NKVD colonels on my trail,' I began. 'They're actually in the building.' 'Of course,' was the reply, 'I've invited them for dinner' ... During the course of a party at Hill's flat one evening, he happened to run short of brandy. I suppose the time must have been ten o'clock and no shops were open. Hill picked up the telephone ... within half an hour a man in a black uniform arrived with a case of the stuff. I wonder whether MI5 would have been equally helpful if a foreign Embassy in London had run short of liquor.[120]

'Pop' Hill, Barman concluded, was one of the very few Britons in Moscow who actually 'managed to come to terms with the Russians and talk to them' as equals.[121] Yet whether 'coming to terms with them' was appropriate behaviour for a senior MI6 officer seems hard to answer. On the one hand, he was doing what he was ordered; on the other, one cannot help feeling that an experienced agent like Hill ought not to have dropped his guard. What is more, the Russians did not reciprocate.

As Barman explains, the Russians continued to trail all Britons in Moscow:

We even tried to laugh at the snoopers and get them to join in our laughter. When I celebrated my 40th birthday in the Aragvi restaurant in Moscow in December 1943, one of my guests suddenly left the table ... to face the grating high up on the wall. Then he recited a verse or two of Pushkin ... and called down the ventilation shaft, 'Take that you blighters.' I myself tried to help the snoopers by providing them with secret documents of various kinds. I had taken with me to Moscow a rubber stamp with the lettering 'top secret' ... and when I found something interesting in the London papers, I cut it out and pasted it on a sheet of plain paper. This I stamped 'top secret' and left under a bundle of shirts. I did the same thing with harmless documents of various kinds so if my belongings were searched at some time or other, the secret police would always find something. I did not want to send them away [empty-handed].[122]

Barman's recollections are confirmed by David Stafford who writes that after 21–2 June 1941 SOE was ready to co-operate on joint initiatives for sabotage and 'subversive propaganda to the European working class' with the Russians. Dalton was enthusiastic about such collaborative ventures but anxious lest the British public discover this was going on.[123] Yet it is clear that nothing of practical value emerged (not least because the Russians were getting most of what they wanted by other means; see p. 140).

Even if these people had tried to get on with a bit of quiet espionage work, they would not have had much success. For the fact was that life in Moscow was extremely restricted; Britons and Americans were simply not able to meet easily or privately with Russians. Sir Patrick Reilly has stated that in his opinion Moscow itself was one of the least useful sources of intelligence about Russian plans and secrets. There was very little anyone could uncover with the possible exception of technical activity, though the opportunities for that, too, were limited.[124]

Ought individual officers to have risked dismissal by disobeying orders and indulging in a little covert intelligence work off their own bat? Such actions would have been impossible to justify. In addition, foreigners in Moscow were sealed in their compounds, spied upon, and even their rooms were searched. Any officer who disobeyed his orders would have been in terrible danger from the Russians, in terrible trouble from the British, and would probably have nothing to show for his efforts in any case. The chances of establishing British moles within the Soviet institutions of State were nil. If Britain paid the price of being an open society, Russia gained all the advantages of being a closed one.

Yet the overriding explanation for British inactivity was the fact that officers were not under orders to gain secret intelligence. Barman goes out of his way to state:

> I do not want to leave the reader with the impression that most of us came to the Soviet Union in a hostile and critical mood, always anxious to put the worst possible construction on things. This would be quite wrong. Clark Kerr would not have tolerated such an attitude for a moment. Rabid anti-Communism with a high emotional content was anathema to him. He was determined to get on with the Russians; he tried to establish relations that would make it possible in the future to talk things over without friction ... If relations between Britain and the Soviet Union worsened steadily after September 1944 ... the fault was not Clark Kerr's. No British Ambassador is remembered in Moscow ... as Clark Kerr: with respect and determination ... If only the Soviets had treated [the Embassy staff] a little more intelligently, [with] a little more co-operation [and had been] a little less offensive and high-handed ... they would have found a friend in every member of the British Embassy staff. The same can be said about the United States Embassy under Averell Harriman and George Kennan. But Stalin would not allow Soviet officials to behave like human beings ...[125]

What is more, the most senior British official in Moscow (who would have had to sanction any spying) was in fact the most enthusiastically pro-Soviet. Barman makes it plain that Clark Kerr was at all times determined to put the best possible gloss on Soviet actions: at the turn of the year, in 1944–5, he visited England briefly and got in touch with several journalists, begging them to 'subordinate their understandable and natural anti-Stalinism to the overriding need to defeat the enemy with Russian co-operation'.[126]

Barman emphasises that the British refused to take an anti-Soviet line during the entire period – 'if the Government erred, it erred in the opposite direction'.[127] When, at the end of 1944, Stalin told Eden, 'Poland will live under a parliamentary system like Czechoslovakia, Belgium and Holland. Any talk of an intention to sovietize Poland is stupid', he was believed.[128] Much of the responsibility for this myopic British attitude towards the Soviet Union in the field, as it were, must rest with Clark Kerr himself.

Clark Kerr was, by all accounts, a curious man; he developed a close friendship with his man-servant, Yost – so much so that when he left Moscow in 1945, Stalin presented him with the servant as a gift.[129] The Ambassador was rather a lonely man, and although he had wanted Barman as an adviser because he claimed he needed someone to contradict him, he could be very rough if anyone ever tried to do so.

He was also a little careless in the choice of his friends. Chapman Pincher states that during the war Clark Kerr attended at least one meeting arranged by Guy Burgess at which Clark Kerr met 'Anatoli Gorski':

> The Soviet spymaster who was later found to have controlled Blunt and others under the code name 'Henry' ... The meeting had been arranged at the request of another KGB agent ... Peter Smollett ... MI5 had been disinclined to question Clark Kerr who could easily have fabricated an excuse for meeting a Russian 'diplomat' ... Many doubts have since been raised about Clark Kerr who had once worked in China where he had been associated with the KGB recruiter Agnes Smedley ...[130]

It is perhaps symptomatic of Chapman Pincher's analysis that he cannot conceive of a foolishly pro-Soviet British Ambassador except as a Soviet mole. But of this there is absolutely no evidence. Like 'Pop' Hill, Bruce Lockhart and others, Clark Kerr was an eccentric pro-Bolshevik and because he was quite open about this, the chances that he was subverted are virtually non-existent.

So much for the Moscow end. As far as Whitehall itself was concerned, the documentary evidence reveals a slightly different picture. Here there were, perhaps, far better opportunities for watching the USSR. Yet these were also stymied, mainly because of high policy, but also perhaps because a Communist sympathiser occupied a position of importance on the Russian Desk of the Foreign Office.

In addition, there are some indications that not everyone in London liked high policy towards Russia in all its ramifications. It seems that the keynote of Anglo-Soviet co-operation in Britain was struck by Bruce Lockhart, the most senior Russian specialist. He was not only a sought-after adviser, but by virtue of his overlord role in propaganda, his duties impinged directly on the area where Soviet intentions most crassly collided with British and American misconceptions about them.

Although in London there were examples of official doubts being expressed about Soviet aims, particularly by military officials, the overall line remained the same, and Bruce Lockhart was determined to ensure that it was maintained.

As enthusiasm for Russia increased, so did the British willingness to co-operate:

> The spring and early summer of 1942 had a decisive influence on the course of the war. It was then that our future relations with Russia took their definite shape ... The success of the Russian campaign had aroused the greatest enthusiasm amongst the British people ... Our desire to help Russia was inspired as much by national interest as by natural sympathy with a gallant ally ... Even in Britain there was a strong tendency to assume that the military successes of the Russians were due to some inherent virtue in the Russian system of government.[131]

As he himself would have admitted, Bruce Lockhart was convinced that, given good will on the Russian part, there were no grounds for any deterioration in Anglo-Soviet relations. This extended to making jokes about the Soviet secret service, which Bruce Lockhart really ought to have known was little better than an instrument of terror. At a lunch for a visiting Soviet Politburo member, M. Shervnik, Eden asked Bruce Lockhart (who spoke Russian) to introduce Herbert Morrison, who was the minister responsible for MI5, as the Minister for Home Security:

> Not wishing to make a dangerous comparison I translated Minister of Security as 'head of the Okhrana' that being the word for the old Tsarist security organisation. Shervnik smiled, 'Ah I see, the Head of your Ogpu' ...[132]

When the Russians asked about Hess, Eden told them they could see all the documents provided they kept them secret. This was done.[133] Eden also said specifically that the only way to get rid of mutual suspicion was to be equally frank in other areas: 'There must be no secrets between Allies.' Shervnik, Bruce Lockhart states, agreed and said he knew that Stalin would approve of such sentiments.[134]

There is no reason to doubt the truthfulness of this record; it conforms with countless other instances of British frankness, even gullibility. It is simply ironic that those who were required to know most about the Soviet Union seemed most ready to fall over themselves in not attributing any underhand motives to the Russians.

If these and similar incidents were the product of the high policy, then the day-to-day work of the organisation which Bruce Lockhart controlled was required to underwrite that policy. It has been argued that propaganda and the Russian attitude towards British propaganda might have given some clue as to Soviet intentions. It is worth noting that propaganda to Russia (as opposed to propaganda with Russia to Europe in general) was not dealt with by PWE because Russia was an ally (it was, instead, the province of the Ministry of Information where it came under the aegis of Peter Smolka).[135]

The overriding demand made upon PWE at office level was once again that it should co-operate with the Russians. Yet, at Anglo-Soviet meetings alert intelligence officers could hardly avoid forming their own judgments about Russian motives. That those judgments, where negative, could have changed high policy, however, proved unthinkable (even if it ought to have been thought about).

This is well illustrated by the secret papers for PWE in 1944 and 1945.[136] According to Professor Michael Balfour, who worked in PWE until October 1944 when he was seconded to SHAEF as chief of the Central Intelligence Directorate, PWE began to take an interest in the Soviet propaganda line to Europe as an indication of Soviet policy aims in the summer of 1943. But this was only a 'vague' recollection. Balfour assumed that the reason was unrest over the 'National Committee of Free Germany' (see p. 188).

The Ministry of Information would not, in Balfour's opinion, have had any interest in doing much about this, since they would have inherited the 'Foreign Office tradition that political intelligence about a country was the responsibility of the British mission in that country'.

PWE's sources were newspapers or, indeed, 'MI6 in the course of gathering intelligence or travellers' tales of which the Stockholm Parrott House [named after Cecil Parrott] provided by far the best'.

PWE took the view that to do good political intelligence 'you needed staff which was distinct from that concerned with policy and output – otherwise people would get their vision distorted by their own hot air'.

Balfour adds:

> The principal point at which I remember intelligence about Russia being done was in PID proper [which ceased to exist in 1944] by a retired Brigadier called Skaife who had been a military attaché in Moscow in the 1930s. He was always said to have produced a much more accurate forecast of the course of events in 1941–2 than anybody else. Like all PID staff, he was very much of a one man band and if he was a Soviet agent, then my name is Konrad Unklebunk ... In the summer of 1943 he presumably moved over to the new Foreign Office research department which was formed by amalgamating PID proper with the ex-Chatham House organisation under Toynbee in Balliol ...[137]

The PWE papers do show a concern for Soviet motives. In January 1944 Pilot (Barman's code name) was asked about Soviet plans for Poland, a 'very delicate point' since there was a rumour that a 'Soviet administration for Poland was being prepared'. Yet mostly the papers bespeak an almost frenetic attempt to get Soviet co-operation (which implicitly was not forthcoming), rather than any shift in attitude towards Russia.[138]

Thus, on 6 February 1944 PWE was told that both the Foreign Office and the State Department had proposed that:

> An invitation should be extended to the Russians to join the new Political Warfare Co-ordinating Committee and send to London a mission to participate with PWE in the drafting of directives for political warfare.[139]

The Russians were not keen: they clearly knew that they might risk giving their game away if they told PWE too much. They also appeared to know that by not co-operating, they were not running any risks of making the West suspicious or even hostile.

There was anxiety in the same month about a report that the OSS officer in Moscow, Sperwack, might not return after a trip to America. 'Pop' Hill had been requested to take this up with Colonel

Donovan. The British Ambassador had spoken to Sperwack who had said he did not know what:

> Arrangements Donovan had made with the Soviet authorities on intelligence or black activities . . . his own view was that in contrast to internal informational work which raises the issue of cultural penetration, the Russians would welcome in principle and in practice very full co-operation in common political warfare, for example, reciprocal exchange between Moscow and London of broadcasting time.[140]

In response to this, PWE formulated a policy statement. It said, in a secret cipher telegram to Clark Kerr, that he should tell the Russians that:

> Both His Majesty's Government and the United States Government are most anxious that in political warfare to Europe, the Soviet Government should be associated with them in their propaganda directives since co-ordination in this sphere of the three principal United Nations is obviously as desirable as in the realms of policy [sic] and strategy.[141]

In short, since the British had no interest in the 'cultural penetration' of the Soviet Union, it was decided to invite the USSR to become a full member of the London Propaganda Committee on its own terms. On 5 April 1944, the War Cabinet Co-ordinating Committee (under the chairmanship of Sir Orme Sargent) agreed that this invitation should be seen as a priority (others at this meeting were David Bowes-Lyon, the King's brother-in-law, and Bruce Lockhart).

The Russians refused to reply to it, however, and the British adduced all sorts of reasons. Bruce Lockhart began to have doubts about the Soviet motives, arguing that unless they could agree to co-operate more successfully with Barman in Moscow, they might cause trouble in London at a more junior level. Orme Sargent said the committee would not give the Russians enough information and this should be rectified. Bruce Lockhart, fearing that Sargent was accusing him of being hostile towards the USSR, replied that there had been no 'anti-Russian bias' in his comments, indeed PWE 'was now being widely accused of boosting Russia' by issuing invitations to the Soviet Government which the latter did not bother to answer.

On 1 May 1944 PWE was handed a message from Frank Roberts suggesting that in his view it was time that British propaganda started to 'blow our own trumpet and cease blowing Russia's'. Christopher Warner urged PWE to take note of this. Even the Foreign Office was finding PWE's willingness to co-operate with Russia slightly overdone.

At the more junior level, some PWE staff were of the opinion that high policy directives needed careful re-examination. A paper produced by Thomas Barman in May 1944 entitled 'Keeping a Balanced View on Russia' was an important note of scepticism from an intelligence officer in Moscow. It was not heeded.

Barman warned that:

> Admiration for the Red Army far outweighs its military achieve-
> ments. For it cannot be said that on present evidence the peoples
> of Europe have decided to embrace Communism as a political
> faith [despite the fact] that the Communist-controlled resistance
> movements, especially in France, have shown a vigour and deter-
> mination [which] has indirectly contributed to enhance the prestige
> of the USSR.

He concluded that PWE ought to realise that the likelihood now was that the Russians would be left:

> Well placed to influence the internal affairs of other countries
> through the medium of their Communist parties . . . Surely we can
> refrain from suggesting even indirectly that the Soviet Union is in
> the process of establishing new forms of political liberty or that
> we have anything to learn from the Russians in the matter of
> democratic leadership.[142]

Barman, in a word, had got it right. Yet PWE's response was to seek to co-operate harder still: the Russians were asked once again to join the London Propaganda Committee and it was officially recorded that Cordell Hull, the American Secretary of State, had specifically said that even though they did not want to join at the moment, 'Whenever the Soviet Government does wish to avail itself of the Committee's facilities, the door is open to it.'

Significantly, when Clark Kerr told all this to the Soviet Foreign Ministry, the only question the Russians had was, 'Did the London Committee exercise any control on the British Press?'

In due course, the Russians did send a representative called Saksin to London. In August 1944 he gave the committee full details about the Soviet propaganda directives for Hungary and Poland. They made such alarming reading that Bruce Lockhart sent them immediately to the Foreign Office. The directive for Poland read:

> Show heroic success of Red Army which is liberating Poland. Explain ... the joint struggle of the Red Army and the Polish Armed Forces against the common enemy ... Underline the historic importance of the agreement of 26 July 1944 between the Soviet Government and the Polish Committee of National Liberation as the forerunner of the rebirth of a strong, independent and democratic Poland and of friendly co-operation between the Soviet and Polish peoples ... Underline the full responsibility for the useless sacrifices of the inhabitants of Warsaw as resting entirely on the bankrupt adventurers of the Polish émigré government in London. Continually give information of the sincere joy expressed by the population of liberated Poland when they come into contact with the advancing Red Army ...[143]

Interestingly, some official in the Foreign Office put a very large question mark next to both the last and the penultimate points, as if to suggest that they were rather dubious and out of line with what the British had assumed to be Russian intentions. For both points implied that Russia had designs upon Polish domestic affairs, which made her respect for Poland's independence seem a sham.

This affair had a curious sequel. In the middle of September, Saksin 'suddenly departed for Moscow and all co-ordination of propaganda between PWE and OWI and the Russians' ceased. Had Saksin given too much away? Had someone friendly towards the Soviet cause with access to these documents told the Soviets that Saksin was 'leaky' and ought to be withdrawn? It seems hard to doubt that the answer to both questions is yes. The likely British source is Peter Smolka, but there were other known Soviet sympathisers who would also have read Saksin's papers.

One very important source of scepticism about Anglo-Soviet co-operation was the War Office. On 9 February 1945, it sent a short note to the Foreign Office on the number of military visits arranged for the Soviet Military Mission in London as compared to the number arranged for the British Military Mission in Moscow. The figures were: an average of 269 per annum for 1942–4 arranged by the British, compared with an average of eight arranged by the Russians (with only six in 1944); also in 1944, the Russians had visited seventy-six RAF establishments, the British had visited only one Soviet airbase.[144]

Brigadier R. C. Firebrace, who was in charge of the War Office Russian Liaison Group, compiled a report of its activities in October 1945. It showed, once again, how one-sided co-operation had actually been. The British policy had been based on the wish:

> To do everything to contribute to the Soviet war effort, not merely to assist the USSR in every way but also to dispel any distrust or suspicion on their part and to engender relations of mutual confidence ...

Yet the British Military Mission in Moscow had been subjected by the Russians to a policy of 'deliberate obstructionism [despite] which policy in the UK was rigidly adhered to'. Firebrace added that all Heads of Mission had been unanimous on the extent to which the Soviets had made life impossible for them. They had requested 'curtailing the activities of the Soviet Mission in London', but the answer was always that this 'was not in accordance with higher policy'.

The Russians in London were invited to a weekly meeting where they were presented with a digest of military intelligence as well as the British order of battle. The Russians, on the other hand, either refused to have such meetings (requests for which had to be submitted in writing) or supplied incorrect figures. One specific issue rankled particularly:

> By February 1944, Military Intelligence had established the presence in the German Armed Forces in the West of very considerable numbers of Soviet citizens. The Soviet Military Mission in London was informed that hundreds of thousands of their nationals were serving in the German Army or the paramilitary Todt Organisation. The Russians were given an MI publication which illustrated the insignia of the Russian Liberation Army formed in Germany under the leadership of General Vlassov. But the Head of the Russian Mission showed great indignation and refused to accept the possibility that any Soviet citizen could be in German service. Immediately after D Day, Russians in German uniform were captured in quantity and transferred with other POWs to

camps in the UK ... the Soviet Government then suddenly changed its attitude and launched the accusation against us of retaining liberated Soviet nationals in German POW camps ...[145]

These were, of course, part of the wretched contingent of anti-Soviet White Russians, some of whom were real traitors to Russia, others merely anti-Stalinist and not even Soviet citizens. They were all handed over to the Soviets and, presumably, liquidated.[146] Firebrace added rather ominously that even before the agreement signed at Yalta on 11 February 1945, the British had given British uniforms to some of these POWs who now counted as 'liberated Soviet citizens'. In actual fact, they were counted as something very different.[147]

Firebrace concluded that the moral of all this was that British policy should continue 'to be friendly but it should also be firm'. Firebrace may have been correct, but it is none the less surprising that he never wondered why the Russians were being so secretive and what the implications of this might be.

A Marxist in the Foreign Office

One of the odder side-effects of this policy of co-operation was in the cultural field,[148] where it was decided to set up a Committee on Russian Studies under the leadership of Christopher Hill (who subsequently became Master of Balliol College, Oxford and a well-known historian of the English Revolution). As the documents reveal, Hill was obliged to co-operate closely with the British Council on this matter and he also had dealings with Peter Smolka, with whom he was on first name terms.

Hill had read Russian at university and it was thought that he would be suitable for a role in Anglo-Soviet liaison as part of British military intelligence. He was, it seems, recruited into intelligence in a typically British manner. In the summer of 1940 a Major Kenyon (from SOE) had come to Oxford to look for potential Lawrence of Arabias. Seven Balliol men were produced by the then Master (A. H. Lindsay) of whom Hill was one. The Balliol men were then enlisted into Field Security Police and enrolled on an Officers' Training Course.

It had been intended to drop Hill and the others in the Baltic

States to promote a revolution against the Bolsheviks but the idea was scuppered (and Major Kenyon sacked). One of this group, Dr Zähner, went back to Oxford, while the rest carried on with their intelligence careers. It is a matter of some significance that Hill was taken into Government service without having been vetted but simply on Lindsay's recommendation.[149]

Christopher Hill's case is an interesting and important one for a variety of reasons. For one thing, it shows that before Barbarossa, while Hitler and Stalin were allies, the British did think about sabotage against the USSR (see p. 94). For another, Hill's subsequent appointment to the Northern Department of the Foreign Office (which dealt with Russian affairs) has a number of wider implications. For Hill was a member of the Communist Party.[150]

It was undoubtedly very curious that a Communist should have been employed to give highly secret advice to the Government upon Anglo-Soviet policy and to help formulate that policy. Hill has added that he did not tell anyone he was a member of the Communist Party, although he believed it was widely known that he was 'left-wing'. It should, however, be noted that Hill firmly denies ever taking orders from any Soviet controller and that his pro-Russian sympathies were not merely explicitly recorded in the material that he wrote, but clearly had the support of his more orthodox Foreign Office colleagues.

Even so, Hill's appointment to a highly sensitive post raises three key issues. The first is whether or not he was vetted by MI5. While there may have been, at this time, no specific instruction that Communists were not to be employed upon work of this nature, it was MI5's clear duty to 'keep people away from areas where they might do harm' (see p. 297), and a Communist on the Russian Desk of the Foreign Office would seem to qualify as one such area, even if in Hill's particular case this danger did not apparently arise. It seems impossible to doubt that Churchill or Eden would have gone through the roof had they known of Hill's political affiliation. Second, there is the question of whether Hill would have shown up on MI5's records as a Communist. Third, of course, there is the propriety of some of the things that Hill did.

Professor Hill has stated that he assumed that he had been vetted for the post on the Russian Desk.[151] Yet, as we have seen, he did not volunteer the information that he was a Communist to the authorities. Sir Patrick Reilly, on the other hand, has said that it would not have surprised him if Hill had not been vetted on being appointed to the Foreign Office, since he had previously worked for SOE and it might have been thought that SOE had vetted him (in fact, they had not).[152] Reilly also makes the point that:

> In the circumstances of that time, someone who was a member of the Communist Party might not have been acting dishonourably in not disclosing his political sympathies, provided, of course, he was not acting as a Soviet or a Communist agent.[153]

If Hill had been vetted and found to be a member of the Communist Party it seems hard to conclude that he would have been permitted to occupy that particular post, but would vetting Hill have revealed that he was a member of the Communist Party? The point will be returned to later (see p. 327). Here it must suffice to say that if Hill was a 'secret' member, like Jennifer Hart, his name would not have shown up on MI5's records. If, on the other hand, he was an 'open' member, MI5 would appear to have had the necessary evidence, and the fact that Hill was employed where he was would demonstrate either gross incompetence or treachery within MI5. Professor Hill, however, has (quite fairly) repeatedly refused to say whether he was a 'secret' or an 'open' Communist and he has stated that 'I have no idea when, if ever, my name was on any list of CP members'.[154]

Hill's apparently legitimate position as a Communist in the Foreign Office is thus an example not of Communist subversion but of the extent to which high policy blurred the distinctions between subversion and normal policy-making. He had understood that as long as he obeyed the Official Secrets Act his position was, in fact, quite legal. He never saw any conflict between his Communism and his work for the British Government, and indeed there may, in his case, never have been such a conflict.

Hill has said that his boss in the Northern Department, Christopher Warner, had very little specialist understanding of the Soviet Union (he had been a Scandinavian expert), and this presumably gave Hill ample scope to develop his own ideas. Sir Patrick Reilly, on the other hand, has described Warner as a 'very wise bird'.[155]

We must, furthermore, accept Hill's statement that his attitude towards the Communist Party did not influence the policy he helped make towards Russia, although clearly the dividing line between his own judgment and that of the Communist Party was bound to be a fine one. In addition, it must be stressed that if people like Hill could be acting quite legitimately, it became very difficult for those engaged in MI5 to counter any Communist who may have been acting illegally.

This leads us, then, to the third issue: the propriety of some of Hill's policy-making. A good example of this was the Committee on Russian Studies, which Geoffrey Wilson asked him to lead. It was meant to be one of the cornerstones of Anglo-Soviet co-operation after the end of the war, to be set up, as Geoffrey Wilson told Sargent, despite the fact that:

> It may be argued that the Foreign Office should not support measures for expanding one branch of scholarship rather than another. But in the case of Russia, the circumstances are clearly exceptional. There is a great shortage of personnel in this country with any knowledge of the USSR but co-operation with Russia is the basis of British policy ... It is important that the demand for knowledge of the USSR should be met by solid academic scholarship rather than by propagandists ...[156]

Hill was asked to draw up proposals. He produced a list which in fact appeared to contradict Wilson's final point, namely that 'knowledge of the USSR should be met by ... academic scholarship rather than by propagandists'. Hill proposed, quite reasonably, that Russian should ultimately become a foreign language of equal rank in British schools to French, and that no existing centres of Russian studies should be closed down but new ones opened. He also insisted, however, that the teaching of things Russian should be conducted by Soviet citizens which, in effect, meant Stalinists selected by the KGB. Yet such was the spirit of the time that in Foreign Office minds the term 'propagandists' applied only to anti-Soviet Russians. Hill declared:

> For political reasons, the employment of teachers of Russian origin but non-Soviet citizens should be reduced to a minimum ... Diplomatic channels [should be used] to ask Soviet citizens to become teachers ...

Forty years on in a letter to me, Professor Hill disputes that there was anything remotely distasteful about this. His concern was with the lack of English teachers of Russian:

The phrasing used was a code way of saying we needed more Russian teachers of English origin ... The problem was to get more well-trained English teachers of Russian; the best way to train them was to send them to Russia to learn. How to get permission? By exchanges which have advantages anyway. Exchange Soviet students in Britain could do some teaching in schools and universities. What is totally absurd is to suppose that they could have had any say in or influence on the content of teaching.[157]

Yet the record states otherwise: that phrase 'for political reasons' is the telling one, for Hill had not written 'for academic reasons'; furthermore, Hill at the time proposed that (English) Russian-language teachers should constitute less than one-quarter of the first set of exchangees.

In short, Hill was asking that Communist Russians selected by the Soviet Government should be given responsibility for at least some of the Russian teaching in English schools and universities, and that anti-Soviet Russians should be dismissed or retired 'for political reasons'. Hill also recommended that a list of bodies and people with an interest in this matter should be collated by him. He urged that members of 'The Society for Cultural Relations between Britain and the USSR' be invited, despite the fact that:

It is listed by the Home Office [i.e. MI5] as a Communist-infiltrated organisation but it would be more of a nuisance off our Committee than on it. They have many relatively respectable members who might get the matter raised in Parliament if they are left off ...[158]

Hill suggested that the Foreign Office invite E. H. Carr to take on responsibility for the exchange of teachers in political science, Maurice Dobb in economics, Wilfrid Le Gros Clark in medicine. B. H. Sumner in history and Kenneth Clarke in art. Peter Smolka was also to be invited to join the group. Carr and Dobb were openly sympathetic to Stalinist Russia; Wilfrid Le Gros Clark, the Oxford anatomist, was known by Hill to be 'vaguely left-wing'.[159] A former colleague has recalled that Le Gros Clark had a portrait of Stalin in his office.

This Committee had several meetings at which it was decided that:

Since collaboration [sic] with the Soviet Union lies at the foundation of British policy ... the British public service needs adequately trained personnel and an informed public opinion if this policy is to be a success ...[160]

A cynic might think Foreign Office funds were going to be used to set up what amounted to a school for Soviet sympathisers and Fellow-Travellers. The fact that they were to be given the Stalinist line in their instruction emerges quite clearly from another minute (reinforcing the earlier unpleasant notion that Russian was only to be taught by those who were politically reliable):

> The employment of émigré Russians as teachers of Russian was thought to be undesirable. The Committee also felt that Poles who after the conclusion of hostilities [the date was 3 May 1945] are unable or unwilling to return to Poland should not normally be employed as teachers of Russian.

Plans were so far advanced that on 30 May 1945 Hill sent a letter to the Committee of Vice Chancellors and Principals of all the British universities about his Committee's work and aims. In the event, however, the scheme appears not to have been fully executed. Although the teaching of Russian was reorganised (something for which Professor Hill deserves great credit) and at least one Russian exchange student arrived at St Antony's College in Oxford, the Cold War soon cast its shadow on it.

Hill had tried to get Churchill to raise this matter at Terminal (the Potsdam Conference). But on 17 July 1945 Lord Cherwell's office wrote to him to say:

> Lord Cherwell is a little surprised that the Foreign Office wants to put so small a matter on the Germinal [sic] agenda. Lord Cherwell [further] would prefer that there should not be an exchange of students. It is impossible to guarantee that a man's acquisition of knowledge is confined to his approved line of research. These security considerations naturally only apply to scientific workers, and genuine arts students should create little difficulty.

Cherwell, doubtless with his specific knowledge of the Tube Alloys project, feared that Russian 'exchange students' might prove to be spies. But the Foreign Office was demonstrably furious about his statements. A note made by Thomas Brimelow on 23 July said, 'It is annoying that Lord Cherwell has succeeded in wrecking our plans for having this subject mentioned at Terminal' and Christopher Warner added simply, 'the departure of Cherwell may simplify'. It is, however, important to note that Eden took specific exception to Hill's proposed exclusion of White Russians.

There are two important points to bear in mind about the tawdry aspects of the Committee's work. First, it is significant that MI5 had, in fact, made a note about the Society for Cultural Relations being a suspect organisation. This shows a careful security service at work, quite capable of differentiating between friendly and subversive organisations, and was Roger Hollis's work. It is revealing too that Sargent did not like to see Hollis's doubts expressed in the term 'Communist-infiltrated organisation' and happily ignored them.

Second, of course, there is the question of Hill's objectivity in all of this. Hill argues that the personnel he chose may have been pro-Soviet. 'This made political sense at the time, just as a Committee for Anglo-American co-operation would not have favoured employing professional anti-Americans'.[161] Yet the point is not a fair one: anyone setting up an Anglo-American committee composed only of supporters of President Reagan, with a card-carrying Republican as chairman, would not be seen as acting objectively. The somewhat vindictive refusal to permit anti-Communist Russians to participate in it might be excused on the grounds that, with such Russians in it, the USSR would refuse to co-operate with the Committee. On the other hand, as we have seen, the Committee specifically claimed to want to uphold 'academic' standards rather than further the 'propagandists'. Christopher Hill, one might possibly believe, was surely clever enough to realise that he was doing the precise opposite.

It has to be said, therefore, that there is some evidence to suggest that Hill's Marxism may have got in the way of his own academic objectivity. Further evidence of this emerged in 1945 in the form of a curious little book entitled *The Soviets and Ourselves: Two Commonwealths* written by one K. E. Holme, which, it was pointed out in the preface, was a pseudonym for 'a young Englishman who is peculiarly well-qualified by training and experience to interpret the public life of the Soviets to us in Britain ... He has been in a position to provide his readers with accurate and up-to-date information which it is hard to come by ...' Holme, of course, was none other than Christopher Hill (Hill has never concealed this). As has been revealed by H. J. Kaye (but has for years been apparent to anyone reading the catalogue of the Bodleian Library in Oxford), *Holm* is the Russian word for hill.[162] Kaye also states that Hill visited the Soviet Union in 1935–6, which Professor Hill has confirmed.[163] In addition, the Foreign Office knew about this book; there was nothing underhand about its production.[164]

The basic drift of Hill's book on Russia was, as its title suggests, that Russia, like Britain, was a Commonwealth, run, we learn, 'like an Oxford College', in that they 'preferred unanimity to a majority decision' based on the traditional belief that 'if two heads are better than one, several hundred are better than two, provided they are in agreement on fundamentals'.[165]

Hill argued that Lenin's 'genius is now being recognised outside Russia, as it has long been among his own people'. There were, we learn, 'direct and secret' elections, 'the vote being enjoyed by all Soviet citizens . . .'[166] Most tortured of all, however, were Hill's attempts to portray parliamentary democracy as simply a different way of doing the same thing that the Supreme Soviet did:

A great deal of time is taken up in Parliament by the cut and thrust of debate, the desire to score party points off the Government by asking awkward questions and by answering them in carefully devised formulae which give the minimum of information compatible with the Government's prestige. A group of Soviet officers who were taken to the House of Commons recently were not impressed but were profoundly shocked to find that in the middle of a great war, the Prime Minister's time was regularly taken up by answering comparatively trivial questions . . . In the Supreme Soviet, whether or not we approve of the methods by which this is attained [Hill does not say what these methods are], there is always in fact general agreement on fundamentals of policy and consequently no desire to score debating points. There is no formal opposition and all delegates are interested in government being carried on . . .[167]

This is not the place to offer a detailed refutation of Hill's intriguing arguments, other than to note that it is hard to think of any British Prime Minister who has not considered it one of the most important constitutional duties to answer questions from the House.

Equally inaccurate is Hill's implication that the Stalinist 'Treason Trials' were non-violent and similar to the Chartist movement. Hill quotes the 'considered judgment' of Sir John Maynard on 'one example of Soviet ruthlessness, the purge of the Fifth Column [sic]'. Maynard said the masses supported the purges because they thought the punishments were deserved, 'and in general they probably were'.[168] Hill was also able to defend the lack of personal freedom in Russia:

A great number of the citizens of both Great Britain and the USSR think the other is not free ... British subjects speak of GPU surveillance, of the one-party system, of the fact that public advocacy of capitalism is forbidden as public advocacy of Socialism is not in this country. Soviet citizens complain that in Britain it is not possible for ordinary people to criticise the manager of their factory and if the criticism proves justified, to get him sacked ... It is clear that different things are meant by the word freedom ...[169]

Hill's eulogy on Stalinist Russia included the description of other features of Soviet life; its own party system was no different from what happened to the British party system 'in war or crisis like 1931'.[170] Stalin's aim was to 'build Socialism in One Country, influencing other countries by the propaganda of example' and is favourably compared to the 'desperate and gambling projects of Trotsky [who saw] the Red Army as the torch-bearer of Revolution'. Stalin, on the other hand, 'may consider that other countries would be well-advised to adopt a Socialist system but that is their affair'.[171]

Hill, as one of the Foreign Office's experts on Soviet affairs, felt justified in concluding thus:

The Soviet electoral system is not a denial of parliamentary democracy on a wide suffrage formally established, as the Nazi system was in Germany; it is not a mere party dictatorship imposed from on top. It is an attempt to skip the stage of liberal democracy in politics and pass on to a society in which there shall be no deep conflicts of interests, no fundamental divergencies of opinion on political questions.[172]

It must be emphasised that it is not being suggested that Hill was not entitled to hold these views, but it is legitimate to wonder whether someone who did could take a sufficiently detached and objective view of Stalin's policies, particularly towards the people of continental Europe.

However, it is important to realise that when compared with some of the things his colleagues wrote, Hill's views do not appear in any way extraordinary. Indeed, this illustrates once again the stark truth that the illegal subversion of British policy by secret Communists would become virtually undetectable if, within the Foreign Office, there could sit a man who (perfectly legally, as he states) could put forward pro-Soviet ideas which not only seemed neither odd nor suspicious but were deemed usefully to underwrite British high policy.

If Hill could be acting quite properly, indeed attracting the praise of his superiors, how could any mole, acting covertly, be trapped? Unless a mole were to be caught in the physical act of handing over secrets, he or she would be safe. And, of course, moles did not simply pass secrets to the Russians, they also helped in the policy-making process. Thanks to the Anglo-Soviet Alliance, it became very difficult indeed to uncover their activities by analysing the policy that they made. Who could, with absolute certainty, say at what stage policy was being formulated by a legitimate supporter of high policy and at what stage by someone who owed his or her allegiance not to the Crown but to Joseph Stalin?

Anyone in MI5 charged with protecting Britain against Communist subversion was required to fulfil an almost superhuman task, which called not only for great intellectual resilience but also considerable personal self-confidence and the support and protection of his superiors. For it would be hard to overestimate the problems that might accrue to any MI5 officer who chanced upon Hill's activities in the Northern Department, and who concluded from them the worst, only to discover that they mirrored the Cabinet's policies and found the approval of senior officials in the Foreign Office.

The secret hunt for Hitler

It would be wrong to leave the field of Anglo-Soviet co-operation in intelligence matters without considering one of its most spectacular exploits: Operation Nursery, the secret hunt for Hitler.[173] This operation was led by Dick White, seconded from MI5 to military intelligence with the rank of Brigadier.

The search for Hitler, to discover whether he had died or fled, was conceived as a joint Anglo-Soviet intelligence operation, although it ended like all the other joint intelligence ventures, in a Russian refusal to co-operate properly. There were three major intelligence questions of concern to British, Soviet and American authorities. The first was to establish the precise fate of Adolf Hitler and the leading Nazis. The second was concerned with the way in which active Nazi members would react to defeat. And, third, there was the problem of how to liquidate the Germans' own intelligence community, from the Abwehr to the Gestapo and Sicherheitsdienst or Security Service.

As far as Hitler and his henchmen were concerned, there was some debate in the final weeks of the war as to whether they would try to escape justice, either to assume new identities or to establish a new political following outside Allied jurisdiction. Alternatively, it was conceivable that they might surrender, allowing themselves to be put on trial, or that they might manufacture for themselves a 'hero's death', so becoming potentially dangerous 'martyrs'. As far as the active Nazi members were concerned, there was obviously a real threat that many of them would go underground, possibly as members of the so-called 'Werewolf' brigades, and carry out subversive activities or even try to establish a Nazi 'State' in the so-called Bavarian Redoubt.

The liquidation of the German intelligence community posed its own set of questions. A former British intelligence officer has confirmed that the sheer size of German Intelligence, the vast numbers of units, presented those charged with counter-intelligence with an awesome task.[174]

This issue began to be thought about seriously towards the end of 1943. Dick White was drafted from his work at the Cabinet War Room (which dealt solely with German matters) to SHAEF, where he became the Deputy Head of Allied counter-intelligence under General Sir Kenneth Strong. The Americans took the top job but their nominee appears to have let Dick White run most of the show. As the British and American armies moved deeper into the territory of the Third Reich, Dick White and his unit followed, mopping up the German intelligence units and taking special care to prepare themselves for the surrender of any leading Nazis.

One of the first Nazi bosses to give himself up was Heinrich Himmler, Minister of the Interior and SS Chief. Dick White gave special instructions that Himmler was to be treated with great care but these were disobeyed. He was roughly handled, took fright and bit on his hollow tooth which contained a cyanide capsule, and promptly expired. The American authorities were not pleased with this; they appeared to believe that Dick White and the British had a deliberate policy of not taking prisoners.

In due course, Montgomery appointed White the chief of counter-intelligence for the British zone of occupation. His headquarters were at Bad Oeynhausen. It was at this stage that rumours began to circulate that Hitler was alive; one suggested he was in the Ruhr. The only official reports of Hitler's death had come from Hamburg Radio which had been under Nazi control. On 1 May 1945, it had asked listeners to stand by for an important announcement. It then played music by Wagner and Bruckner's Seventh Symphony. After a while Grand Admiral Dönitz came on the air saying that 'Hitler had fallen this afternoon at his command post at the Reich Chancellery, fighting to his last breath against Bolshevism and for Germany'.

Yet this odd story conflicted with the evidence that Himmler had presented to Count Bernadotte (namely that Hitler had died of a stroke) and there were those in British Intelligence who believed it might well prove in the Nazis' interests to pretend that Hitler was dead, in order to give him a chance to escape the Allied net. Furthermore, the rumours that Hitler might be alive would, it was thought, fuel the Werewolves into acts of sabotage and terror.

It was therefore decided that White should organise a major intelligence operation in order to discover Hitler's true fate, and since Berlin, where it was alleged the Führer had fallen, had been occupied by the Russians, the search for Hitler was considered to be an excellent subject for a joint Anglo-Soviet intelligence effort. White believed that Hitler was, in fact, dead but the issue had to be settled.

Even before this time, the British had tried to get the Russians to agree to a joint counter-intelligence operation against the Nazis once Hitler had been defeated and, at one stage in the negotiations, it had been suggested by General Bedell Smith that White should go to Moscow in order to set this up. This never materialised, possibly because the Russians knew that the Brigadier Dick White of military intelligence was the same Dick White of MI5's counter-espionage division and suspected (quite wrongly) that he would do more in Moscow than simply co-operate with the GRU (Russian military intelligence).

In the event, Montgomery wrote to the Russian Commander-in-Chief Zhukov asking him to accept White's move to Berlin. This was forthcoming, and White and his staff (which included Hugh

Trevor-Roper, seconded from MI6, and Leo Long) went to Berlin early in 1945 to make contact with the GRU. Sir Dick White has confirmed that initially relations with the Soviets were good: this was a military operation in the first instance and the Soviet and the British forces got on extremely well. The Russians had succeeded in overrunning Hitler's bunker on 2 May.[175]

Yet the Russians soon began to put about a variety of stories about Hitler's fate. First, on 9 May, they claimed to have exhumed the bodies of Hitler and Eva Braun; they stated that the teeth matched and that one of the bodies had a bullet hole in the temple. By June the Russians refused to make any further comment; Zhukov made no mention of Hitler's death in a public statement, and one of his associates alleged that Hitler and Eva Braun were in Spain, being entertained by General Franco. At the Potsdam Conference, Stalin told James Byrnes that Hitler was alive either in Spain or Argentina.

White's mission was therefore unlikely to be an easy one. An early stroke of good fortune occurred when British intelligence officers were being shown round the bunker by a Russian officer; one of the Englishmen slid his hand down the side of an armchair and discovered the diary of Heinz Linge, Hitler's man-servant. This provided the names of the people who had been in the bunker and, of course, immediately enabled the British to start rounding them up. The Russians were, at first, quite ready to be helpful. Sir Dick recalled that he had been entertained to a lavish meal and, when he asked the Russians how they could assemble such fare, they replied that the Red Army 'always lived off the land'. Later they told him they had a similar attitude towards intelligence gathering. They were not interested in 'academic intelligence'; they picked their information up 'on the hoof'.

The British soon managed to assemble a fairly accurate picture of the last days of Hitler and his entourage. They also obtained many of Hitler's medical and dental records. In them Hitler was referred to as 'Patient MF' (for Mein Führer) or simply 'Adolf Müller' by one doctor, and as 'AH' by others. At this stage, however, all attempts at further co-operation with the Russians suddenly ceased. They refused to have any more dealings with Dick White.

Three reasons could be adduced for this. First, that the Russians had a clear propaganda incentive for not revealing the truth about Hitler one way or another, since this would imply there was a possibility that he still lived and, if this was the case, he might try to make a come-back. This, in turn, was an argument for viewing the presence of the Red Army in Germany as a real necessity. Indeed, over the years, Soviet misinformation on this issue continued apace. At various times, the Russians produced 'Hitler's false teeth' (he had none), a body which measured 5'6" (Hitler was 5'9"), a body with no left testicle (Hitler had two, although the extant medical evidence does not make it entirely clear whether Hitler's doctor had seen all of him), a body with teeth that did not match the dental records, a body without any gunshot wound, and a body with darned socks (it was thought unlikely that the Führer of the Third Reich would have worn darned socks).

The second reason why the Russians may have pulled out of this operation was that they realised that Dick White's team would soon tumble to the fact that they were not taking the search for Hitler seriously and that they therefore did not wish the truth to come out. This, in turn, might have called their other motives into question. Interestingly enough, Sir Dick's inclination at the time was to publish his results as soon as he could; the Foreign Office, on the other hand, was strongly opposed to what it saw as a unilateral utterance on a major issue. It is also significant that, once the news about Hitler's certain death had come out, Leo Long asked none other than Sefton Delmer to deal with the radio publicity about it in Germany, suggesting that he believed that Delmer would know how best to handle it.

Finally, it seems highly probable that the Russian army officers soon discovered White's true status as an MI5 man. This information could easily have come from Philby, from Blunt or, indeed, from Leo Long.

Despite the Russian withdrawal, White's team achieved a second major breakthrough on 1 November 1945 when a copy of Hitler's will was discovered during a search of a German prisoner. It had been sewn inside the lining of his jacket. British Intelligence reasoned that if the signature on the will proved to be authentic, then the likelihood was that its contents were also authentic, and in the will Hitler made it clear that he would commit suicide. Three copies of the will had been made (together with one copy of Hitler's marriage certificate) and the documents were then given to three officers with orders to escape from the bunker. On 1 December 1945 the signature was shown to Captain Jim Skardon, of MI5 liaison, who verified it. He was MI5's handwriting expert, later to become one of its chief interrogators.

At the end of 1945 Trevor-Roper returned to Oxford; but the

Statement by William James SKARDON, Capt Int Corps, MI 5 Liaison Section.

1. I have to-day made an examination of certain original documents which may be described as follows:-

   (i) HITLER's personal Will

   (ii) HITLER's Political Testament

   (iii) Appendix by GOEBBELS to HITLER's Political Testament.

2. I have compared the signatures to be found on these documents with what have been represented to me as authentic signatures of the signatories.

3. On document no (i) are to be found signatures of HITLER, GOEBBELS and BORMANN. The specimens with which I have been able to compare these signatures leave me in no doubt that the signatures on document no (i) are genuine.

4. Again on document no (ii) the same signatures appear, the same comparison has been made and I have no doubt that they are genuine signatures.

5. On document no (iii) is to be found the signature of Dr GOEBBELS . I have no doubt that this is a genuine signature

6. There is a slight difference to be found as between the signature of GOEBBELS to the first two documents as against that of his in document no (iii). This difference, and I refer only to the writing of the surname, does not detract from my belief that they are all written by the same hand.

7. I have not had the advantage of comparing originals in the case of BORMANN and GOEBBELS but the photostatic copies which I used are said to be authentic and are sufficient for the purpose.

8. I base my opinion upon experience of examining hand writing over a number of years.

Captain I.C.

1 Dec 45

1 MI5's handwriting expert is called in to prove Hitler's death

investigation continued. British intelligence officers visited Berch-
tesgaden where they took evidence from Hitler's domestic staff
(Hitler's chambermaid declared that Hitler and Eva Braun had never
had sexual relations, contrary to popular belief; she was absolutely
certain of this) and continued to round up members of Hitler's
private circle. Thus, by the end of that year British Intelligence was
certain that Hitler had died on 30 April, although Bormann's fate
remained an open question. Sir Dick White was convinced that
Bormann had died near the bunker in an attempt to escape from the
Russians.

Over the following months and years, the Soviet Union continued
to refuse to co-operate in tying up loose ends. It had refused to let
the British interrogate two members of the bunker (Güntsche and
Linge himself) who were kept in the Lubianka gaol in Moscow, and
it was reported in January 1954 that both of them had been warned
by the NKVD that they were never to say anything about the events
they had witnessed in the ruins of Berlin in April 1945. This, then,
was the sordid ending to what had proved to be the last time British
and Soviet Intelligence co-operated.

As we have seen, in the entire field of secret intelligence gathering
during the Second World War period the thrust of British policy was
towards full and frank co-operation with the Soviet Union, with two
chief exceptions. The Soviets were not to know about the Tube
Alloys project, nor were they ever to learn of the real source of Ultra
intelligence. Apart from this, the desire to work together with the
Russians was intense, particularly at the highest policy-making levels.
The meeting in Berlin between a top Russian army intelligence officer
and the man who was to become both Director General of MI5 and
'C' of MI6, and then Intelligence Co-ordinator to the Cabinet, may
seem to some to contain more than an essence of fiction, either
because it is such a good story (which it is) or, more pertinently,
because in the popular imagination the Russians were thought by
British leaders to be only one level lower than the Nazis in terms of
being an enemy of this country. However, the real fiction in this case
is what the popular imagination thinks must have been true; the
actual truth was very different.

8

The Secrets of the Service: MI5 and Communist Subversion

Who was Roger Hollis?

It seems hard to doubt that there is considerable evidence of attempted Communist subversion in Britain during the Second World War, whether in terms of the injection of Soviet moles into various high offices of the British State, or in the several methods adopted by the Kremlin to advance its own war aims to the detriment of Britain's interests. These, it should not be forgotten, were executed in flagrant contradiction of its own formal treaty commitments not to interfere in the internal affairs of other States. That subversion was particularly crass, bearing in mind the overriding British desire to co-operate fully with the Soviet Union in all aspects of Anglo-Soviet affairs. And it was particularly dangerous when we consider the effects that subversion could have upon British foreign policy and within British Intelligence.

We have seen how Communist subversion achieved its successes, such as they were, thanks to a mélange of high policy, of a lack of political judgment in certain detailed areas and, finally, of the penetration of the intelligence services themselves. What must now be addressed is the final, perhaps the most tantalising question of all: the failure of British Intelligence to realise that, within its own ranks, it contained agents of Stalinist Communism, commonly and not inaccurately known as moles.

It was MI5's job to protect Britain's domestic security by acting against hostile agents. If MI6 was stymied chiefly by high policy, in particular by the decision to cease decoding Soviet wireless traffic and to make MI6's Soviet specialists spy with Russia rather than against her, the same explanations cannot be adduced for all of MI5's failures. For although the wireless traffic decision did affect MI5 as well, it is not true that MI5's Communist specialists were obliged to act in the same way as MI6's. MI5 was not ordered to co-operate with Communists in the same way as MI6 had been. What is more, precisely because MI6 was *hors de combat* but MI5 supposed most definitely not to be, a very heavy burden of responsibility was to fall on MI5 and on its chief Communist specialist. Roger Hollis. At the end of the day, almost everything could come to depend on him.

We shall now trace out both the arguments and the evidence connected with an evaluation of Roger Hollis's role in MI5 in this highly critical wartime period: the period of maximum penetration and, almost certainly, maximum damage. Did Hollis fail because it was simply impossible for him to succeed? Was he incompetent and ought never to have been given this task? Or did he fail because he, like Kim Philby in MI6, was himself one of Stalin's Englishmen?

In different ways and to different degrees, the moles and the agents not only helped to maintain a smokescreen of ignorance about Soviet intentions but also, in the case of moles, wherever possible tried to influence the actual outcome of policy. In addition, of course, moles and agents could help the cause of Communism by passing secrets to the Russians. These could vary from the most secret secrets of the Anglo-American nuclear programme to apparently insignificant facts and figures about British life in general. For Soviet Intelligence was based on the principle that the more facts that Russia possessed, the better its knowledge of the West would become, and that facts that might be irrelevant today could, in due course, become highly significant.

Despite this, however, it is important to realise that what the moles and agents hoped to do and what they actually did are two different things. The end result of their actions was, as has been suggested, to help the Soviet Union to achieve a dominant political position in 1945. However, even if there had been no moles or agents, Stalin's Russia would still have achieved its dominance in the central and eastern part of the European continent. For the major source of Stalin's power was the Red Army and not the mole army. In some senses, then, the individual machinations of the agents and moles had very little effect.

There were, of course, exceptions to this rule. Although the hallmark of many of Stalin's Englishmen and women was extreme arrogance (they were the 'best and the brightest', destined for plum positions), this does not necessarily mean they and others have overestimated their own importance. Britain did possess a small political class, allowing its members considerable influence on the margin of British affairs. Later on, the fact that a number of them did achieve high positions within the British Establishment seems to confirm their leadership potential.

Of course, on achieving those positions, some evidently renounced their former Communist sympathies. The late Philip Williams, who had kept a record of a number of people whom he believed had been secret Communists since their student days at Oxford, noted wryly that certain individuals, many of whom went on to occupy important positions in the Civil Service and in academic life, nevertheless made no attempt to use their positions of influence seriously to undermine parliamentary liberal democracy.[1]

This should not be taken to imply that the present study believes that any who were moles and agents did no harm; when compounded, their actions were very serious. Yet, as a former senior MI6 officer has rightly argued, a true assessment of the damage that they did must take into account the enormous variation in their activities. Some were able to kill for Stalin; others merely told the Russians what they knew already.[2]

The questions surrounding Communist subversion and British Intelligence do have a bearing upon contemporary British political history. First of all, they throw light on the nature of a security service in a pluralistic liberal democracy. This is, of course, an issue which still causes controversy today. Petrie, White and Hollis, when they were MI5's Director Generals, believed very strongly in a service which operated in great secrecy but with great responsibility. Its object was not to lock people up, but to ensure that subversives were kept away from the areas where it was possible for them to do real damage.

As we have seen, from 1939–51 MI5 was not conspicuously successful at this as far as Communist subversives were concerned, for reasons we shall shortly explore. Nevertheless, its lack of success ought not to be permitted to bulldoze today's public into demanding a quite different sort of secret service where no mistakes could be made.

It is a fact that all intelligence services in liberal democracies, particularly in recent times the American, the West German and the French, have suffered major defeats. A comparative study of Western intelligence services would suggest that Britain's record is, on the whole, by no means bad. Furthermore, it is hard for any intelligence service in a free society to get a good press: if spies are not caught, it is taken as an indication that the security service is not doing its job. If they are caught, that too is taken as an indication that it is not working properly, since the spies ought not to have existed in the first place.

Partly, then, the bad press that MI5 has received is not its own fault. It does, however, seem legitimate today to question the excessive secrecy that the security service exhibits. The identity of 'C' has, until recently, been regarded as a major state secret, affecting the security of the realm. When a former 'C' was prepared to give me his permission to reproduce the first photograph of himself which had ever been published (apart from a snap from his student days), it was only after considerable heart-searching on his part, despite the fact that the photograph was forty years old and of a man who technically was an army officer at the time it was taken.

Such secrecy not only permits wild and sometimes absurd allegations to be made about British Intelligence, but it also implies that MI5's work is more sinister than it usually is. This undermines public confidence in what is, after all, the public's security service and has also evidently undermined confidence within the service itself. This has spawned new and wide-reaching political difficulties.

The chief cause of anxiety has been the public activities of the mole-hunters themselves, which have given grounds for legitimate disquiet. The open probing of Roger Hollis by at least three of them (Peter Wright, Arthur Martin and Stephen de Mowbray) without, as we shall see, any firm proof must make the ordinary citizen wonder at what stage some of Britain's intelligence officers think investigation ceases and persecution begins.

It is hard to disagree with Sir William Hayter's assessment when he wrote:

> If Mr Wright's performance (on Granada TV, 16 July 1984) is typical of the reasoning of professional intelligence officers, it only shows on what slender and ill thought-out evidence they arrive at damaging and indeed dangerous decisions ... If this is the best the critics of Roger Hollis can do they had better shut up ...[3]

MI5's reputation has quite obviously been seriously damaged by the Hollis saga. Indeed, this damage may itself be one clue to the existence of so many damaging allegations against him. So how can MI5's morale be restored?

One, simple, answer would be for MI5 to be less secret about things that are irrelevant to the present security of Britain and more open about both its recruitment and its other monitoring activities.

It ought to have an official spokesman and offer the public a well-ordered set of archives setting out MI5's past activities in a historical context. Another answer has been provided by Chapman Pincher who urges political 'overview'.[4]

But Chapman Pincher is probably wrong. It seems fair to claim that the strength of a parliamentary liberal democracy depends in large part on the resilience and independence of its important offices of State, whether they be the great ministries or its security service. There should of course be overall political control of MI5's activities, but this has always existed in the person of the Home Secretary of the day. He is kept in close touch with MI5's activities, and the Permanent Under-Secretaries at the Home Office meet at least weekly with the Director General of MI5, as two of them have confirmed. Beneath that overall political control, however, MI5 should be able to pursue its current work in secrecy subject to the laws of the land. The principle of preventing damage to democracy by keeping its enemies away from places where they could harm it is perfectly acceptable. What is never acceptable is either that people should be persecuted for their political views or that 'damage to democracy' should have any definition other than an extremely tight and narrow one.

As many former MI5 and MI6 officials have testified, no Director General of MI5 believed this more firmly than Roger Hollis. It is, therefore, more than a little ironic that he himself has now become the object of so much uncertainty.

Why has this had such a devastating impact on the public perception of MI5? This is in part, of course, a naive question. For how can the public be expected to have confidence in an organisation which is supposed to protect British security, if its boss was an agent of the Soviet Union? But the impact of the Hollis case may have far deeper causes. It could be said to be part of the general lack of self-esteem which has been a feature of British life since the 1950s, to which many authors have drawn our attention. British institutions – whether the Civil Service, the BBC, the universities, or even MI5 and MI6 – have often been blamed for Britain's failures, usually with little justification. Furthermore, we should not forget that the undermining of public confidence in MI5 is of most practical use to those who wish to subvert it. That is why the allegations made against Hollis are desperately serious.

The Hollis case is also important from a different aspect. If, as I believe, Hollis is innocent of the charge of treachery, then those who have pursued him, in the absence of proof, are making him a scapegoat for all the factors (outlined above) which came together to make the story of Communist subversion. One needs only to recall the Dreyfus case of nineteenth-century France to see the dangers and injustices of blaming one man for a vast catalogue of public and private errors. Nor should one minimise the seriousness of the charge that has been made: to accuse the head of MI5 of betraying the security of his country (of which he is one of the most important guardians) is to make what would, before the abolition of the death penalty, have been a capital charge and thereafter has meant a very long prison sentence. Michael Bettaney was gaoled in 1983 for twenty-three years for betraying British secrets to the Soviet Union.

In Hollis's case, of course, the charge was made publicly only after his death. Privately Hollis knew of it in 1965. But the charge of treachery has a sinister and menacing ring which echoes beyond the grave on to the family of the person involved. With the exception of Kim Philby, no one could have done greater damage to Britain's defences against Communist subversion than Roger Hollis, had he been a mole. Correspondingly, the verdict of history upon Hollis would, were the allegations true, be an appalling one. But are they true?

We must now examine in some detail the allegations themselves. Although it is impossible ever to be entirely certain about anyone, whether in the world of intelligence or elsewhere, most of the evidence we possess, both documentary and verbal, suggests that Hollis is innocent of the charge that he was a traitor to Britain and another of Stalin's Englishmen. Those who accuse him of treachery appear to do so without having a shred of substantive evidence linking him with the cause of Communism.

Although there are those, such as Peter Wright and Chapman Pincher, who have alleged that there is a whole string of incidents from 1939 until Hollis's retirement and even after which must serve to condemn him, the most serious allegations cannot actually concern the period when Hollis was Director General of MI5. It is a matter of historical record that during his period in office MI5 had a truly impressive record of counter-espionage successes: Communist agents such as Wraight, Vassall, Blake, Houghton, Gee, Lonsdale and the Kroegers were all apprehended. Some former senior officers in MI5 and MI6 make this point in private with the greatest vehemence, arguing that it destroys the Wright case at once.

Rather, the real basis of uncertainty about Hollis stems from an analysis of the time before he became Director General of MI5, the period from 1939 until 1951. For as we have seen, it was during this period that Communist subversion was most rampant and that the most important moles – Philby, Blunt, Burgess, Maclean, Long, Hart and, indeed, Klaus Fuchs – were all able to infiltrate into Britain's wider government, apparently, and surprisingly, with no fear of detection. Yet at this very period the person in MI5 required to counter such subversion was Roger Hollis. Hollis was convinced, according to fellow-officers, of the need for a security service which kept dangerous people away from areas where they might do harm. He obviously failed. And these moles were potentially the most dangerous of all the agents of Communism. Why were they not caught? Was it possible to catch them? Or did Hollis choose not to catch them? Did he want to fail?

Although there is some public debate about the precise date that Hollis embarked upon his career (it was in fact in the spring of 1938), there can be no doubt that by 1941, when he was thirty-five, Hollis had become MI5's chief expert on Communist subversion (as former MI5 officers have confirmed; see p. 179).

We now know that on first entering MI5 Hollis worked for Jane Archer who was compiling material on the Comintern. In due course, he seems to have made surveillance of the Communist Party his special subject, later extending his professional interests to the gathering of intelligence about international Communism and Russian-directed Communism (which were not entirely the same). Hollis, then, was undoubtedly the person who ought to have known about the aims and strategies of Communist subversion in Britain and about the moles and the agents, but plainly he did not.

One former MI5 officer has recalled that there may also have been a small counter-espionage unit attached to Hollis's department, but that basically it was never Hollis's job to deal with Communist agents and moles in terms of counter-espionage in the strict sense (by neutralising them, locking them up or turning them into double agents for Britain), but rather to find out all he could about Communist subversive activities.[5]

Thus Hollis was, at this stage, primarily an intelligence-gatherer rather than an expert in counter-intelligence.[6] Although he had the status of a divisional director during the war, he was relatively junior. By the end of the war, however, former MI5 and MI6 officers have declared that Hollis's personal standing and authority had greatly increased. His superiors believed that he had gained considerable experience of Communism which would, in the post-1945 climate, be much in demand. Hollis was soon asked to undertake a series of top secret and highly sensitive missions to various Commonwealth countries, beginning with Canada in 1945, advising them on how to set up systems of security to guard against Communist subversion. Indeed, Hollis is remembered in Canada and Australia (where he set up both the Australian counter-espionage organisation ASIO and its spying counterpart, ASIS) as someone who persistently argued that increased resources should be put into Communist counter-subversion.

Against this record, however, we now have to set the incontrovertible fact that during the war Hollis did not spot the moles, the very people about whom he, more than anyone else in Britain, ought to have been aware. Now, it has to be said that there are those who refuse to accept that Hollis really did fail. They suggest that he did know about the extent of Communist penetration but did nothing openly, working behind the scenes to ensure no harm could be done, and even going so far as to run a number of moles as double agents for Britain. Sadly, perhaps, both for Hollis and for Britain, this natty little theory can be totally discounted as the subsequent history of the moles proves.

The real debate is between those who believe that Roger Hollis failed for perfectly straightforward and honourable reasons, and those who adduce a far more sinister explanation for his failure; that is, that Hollis was himself a Communist mole. He thus purposely failed to identify the moles during the war and, after 1945, he continued to protect them and prevent their subsequent discovery.

As we will see later, it has been alleged that it was Hollis who enabled Burgess and Maclean to defect, that it was he who concealed the existence of a whole host of secret Communists, ranging from the home-grown kind like Hart to the more exotic Kuczynski clan, and that it was he who 'permitted' Philby to escape British justice. Indeed, the list of his alleged transgressions has become almost endless. Every new mole or closet Communist has been used by Hollis's critics to imply that Hollis was the most important Communist mole of all.[7]

Hollis's detractors argue that the list has to be virtually endless, because Hollis's formal duties connect him with every case of Communist subversion in Britain until his retirement in 1965. In addition, since 'moles breed', Hollis may, they argue, have been able to inject other like-minded Soviet agents into MI5 who continued to work for Russia even after he left it.

Yet are his critics right to see the Hollis case as one of mole-hunting *par excellence*? Hollis did not hunt moles properly, so the charge runs, therefore he must have been one himself. The fact that the case against Hollis seems on the face of it to be hopelessly circumstantial does not, however, mean it can be ruled out of court at once. Intelligence work is often about circumstantial evidence, much of it very detailed and obscure. Piecing bits of it together to make something comprehensible is what intelligence officers have always been paid to do. This approach has been neatly summarised by a former intelligence officer:

> Intelligence is like kippers. Individually each tiny bone amounts to little but all together are of immense importance to the kipper ... nothing we find and put together is valueless. All should be carefully documented and studied.[8]

In the final analysis, however, even this sort of activity has to deal with real facts and real evidence. Grand sweeps and hunches are of little value unless they can be fixed to actual events and actual people. Now, in Hollis's case no such linkage has ever been demonstrated. Instead, we have been treated to ever increasing amounts of circumstantial evidence, none of which has actually generated a guilty verdict upon Hollis, and all of which is capable of a perfectly straightforward explanation.

One cannot help feeling that both Hollis and White were perfectly correct to fear the mole-hunters' endless circumstantial investigations and not because they were anxious about what they might come up with. Rather, they could foresee the damage the mole-hunters might do to MI5 by undermining both its morale and, more important, the liberal essence of British security work. For to accuse someone repeatedly of being a mole without providing any proof is, in a curious way, not wholly dissimilar from the mole-hunting that Stalin and the KGB indulged in under the pretence of 'purging' Russia of 'traitors'. Suspicion is taken as proof of guilt, innocence is held not to exist. This accounts for the heavy heart with which Hollis and White permitted at least two mole-hunts which involved Hollis himself. It was therefore not unreasonable that when one of the mole-hunters, Arthur Martin, refused to accept that his findings were negative, he was told to leave MI5 for MI6 and turn his mind to new problems.[9]

It goes without saying that to cast Hollis as a mole would obviously provide a neat and easy ending to this sorry tale. Yet to do so might not merely be historically inaccurate and unjust, but also be to forget that easy endings are more common in fiction than in life. Here, we are dealing with reality; and in order to prove a 'spy case' against Hollis we must firmly establish either that there is a direct link between Hollis and definite evidence of subverted intelligence, or that he possessed a secret motive for betraying Britain to Russia. Without any such direct link, or any such motive, the case against him must fail. It is as clear-cut as that.

Let us begin by examining the charges against Hollis under three headings: the charges made by Peter Wright which formed the basis of Chapman Pincher's account, the related charge that Hollis failed during the Second World War to prevent Communist penetration of British Intelligence and other high offices of State, and, finally, the charge relating to motive. If Hollis can be shown to have failed over and above what might be considered a normal frequency for democratically accountable intelligence work, we must then decide whether the explanation for the failure was Hollis's incompetence, or his treachery.

The case against Roger Hollis: Peter Wright's charges

Since Hollis played such a decisive role in British attempts to counter Soviet subversion, the charges against him relate to allegations of treachery arising from faulty intelligence gathering and the failure to remove Britain's moles from positions where they could do damage.

We begin, then, with the case presented by Peter Wright, the former MI5 officer charged with investigating the penetration of British Intelligence, who supplied Chapman Pincher with much of his material. He has concluded after a very full and careful study of the documentary material that Hollis was a Communist mole and that he had almost certainly been one ever since 1938 when he entered MI5. Some former MI5 and MI6 officers have stated that they find Wright's charges so absurd that they can be dismissed out of hand. While being sympathetic to this view, it seems hard to dismiss those charges without further consideration: they are not flippant ones.

Wright's case is, superficially at any rate, not a weak one.[10]

It has been reliably reported that Wright entered MI5 in 1953,[11] and that he was recruited for his technical expertise rather than any proven analytical or detective skills. He then worked as Arthur Martin's deputy. It is important to note that, according to his own testimony, Wright did not initially come to his conclusions about Hollis from any direct analysis of the penetration achieved by the moles and their agents during the Second World War period, but only indirectly from two quite different sources.

The first was the defection of Anatoli Golitsin in 1961. In December of that year, Golitsin, a KGB officer at the Russian Embassy in Helsinki, Finland, presented himself to the American Embassy, offering to supply information about Soviet intelligence operations in the West.[12] Golitsin was flown first to an American base in West Germany and from there to the United States.

Golitsin knew a great deal and gave an enormous amount of information to the Americans and through them to the British. His defection produced the arrests of George Blake and William Vassall, and confirmation that Kim Philby had indeed been a senior Soviet agent of many years' standing. So great was Golitsin's contribution that two British officers were sent to America to interview him, one from MI6 and one, Arthur Martin, from MI5. When they spoke to him, Golitsin told them one further very important detail: it had not only been MI6 that had been penetrated; MI5 too had been the object of subversion and at a high level. As Wright stated on Granada TV:

> He told us that he had seen a document in the British Department of the KGB about all the technical work and research for both MI5 and MI6. He knew the date when he'd seen it and from this we were able to pin it down almost certainly to one document. It was one I had written to brief the Defence Research Policy Committee about the requirements of MI5 and MI6 in the technical field.

This particular document was important not simply because it showed that the KGB had an agent in MI5, but also because it gave an indication that the agent operated at a senior level, since otherwise he would not have had access to it.

Now, the significance which has been attached to defectors cannot be minimised, particularly in a free society which would not tolerate the levels of surveillance that would be needed to ensure the uncovering of every single Communist agent. Equally, however, precisely because this is the case, a defector must always be treated with suspicion. He might be a plant, for example, and even if his information were to lead to a successful conclusion, it may simply be decoy information, the attempt to deflect attention from a more important fact or an agent whom he may wish to protect.

Golitsin was clearly a somewhat bizarre individual who eventually became demented. Yet both Wright and Martin continued to underwrite his credibility long after Golitsin had begun to propound utterly absurd theories about the Sino-Soviet split (which he claimed never existed) and about respected Western statesmen (who he said were secret agents of Communism).[13]

On the other hand, there is absolutely no doubt that senior MI5 and MI6 officers did accept that a serious penetration of MI5 appeared to have taken place at a high level and a 'warning was called'. Neither Hollis in MI5 nor White in MI6 disputed the possibility that someone might be leaking information to the Russians and that the someone, if he or she existed, would be a dangerous mole. However, they believed that if a leaker existed, then his or her identity could with hard work ultimately be established. For the number of people that had possessed a copy of the document to which Golitsin referred was small and MI5 knew who they all were. West reports that the list of possible suspects was limited to five: Hollis; Graham Mitchell, his deputy; Malcolm Cumming; Arthur Martin; and Martin's secretary.

Presumably, however, there was a sixth candidate: Wright himself, because he said that he had written the document that Golitsin had seen. Martin, who is one of those known to take Wright's view on Hollis, believed that the field could be narrowed down to two candidates, Hollis and Mitchell.[14]

Meanwhile, however, while Wright and his colleagues investigated this matter, they also delved into a second source, the Venona or 'V' material.

It will be recalled that on 22 June 1941 Churchill, almost certainly personally, ordered that MI6 should cease to decode Soviet wireless traffic since it would be wrong to 'spy on one's friends' (see p. 252). This material would, had it been decoded, undoubtedly have pointed to the existence of most, if not all, Soviet moles and agents during the Second World War (for the debate about whether it could have been deciphered see p. 249). It was the Russian version of the Enigma material, but it had not been utilised. After the outbreak of the Cold War, the Americans and the British decided to try to decode this material.[15]

Chapman Pincher points out that it was Venona evidence which in 1949 alerted MI5 to the fact that Klaus Fuchs was a spy.[16] Peter Wright, who has seen the Venona material, has stated that it contained the names of over 2,000 spies operating in the West for either the KGB or the GRU and that it was:

> Irrefutable evidence about the Russian penetration of the West; irrefutable because it was in cipher.

It was in cipher, of course, because the Russians did not intend it to be decoded by the British; it was therefore safe to conclude that it was authentic and not misinformation. The Venona material showed:

> That there were at least eight very important spies. It showed that Philby, Burgess and Blunt were spies and there were five others that were undoubtedly of the same calibre.

These two prime sources, Golitsin and the Venona material, raised the question of whether there were any other pieces of relevant evidence at which MI5 should look. It was at this point, according to Wright, in 1965, that a working party was set up, at MI5's old headquarters, Leconfield House. It consisted of seven officers and was chaired by Wright himself. Its purpose was straightforward: to resolve once and for all whether there had been a serious penetration of MI5 over and above that of Anthony Blunt, who had confessed in 1964 (in return for immunity) that he, too, had been a Communist mole. The committee, which was called Fluency (this was merely a code word), decided to look once again at one other important source: the testimony of two further defectors, Volkov and Gouzenko.

Konstantin Volkov had attempted to defect to Britain in Istanbul in 1945 (see p. 217). In the event, Philby was able to betray him but not before Volkov, in order to establish his credentials, had provided a list pointing to Soviet agents active in British Intelligence.[17]

Wright has now stated that one entry on Volkov's list referred to a Soviet mole who:

Was fulfilling the duties of Head of a department of British counter-intelligence.

This, Wright said, had 'for years been assumed to refer to Kim Philby'. Philby could, theoretically, have been referred to in this way after November or December of 1944 when he became head of Section IX of MI6.[18] As we have already seen (see p. 216), there has been some confusion, and one might cynically suggest that it had been inspired by the intelligence services themselves, as to whether Section IX was simply 'intelligence' or 'counter-intelligence'. Cecil repeatedly refers to 'counter-espionage' and 'the new anti-Communist section'.[19] Yet it was also true that counter-espionage was chiefly and most importantly MI5's work rather than MI6's. Thus Volkov's information could be construed as applying not to Philby in MI6 but to Roger Hollis in MI5.

Wright has also claimed that the original translation of Volkov's item had been wrong. GCHQ (the post-war successor to Bletchley Park) re-translated it, coming up with:

The acting head of a section of the British Counter-Intelligence Directorate.

This, Wright argues, could only have meant MI5, since the Russians referred to MI6 in another way. This appeared to confirm that the spy could not be Philby but must be someone in MI5. What is more, it could not have been Professor Anthony Blunt, because he had never been either head or acting head of anything except the Courtauld Institute and the Queen's picture collection.

Wright's case is therefore a strong one, but there are important grounds for treating it as less watertight than it at first appears. For one thing, we are obliged to take Wright's word for the correct translation of the item, although it has to be said that former MI5 and MI6 officers have confirmed that an investigation was carried out as if Wright's version was correct (see p. 322). This does not mean, however, that it was correctly translated. Translation is, in fact, never straightforward. For another, it is unclear why Wright assumed 'counter-intelligence' to mean *Soviet* counter-intelligence; it could, depending on the dating, have meant German counter-intelligence. It was a Cold War assumption to think it must apply to Russia only.

Next, there was the important question of when the individual in question was 'acting head'. For as far as Hollis was concerned, he had been severely ill with a recurrence of tuberculosis from March until October 1942 and his place had been taken by Roger (later Sir Roger) Fulford.[20]

Fourth, it was not inconceivable that the precise description of the individual's duties had been either incorrectly recalled by Volkov or incorrectly recorded by the individual himself.

Finally, it should be emphasised that Wright has never suggested that the original mistranslation, if that is what it was, was in any way at all attributable to Hollis. Thus Hollis, like everyone else in MI5 and MI6 who knew about it, was acting entirely properly in assuming that the translation they were given was correct.

In addition, however, there was a second piece of important circumstantial evidence emanating from a defector; the Gouzenko testimony. Igor Gouzenko had been a Soviet cipher clerk in the Russian Embassy in Ottawa. He defected in 1945 (see p. 217). Gouzenko's book, published in London in 1948,[21] is a fascinating account of his life working for Soviet Military Intelligence, the GRU. After 1943, Gouzenko claimed:

> Military intelligence took over the old chores of the Comintern. It became an active part of the Soviet Fifth Column in democratic countries. Its ultimate aim, as outlined in black and white ... was 'the undermining of democratic countries from within. The best way of achieving this ultimate aim as well as worthwhile daily results in obtaining information was to "infiltrate unnoticed into the vital organs of Government".'[22]

Gouzenko repeated this point a little later:

> America and England are particularly well-covered by Soviet agents. When I worked in the special communications branch the vast majority of the telegrams came from England and the United States ... 'How is it,' I once asked, 'the authorities of America and England are unable to uncover our agents when there are so many of them?' Our section chief smiled warily. 'The large numbers are our strength. The authorities nip one and then turn to another interest while nine agents stay free ... We are also materially aided in our work by influential friends of the Soviet Union.' He showed me a still coded telegram. 'This is information from an American who holds a high post in the United States Government. He not

only supplies our military attaché with any data on request but
is also in a position to influence questions of national political
importance. A man like that is worth twenty agents to us.'[23]

This, of course, was the published record. What Gouzenko said
privately was even more detailed. But it does show very clearly that
one explanation for MI5's failures, which rests on the assertion that
the very concept of the mole was not something that was known
about, collapses. MI5 did know that moles might exist even if they
did not know their names and addresses (in fact, the first major
warning had been delivered by an earlier defector, Walter Krivitsky,
in 1939; see p. 336).

Gouzenko's most intriguing confidential testimony concerned the
spy called Elli. Those who have seen the full account given by
Gouzenko state that he made it clear that Elli worked for Soviet
military intelligence, the GRU (and not the KGB), and he claimed
that Elli had such high-level access inside MI5 that his reports were
sometimes taken directly to Stalin himself. Wright stated:

Elli was working for the GRU whereas Blunt and Philby were
working for the KGB. [Furthermore] Gouzenko said there was
something Russian about Elli. It could mean that he had visited
Russia. Hollis had visited Russia [see p. 385]. Secondly, Gouzenko
said Elli was able to bring out the files of Russians serving in
London. Hollis's branch in MI5 handled these files as a matter of
business . . . But Hollis, who had visited Gouzenko in Canada and
written a report advising MI5 to disregard his evidence about Elli,
had tried to discredit Gouzenko by implying that he did not know
anything about British intelligence and that Hollis didn't believe
that it was even MI5 to which he was referring. Later when he
saw Gouzenko during the Hollis investigation, Gouzenko was
shown a copy of the telegram that Hollis sent back and he denied
that he had ever said any of that . . . His reaction was that Hollis
must be a spy, probably Elli . . .

This story was first revealed by Chapman Pincher whose source,
of course, had mainly been Wright (MI5 knew this because they had
traced Chapman Pincher's airline tickets to Australia where Wright
lived). Chapman Pincher had been the first person to state publicly
that Gouzenko's interviewer had been Hollis. He also claimed that
Hollis had not listened properly to Gouzenko and had not taken full

notes. The implication of these remarks was quite clear: Hollis realised that unless he made Gouzenko's testimony seem worthless, he, Hollis, was in danger of being caught.

Peter Hennessy, a respected journalist, went to Canada to test this account. He managed to speak to Gouzenko (who has since died, after living in the constant fear that the Russians would murder him; a not unreasonable assumption given the circumstances). Gouzenko could not confirm that Hollis had interrogated him but, according to Hennessy's account, he was:

Adamant that the report [made by the MI5 officer] had been a travesty of what he had said ... 'I told him what I tell you about Elli. We were standing. We did not even sit down. It was very short. He just listened. He didn't write one word. Maybe he asked me one or two questions ...'[24]

Former officers of MI5 have now confirmed that it was indeed Hollis who visited Gouzenko. Yet it is important to realise that Wright's account assumes that Gouzenko's Elli and Volkov's counter-espionage chief are the same person. In Gouzenko's original statement to Mr Justice Taschereau, however, he made it clear that he did not know Elli's identity, nor did he know Elli's sex. This point was not unimportant, since the code name Elli had been used before, to refer to a female, a Miss Willsher. Elli is, indeed, a woman's name and not a man's, and those code names used by the Russians that we do know about seem rarely to contradict the gender of the agent by the choice of a code name.

This has been disputed by some commentators who have declared that male and female code names were interchangeable. Indeed, in 1952 Gouzenko was asked by the Royal Canadian Mounted Police, presumably at the request of MI5, to elaborate on this point. Gouzenko said that he had by then forgotten the precise cover name ('Elli') but:

The cover name in this case was of female character. But of course it is not necessary that the person was a woman. There were some cases when Moscow gave male agents female cover names and vice versa.

Yet the record of most of the Soviet cover names that can be readily researched shows that they appear not to mix sexes. The most important exception that I have been able to find is in Alexander Foote's account.[25] Foote writes:

> All agents have code names. English Christian names are most commonly used and both male and female names are employed indiscriminately without regard to sex.[26]

Foote's account not only differs from Gouzenko's original testimony,[27] but his own narrative contains only one example of a female name being used for a male – the legendary leader of the Lucy ring, Lucy 'himself' (Lussi (i.e. Lucy) is, in fact, a male name in German-speaking countries). Furthermore, when we recall that Foote's book was written with the close assistance of MI5 in a deliberate attempt at misinformation, and that 'Lucy' was almost certainly not a person but a convenient means of passing Ultra intelligence to Russia without identifying its source, it seems most likely that Foote also supplies deliberate misinformation on this point.[28]

Gouzenko also elaborated in the RCMP letter on the 'something Russian about Elli'. It could mean the person was a:

> White Russian or that his (or her) relatives came from Russia. He could be 100% English but was in Russia ... on official duties or as a tourist; or he has some friends of Russian origin (less probable) and to stretch the words, he could have attended some Russian courses.[29]

Chapman Pincher has suggested that here too there is a link with Hollis, for there was a story within the Hollis family that they were distantly related to Peter the Great, the Russian Tsar.[30] But there was another 'Russian dimension' to Hollis's background for, as I revealed in *The Times* of 3 April 1982, Hollis had actually visited the Soviet Union in 1934 (see p. 385).

Gouzenko's testimony resulted in the direct conviction of Alan Nunn May (whose code name was Alek), who was arrested in March 1946 by Special Branch officers acting for MI5.[31] Nunn May pleaded guilty and at his trial Mr Justice Oliver told him:

> I have listened with some slight surprise to the picture of you as a man of honour who had only done what he believed to be right ... I think that you acted not as an honourable man but as a dishonourable man. I think that you acted with degradation.

Whether money was the object of what you did, in fact you did get money ... [32]

Wright adduced one final major piece of evidence in his television case against Hollis. Venona material showed that contemporaneously with Hollis's move to Blenheim in 1940 a 'top GRU radio controller had moved nearby'. Her name was Ruth Kuczynski, whose code name was Sonia, and she was a member of a prominent German refugee family. Her father and her brother (René Robert and Jürgen) were leading members of the exiled German Communist Party in London and they played an active part in trying to set up a 'Free German Committee' in London in 1943. [33]

According to Wright, the Fluency Committee tried very hard to find out precisely whom Sonia was running at this time, but to no avail. Chapman Pincher, however, argues that it was none other than Roger Hollis (although Sonia subsequently went on to run Fuchs, who was already in England, escaping to East Germany in 1950 after Fuchs himself had been arrested). [34]

It was at this stage that Wright decided to confront Hollis with his evidence:

Hollis called me into his office just before he retired. He sat down beside me and smiled at me and said: 'Why do you think I am a spy?' I thought very quickly because I felt I could not tell him a lie so I gave him a summary of the Fluency assessment at present and pointed out that he was by far the best suspect. His reply to that, 'Peter you have got the manacles on me. I can only tell you that I am not a spy' and I shrugged my shoulders and that was that ...

But Wright was not convinced by Hollis's answer and decided to pursue the issue. He suggested to Hollis's successor, Sir Martin Furnival Jones, that a new group called K7 should be established in order to investigate this matter for a third and final time. It was Wright himself, according to his own testimony, who made the proposal that the members of K7 should not be the same officers who had sat on the Fluency Committee. The chairmanship of this committee was to go to an officer named John Day.

According to Wright, Day came up to him one day and said:

He had always regarded me as seeing 'Reds under the beds' but he now wanted to tell me that he'd come to the conclusion that Hollis was a spy. This was very important because it was a completely new assessment of the case.

As a result of Day's conclusion, Hollis was called in from retirement in the Somerset village of Catcott to face his accusers. He was interrogated in a house in Mayfair with Peter Wright listening secretly through earphones next door. This rather squalid investigation continued for two days.

It is, however, vitally important to realise that Wright has declared that he found Hollis's testimony entirely satisfactory except for the account he gave of his activities in the two 'missing years' from 1936 until 1938.

Wright has stated:

Sir Roger dealt convincingly with questions about his career, except for a two year period immediately before joining MI5. We were of the opinion that he was hiding something. He seemed unprepared to tell us what went on. He avoided telling us exactly who he was meeting at that time, what he was doing. He was given a second short interrogation to clear this up and failed to do it. We can only conclude that something happened during that period which he was anxious that we should not be able to investigate. We consider that it could well have been that either he was recruited in that period or he was reactivated as a spy ...

Wright's charges, then, represent the base-line of the case against Hollis. While it may be true that the Granada television interview given by Wright was only a selection of the evidence against him, it seems fair to assume that it was Wright's best evidence. Even so, on his own admission, Wright had no evidence to link Hollis himself either with MI5's failures or with the KGB in any way. In the attempt to substantiate his suspicions against Hollis Wright had to go beyond the original spectrum of evidence – Golitsin, Venona, Volkov, Gouzenko and what appear to be the tip-offs to Burgess, Maclean and Philby.

In this way, Wright comes to confuse two quite distinct intelligence matters. The first is whether there was any evidence to suggest that Hollis had failed in his duties as MI5's chief mole-catcher. The second is whether there was any evidence to bring Hollis into actual contact with the KGB or the GRU. Throughout his own account of his investigations, Wright slips from the one issue into the other and then back again.

Yet, strictly speaking, the latter was only a relevant question to put to Hollis if he had failed to answer the former satisfactorily. And, as Wright stated, he had in fact provided satisfactory answers to his failures (for a discussion of the 'missing years', 1936 until 1938, see p. 389). What Wright and his colleagues had as the basis of their mole-hunt was an important piece of evidence that MI5 had been penetrated at a high level, a clue about a spy called Elli (whose gender was unknown), and a clue that a Soviet radio operator had been near Blenheim during the years that Hollis worked there; to which one might add MI5's failures during Hollis's overlordship to protect Britain from Communist subversion.

Nevertheless, as they have admitted, none of these leads, after careful investigation, produced any firm evidence to incriminate Hollis. The less evidence there was, however, the more Wright and his supporters believed in the presence of a super-mole. This produced an eccentric and obsessive mode of enquiry.

Wright himself said:

> It's no good clearing Hollis if you accept that there was a high-level penetration without providing another candidate ... Hollis is the best candidate. And if it wasn't Hollis, who was it?

That final throwaway line is significant. For what Wright was saying, in effect, was that *somebody* had to fit the evidence, and that somebody ought to be Hollis, but if it could not be him, it had to be somebody else. If Wright is saying that the same evidence will do for more than one person, what he is really implying is that the evidence is weak, applying to anyone in general but no one in particular.

What is equally remarkable is that Wright fails to emphasise that the Golitsin evidence pointed not to Hollis at all but to his deputy, Graham Mitchell. Wright himself appears to sense the shaky ground upon which he was walking. In an important passage he stated that he was himself convinced of Hollis's guilt because:

> Intelligence-wise it is 99% certain that he was a spy ... I think in a case like this, the country should be given the benefit of the doubt, not the individual ...

Yet what exactly does 'intelligence-wise' mean? As several former

MI5 and MI6 officers have pointed out, it suggests that there is one sort of logic for the world in general and another sort for the intelligence community. Since this is not so, Wright's phrase is merely another way of saying 'despite the facts'.

None of this means that Wright was acting incorrectly in 'calling a warning' about Hollis and Mitchell, and one has, of course, to appreciate the difficulties with which he and his colleagues were faced; for the charge that he made was a terribly serious one, but not implausible. After all, Hollis's opposite number in MI6, Kim Philby, had been proved to have been a Soviet agent, and Hollis's failures could not be ignored.

The insufficiency of the existing case against Hollis is something that has been unwittingly conceded by at least one of his inquisitors, Arthur Martin. He has stated that the existing evidence does not indict Hollis. So, he has suggested, new evidence must be sought. He has written:

> Peter Wright said he was 99% certain that Hollis was a spy. I think that was an exaggeration. My recollection is that, while Hollis fitted the circumstantial evidence more closely than any other candidate, the case against him was not conclusive ... It has been suggested from time to time that yet another official enquiry should be made. In my view this would be pointless. No amount of re-examination can resolve the case, only new evidence will do that. New evidence, if it comes, will be by chance or renewed security service effort.[35]

However, where there was evidence, some of it very significant, that Hollis was innocent of the charges made against him, it was apparently overlooked, as it was by Stephen de Mowbray in his *Encounter* article (see p. 196).

Some former MI5 and MI6 officers have argued that Wright has become the victim of his own profession; that his duties, which involved him in investigating possible conspiracies (despite his original appointment as a technical specialist), have made him lose touch with the dictates of reality.

It is always easy to attempt to dismiss someone with whom one disagrees, and those former MI5 and MI6 officers may be unfair in questioning Wright's sanity. There is, after all, such a thing as Communist subversion and it does operate on the basis of conspiracy. But anyone could be forgiven for questioning his state of mind when he comes out with statements such as 'the Hollis case rewrites the whole history of what the Russians have done against the West'.[36] Even if Hollis had been a mole, it would not cause history to be rewritten.

A serious investigation of Hollis ought to have proceeded on two quite separate lines. They were: what was the evidence of subversion and treachery within MI5, and what evidence was there that might produce a direct personal link between Hollis and the KGB? Negative results in either case would mean Hollis almost certainly was not a mole. Wright had asked reasonable questions but he had not delivered the proof. There was clearly no evidence of any treacherous conduct in MI5 on Hollis's part during the period when he was Director General. Indeed, MI5's successes against Communism at this time were probably more impressive than during any of his successors' periods in office. Wright himself conceded that: 'Sir Roger dealt convincingly with questions about his career.'

But what of Wright's insinuation that it is the earlier period of Hollis's activities that raises the most serious doubts? That Hollis's alleged treachery may have much to do with his failure to identify the moles who penetrated the high offices of the British State during the Second World War? This is something that Wright appears not to have investigated, but it undoubtedly holds the key to the real Roger Hollis.

9

The Real Roger Hollis

The case for Roger Hollis

What we have just seen represents the case for the prosecution. It is in some ways a very strong case, in others appallingly weak. What we must now proceed to do is present the case for the defence. The charges against Roger Hollis relate to three distinct areas of assessment. First, the information from the three defectors and the Venona material. Second, the successful penetration of British Intelligence and other institutions by Soviet agents which took place from 1939 to 1945 and often resulted in subversion. Third, and most testing of all, there is the question of motive and the assertion that Hollis himself was a secret Communist. We shall now deal with these in turn.

First, however, a word about the evidence to be adduced. Without open access to MI5's documents, it is obvious that the material here presented cannot constitute anything like the total body of evidence. In addition, although some of it emanates from official documents, other pieces have come from a variety of written and verbal sources, some of them given on condition that the names of those who have provided them will not be revealed. It is sometimes claimed that such evidence must be suspect. In this instance, however, it must be emphasised that the individuals concerned were all former officers in MI5 or MI6 and that they believed very strongly, particularly those in MI5, that since their professional lives had been concerned with keeping secrets, they could not now be seen to contradict that.

With very few exceptions, all those who wished to have their views recorded were convinced that Roger Hollis was totally innocent of the charges made against him. What is more, most of them stated that Hollis was associated in their minds with being one of the few MI5 officers who consistently and, above all, early on during the war itself, warned against the dangers of Communist subversion at a time when others, whether in intelligence or in Government, were, perhaps, less than keen to hear about it. It was therefore, in the view of his former colleagues, more than a little curious that Hollis of all people should be under suspicion of having tried to conceal the existence of moles and of being one himself.

Finally, most of them stressed that Hollis was also a very liberal intelligence officer. He not only took Communist subversion very seriously, repeatedly urging that full resources be devoted to countering it, but was also adamant that this should be done in a fair and democratically responsible manner.

Hollis stood for a security service whose job was not to intern people or interfere with their basic liberties but to keep them away from areas where they could do damage. One former colleague described him as a decent and humane person:

> The last thing that Roger would ever have wanted, was to see people prosecuted for their political views. He simply believed that they should not be given access which might prove dangerous to Britain.[1]

Cynics might argue that his former associates would have a vested interest in speaking up for Hollis. Chapman Pincher has even written:

> Parliament and the Public have been systematically misled by official statements and reports on security and espionage affairs ... the truth has been repeatedly suppressed, distorted, manipulated and on occasion, falsified on spurious grounds of national interest ... This is an indictment of the past behaviour of the Whitehall and Westminster machinery ... British Governments hate to be accused of cover-ups but there is nothing of which they are more consistently guilty.[2]

It is, of course, technically just about feasible to imagine that all those who have vouched for Hollis's innocence and his general attitude towards these matters, and they include some of the most senior figures in the British political establishment, are engaging in a cover-up.

Indeed, cover-ups do exist; but the scale of the cover-up that has to be posited if the statements in support of Hollis were untrue would be of a scale exceeding the bounds of credibility. Nothing is impossible, but it has to be admitted that a cover-up is really most unlikely.

What is more, a cover-up could have only two aims: to protect the British Establishment or to hide a deep and widespread Communist conspiracy in Britain. Of the latter there is not a shred of evidence. Of the former it has to be said that, although there might be a natural tendency for the Establishment to close ranks behind one of their number at bay, it is quite inconceivable to me that it should do so in this case, using people whose integrity has been repeatedly vouched for during long years of distinguished public service.

It should of course be stressed, and it is an important point, that the vast majority of people who have publicly and privately spoken out for Hollis have judged him on their knowledge of his record and on his character. Over a dozen of these were privy to the actual details of his work at various stages of his professional career. Yet none of them knew everything about Roger Hollis. One former colleague, convinced of his innocence, nevertheless added: 'Of course, at that time, I didn't know everything about him.'[3]

Hollis was a very secretive person (he believed he had to be) and this makes any account of his activities complex, whether or not it sustains his reputation or destroys it.

Let us now turn to the first specific charge against Hollis. Golitsin suggested that there was high-level leaking to the Russians within MI5. The first point to realise is that Golitsin's evidence was very thoroughly investigated and that Hollis himself played a full role in the investigation. Furthermore, as a number of former senior MI5 and MI6 officers have pointed out, once the investigation was complete it was not to Hollis that the leads pointed, but to Graham Mitchell, his deputy. If, as even Wright has had to admit, the evidence led so clearly to Mitchell, it is hard to see how this can be adduced as evidence of equal force against Hollis.

Graham Mitchell, CB, OBE, died on 19 November 1984 at the age of seventy-nine.[4] He had read PPE at Magdalen College, Oxford, where his tutor had been Harry Weldon (who had accompanied Hugh Dalton on his trip to Russia in 1932; see p. 93). Before the war he had worked both for Conservative Central Office and the *Illustrated London News*. He joined MI5 in 1939, becoming Deputy Director General in 1956. *The Times* obituary states with some authority that:

> In the late 1940s and early 1950s he played a leading part in the construction of anti-penetration devices, designed to keep the KGB out of Whitehall and was one of the chief architects of

positive vetting for officials in sensitive posts. With senior civil servants in the Treasury and the Cabinet Office, he was instrumental in ensuring that Britain's Cold War security purge avoided the excesses of McCarthyism and the aim was that there should be no public pillorying of those transferred to non-sensitive work or asked to resign ... It fell to him to stimulate and expand the scope of the Service's counter-espionage effort. In this he was outstandingly successful particularly in the later stages of the Burgess and Maclean case ...[5]

It is, of course, impossible to know who the author or authors of this obituary were, but it is clear from this account (if it is true) that in theory Mitchell was certainly in a position to help conceal moles after the war. On the other hand, we know that he was not in a position to help the Soviet moles penetrate Britain during the war, because his duties lay in the surveillance of the extreme right. It is, nevertheless, a matter of record that Mitchell spoke up for Kim Philby on several occasions.[6] Had there been any firm proof, however, that Mitchell had acted improperly, either in this or in tipping off Burgess and Maclean, Wright and the Fluency Committee would have known about it.

What evidence there is about Mitchell supports Wright's own conclusion that he was innocent, although one former MI5 officer did intimate to me that some doubts remained about whether Mitchell's general low morale might not have caused some carelessness. Mitchell had sought and been granted early retirement; there is no doubt that he had suffered from the pressures of security work. It is, however, quite untrue that he accepted Chapman Pincher's account of the investigation into his activities and, in particular, the implication that he had actually given details of it to Chapman Pincher.[7] In a private letter, Mitchell demonstrated the deep hurt he had felt both at his ordeal during the 'Peters' case (Peters was his code name) and at Chapman Pincher's allegations which he knew were inaccurate but felt unable to contradict in public. As Mitchell wrote:

I await with foreboding a new edition of Pincher's book. I am not likely to be his favourite man and in a new edition he will almost certainly tell new lies about me. Soon after publication of his book last March, Pincher wrote me and asked two questions: was it true that I had publicly announced that I was Peters and were there any inaccuracies which I could correct for him for future editions.

I replied that I had not volunteered to anybody that I was Peters
... and that his Peters chapter was such a tissue of falsehoods and
distortions that no emendations would suffice short of re-writing
the chapter and I had no intention of entering into literary collaboration with him ...[8]

There is no doubt that Hollis felt he had to subject his deputy to
the ordeal of interrogation but that he stood by Mitchell during
it. In a further letter (to Hollis's son), Mitchell not only declared
his complete confidence in and loyalty to Hollis, but revealed that
he had not been aware until 1970 that Hollis had himself been investigated:

I first heard of the suspicions about your father in 1970 when I
was told that I too had been under investigation. I did not believe
them then, and I do not believe them now. For one who perhaps
worked more closely with Roger Hollis and for a longer period
than anyone else, his name needs no vindication ...[9]

What this material suggests, therefore, is that MI5's self-
investigation was carried out very seriously. More than this,
however, Hollis, despite great personal affection for Mitchell, did
not tell him or 'tip him off' but acted both decently and with
decorum. Any suggestion that Hollis and Mitchell were in league
with each other must therefore be considered ridiculous; and
Mitchell's evidence and his support for Hollis are thereby enhanced.

There is one further point. If we posit that Hollis had been a mole,
and bearing in mind that all the leads pointed to Mitchell (the last
letters of his name even suggested an 'Elli' link), Hollis would have
been a complete idiot not to have let Mitchell fall, knowing that the
Elli case would thereby be closed and that he would no longer be
suspect. In fact, he did the precise reverse, despite the knowledge
that he would then have to be investigated himself. There is no doubt
about what Philby would have done under the circumstances. The
fact is that Hollis acted blamelessly.

In addition, we do now know a little about how moles behave
when under the pressure of surveillance. Hollis did not 'flip his lid'.
Indeed, John le Carré claims to have met Hollis on several occasions
while he was being investigated: Hollis seemed miserable, as one
would expect, but certainly not like a fish on a hook.[10]

Chapman Pincher and a good story

What, then, of the Venona material and the Volkov list? They indicated that a top Soviet wireless operator by the name of Ruth Kuczynski (code name Sonia) had operated from the Oxford area during the war years and that a Soviet mole was 'fulfilling the duties of the Head of a department of British counter-intelligence'.

As far as the latter is concerned, there is no doubt that if that is what Volkov truly said (and that it applied to the USSR), then either he meant Philby (after 1944) but was given or gave the wrong description of him, or he meant Hollis or one of his deputies. He may even have provided what was a deliberate piece of Soviet misinformation. It seems fair, however, to deduce that the evidence cannot have pointed so directly to Hollis that there was no reasonable doubt about it, for otherwise Wright would have been able to prove Hollis's guilt, which he patently was not. But until this material is made freely available, we cannot say more than this.

It is, however, possible to add a little to the Kuczynski story. Chapman Pincher has, of course, used 'Sonia' as the fuse for his massive work, *Too Secret, Too Long*. As we have noted, the essence of the Wright–Pincher approach is that where specific and positive charges cannot be made to stick, a remedy is sought by adducing ever more detailed circumstantial evidence. Common sense dictates that the best way of refuting such a plethora of circumstance is not to adduce additional circumstantial evidence but simply to point out that the actual case, the bringing together of Hollis with the KGB or GRU, is never made.

Let us first consider the general flavour of Chapman Pincher's use of circumstantial evidence. He is a very experienced and wise journalist, and to have gained information that a former head of MI5 had been investigated to see whether he had been a mole could be said (as several former MI5 and MI6 officers have admitted to me) to have been the scoop of a lifetime. He could not afford to ignore it. And in his first book, *Their Trade is Treachery*, he gave a reasonable, if one-sided, account of the case against Hollis.

His second book, *Too Secret, Too Long*, is a different matter. It has been constructed in such a way that every single point indicts Hollis at such a detailed level that it would take a book even longer to make the case for Hollis's innocence. Yet some of those details are in fact very misleading, possibly even fictional.

The only way this sort of indictment could have been assembled is from within intelligence itself, and the testimony of Peter Wright and Arthur Martin may be one explanation for the intricacy of the material. Equally, however, it does not seem to be implausible that, entirely unbeknown to Chapman Pincher, he has also been supplied with a very liberal dose of misinformation emanating from the KGB itself. A case is built on a very specific matter which presupposes very detailed knowledge. This is then given an interpretation very damaging to Hollis. Some of Pincher's best written sources do emanate from behind the Iron Curtain. Autobiographies, whether by Philby or by Sonia, must be treated with the greatest care for their chief aim is not information but misinformation (indeed, Philby goes out of his way to mention his friendship with Hollis in his book. Would he have done so, had Hollis really been a mole? See p. 146).

It must, however, be emphasised that Chapman Pincher himself is as anxious to get at the truth as anyone else and would be the first to be horrified at the discovery that some of his information may have been doctored.

Let us take an example; it concerns the allegation that in some way Hollis failed to act on the illegal wireless intercepts which would have proved that Sonia was a Communist agent. This is indeed an important matter, but is Chapman Pincher right to 'Hollisise' it? He states that even before the decision taken on 22 June 1941 to cease decoding Soviet wireless traffic, Hollis failed to decode wireless traffic which would have pointed to the existence of Soviet agents, if not to Sonia.[11]

The flaw in this theory is that it was not Hollis's job to decode wireless traffic (this was an enormously difficult, highly technical operation). Sir Patrick Reilly, who from April 1942 until October 1943 was personal assistant to 'C', virtually living in his office at this time, who knew Hollis and his work, has confirmed this.[12] He has stated that it is ludicrous to suggest that Hollis's job involved any decoding at all, and that Russian codes were in any case almost indecipherable even before 1941 (for the debate about this see p. 249).

Chapman Pincher then alleges that after the decision of 22 June 1941, which applied only to 'legal' wireless traffic (that is, Soviet Embassy traffic), Hollis continued to fail to decode illegal Soviet traffic. Yet in reality it was still not Hollis's job to decode wireless traffic at all.

Furthermore, one former MI5 officer has stated that if such illegal wireless traffic had existed, it would certainly have been located by the officers concerned, if only because wireless signals coming from the wrong places might indicate German spy transmissions. The fact that Sonia was not discovered, therefore, indicated to this officer that no such traffic existed at this time or that, in the improbable case that it did exist, the technical monitoring (again not Hollis's job) had not been done properly. It would have been quite inconceivable for Hollis to have ordered the interceptors to destroy all records of Sonia's traffic, as another former MI5 officer has made plain, for if he had, this would certainly have come to light eventually.[13] This former MI5 officer emphasised that 'an unknown person transmitting would immediately have been investigated; a known person, like an Embassy official, would simply have had his traffic monitored'.

Yet Chapman Pincher then proceeds to allege that Hollis did not decode the 'illegal' traffic for the simple reason that his own communications via Sonia would thereby have been discovered. Such a premise is, however, totally ridiculous on Pincher's own terms (not to mention the historical fact that decoding intercepts was not Hollis's job). For if Hollis had been a mole, the first thing he would have told Sonia was that there was no point in using her little wireless set at home in Oxfordshire because she would probably end up getting caught. He would have known that an interceptor would soon pick her up: she was a German; MI5 was on the look-out for German spies and someone sending wireless traffic from an 'illegal source' would have been picked up before they had time to clear their throats. Thus the correct advice for Sonia would have been to go to the Russian Embassy in London and send 'legal' traffic, traffic that was being monitored but not decoded as a result of the directive of 22 June 1941. Hollis knew about this directive and had he been a mole, he would have told Sonia this. Yet if Pincher is right about Sonia's wireless traffic, she cannot have been told to send 'legal' messages, in which case Hollis cannot have been a mole. Indeed, if, as Chapman Pincher alleges, Sonia was sending wireless messages from her home, she was almost certainly not in contact with any mole inside MI5 (or MI6) at this time.

If Hollis had been a mole, he would not have used Sonia for communications with Russia in any case, precisely because he knew that they could be easily conducted via London (where he could go at will) and the Soviet Embassy (whose radios were, it so happened, supplied by the British Government). This was the route used by the other moles and agents. Indeed, it appears that in November 1981 Gouzenko told William Bemister, an Australian TV producer, that the wireless message from Elli had arrived in Moscow via the Soviet military attaché in London, in other words 'legally' from the Russian Embassy in Kensington.[14]

In short, if Hollis were guilty of being Sonia's contact, it would be the absence of a wireless, rather than its presence, which would be suspicious.

Thus while Chapman Pincher's (unnamed) source may well have been acting in good faith, his or her evidence was nonsense. If Sonia had a wireless, it can only have been to service a mole who had no knowledge of British secret intelligence policy. It is just possible that Sonia was trying to spy on MI5 at Blenheim (although Anthony Blunt, who did work at Blenheim, was a considerably better and less endangered spy). It is far more likely, however, that if she was doing anything other than waiting for Hitler to be defeated, she was servicing Klaus Fuchs. If she was also sending wireless traffic she was very lucky indeed not to be caught. But she cannot have had dealings with Hollis.

There are countless other examples of the same analytical method throughout Chapman Pincher's book; circumstantial evidence is added to more circumstantial evidence as each successive stage in his case begins to evaporate.

Let us look at another specific allegation: the charge that Hollis failed to make any mention of the Kuczynski family in any of the MI5 reports his section compiled during the war. Pincher states:

> Dr Anthony Glees who has examined most and possibly all of the MI5 documents concerning wartime German exiles ... has noted that the Kuczynskis, who were probably the most important among the Communists, are never mentioned.

My book *Exile Politics* is given as the source of this statement. In fact, I make no such statement. Indeed, the reverse is the case.

Now, there is a document which Chapman Pincher has come across (and which he has been good enough to pass to me) consisting of a 'List of Foreign Communists considered dangerous by MI5' – significantly, all of them were German – and passed by Hollis's section to the US Embassy on 26 December 1940. The names of the Kuczynski family are not on it, and Chapman Pincher has suggested that Hollis may have been 'protecting' them. Yet not only is it not clear from the document what the list was for, but, in addition, the MI5 reports that I have seen do in fact make repeated mention of Kuczynski père et fils (though not of Sonia). The report made on 7 October 1943,[15] for example, points out that Kuczynski père was made Chairman of a Free German Committee.

If Hollis failed to draw attention to Sonia this does not necessarily mean he was protecting her. He probably did not know about her, for she was not an active Party member but a secret Communist. Indeed, there are many other explanations for this failure without having to resort to the charge of treachery.

Indeed, MI5's record in trying to alert the Foreign Office to the dangers of Communist subversion, particularly with regard to German Communists, is unimpeachable. In November 1943, for example, Hollis's section of MI5 asked the Foreign Office to license a non-Communist German trade union paper because – in their words 'it is not in Britain's interests for the Communists and Russians to control everything'.[16] If anyone's attitude towards this matter gave rise for concern, it was not Hollis's but that of the Foreign Office which found MI5's behaviour ludicrous:

MI5 exaggerates the danger ... of Communist influence ... and suffers from so many delusions ... that the Foreign Office will have to educate them.

In September 1945 Hollis (who was still in Oxford) sent the Foreign Office more detailed evidence about the ways in which German Communists were being used by the Russians in the 'Berlin Shadow Cabinet set up by the Russians'. He enclosed an important six-page report 'from a source in this country which has proved reliable on other occasions'. Almost uniquely, the 'weeders' who remove sensitive material from the archives not only failed to remove this report, but left Hollis's name and his signature on it. There is thus direct evidence to link Hollis personally with an alert anti-Soviet counter-espionage section.[17]

This report warned that the Sovietisation of the Russian zone of Germany was proceeding even without the assistance of the German Communists in London, and that the Russians were taking steps to ensure that their part of Germany, like the rest of central Europe, 'will not be exposed in any circumstances to the influence of parliamentary democracy'. For the Bolsheviks:

The victory over Germany is the long awaited opportunity to revolutionise the Eastern part of Europe as a safeguard against any possible aggression on the part of the capitalist powers ... The people of all European countries ... together with the Resistance movements ... blended with Communist elements ... will not or cannot realise that the victors of Nazism do not stand for democracy but for a totalitarian system ...

This document is of special importance. First, because it shows so clearly that Hollis was both aware of the Communist threat and sought to provide political intelligence about it to the Foreign Office. Second, however, when we consider that most MI5 material never gets into the Public Records, it is surely clear that when we look at this document and the ones already discussed, there is a consistency about MI5's line which proves that Hollis's own concerns were as I have claimed and not as described by Wright and Pincher. (This document may have slipped through because it does not actually say MI5 on it; the covering letter is headed Box no. 500, GPO, Oxford and gives its telegraphic address as 'Snuffbox'.)

Chapman Pincher (to whom I showed a copy of this document) discounts its significance:

It has been suggested that this is prima-facie evidence that Hollis was loyal but there is little else he could have said at the time because it was self-evident.[18]

This is, of course, not true. As we have seen, it ought to have been self-evident (and it was evident to Roger Hollis), but it was definitely not evident to those to whom the report was addressed – the Foreign Office. (Curiously, the significance of the report is confirmed by another of Pincher's sources, de Mowbray. He points out that this paper did, indeed, go against the accepted view in the Foreign Office at the time, but he fails to state that the report emanated from Roger Hollis (see p. 196).)

The Fulford testimony and supporting evidence

Documentary evidence of Hollis's concerns about the Communist threat throughout the war has been corroborated by a number of former MI5 officers. Two of them were prepared to write a formal account of their knowledge of Hollis at the time. They are the Hon. Hugh Astor and the late Roger Fulford. Both these accounts are cautious, not because either man doubted his judgment of Hollis, but because they wished to speak only of the time that they actually knew him. There are those who will dispute the importance of the accounts for this reason; but, in fact, their accuracy is thereby enhanced. It is because they are precise accounts that they are worth taking seriously (Fulford also supplied a note on Hollis's character which is considered separately; see p. 378).

Fulford wrote that he had first met Hollis in 1924 when Hollis came up to Worcester College. He recalled that Hollis had been a good golfer and played regularly with 'Sam' (as he was then known) Gaitskell. He left Oxford in 1926 without taking a degree and he had become 'rather dissipated' by this time, although in due course he 'shut the door on his ill behaviour'. Fulford believes that Hollis joined MI5 in 1937 or 1938 (it was the latter date; see p. 392). He and Fulford renewed their friendship at this time (they had kept in touch in the intervening years).

Hollis was working in 'A' Division (MI5's administration); Fulford in the Wormwood Scrubs 'B' Division, doing counter-espionage work:

> I was doing postal and telegraph censorship – very similar work to the work he [Hollis] was now [in 1940] doing and he asked me to join him in that spring. We worked in adjoining cells at the Scrubs and talked of our cases each day, going through them without any sort of reticence and doing it completely openly ... That September the bombing began and our office was hit by the enemy in that month. My memory may be wrong but our records were kept under the careful eye of Miss Beeching. It is obvious that for the records of an office of this kind, their safety was of the first importance ... I know that the MI5 records, though never severely bombed, were in some disorder as a result of the bombing.
>
> We had always thought that the removal from London might

be necessary to safeguard ourselves and accordingly we went in October. There was a good deal of chaos naturally while we were moving down from London and there was a good deal of confusion between London and Oxford. During that period, the various spies were, of course, active and no doubt did much harm. Roger came down to Oxford and [soon] developed TB. He was sent out to a sanatorium near Cirencester. I went over to see him several times to discuss cases in which we were interested and I generally went accompanied by the Head of a Branch.

I remember saying to Roger on one of those occasions after the Russians had come in against the Germans, 'You know, I think we spend too much time worrying over the Russians. What do you say?' He answered, 'I do not think that I should think that if I were you' . . . The points to notice carefully are these. Roger was thoroughly grounded in the position of the office under dear Sir Vernon Kell who was wantonly sacked by Churchill. Kell was a very fine man and very carefully guarded the secrets of the Service. Roger Hollis – and I remember this very well – acknowledged these traditions as the main block of the Service.

In the summer of 1940, they allowed far too many people to swarm in and really of course to suffer from far too much manpower. Hollis was totally different from many other people in the office in that he never wanted to impel people. 'B' Section . . . were far too anxious, in my opinion, to see results for all their work, in imprisonment and the rest of the punishments. Roger always believed that the right thing to do was to know everything about your quarry but not to put them inside, though naturally it might have to be done on occasions.

The Communists were leniently treated [but] the opposite was always dangerous. I remember there was one occasion when I had a microphone fitted up inside a public meeting and unfortunately a plain-clothes policeman tripped over the wire and alerted the whole hall to what we were doing. Morrison, the Home Secretary at this time, summoned me to him to explain the danger of what we had done and we certainly did not do that unless there were good reasons. I had no experience or knowledge of savagery by the Police, as they were always, in my opinion, most understanding of those they pursued and to prosecute them or not was naturally a matter for the people in the Office. Certainly so far as I knew, the Heads in the Office knew that Roger Hollis had no marks of the traitor about him.[19]

Hugh Astor recalled:

> Roger Hollis's cynical amusement which he derived from the contradictory instructions issued to the CPGB when Russia came into the war on our side. With regard to his taking the Russian-CPGB threat seriously, there is no doubt in my mind that he did so.[20]

Astor had been Hollis's personal assistant for a few months in the summer of 1941 and had continued to work in Hollis's office for a time after this. Astor has also written that, had Hollis been a spy, he would not, of course, have told this to his PA but:

> I believe that he is innocent and that the allegations made by Pincher and Wright (I may not have seen them all) although damaging, do not convince me. I have not seen the evidence which was submitted to the Trend Committee but possibly this would throw more light on the matter. It will be difficult for anyone to produce evidence of innocence ... but if he were guilty, I am surprised that much more evidence has not already been brought to light.[21]

Sir Patrick Reilly who, as we have said, knew Hollis well throughout his career, has declared that in all his copious dealings with him there was, at no time, the least hint of any Soviet sympathies. Indeed, the reverse was the case. In addition, he believed that there was nothing remotely suspicious about Hollis's professional activities against Communism both during the war and after.

Plainly Hollis's work was severely stymied by the high policy decision on wireless traffic. While there is some doubt as to whether MI6 could actually read Soviet codes at this time, it seems to be the case that it could read Comintern messages.[22] Thus it is plausible to suppose that had Hollis had the benefit of Comintern messages, he might have been able to identify at least some of the moles operating at the time. We do not know what Hollis thought about the decision (although Hugh Astor has pointed to his 'cynical amusement' in respect of Communist tactics), but the chances are that he did not like it. Equally, however, it would have been impossible for him to do anything about it. He had no access to any political leader and, as one former MI5 officer has stressed, had Hollis tried to make an issue out of this to Petrie or an even higher authority, he would have been told in no uncertain terms that he was obliged to obey orders.[23]

An unnamed former officer who knew Hollis well recalled clearly that Hollis had always argued that, although Russia was a wartime ally, she would certainly become a peacetime danger.[24] This officer had been dumbfounded by Wright's allegations. He had possessed the highest regard for Hollis who never showed the slightest trace of sympathy for the Communists. This made him very different, in this officer's recollection, from both Blunt and Philby, who had openly expressed Communist sympathies during the war.

Hollis was associated in this officer's mind with being 'exceedingly well-informed' about the activities of the Communists in Britain, and he specifically recalled Hollis's anxieties about the 'Communist sympathies of people in high places, like Stafford Cripps'. Hollis, he recalled, had been one of the few MI5 officers who had consistently warned Whitehall about the dangers posed by the Russians. He possessed an excellent knowledge of Communists in the trade union movement, he knew about the sabotage they undertook and he knew too how well organised they were and with what large funds they were able to work.

Yet this officer recalled that Hollis could not speak Russian or German and this, he believed, might have hindered his efforts. Furthermore, he recalled that in 1941 there had been a directive that MI5 was to scale down its surveillance of the Russians in London. This was matched by the fact that the Communists ceased to sabotage the British war effort: 'they stopped being a pain in the neck', and the British used the effort made by Stalin and the Russians as a specific incentive to the British working class in order to achieve a boost in productivity.

The officer emphasised, however, that the keynote of Hollis's approach was 'passive observation without intervention'. The failure to arrest an individual did not necessarily mean that that individual was not known about. In addition, all information was pooled so that no single officer could ever have sole responsibility for any specific intelligence case. For all these reasons, then, Chapman Pincher's allegations seem, according to this officer's personal experience, totally unwarranted.

In a subsequent interview, this former officer argued that Hollis's method of surveillance was appropriate to the sort of security MI5 was asked to provide: he watched, without necessarily intervening. Before Barbarossa, Communists had sabotaged the war effort because they were ordered to sustain the Hitler–Stalin Pact and

British Communists were told to help Hitler to defeat Britain. After 22 June 1941 all this changed. Hollis, this officer added, had a very strong reputation for knowing what the Russian directives to British Communists were and even suspected the part moles might play in executing them, but there was a 'certain slackness in the system' which got worse as the war went on, so that the already enormous difficulties in spotting subversives increased (see p. 336).[25]

Thus, if these testimonies are correct (and there seem no grounds for doubting their veracity), it would appear that Hollis cannot be charged either with absolute ignorance about Communist subversion or indeed with general incompetence.

Yet it is a fact that Hollis failed to identify and counter Britain's moles: why, if he was all his former colleagues have claimed? There is no doubt that he spotted the overt Communists, whether German refugees or members of the CPGB. Yet he clearly missed the covert Communists. Was it that they were so well hidden? Or can it really be claimed in the face of all the factual evidence that he was acting under orders from Moscow not to find them?

Mole-hunting in England

It will already be clear that my own answer to the question of why Hollis failed to detect the large number of wartime Communist moles and agents was because there was no actual way of detecting them at that point in time. They were almost certainly protected not by Roger Hollis (or any of his colleagues in 'F' Division) but by a mixture of high policy directives pertaining to the Anglo-Soviet Alliance, primitive methods of surveillance and the constraints on surveillance properly imposed in a liberal democracy, and, finally, by the skills and sheer cleverness of the moles themselves.

There were, generally speaking, five ways of discovering moles and agents. The first was to gain access to a list of their names, or to screen every appointee to a sensitive post very thoroughly indeed. As we shall examine later there were, in the period under review, real difficulties in achieving either of these ends, for reasons which had nothing to do with Hollis himself. The second way was to catch moles in the act of taking orders or passing secrets to the Soviets. Yet, as former MI5 and MI6 officers have pointed out, surveillance is one of the most difficult and testing security tasks, even when one has large financial and manpower resources at one's disposal. Hollis had neither. Furthermore, Britain was a democracy and it was quite inconceivable that any MI5 officer should start behaving as though Britain was run like Russia or Nazi Germany and order endless surveillance of everyone in sensitive positions.

The third way of catching moles was by decoding the wireless traffic which conveyed their orders or passed on their intelligence. In the case of the Soviet Union this option was ruled out after 1941 for political reasons, which again had nothing to do with Hollis. The fourth means was to hope that a defector would give the moles away. In a free democratic society defectors play an invaluable role, for they permit security successes without a more general infringement of liberties. And, indeed, there had been defectors who had pointed to the moles.

The fifth way of identifying moles was to judge them by their works. We have seen, in this study, numerous examples of policies, of networks and of decisions which, with hindsight, appear to have had subverted inputs. The operative phrase here is 'with hindsight'. For we have also seen how well and with what ease subverted policy slipped into perfectly legal high policy (and could be justified on that basis). This had two major consequences for MI5: not only was it impossible to tell from such blatantly pro-Soviet policies that they were suspect at the time, but it was also impossible to distinguish quite reputable policies from ones which were subverted.

If a man like Christopher Hill could, apparently quite properly, advance his own views in the Foreign Office and actually formulate policy on the basis of them while doing, it would seem, absolutely nothing illegal, then how could a man like Hollis track down a Blunt, a Philby, a Long, or their many colleagues? It was only after the post-1945 change in the political climate that what the secret moles were doing could become evident; before that time, they were, in terms of their policy advice, simply invisible.

Even if Hollis had managed to come by documentary evidence tending to cast doubts upon the political allegiance of any of the moles, had he tried to convince his superiors that they were secret Communists on the basis of that evidence, he would have been considered demented. Furthermore, Hollis was probably less bright than most of the moles he was up against. To catch a Philby, one needed to be a Philby. Hollis was almost certainly honest, loyal, secretive, very thorough and careful but not very imaginative or in any way adventurous. Ideally, MI5 might have been better served if he had been a trifle more enterprising. Yet despite his failures, it seems hard to doubt that he was an acceptable intelligence officer for a liberal democracy like Britain.

What all this means is that MI5's failures during this period can be explained (I believe satisfactorily) without seeking recourse to the claim that Hollis himself was a mole. This does not, of course, mean that he was definitely not a mole. For one thing, we know that the Communists tried to penetrate MI5 in the same way as they penetrated MI6; and it is never possible to be totally certain about anyone's true allegiance.

Furthermore, as many former MI5 and MI6 officers now openly accept, Hollis, even if he could not help it, made a number of mistakes. While good reasons can be adduced for explaining them, it is still conceivable that all of those who admired his work were entirely wrong about him, and that his mistakes were not inevitable but the result of shrewd tactical plotting. Those who state the latter view do so ultimately by introducing a theory for his alleged motivation, namely that he was himself a Communist or that he was bribed into acting on Russia's behalf. Without the full facts, a definitive answer can naturally not be given. Yet it is possible to give a firm, if provisional, verdict based on the existing evidence. It is to this evidence that we should now turn.

As far as Hollis's general efforts against Communism in Britain were concerned, there are good grounds for arguing that his personal record was first-rate. The best example of this was the detection of Douglas Springhall and Ormond Uren. Springhall had been a leading member of the British Communist Party since 1932 and was, according to Nigel West, a routine subject of MI5 surveillance.[26] Springhall led MI5 to two agents, a Mrs Sheehan and Uren, who worked in SOE. West states that Uren handed over highly sensitive information about SOE policy in the Mediterranean area which ended up with 'Anatoli Gorski', one of the CPGB's controllers at the Russian Embassy. Springhall and Uren both got seven-year sentences.

Yet Hollis's successes here, which have been described by some former MI5 and MI6 officers as proof that 'the work against Communists at home was kept alive by Hollis and is an example of an alert counter-intelligence system',[27] also shed light on two other matters which could have been explored to MI5's advantage but were not. The first was that SOE policy was something in which the USSR was very interested. To attempt to conceal this point,

Springhall was expelled from the CPGB so as to convey the impression that he had not acted under orders. This was a ruse that should have been seen through. The second matter, of course, was that the Russians had actually hereby managed to penetrate into the British intelligence community itself. Furthermore, Uren was an intellectual and a Communist by conviction. Thus, one might assume, Uren's activities ought to have alerted Hollis and MI5 to the proposition that there might be more moles of his ilk. But it did not.

One explanation that has often been advanced for this is that MI5 was simply unaware there was such a thing as a mole strategy. It has been argued that MI5 could not detect the Blunts and the Philbys because it did not know the species existed. This suggestion has however been very firmly rejected by several former officers who drew attention to the fact that one of the first major Soviet intelligence defectors, Walter Krivitsky, had specifically told MI5 about the mole strategy.

Krivitsky, who had been head of Soviet military intelligence for Western Europe, defected in 1937.[28] He not only gave MI5, who interviewed him in 1939, full details about the organisation of the GRU, but also specifically pointed out that the Kremlin had received documents which only someone on the inside of Whitehall could have provided. Krivitsky was almost certainly pointing at Maclean.[29]

It is therefore not unreasonable to wonder why, if the existence of moles was known about, MI5 did not proceed to round them up? Indeed, one former MI6 officer (who was in a junior position at the time) himself told me that he had never understood why MI5 had not taken Krivitsky's testimony more seriously. He knew, he said, that highly placed moles had not been uncovered despite the fact that he had been told during the war itself that Krivitsky 'had blown the gaff' on the mole strategy.[30] But another former officer, who was in a more senior position, stated that it was complete nonsense to imagine that MI5 had not taken Krivitsky's warnings seriously. Indeed, 'one minor official' (King) had been arrested and given ten years. MI5 knew that the person to whom Krivitsky referred had had access to the minutes of a top Government committee. Despite a major investigation, they had simply not been able to find the mole.[31]

Further confirmation of the mole strategy came in 1945 from yet another defector, Igor Gouzenko (see p. 309). Once again, it might appear that Gouzenko's testimony had been disregarded, a particularly damaging charge in this case since Gouzenko had been interviewed by Roger Hollis.[32]

Against this, however, several former MI5 and MI6 officers have stated that Hollis took what Gouzenko said very seriously indeed. If Hollis did not give him much time, this was because Gouzenko did not have a great deal to say about Britain other than what has already been noted. In addition, Hollis knew that the Royal Canadian Mounted Police were going to give MI5 a full report on this matter.[33] One former MI5 officer added that it had not been Hollis's task at that time to deal with counter-espionage matters but that he was an expert in intelligence; indeed, he had come to Canada not to interview Gouzenko at all but to advise the Canadian Government on the setting up of an organisation to counter the Communist threat in Canada. Hollis then went on to other Commonwealth nations to undertake similar work. Furthermore, Volkov's list had been more helpful to counter-intelligence than Gouzenko's.

In any case, by 1945 Hollis was too senior personally to follow up leads like those provided by Gouzenko and Volkov. But they were followed up by more junior officers.[34] The real problem, according to former MI5 and MI6 officers, was that the leads did not produce proof, merely suspicions, and they were not enough to allow MI5 to act decisively, let alone to gain convictions in British courts.

Yet if Hollis was by 1945 too senior to deal personally with moles, this does not, of course, exonerate him from the failure to deal with them before 1945. Since, broadly speaking. Gouzenko and Volkov had simply provided more details about a strategy which MI5 already understood, why had Hollis not discovered the moles during the war itself?

One former MI5 officer has provided an answer: there was no proper vetting. It was, therefore, largely a matter of chance as to whether MI5 would know who might be a hazard. It cannot be doubted that the best means of effectively countering Communist subversion was a combination of careful surveillance, good intelligence and the thorough use of accurate records. For Hollis both the first and the last were difficult to achieve; the first because of the order forbidding the decoding of Soviet wireless traffic and the last because of the paucity of records detailing Communist sympathies or affiliations.

Had there been proper vetting, MI5 could have ensured that Communists were kept away from sensitive posts, although we should not forget that a blanket ruling on this issue was not made until 1948. As far as one can tell, Communist sympathies were not automatically a disqualification from Government service. Certainly, removal from sensitive posts was the worst that Communists had to fear. Neither the British public nor its political leadership would have countenanced any stronger action against them, such as internment. MI5, which had organised the odious internment of 'enemy aliens', mainly Jewish refugees, had found the exercise repugnant, resorted to only in Britain's darkest hour.[35]

Yet it cannot be denied that Communists did succeed in penetrating precisely those areas from which, on its own terms, MI5 ought to have excluded them. We need only recall Hart at the Home Office, Hill at the Foreign Office and Philby in MI6, to name but three.

The view that the lack of proper vetting was a prime explanation for the success of some of the moles receives, perhaps not surprisingly, considerable support from several former MI5 and MI6 officers. A number of them have confirmed that before the introduction of positive vetting in 1951, MI5's records were an inadequate source of information about the extent of Communist subversion. MI5 had, it seems, lists of all 'open' Communist Party members but no record, for obvious reasons, of any of the 'secret' or closed Communists (see p. 20). There were, for example, no 'Cambridge or Oxford catalogues' (records of the names of Oxford and Cambridge undergraduates who had supported extremist political movements during their student days). The only vetting that could be done in the absence of positive investigation of Government employees was a basic 'reference to records'. If there was no record of any known Communist activity, 'NRA' (nothing recorded against) was noted against the individual's name and he or she was free to enter Government service. After the introduction of positive vetting late in 1951, candidates for high office were actively investigated and there were, as a result, fewer cases of penetration by Communists (although they did not cease altogether).

Thus it is not the case that there was, generally speaking, no vetting at all, as has sometimes been alleged. Sir Hugh Greene, for example, subsequently Director General of the BBC, was right to think that he probably had been vetted in 1939 on suspicion of being a Communist (he was not one). Some vetting did take place but it was very haphazard.

In Anthony Blunt's celebrated interview for *The Times*[36] he was specifically asked if he had been vetted:

Q: When you applied to MI5 in 1940, did they vet you? A: Only in a very routine sort of way. Q: Why was that? A: I think I was vetted when I joined the Intelligence Corps in 1939 ... and it was a moment when owing to pressure, vetting was undoubtedly very brief ... Q: So when you applied for MI5 you say you were vetted in a routine way. Was that because they were so busy? A: Well, I think it was. Q: Presumably the old boy who recruited you to MI5 would have been aware of your open past convictions? A: Yes.

Since some vetting was unquestionably carried out, it is not unfair to ask why it was so unsuccessful (we do not know how many Communists, if any, were not allowed through by MI5, but we do know that many were). Are the Service's explanations satisfactory, or is it possible that what we are dealing with here is simply yet another example of subversion: that officials in MI5 deliberately permitted Communists to slip through the net? Let us examine these propositions.

The Government's own statements about these matters merely add to the confusion. The 1955 White Paper, for example, stated that it was 'known' that Burgess and Maclean had 'gone through a period of Communist leanings' and afterwards they 'openly renounced' them.[37]

This implied that the authorities had known about their student Communism, that it was therefore considered a relevant issue, but that assurances given by Burgess and Maclean were sufficient to placate British Security; in other words, that vetting had taken place but that, through no fault of its own, MI5 had failed. Against this, however, must be set the fact that people could be found who attested that they had not been in any doubt about their Communist affiliations long after leaving university. Lord Hailsham, for example, stated that 'Burgess made no secret of his pronounced Left-wing opinions' in the period from 1941–4 while he worked for the BBC.[38] Sir Harold Nicolson said that 'Burgess publicly announced his sympathies with Communism'.[39]

The government of the day seemed to realise the deficiency of its response, for it then stated that MI5 had not been 'aware of Burgess's association with Communist circles of a kind which threw doubt on his reliability' and he had not been vetted during the war when he was only a temporary civil servant, although he had been subject to the 'usual routine screening' when he was taken on the permanent staff in 1947.[40] This did not exonerate MI5, but two features suggested the mistakes were excusable; the first was that MI5 knew that he had associated with Communists but that this did not automatically imply he was a danger to Britain's security, and the second was that, once in the Government service, it was not too difficult to stay in.

If these two deductions are reasonable they throw considerable light on Christopher Hill's case (although it is not being suggested that he behaved in any way like Guy Burgess). When today we see that, as a member of the Communist Party, he was permitted to serve on the Russian Desk of the Foreign Office, it is not difficult to believe that on the face of it something had gone very wrong. Had Hill been vetted but assumed to be without risk? If so, was MI5 right to assume there was no risk attached to employing a Communist in that position? Or had Hill in fact not been vetted at all? Professor Hill assumed that he had been vetted, not by any 'face to face interview or confrontation' but by 'secret referral to MI5 for checking' although, as we have seen, he did not volunteer the information that he was a Communist Party member (p. 280).[41] It does not seem unreasonable to argue that if MI5 had vetted Hill but not raised any doubts about his suitability for office, it was, strictly speaking, acting with amazing irresponsibility, since there was a clear risk that a Communist would pass on sensitive information to the Russians, however loyal and patriotic his or her intentions might be. Any Soviet official, learning of the existence of a Communist on the Russian Desk of the Foreign Office, would have been bound to put the greatest pressure upon him or her to reveal all that they knew.

Yet it is by no means certain that Hill actually was vetted: Sir Patrick Reilly has said that at this time vetting was a 'hit and miss affair nothing like the positive vetting introduced after 1951'. He would 'not have been surprised if they had not vetted Hill'. At the same time, he guessed that his colleagues in the Foreign Office did not know of Hill's Communist affiliation although:

It is conceivable that in the atmosphere of that time, the person who took him on did know but did not think it mattered then.[42]

Subsequently, Sir Patrick wrote:

I would guess that there were plenty of Communists in sensitive parts of the Government machine and that they stayed there however much Churchill and Eden fulminated against them ...

the USSR was a noble and extremely popular Ally.[43]

A former colleague of Hill's, Sir Geoffrey Wilson, confirms this line of reasoning:

The obsession with security, vetting and all that is comparatively recent and the whole atmosphere was totally different in 1943 ... For instance, I have no idea whether I was vetted or not. If I was, then I'm a bit surprised that I was employed in the FO if you apply present standards. I was never a member of the Communist Party, but I consorted with them regularly and frequently in the late 1930s at the time of the Spanish civil war. We were all fairly Left-wing and it never occurred to me to ask whether any particular person was a Party member or not, some were, some weren't. Hill came from the same sort of 1930s background. I went to the FO via our Embassy in Moscow where I had gone as a personal acolyte of Sir Stafford Cripps. When I came back to London in 1942 I was asked to join the Northern Department. I told them that I was about to register as a conscientious objector assuming that this would rule me out. They said immediately, apparently without consulting anybody, that it made no difference as far as they were concerned.

As for Hill himself, Sir Geoffrey added:

He was the sort of person I had consorted with before the war, he knew something about Russia, he was highly intelligent and an obvious asset in the Russian Department. I knew he was very Left-wing, but had no idea whether he was a Communist Party member or not and I am not prepared to speculate, after more than forty years, what my reaction would have been at that time if I had known.[44]

What does all of this show? Its most striking feature is surely the fact that Communist 'sympathies' were simply not considered a bar to employment in sensitive Government positions, MI5 or no MI5. Thus, even if MI5 had attempted to convince the mandarins that to employ Communists was unwise, it is certain that the security service would not have been listened to. Second, however, it seems highly likely that in Hill's case this situation never arose, that Hill was never vetted at all.

Third, however, one cannot run away from the possibility that such explanations are in reality nothing more than 'Establishment cover-ups'. Is one being taken for an elaborate ride by those who held high office? The answer is a matter of judgment, but on the basis of all the evidence we possess today it has to be a firm 'no', in historical terms at any rate. People then simply did not believe that Communist Party membership, let alone Communist sympathies, represented a prima-facie risk to British security. This does not mean that they were right to hold this belief: they were wrong; but there seems no reason to doubt that they held it in good faith. This is not to say that Communists could not behave patriotically; each case might have been different (that was for MI5 to decide). Broadly speaking, however, Communists did represent a risk and needed to be screened very carefully if given sensitive posts, to protect themselves as much as Britain.

For the mandarins, however, what was decisive was, on the one hand, the wish to be liberal and the notion that the institution itself would ensure everyone acted honourably and, on the other, an ignorance about the true nature of Stalinism and Communism. Indeed, one reason why the defection of Burgess and Maclean in 1951 caused such a devastating impact within the Civil Service was that, prior to their defection, it had seemed unthinkable that an individual would put his private politics before his public duty. Burgess and Maclean showed the civil servants how wrong they had been.

MI5 had to operate within the confines of British society as then composed and with the attitudes that existed at the time. Clearly the penetration of Britain's high offices of State by Communists which, at any rate after 1951, was seen to be damaging, was not something which before 1951 was understood, still less which caused alarm, given the spirit of the times.

There was, of course, one further difficulty about adequate vetting: the existence of 'secret' members of the British Communist Party. These people were known only to individual Communist Party leaders or to their Soviet controllers. The CPGB obviously adopted this strategy because it knew the ways in which MI5 vetted British Communists. What this meant was that if a mole were a secret Communist, MI5's vetting procedures, such as they were, might well not produce a positive response. For anyone might be a secret member of the CPGB. The problem facing MI5 was thus insuperable.

Paradoxically, then, one result of the wartime procedures was that secret Communists were able to have an NRA chalked against their name with far greater ease than the less problematical individuals who were paid-up Communist Party members. This explains the confusion in the minds of some former officers of MI5 and MI6 who recalled that the Marxist sympathies of some of the moles were well-known.

Hugh Trevor-Roper, for example, has written:

I admit that Philby's appointment astonished me at the time for [an] old Oxford friend had told me ... that he was a Communist. By now I assumed of course that he was an ex-Communist but even so I was surprised for no one was more fanatically anti-Communist at that time than the regular members of MI6 and MI5 ... That these men should have suspended their deepest convictions in favour of the ex-Communist Philby was indeed remarkable. Since it never occurred to me that they could be ignorant of the facts (which were widely known) I assumed that Philby had particular virtues which made him indispensible ...[45]

Here we should first note confirmation of the assertion that members of the Communist Party (even former members, which is what Philby counted as) were at the time not considered suitable candidates for Government office where sensitive issues would be dealt with by those in MI5 and MI6. This may have been, however, merely informal practice and not the law. But it is also strange that Trevor-Roper states that he continued to think of Philby as a former Communist, when Philby had in fact after 1934 openly moved far to the right by joining a pro-Nazi organisation, the Anglo-German Fellowship, and had received a medal from General Franco.

Corroboration of Trevor-Roper's recollection comes from another former MI6 officer. He told me that he had, while in MI6, always been given to understand that Roger Hollis had known that Philby had been a Marxist but believed that Philby had mended his ways.[46]

We must realise that a number of uncovered moles, ranging from Fuchs to Blunt (and perhaps beyond), intimated that they had never concealed their true allegiance and that therefore the real culprits were MI5 and not themselves. Blunt, for instance, said explicitly that Guy Burgess had been an 'open' Communist Party member. It was clearly in their interests to discredit MI5 and thus compensate for the damage their uncovering had done to the Communist cause. In Blunt's own case we do not know what, if anything, he said to MI5 in 1940 which might have convinced them that he was now reliable, but it was obvious why he should seek to make them guilty for failing to spot him. Christopher Hill has stated that he never volunteered the information that he was a Communist Party Member. And in Philby's case, what was odd was that Trevor-Roper should have continued to regard him as a Communist long after Philby had gone out of his way to demonstrate a right-wing allegiance. (A former MI5 officer emphasised to me very forcefully indeed that MI5 had not known about Philby in 1939, although during the war (possibly in 1944) Philby had been more thoroughly looked at.[47] In other words, when we add to the haphazard vetting, possible mis-information and the fact that alleged 'Communist' sympathies unsupported by any hard evidence may not always have been an automatic disqualification from sensitive office, it is possible to argue that MI5's mistakes were the result of perfectly straightforward errors. If that is the case, it was nevertheless a remarkable coincidence that moles such as Blunt, Burgess and Philby got through despite their past.

Whether or not Philby's pro-Fascist sympathies had, indeed, (fool-ishly) cancelled out his Communist reputation, the likelihood is that he had an 'NRA' next to his name until Hollis and White began to suspect him in the late 1940s. Since Philby was, in the words of the former officer, 'laid down as part of a long-term strategy', it seems fair to presume that steps were taken to distance him from his past affiliations. In theory, the notion that Philby's Fascist proclivities and his Communist ones cancelled each other out in Hollis's mind seems plausible; the one without the other would certainly have made Philby a very peculiar choice for SOE and then MI6.

Klaus Fuchs and Roger Hollis

As far as non-British Communists were concerned, it is the case of Klaus Fuchs, the atom spy, which has generated the most unease about Hollis's actions in respect of vetting procedures.

Fuchs's detection had been preceded by another defection to the West, if that is what it truly was; important because it gives us a good idea of the state of MI5's knowledge about Communist penetration at this time. In August 1947 a Soviet agent by the name of Alexander Foote decided to return to Britain after having spent eleven years working for the Russians. He produced a fascinating account of his work.[48] Foote stressed, for example, that a mole should 'have no obvious links with the Communist Party'. If they did have such links, they ought, he suggested, to drop them before dealing with sensitive material. This proves that MI5 had, by this time, clearly understood about the dangers posed by secret members of the Communist Party.[49]

Fuchs was caught as the result of successfully decoded wireless traffic which had been transmitted during the war and monitored by MI6 but not decoded. The fact was that he had not been detected during the war itself but only after it (when he had already accomplished his chief task, informing the Russians about the A-bomb). In 1949 two decrypts identified two different Soviet moles working in Britain. The decoding was done, according to Professor Robert Williams, by members of the US Armed Forces Security Agency, a forerunner of the National Security Agency.[50] One of the moles (code name Homer) was known to work for the Foreign Office and to be a Communist by conviction. He was later identified as Donald Maclean (see p. 359). The other appeared to be a naturalised British nuclear scientist, also a Communist by conviction. This was Klaus Fuchs.

In January 1950 Fuchs was interrogated by Jim Skardon who, despite his original trade as a handwriting expert, had become MI5's ace interrogator. Fuchs admitted that he had been passing secrets to the Russians since 1942 when he had been introduced by Jürgen Kuczynski to a Soviet intelligence officer, subsequently identified as 'Sonia', Jürgen's sister.[51] On 10 February 1950 Fuchs appeared before Lord Justice Goddard and received a fourteen-year gaol sentence.

The Fuchs case raised many critical issues for British security. One of the most important was the allegation that Fuchs had never concealed his Communist beliefs and that MI5 had therefore been culpable by failing to ensure that Fuchs was kept away from secret work. At his trial, for example, in his defence, Hartley Shawcross (later Lord Shawcross) claimed that:

It was realised when Fuchs was examined by the enemy aliens tribunal at the beginning of the war that ... he was a Communist. All investigations at that time and since have not shown that he had any association with British members of the Communist Party [implying, as was true, that he had associated with German Communists].[52]

Furthermore, it was accepted that for a Communist to pass secrets to Russia was not, technically, high treason since Britain and Russia were allies. In passing his verdict, Goddard agreed that Fuchs's crime was not treason, even if it was only thinly differentiated from it.

The Fuchs case was without doubt one of the most important examples of wartime penetration achieved by the Communists. It concerned Britain's most secret secret, the strategic key to the nuclear age. As is well known, Roosevelt and Churchill decided that both Russia and France were to be excluded from the secret for the time being, and it became MI5's job to keep the secret secure. Thanks to Fuchs, MI5 failed.

There seems every reason to believe that Fuchs, who became a British subject in 1942, genuinely believed – like many other nuclear scientists – that the nuclear secret was not the preserve of any single nation; Niels Bohr, the 'father' of nuclear weapons research, took the same line. Lord Sherfield, who knows more about this issue than most, has argued that Fuchs helped the Russians to build their bomb two or three years sooner than they would otherwise have done.[53] (It is well known that the Russian nuclear programme was started early in 1942 and Fuchs had only a marginal effect on it.) In the final analysis it was an illusion to imagine that the nuclear secret could be kept from them.[54]

On the other hand, of course, Fuchs had given the Russians everything he knew. He had signed the Official Secrets Act and, had he not felt able to live within it, he ought not to have accepted employment on the Tube Alloys project. Furthermore, he supported an illiberal and anti-democratic political system led by a brutal dictator even if, after 1941, that dictator became Britain's close ally.

What the Fuchs case clearly provides is a grave example of the way in which Communist agents subverted British policy, and because of this MI5's lack of success does require detailed scrutiny. For it could be suggested (and has been by Chapman Pincher) that someone in MI5 was trying to prevent Fuchs from being detected. It may certainly be thought that if Stalin had anyone in MI5 in a position to protect moles, the one mole who would have made the whole of this highly dangerous strategy worth while was Klaus Fuchs. Thus, if Chapman Pincher is right that it was one of Hollis's duties to ensure that Fuchs did not get caught for as long as possible, it would be reasonable to conclude that this would have been Hollis's most vital duty.

In addition, if Fuchs had been caught before 1945, it would have meant that Britain would have been alerted to the existence of Soviet-sponsored espionage against Britain at a time when there was, effectively, no British espionage against Russia (we may recall that Springhall and Uren were presented as people acting off their own bats). It would have provided a line to the Kuczynski family; that in turn might have revealed the part that European Communists were supposed to play in Stalin's new order.

It is, as Professor Robert Williams has pointed out, possible to put a highly sinister interpretation on all of this. For while Fuchs's conviction led to the capture of his American contacts, the Rosenbergs and Harry Gold, no similar arrests took place in Britain. Fuchs's apparently most important British contact, Sonia, had been interviewed by MI5 as early as 1947 and because of this fled to East Germany.

One possible reason, Professor Williams has suggested, for MI5's unwillingness to arrest her could have been the British wish to conceal the significance that Western Intelligence placed on intercepted wireless traffic. If Sonia had been caught, the Russians and East Germans would have realised that Sonia's wireless activities had been blown and they would, so the argument runs, have been alerted to the role that interception was playing in counter-espionage. Fuchs's arrest was publicly attributed to his being caught red-handed (in fact, on the basis of MI5's signals intelligence, Skardon got a confession out of him). Sonia, on the other hand, would have been harder to trap in this way.

It is, of course, true that officially it was not until 1974 that the role played by radio intercepts in the intelligence war was revealed. It is possible that before the first positive suspicions of Philby emerged in 1951, British Intelligence might have assumed that the Soviets did not appreciate the significance placed upon wireless interception. On the other hand, it seems unlikely to suggest that Sonia was allowed to get away for this reason; MI5 could have produced a charge against her which would have concealed her alleged wireless activities.

Another possible (although I believe implausible) explanation is, of course, that both Sonia and Fuchs had been systematically protected by Roger Hollis. Was Hollis's failure to catch Fuchs a sad mistake or was it a deliberate act? Was Hollis himself even involved in the case? Former MI5 and MI6 officers have stressed that it was not Hollis's job to advise on the security clearance of every person referred to MI5 before 1945. One former MI5 officer described the procedure.[55] Each week large numbers of names would come into MI5; they would be checked against the record. Only very important cases would have been referred to Hollis as chief. Fuchs became important but might not have been important enough to have been taken to Hollis before 1941 and, once given an NRA, a precedent would have been set which would have been hard to overturn.

However, another former officer emphasised that even if Hollis had not initially seen Fuchs's card, such was the importance of the Tube Alloys project into which Fuchs was to be recruited that Hollis would have been given the card and the final say.[56] In actual fact, the inference that can be drawn from available documentary evidence suggests that the second officer's version is the correct one. Hollis was indeed personally involved in the Fuchs case at all times, even if there is no reason to believe that the NRA decision giving him security clearance was taken by Hollis alone, for it was a general rule that decisions of this nature were taken collectively to avoid responsibility for a wrong decision falling on any individual.

There was no doubt that MI5 knew Klaus Fuchs had been a 'Marxist' student in Berlin before the war, but this information had emanated from a Nazi source and 'Marxist' was a fairly general term of political abuse (which was also applied to the anti-Communist Social Democrats). By the end of May 1941 Fuchs was working with Professor Rudolf Peierls in Birmingham.[57] From that time on, until the spring of 1949, Fuchs began to pass secrets to the Russians. He passed over a large amount of very important material about the bomb itself:

> Including a full account of the make-up of the Plutonium bomb tested at New Mexico in July 1945. He gave all he had known of the general principles underlying the bomb.[58]

As to Hollis's role in this affair, Professor Gowing's extremely careful account (which was based upon the documentary records) shows MI5 (and thus Hollis) in a favourable light. She suggests that once the initial decision was taken to give Fuchs security clearance – a decision which MI5 was reluctant to make by itself – the damage had been done, but it was not a decision for which Hollis could in any way be personally blamed. Against this, however, we must set more recent documentary evidence uncovered by Chapman Pincher which shows a serious discrepancy between Professor Gowing's account and Hollis's own version. As this discrepancy could be used to cast very damaging aspersions upon Hollis, it must be looked at carefully.

Professor Gowing has written:

The question was often asked: why were men with political affiliations far to the Left employed on the project at all? The reply has often been given. Firstly the war was against Fascism [and] from the summer of 1941 Russia was a valuable if difficult ally. Secondly to have excluded from wartime work people [on the Left] would have meant excluding a very large number of intelligent and able members of the country. In Britain, students of the 1930s had turned to Left-wing policies, moved by the depression ... Thirdly, the Security Service had a very minor place in Britain in the 1930s. It was not considered necessary or desirable to check systematically on people's political affiliations.[59]

Professor Gowing adds that some known members of the Communist Party were excluded from the Tube Alloys project. In Fuchs's case, she suggests, the details were more involved. In 1941 a German refugee had informed MI5 that Fuchs was well-known in Communist circles, although it was not clear whether he was a Party member. MI5 told this to the Ministry of Aircraft Production, 'pointing out that any leakage ... would lead to Russia'.[60]

Later in 1941, the Americans desired to know whether Fuchs would be suitable in terms of their own security clearance. According to Professor Gowing, MI5 had doubts about this and the matter was resolved by Sir Edward Appleton, a civil servant, who argued that Fuchs's importance to Tube Alloys outweighed the possible dangers.

In 1942 Fuchs was naturalised. MI5 had no objections to this. Then two further reports were made. The first stated that Fuchs had associated with Communists in internment in Canada, which did not appear to upset MI5; the second that Fuchs was said to be a former member of the German Communist Party and to be playing a part in Communist activities in Birmingham where a Free German Committee had been set up. MI5 decided that there were no objections against him on this score either 'as he probably had never been active ... recent reports endorsed his good behaviour in Britain'.[61] Thus MI5 concluded the risk of Fuchs betraying Britain was 'slight'.

When, however, the FBI later interrogated Fuchs in America, he gave them the impression that he had been more active in Communist affairs in Britain than the security service realised. Yet this still did not cause alarm since 'the border lines between Communist and ordinary Left-wing groups was difficult to draw in the 1930s'.[62] This assessment (presumably made by the FBI) was, as a matter of fact, nonsense. What is more, since it was a common practice for Communist moles who were uncovered to allege that they had been open Communists for years in order to try (often with great success) to discredit MI5 and other Western security services, one might be forgiven for thinking that if Fuchs actually had been protected, he would not have made this point since its implication was so obvious.

Certainly, Professor Peierls has testified that he was specifically asked whether Fuchs had expressed Communist views. His reply was unequivocal:

> No, he never talked much [about politics] but gave the impression that he shared our general views. I knew of course that he had been strongly Left-wing as a student but that was very common with young people.[63]

There can, however, be no doubt that Fuchs's clearance by MI5 turned out to be a major mistake. One former MI5 officer who knew something of this case was convinced that the first suspicions about Fuchs had been expressed by Hollis, and that it had been Hollis who had been reluctant to give Fuchs clearance and had asked Sir Edward Appleton to decide.[64] But Fuchs, he recalled, was in great demand. He was a brilliant scientist and very forceful. He ought, in theory, in the view of this officer, to have been 'picked up' subsequently, but the responsibility for MI5's failure here was not Hollis's either. The view inside MI5, then, seems to have been that once Fuchs had got through the initial hurdle (one which Hollis had presented), he could count on continued clearance. Hollis himself would not have stood in their way, although he would not have liked the first decision to clear him.

Chapman Pincher, however, possesses important evidence apparently contradicting this: he has made available the official record of Hollis's testimony on this case at the Tripartite Talks on Security Standards held in Washington in June 1950. Hollis began by making it clear that he had personally dealt with Fuchs from 1940 on. He stated:

> He [Hollis] had, throughout, been concerned with all the security aspects of the case. Fuchs had come to England in 1933 and took

up University work at Bristol. In 1934 the German Consul there reported that Fuchs was a Communist. This was based on a Gestapo claim ... and the source was regarded as tainted and the claim not considered to be of real significance.

In June 1940 Fuchs was interned. In the confusion then existing he was sent to a camp in Canada which was intended for active Nazis only. Also by mistake a well-known Communist was sent to the same camp and it was known that Fuchs associated with him there. This however was again judged to be of relatively little significance and a natural result of the presence of two anti-Nazis in a crowd of active sympathisers. Fuchs was released from internment and came to Edinburgh University ... There were no police reports showing any political activity. At the end of 1941 his potential use for the Tube Alloys project was recognised ... The DSIR [Department in charge of the project] was very anxious to get the services of Fuchs. When his security clearance came up for consideration, the Security Service reported the adverse information known to them, explained their reasons for doubting its validity and pointed out that they had no positive adverse information on his activities.

In 1942 Fuchs was naturalised ... the proceedings involve the active participation of the individual and an open investigation is carried out ... This disclosed no adverse information ... On his return to Harwell in 1946 Fuchs was given a post as an established civil servant. Because he was not British born of British parents, his case was very specially considered and the Security Service maintained, for several months, a very careful secret check on his activities. This disclosed nothing derogatory and it has subsequently transpired that during this particular period, he was not engaged in any espionage activities.

In summing up, it was pointed out that a serious mistake had undoubtedly been made but that a type of espionage was involved which necessitated positive action only during a few periods in a year each of which might not last more than half an hour. Three detailed Police reports, one thorough covert investigation by the Security Service and naturalisation proceedings disclosed nothing adverse ... [What Hollis said was accepted as satisfactory and the report of his statement concluded] This account was sympathetically received and the US representatives expressed their gratitude for having been given a first-hand explanation.[65]

Interestingly, it transpired from a question asked at this meeting that the British doubts about Fuchs had not been communicated to the Americans as this was not standard practice.

It is clear that Professor Gowing's account gives the impression that MI5, namely Hollis, was uncertain about Fuchs and did not wish to take the responsibility for clearing him. It was, she implies, Sir Edward Appleton, mindful of the needs of the atomic project, who took him on despite MI5's anxieties. If this was the case, however, it is surely very peculiar that Hollis did not mention these facts in America? If what Hollis told the Americans was true, Sir Edward had not been the main reason why Fuchs was cleared; indeed, he seemed to have nothing to do with it at all. This, it could be said, makes Hollis appear in a decidedly suspicious light.

Why should Hollis have failed to mention Sir Edward's role in the affair? Hollis's detractors might claim that what he did in America was to own up because he realised that the risks of trying to blame Sir Edward were too great. He knew, they might allege, that the Fuchs case could blow his cover. Were Hollis to have attempted to blame Sir Edward but subsequently be found to have lied, he would have been caught, so the theory goes, and therefore he decided to do what Philby had done under very similar circumstances: bluff it out. Sir Edward could so easily have been asked about his part in it, and thus on balance it was best not to lie to the Americans who might well ask him. And, since Hollis could ensure that the British authorities would never challenge his story, the only real risk did, indeed, come from the Americans.

Thus he admitted a 'serious mistake' and waited to see if they would call for his head. They did not and so, the charge runs, Hollis managed to 'get away'.

Indeed, we know that Hollis's performance, which obviously impressed the Americans, was a source of great pride to British circles generally. When Malcolm Macdonald reported this incident to Roger Hollis's brother, the Bishop of Madras, he told him that Roger had been able to squash American suspicions about MI5 by 'making rings round them'.[66]

Yet it is possible to put a quite different interpretation on Hollis's statement in America. It was true that he did not attempt to whitewash MI5 and that he assumed full personal responsibility for clearing Fuchs; but this could be an indication of his own clear conscience. He felt totally confident about MI5's role and, indeed, his own part in the matter, because he thought Fuchs had been an unavoidable accident. Furthermore, the document states that Hollis 'had not been briefed in detail and was speaking off the record'. It is therefore plausible (if not altogether likely) that even though his report showed MI5 in a far more unfavourable light than was in fact the case, he had simply forgotten to include the Appleton decision.

In short, what this issue hinges on is whether Sir Edward did ultimately clear Fuchs, as Professor Gowing has alleged or whether Hollis provided the full version of events in America. If it was the latter, things look very bad for Hollis, but if it was the former, it suggests not only that Hollis had behaved responsibly and properly, but that he was so totally unaware that anyone might adduce sinister motives that he missed out a vital piece of evidence in the jigsaw.

This interpretation that Sir Edward was responsible for Fuchs's clearance appears well-founded in fact. Professor Margaret Gowing, a very careful scholar, has confirmed that her own account of this incident was fully based on the documentary record which was produced at the time; it was not written from verbal testimony or from any report specially prepared for her which could have been produced by Hollis with this very aim in mind.[67] Anyone reading her account would clearly deduce that Hollis had, in fact, come out of the Fuchs case rather well. She could recall that Sir Edward Appleton had taken the final decision in 1941, and that Hollis and MI5 had made quite plain their serious misgivings about Fuchs, but that the urgency of the Tube Alloys project made it imperative for Appleton to engage Fuchs. Once cleared, Fuchs stayed cleared. In short, if MI5 allowed Fuchs to slip through the net it was despite Hollis's personal actions and not because of them. But as the senior officer, he accepted full responsibility for it. Once again, then, the documentary record shows Hollis to have acted entirely properly. Professor Gowing's account, rather than Chapman Pincher's, is the one which the fuller record confirms.

There is one final incident to which we must turn because it, too, has been the subject of detailed comment. This concerns the defection of Burgess and Maclean on 25 May 1951.

Burgess and Maclean

Much has been said about this matter, both in terms of the damage that Burgess and Maclean might have done and in terms of the actual circumstances of their escape. For the fact was that they both defected on the Friday before the Monday when Maclean's interrogation by MI5 was about to begin. It seems hard to doubt that someone had tipped Maclean off. But who? And how?

Let us first of all try to assess the damage these individuals caused. It seems plausible to argue that they did cause damage before 1945, although that damage is likely to have confirmed the line the British Government had decided to adopt towards Stalin in any case. After 1945, when the British line began to change, both of them were, at different times and in different places, able to do serious harm to British Security. They could continue to help with the formulation of British policy and they could also pass secrets to the Russians, particularly about the British base-line in any negotiations with the Communist bloc or, in Maclean's case, over atomic secrets.

There is documentary evidence (in the Foreign Office papers for 1951) of the way in which Maclean tried to influence the making of British policy in order to assist the Soviet Union. There is, however, also some reason to believe that Maclean could have done worse damage than he did. A senior academic source has pointed out that one of the most important issues at the time of Maclean's defection concerned the provision of uranium from the Belgian Congo. The Communists in the Belgian Parliament could have made matters very difficult for M. Paul Spaak, the Belgian leader, had they known about the secret deal he was prepared to make with Britain and America to supply them with it. Yet they did not discover the secret deal; Maclean, it has been said, could have enabled them to do so, with very damaging effects, but he evidently stayed silent.

It is thus not ridiculous to argue that one of the most damaging things Burgess and Maclean did was, in fact, to defect. For not only did their defection undermine morale in the intelligence community and Whitehall generally, but once it became public knowledge it also undermined the self-respect of Britain as a whole. If British institutions could harbour men like Burgess and Maclean, it seemed to considerable numbers of people that those institutions were themselves unreliable and suspect.

Lord Sherfield has told me that he believes the damage Maclean did before he defected has been seriously exaggerated.[68] Both in Washington and then in London, from 1946 until the defection, Sherfield knew what Maclean knew. In subsequent years he had often asked himself what he could have passed to the Russians had he been a spy:

> I had no technical knowledge. But then they had got this from Fuchs, Rosenberg and Nunn May. I could have told them how the organisation worked and my assessment of the people who worked in it; where the uranium came from.

While this might have made some difference at the time, in the longer term such matters were really no more than 'gossip'. As for the strategic issues of nuclear energy, Maclean would have had no knowledge of under what circumstances and where Britain and America would have exploded nuclear devices.

According to Sherfield, what the Russians wanted more than anything was technical knowledge and, quite apart from the activities of their agents, they were able, rather surprisingly, to gain a great deal of information perfectly legally from none other than the Americans. For Sherfield had argued at the time that in their scientific papers American scientists were giving far too much away and he, Owen Chadwick and Donald Maclean spent some of their time modifying American offerings to exclude sensitive material left by American scientists in research reports destined for Russia.

Sherfield did not believe that Maclean had been an influence on the thinking of others in the Foreign Office, although no one had suspected him in any way and he had therefore played a full part in official life. There was only one thing about him that Sherfield ever found disquieting. When asked a question, Maclean would take an inordinately long time in answering. Sherfield had put this down to his 'Scottish caution'.

While Maclean had indeed passed over valuable information during his time in Washington, subsequently, in London, Lord Sherfield honestly did not think Maclean handed over anything of any great significance. It was true that he had always regarded Maclean as very able (to which, with hindsight, clear risks had been attached), although after the Cairo incident in May 1950, when Maclean clearly 'went berserk' as a result of his double life and his alcohol intake, his chances of high promotion were finished. In Washington, Maclean had been an 'extremely good officer, after Cairo he was a liability'. In some ways, then, like some of the other moles, Maclean had been beached by the change in the world's political climate. He could not fit in to post-war Britain in the same way as he had belonged to the Britain of the 1930s and the era of the Anglo-Soviet Treaty. Thus, sooner or later, Maclean's treachery would either have had to be repressed or it would have come to light. By 1950 his time was running out. But how was it that Burgess and Maclean were able to defect? Who tipped them off? Was the failure to prevent them from escaping merely another example of MI5's incompetence or was there something rather more sinister at play here?

For Chapman Pincher and for many others mere bungling is not a satisfactory explanation. Someone had clearly tipped off Maclean. But who? Two names have frequently been mentioned as likely candidates, Kim Philby in MI6 and Anthony Blunt. Pincher claims that neither of them can have been the culprit. Thus, in his eyes, there can be little doubt that the tip-off came from none other than Roger Hollis, who was unquestionably one of the few people who knew exactly when Maclean was going to be picked up.[69] This extremely grave charge, if it could be made to stick, would of course be sufficient by itself to indict Hollis as a traitor and it would carry with it the most serious consequences for a judgment on the whole of Hollis's career. But is there any truth in it? Who did tip off Maclean?

It cannot have been Blunt, who had of course left MI5 by this time, preferring the culture of the Courtauld to the secrecy of MI5, and although he was involved in the affair from outside the service (he took a group of MI5 men to Burgess's flat in New Bond Street for which he had a key), he could not possibly have known of the date unless someone within MI5 had told him it.[70]

Blunt was in fact asked by *The Times* reporters about his dealings with intelligence after his formal resignation from MI5 in 1945:

Q: What kind of relationship did you have with Burgess from 1945–51? A: Oh we met frequently, we belonged to the same clubs and we frequently used to meet and have long discussions about almost everything except politics ... Q: How much contact were you in with former [sic] members [colleagues is meant] of the intelligence service? A: None, except I suppose I would occasionally have met one or two of them over a drink, no formal contact of any sort and very little contact. Q: Whom would you have met socially? A: Guy Liddell ... Q: I remember reading somewhere that you used to meet with Sir Dick White, who is high up? A: Well I knew him; Dick White was my boss during the war but no, I met him rarely. I met him naturally in 1951 over the inquiry and so on but I never knew him personally very well ... and he was not much of a person for parties ...

The Times reporters then asked him specifically whether he had tipped off Burgess and Maclean:

Q: Did you warn Burgess and Maclean? A: No I did not and could not have. Philby warned them, as has been publicly stated and I could not have had any knowledge of this. It is inconceivable that I should have gone to Dick White and said look, can you tell me this very highly secret information. It is absolute nonsense and I did not. It was simply Philby ... Q: How did you come to know of Burgess's and Maclean's situation? A: Simply through Guy, from Philby. When Guy came back from America which was a week or ten days before they left. He came back with the information from ... Q: And he told you that Philby had told him that they were closing in? A: Yes. Q: And you did not feel obliged to warn the security services? A: No, because they were my friends. Q: You said in your statement that you had contact on behalf of Guy in 1951 with the Russians? A: Well, when Guy came back he put me in direct contact and after they had gone I had to take up this contact, and it was at this point that I had orders to go to Russia and I refused. Q: You use the term 'orders'. In what sense orders? A: Well, I had not formally broken ... and they assumed I was probably still with them ... Q: But were you able to help Guy in any way? A: No, in no way ...[71]

What Blunt's testimony suggests is that although he retained contact both with MI5 and with Soviet Intelligence, he was not in any position to tip off Burgess and Maclean; it had, he says, been Philby's work. Yet, according to Chapman Pincher, there are grounds for dismissing this explanation. For one thing, there is the actual timing of the tip-off. In the House of Commons, Morrison, then Foreign Secretary, stated that he had only signed the order authorising Maclean's arrest on the Friday (25 May 1951). Thus, Chapman Pincher claims, even if we suppose that Philby had been able to issue a general warning to Maclean, it was impossible because of the time difference for the information to travel from London to

Washington (and Philby) and then back from Washington to London on the same day. Furthermore, we know that Burgess had spent the period after 14.00 on the Friday preparing the escape (it was at 14.00 that he hired a cream Austin A40 from Welbeck Motors in London).[72]

This line of reasoning is, however, not adopted by other authors. Robert Cecil is certain that the original tip-off came from Philby; he is clearly unconcerned by the question of its timing.[73] Andrew Boyle also states that Philby was the culprit and claims, without giving any source, that the defection confirmed in Dick White's mind, at any rate, that Philby was the mole referred to all those years ago by Krivitsky.[74] Boyle adds that the decision to interrogate Maclean was not taken on the 25th but in the week which ended on the 25th, thus giving Philby enough time to turn the information round.

Chapman Pincher, however, disputes this. He points out that his date is the one that was officially given and that it was confirmed by Morrison himself in the House of Commons (see p. 11). To these objections, Chapman Pincher has now added another: that Philby could not have tipped off Maclean in any case because Philby had not after all been told of the precise date for Maclean's arrest. The reasons for this were that MI5 had determined that the FBI should not be told of it. Chapman Pincher suggests that between them MI5 and the Foreign Office did not want to prosecute Maclean and were simply waiting for him to defect and thus escape punishment.

Strong support for Chapman Pincher's allegations has recently come from a book published by a former FBI officer, Robert Lamphere.[75] Lamphere, who claims he was in charge of the American end of the investigation into the Maclean–Philby affair, has alleged that MI5 misled and repeatedly lied to the Americans about the events which led up to the identification of Maclean. He states that the Americans were not told anything at all about Maclean until after he had defected, and that both he and Hoover were furious about what they saw as a British 'double-cross'. In addition, Lamphere quotes Arthur Martin of MI5 as telling him that MI5 had insisted the FBI not be told about Maclean.

As Chapman Pincher rightly observes, if this is true then Philby cannot have tipped off Maclean, since Philby would have known about Maclean and the date of his interrogation only in his capacity as MI5's postman to the FBI.[76] But is it true? The answer must be 'no'.

For against these allegations we must set the far more authoritative testimony of Sir Patrick Reilly, who has set down the actual events for the record in this book. Sir Patrick was, from December 1949 until June 1953, an Under-Secretary with special responsibilities for intelligence and security matters and Chairman of the Joint Intelligence Committee. His first concern now is that the full story of Maclean's identification be told. Radio traffic sent from New York to Moscow in 1944 and 1945 was decrypted, identifying Maclean:

I have lived with the story of how Maclean was identified for so long that I do not know how much of it is now public knowledge. One important stage in the investigation has, however, been overlooked. This is that at a fairly late stage a message became available showing that Homer was being consulted by the Russians. The original list of possible suspects was 35, including cipher officers, clerks etc. among whom we at first expected to find the spy. The investigation of all these people was a long and tedious job and so it was not surprising that for a long time MI5 had nothing to report. The new message however showed that the spy was someone of some importance and we were then able to produce what was a relatively short list, about 9, I think. But we still had nothing special pointing to Maclean and indeed I remember clearly that we thought someone else was a more likely suspect.

The other part of the story quoted by Pincher is pure fabrication; it is totally untrue that the Foreign Office told MI5 not to inform the FBI that Maclean had been identified. On the contrary, Sir Percy Sillitoe [head of MI5] was absolutely determined not to put a foot wrong with Hoover since he had had such a lot of trouble with the latter over the Fuchs and Nunn May cases. He kept Hoover informed with messages which were sent over for special security (!) through MI6 and therefore, of course, through Philby. And there is not the slightest doubt that it was Philby who was thus able to set Maclean's escape in train. Indeed, I remember that when we in the FO were getting impatient about the delay in interrogating Maclean we were told that Sillitoe wanted to be quite sure we were in step with the FBI before the interrogation took place.

The allegation that Maclean was not going to be prosecuted is also totally untrue. The long delay in interrogating him was due to the fact that it was considered that the evidence from the deciphered telegrams could not be used in court. This was either because it was thought essential not to reveal that Soviet ciphers had been broken or because the evidence would have been legally inadmissible. I think probably the former. MI5 therefore considered that a conviction could only be obtained by a confession and in order to obtain a conviction their star interrogator, Skardon, needed much more information about Maclean. Hence the long delay which proved disastrous, especially as MI5 did not have enough men to keep Maclean under continuous observation.[77]

In a subsequent letter, Sir Patrick completed the account of what had really gone on. His first point, which it seems impossible not to accept, is that the actual dating of the order to arrest Maclean ought not to be taken as the dating of the *decision* to arrest him:

Morrison would certainly have had before him a written submission, certainly already signed and approved by Strang, drafted by me or Carey Foster. That submission would certainly have been the result of prior discussion among officials and the Home Secretary's concurrence would have been obtained. All this would have taken time. I think it is certain that Sillitoe would have informed Hoover of the proposed date for the interrogation as soon as the officials had agreed on their recommendation. Philby knew of the investigation from the time he went to Washington: he was briefed about it in London in August 1949 on his way from Turkey to the US.[78]

Philby, Sir Patrick believes, must have warned the Russians about this investigation at a very early stage and, what is more, Maclean was probably warned too while he was in Cairo, which would help explain his peculiar behaviour there. Sir Patrick continued:

All Sillitoe's messages to Hoover went through Philby who was thus able to arrange for Burgess to get himself sent home to alert Maclean without the latter's Russian contact in the UK having to contact him. Philby would of course have been on the alert for information about the date of the interrogation. He would certainly not have telephoned to Maclean whose telephones were of course being tapped. He could have telephoned to Burgess who was not then suspected or under observation. But it is surely much more likely that he would have used the safe channel of his Soviet contacts in Washington who would have informed their colleagues in London who must have told Burgess by the morning of the

25th since the latter spent the day preparing for the escape.

Sir Patrick has also provided a copy of his own record of the final days:

At last, towards the end of May, MI5 declared themselves ready to interrogate. Full details of the plan were telegraphed to Washington (via Philby). I seem to remember that some hitch with the FBI caused a last minute delay. A meeting chaired by Strang fixed the final instructions for the interrogation to be held on the week of May 28th, probably on the Monday. Andrew Boyle says that Morrison overruled the recommendations of his senior advisors that there should be some further delay and approved MI5's proposal for an immediate interrogation. This is pure invention. In the FO we had no conceivable motive for further delay. We were longing for the end of three months of intense suspense.

It is perhaps difficult after all this time and after all the spy stories since to understand what an intensely traumatic experience this was for those of us in the FO directly involved. Our service had the tradition of a closely knit family. That one of us, the son of a Cabinet Minister, should be a Soviet spy was something quite horrible and we had been living with this knowledge for months. But that doesn't mean that we wanted to hush up his guilt, shirk a prosecution and give him a comfortable retirement. Absolutely not. We wanted to get on with his confrontation.

Sir Patrick concludes:

What is of course impossible to understand is that Arthur Martin should have told Lamphere (if he really did) that the FO told MI5 not to keep the FBI informed. Martin was unquestionably closely involved in the investigation which led to Maclean's identification with Dick White and Carey Foster. Either his memory has deceived him or he did not know what was being done once Maclean had been identified. If he is concerned to incriminate Hollis and therefore wants to minimise Philby's part, he is being deliberately untruthful. I am absolutely astounded that it is possible for any doubt to be cast on the fact that it was Philby who warned the Russians of the investigation of Maclean and thus enabled them to plan his escape. The statement that the FO had told MI5 not to inform the FBI is false. I say that with complete certainty. If MI5 had accepted any such instruction, it would have come from me or Carey Foster on my instructions.

In short, then, the full truth about the defection of Burgess and Maclean serves to incriminate Philby and to exonerate MI5 and Roger Hollis in particular. As we have seen in the discussion of Hollis's wartime role, the information that Chapman Pincher has been supplied with is extremely elaborate but in fact totally incorrect. It would be naive to the point of stupidity not to sense, at its root, misinformation of a highly sophisticated nature which, although this cannot be proved, is either the product of the over-fertile imagination of an MI5 'insider' or of the Soviets themselves.

Before we leave the subject, however, we should briefly look at a charge which Robert Cecil has made in respect of the apparent ease with which Maclean was able to defect. For the issue of the tip-off is one thing, the reason why Maclean could slip the net another. In his scholarly study of this issue, Cecil adduces a new culprit, Lord Sherfield himself:

> The only official against whom some criticism might be levelled was Makins [Lord Sherfield] who failed to pass on to Carey Foster [the Foreign Office security officer] for the information of MI5 that Maclean had asked to be excused from coming to work on Saturday, 26 May.[79]

This is, of course, a very damaging allegation because it implies that Lord Sherfield was, in the final analysis, responsible for Burgess and Maclean's defection, since if he had told Carey Foster of Maclean's request, MI5 would have been alerted and steps taken to prevent Maclean from leaving England (Burgess appeared to decide to go with Maclean at the last minute).

This interpretation seems very unfair, and not only because it has generated a certain amount of innuendo against a respected diplomat. It does, however, appear to exonerate MI5 from the specific charge that it permitted the two to get away. MI5 had, in fact, been watching Maclean only in London (he lived in Sussex), and thus it is arguable that even if Maclean had come into his office on Saturday morning, he could still have defected perfectly happily on the afternoon or in the evening; MI5 would only have suspected something had he failed to show up on Monday morning at Charing

Cross station. Yet it would be plausible to suggest that if Sherfield had told MI5 that Maclean had asked for Saturday off, MI5 might have suspected that this had something to do with the Monday interrogation and Maclean might have been picked up.

Lord Sherfield has said that he had known for several months of the suspicions against Maclean. But as it was known that Sherfield had liked Maclean, he was asked to employ him in Whitehall in order to keep an eye on what he did. Furthermore, MI5 had told Sherfield that Maclean was only being trailed in London. Cecil, it should be added, has also criticised Sherfield for putting Maclean in such an important post as Head of the American Department.[80] Lord Sherfield's riposte is that this post was not particularly important, but was in many ways the least sensitive place that could be found without arousing Maclean's suspicions. The fact was that all the sensitive issues were dealt with by Sherfield himself or by the territorial departments – aviation was dealt with by a department under Sherfield's supervision; nuclear energy was something he did by himself.[81]

On the Friday night Lord Sherfield had been working at the Foreign Office rather late; he was due to go out to dinner at 19.30:

I saw Donald in the courtyard of the Foreign Office. He said his sister-in-law was staying and was it alright for him to have the Saturday off. It couldn't have mattered less whether he was in the Department on Saturday or not. Uppermost in my mind was the question of whether he was acting suspiciously or not. There was nothing fishy about him. In any case, I knew he was being trailed. So I went to see Carey Foster but he had gone home. So I then thought: ought I to raise a great hue and cry. I saw no reason to do so, since I knew he was being trailed.[82]

Lord Sherfield added that no one had ever blamed him for this; had he not happened to be in the Foreign Office late, he would not have bumped into Maclean in the first place. He furthermore believed that Burgess, a 'dissolute, disagreeable person with whom I had nothing to do', had decided to defect only at the last minute.

Sir Patrick Reilly has stressed that both Dick White and Roger Hollis were convinced of the need to secure Maclean's conviction by confession, and for this MI5 wished to subject Maclean to full observation. It was Sir Dick White, therefore, who had insisted on a period of watching and waiting. The Foreign Office did not have discretion in this matter. Indeed, once Herbert Morrison, the Foreign Secretary, had on 17 April 1951 signed the order permitting MI5 to put Maclean under surveillance (this was not the order to arrest on Monday 28 May, discussed earlier), the mandarins of the Foreign Office ceased to have any further responsibility for him. At the time, Sir Patrick had assumed that 'full observation' implied full surveillance at home and at work, and telephone and mail censorship. Afterwards, of course, it transpired that MI5 simply did not have enough men to do this properly.

As for Philby's role, Sir Patrick naturally accepts that the incident was a failure, although he has told me that critics of British Intelligence have paid far too little attention to the fact that Philby was retired from MI6 as a result of pressure from Dick White, Hollis, Carey-Foster and himself. And he strongly disputes that any conspiracy, or indeed any great level of incompetence, precipitated a cover-up. However difficult it was to accept and however unfair it might seem, the fact was that Philby had been subjected to a thorough interrogation by a star lawyer, Helenus Milmo, but that Philby had simply defeated him; the harsh truth was that MI5 possessed no decisive evidence which might lead to a prosecution. As for Philby's partial re-employment afterwards, Sir Patrick has said that this was a personal decision taken by Sinclair, the new 'C', against advice. Philby was Sinclair's 'blue-eyed boy'. Sinclair believed that Philby was totally innocent and he had long held the view that Philby ought to be the first 'C' to come from within the service itself. It had been Sinclair who had arranged for Philby to work for the *Observer* and he had provided payment for his espionage in Beirut.

However, Sir Patrick is absolutely certain that there was no institutional cover-up within MI5 or MI6. When Dick White became 'C' in 1955 he had been appalled to discover what had been done for Philby. Hollis, White and Reilly all believed the further semi-employment of Philby had been an utter absurdity. As for Macmillan's exoneration of Philby (prepared, it seems, by Graham Mitchell of MI5; see p. 321), Sir Patrick Reilly has told me that he believed Harold Macmillan erred here. He himself would not have wished the Prime Minister to have been as generous towards Philby as he had been. But much to his disquiet, Patrick Dean, Reilly's successor as Chairman of the Joint Intelligence Committee, did not consult him about the advice that was to be given to Harold Macmillan about Philby.

In some ways, Lord Sherfield still finds it curious that Maclean should have defected. In his view, Maclean had done serious damage but it had not been *that* serious. What undoubtedly did cause very major problems, however, was the act of defection itself. At first, Sherfield recalled, the Americans were prepared to be understanding: at a 4th of July celebration at the American Embassy he was introduced by the Ambassador Arthur Goodhart as 'Makins of the Foreign Office and we're glad he's still with us'. But in due course, relations became very strained indeed:

> The defection did an enormous lot of damage. It had a very serious effect on our reputation at a time when we were negotiating for a resumption of atomic collaboration [which had ceased after the passing of the McMahon Act in 1945]. It was very bad. The great argument was: the British aren't secure.

Yet, Sherfield says, the defection did not do lasting damage to Anglo-American co-operation. By 1955 full collaboration had been restored. It had taken five to six years of hard work to rebuild trust, although there had been no break in co-operation over the provision of atomic raw materials. Lord Sherfield's own conclusion is that the important thing was to realise that over a forty-year time span Maclean's machinations had done very little real harm, even if this could not be said of the other moles. And, of course, it was the succession of defectors which had compounded the problem of Communist subversion that faced Britain.

However, former officers in MI5 and MI6 still argue that Maclean could have been arrested if only Sherfield had told them about Maclean's request to have the Saturday off. Furthermore, if they had caught Maclean, they would also have got Guy Burgess.

At any rate, not only must Cecil's criticism of Lord Sherfield be considered unduly harsh, but it is also plain that there is still no hard evidence suggesting that anyone in MI5 wanted Burgess and Maclean to defect, and absolutely no evidence to make any direct connection between Hollis and their defection.

We should, of course, not forget that the discovery of nuclear energy introduced a new and frightening element into espionage and counter-espionage, which required greater professionalism from MI5. Although the nuclear secret did not belong to any one nation, the need for secrecy was not exaggerated either in respect of Nazi Germany or in terms of the Soviet Union, both of which were totalitarian dictatorships.

Niels Bohr himself was unfairly suspected by Churchill of being a
potential source of disloyalty, to the distress of a number of his
colleagues, including Lord Cherwell.[83] In April 1944 Bohr returned
to London from America, and found waiting for him a letter from
a Russian scientist who had been part of the Cambridge Cavendish
team until 1934. Bohr formed a 'strong impression' that the Russians
knew about the Tube Alloys project (he was right; they did, thanks
to Nunn May and Fuchs) and Bohr was invited to visit Russia to
discuss his work in detail.

Bohr replied in a non-committal letter which had the full agreement of MI5; he then attempted to persuade both Churchill and
Roosevelt to tell the Russians the secret behind the Tube Alloys
project. Roosevelt had originally agreed that the Russians ought to
be told about the bomb, and he claimed that the secrecy about it
'worried him to death'. But Churchill was infuriated by Bohr's
behaviour – 'he ought to be confined [i.e. interned] or made to see
that he is very near the edge of mortal crimes'.[84]

Indeed, so upset was Churchill that he had written into the September 1944 Hyde Park Agreement that:

Enquiries should be made regarding the activities of Professor
Bohr and steps taken to ensure that he is responsible for no leakage
... to the Russians.

Furthermore, when in the summer of 1945 forty distinguished
British scientists were invited to visit Russia: 'on Churchill's instructions, all those having any knowledge of Tube Alloys were prevented
from going'.[85] Since Fuchs and Nunn May had already spilt the
beans, the moral seems to be that the political control of knowledge,
particularly scientific knowledge, is, in a free society, a good deal
harder to secure than many politicians would want. It is probably
just as well.

There is, therefore, no firm evidence on which to 'start a spy case'
against Roger Hollis in terms of the Fuchs, Burgess and Maclean
cases; indeed, a number of the allegations that have been made
against him personally are very difficult to sustain.

At the end of the day, however, Maclean and Burgess, and indeed
Philby himself, did get away. There is no doubt that the full explanations that have been offered for this make it quite plain that Hollis
was in no way guilty of suspicious behaviour, let alone of acting on
behalf of the Russians. None of these moles was being 'protected'

by either Hollis or the 'Establishment', save in being treated fairly and properly. Yet the fact remains that MI5 failed and failed badly. This failure could be attributed to sheer incompetence (and to factors like a shortage of manpower). It could also be attributed, and arguably more accurately, both to the difficulty of detecting moles against the political climate of the Grand Alliance and to the checks which operated on a security service which was responsive to British democracy and the special historical position which had developed as a result of the onset of the Cold War. MI5 did not want to intern people; it did not want to be a secret police. There was, however, a price to be paid for this, although one cannot help agreeing with the view put forward by several former MI5 and MI6 officers that this price was not too high if the end result was an enlightened secret service.

It is, perhaps, not entirely coincidental that Tom Driberg, who himself appears to have worked as a double agent for MI5, made this very case in 1955:

I say it is better that there should be a few Burgess and Maclean cases than that our nation should be like a McCarthyite police state with elaborate checks on people's movements.[86]

Of course, those hostile to this view will point out that it appears to give all the benefits to those who sought to betray Britain and none to Britain itself. This is, however, a gross exaggeration of the position: in an efficient police state, the innocent suffer almost as much as the guilty. (It is hardly a coincidence that Hitler should have said 'terror is good for people' or that Stalin would certainly have concurred with this sentiment.)

Finally, it must be stressed that the activities of the moles did great damage; that British and Soviet interests were patently not 'the same'. The very fact that Moscow felt constrained to give these people their orders proves this was the case even if, for historical reasons, the truth was virtually impossible to perceive. That is why it is correct to speak of Communist subversion; to make it absolutely clear that these people acted surreptitiously and secretly because they knew that what they were doing would undermine Britain and the West.

It is important not to exaggerate the net effect of Communist subversion and hence overestimate the damage that was done. The defection of Burgess and Maclean was a severe blow to British morale. But it was not a fatal one. Emotionally, treachery seems an absolute offence. History, however, knows of far worse crimes committed in worse ways at this very point in time. Popular outrage is often an unreliable guide to interpretation. Lord Sherfield's testimony may, for some tastes, err in the direction of lenience towards Maclean, but his insistence that blanket indictments of treachery should not be permitted to suffocate a rational assessment of the damage caused by individual moles is entirely correct.

One immediate result of Burgess and Maclean's flight was that on 4 September 1951 the then Prime Minister, Attlee, reluctantly agreed to far more stringent vetting procedures for officials in sensitive posts. Such people were henceforward to be actively investigated (by 'positive vetting') rather than checked against a card index. Had Burgess and Maclean not disappeared, this might not have happened for a decade or longer. Indeed, it is intriguing to speculate on what might have happened had Burgess and Maclean not defected. It seems likely that Maclean would have received a prison term although this may not have been excessive. Burgess and Philby would have been less vulnerable; indeed, the KGB could have foreseen that Burgess's defection would draw attention to Philby, suggesting that his was indeed a last-minute decision, one not wanted by the Russians. Having said this, however, it is important to realise that by 1951 the Russians knew that Maclean's usefulness to them was over. As can be argued in the case of Otto John, they may have reasoned that a defection would be the best way of inflicting a last blow to British interests, a final flourish that, if Sherfield is correct, was probably more damaging *in toto* than all of the two moles' other works.

A man and his character; a man and his motives

As we have seen, there is ample evidence to suggest that some of the theories that have been advanced for Hollis's failure to catch the major British Communist moles during the period of their maximum penetration quite simply hold no water. It is not true that no one in MI5 kept tabs on the Communists during the Second World War; it is not true that MI5 as an institution was incompetent. What can, however, be held up as a reasonable prima-facie charge against Hollis, namely that he does not appear to have known about the secret Communist agents within the high offices of the British State, could have been the outcome of genuine and unavoidable ignorance. Yet it has to be admitted that it could also be explained by Hollis being a mole.

Was the reason for MI5's lack of real success in exposing the moles the fact that its chief expert on Communism was incompetent? Or was he a traitor? We have pursued the various charges against him and we have seen that he was not incompetent when dealing with Communism generally, although his mole-hunting was clearly poor. Do the few moles that he did catch scotch any notion of treachery? Hollis's detractors reject this, arguing that Hollis appears to have been selectively incompetent, that is, catching some minor Communist agents but letting the major ones have their freedom.

So was Hollis's treachery the real secret of the service? Was it that Hollis was in truth a secret Communist, thus making nugatory the whole series of reasonable counter-explanations discussed earlier? Were the arguments put forward on his behalf simply parts of an alibi constructed by him, and perhaps by others, to save his skin and ensure that he could continue to work for the Soviet Union? Or was the real secret of the service the stark fact that the moles were simply undetectable; that, short of catching them in the act of treachery, they could be detected neither by Roger Hollis nor, indeed, by anyone else?

Those who posit that Hollis was a mole, and they include, of course, a number of former MI5 and MI6 officers and not just Chapman Pincher, cannot bring together MI5's failures and Hollis's activities except in the non-specific sense that he was MI5's Communist expert during the war. To condemn Hollis, however, one has to do more than this. One needs to prove that he had a motive. Have they done so? The answer is no.

The facts revealed by the late Sir John Masterman proved that MI5 had successfully contained the Nazi espionage assault on this country.[87] There was virtually no German spy in Britain who had not been uncovered and a great many of them were then 'turned' into British double agents.

The question must therefore be put: MI6's failures may be attributed to a mixture of high policy and Kim Philby, where the former was very much more significant than the latter. To what may MI5's failures be attributed, bearing in mind that high policy decisions did not rule out all its surveillance of Communist activities and that Roger Hollis was demonstrably neither inactive in working against some forms of Communist subversion nor ignorant in principle about Stalin's mole strategy?

Is there any justification for Chapman Pincher's blunt reply to this question?

> The basic answer is straightforward: the Germans were totally unable to penetrate the British secret services. Against the Soviets ... performance has been pathetic because both MI5 and MI6 ... have been deeply penetrated by Soviet agents.[88]

Of whom the major example, in Chapman Pincher's view, is Hollis himself. As we have seen, Chapman Pincher's entire attack on British Intelligence emanates from a gross oversimplification of a complex historical issue. Yet his writings based on the testimony of Peter Wright do raise important issues (not all of them ones of his choosing) and there is no doubt that he has successfully called Roger Hollis's reputation into question, and that for many people, both in Britain and abroad, Hollis's career has been badly, perhaps irreparably, tarnished. While many senior figures in the British political establishment who knew Hollis and worked with him have no doubts about his loyalty, the wider public is far less certain about its verdict upon him.

Hollis's detractors have pursued two different lines of enquiry in trying to establish a motive. There are those, like Chapman Pincher, who have suggested that both the connection between Hollis and the Russians, as well as a motive, are to be sought in the time he spent in China. Others (possibly after considering evidence I discussed in *The Times* on 3 April 1982) have argued that the Chinese days do not provide the answer. Instead they adduce the theory of the 'missing two years', the period from Hollis's return from China in 1936 to his appointment to MI5 in 1938.

Before we explore the detailed evidence supporting these two theories, however, we must spend some time considering the nature of Hollis's character. Many historians would doubt that character studies have any part to play in historical analysis. Their reason is that the most important factors in political and social change are vast and impersonal. While this may possibly be true in the wider political context, in any analysis of intelligence matters character must play a vital role.

It is very important, for a variety of reasons, to try to establish an accurate picture of Hollis's character. For one thing, what might be called a weak character could indicate a possible area which might be exploited by a blackmailer. For another, it might indicate mendacity, which would suggest the ability to deceive others. Finally, whether in high politics or in low spying terms, much depends on whether one can really trust an individual, whether they are truly what they say they are. No one can ever be entirely certain about anybody: what helps one to decide whether to trust them or not is very often their character.

On the face of it, Hollis has virtually impeccable character references for every stage of his career apart from his time as an undergraduate at Oxford. When I first began to take an interest in Hollis's activities, I received many letters from people who had known him. One letter came from a farmer who wrote:

This is just to thank you for vindicating my friend Roger Hollis so convincingly. I was at Clifton, as a contemporary with Roger. The whole family seemed to be thoroughly nice, well-affected, all being on good terms with each other. Roger at school seemed quite normal, taking several wickets in house-matches and being quite good at fives. After I left school, I met Roger only once. He was posting late letters at a city post office, on behalf of some foreign bank, I think, while I happened to be an office boy for an insurance company, doing likewise. He did not seem too pleased to be caught on such a menial task. You have put my mind at rest after the horrifying accusations of Mr Chapman Pincher.[89]

Another communication came from a former secretary:

At last someone has written with justice and common sense about poor Roger Hollis. I was a secretary in MI5 a lot of that time at Blenheim. Speaking both for myself and other secretaries of that period that I have asked, we could not conceive how anyone could seriously suppose that Roger Hollis was a traitor. Good secretaries in any organisation normally have a thorough grasp of the character and capabilities of the people they work for. Hollis was a man of integrity; ordinary, unimaginative, conscientious, hardworking, though not a particularly clever man. We were somewhat surprised when we heard that he had been made DG as we realised that he had always been appointed above his station.

We were not in the least surprised when we heard that Anthony Blunt was a traitor. He was always said to be charming by the people who worked in his section but the rest of us tended to regard him as an ice cold bastard, knowing that anyone who was not important to him did not exist. PS Maybe 'Elli' was a woman in the registry![90]

And, concerning Hollis's final years, the former headmaster of Wells Cathedral School, Alan Quilter, wrote:

Roger Hollis moved to Wells on his retirement and became a Governor of the School just after I arrived. He was always ready to be helpful in all matters concerning the welfare of the School. I liked Sir Roger. He was obviously a highly intelligent, thoughtful man. He was kindly and very supportive. He was well-liked by all those with whom he came into contact in the school. I was genuinely surprised to hear of his divorce; it seemed perfectly in character with him that he decided that he should resign as Governor and I was very sorry to lose contact with such a friendly, helpful person.[91]

A cynic would, of course, argue that such character references merely bespeak Hollis's great skill in presenting a false picture to the world. But a senior former MI5 officer, who had personal experience of all the moles, has stated that none of them could ever have got such comprehensive testimonials.[92] This does not mean that Hollis was an easy person. A number of former MI5 and MI6 officers have declared that Hollis was always a very decent man, but he was not generally liked in the office; he found it hard to relate to his junior staff and he was not good at being one of a group. In a phrase used by more than one officer, he was summed up as 'a reserved and very secret man'.

Lord Sherfield, who met him on several occasions, said:

Hollis appeared to be a Black Catholic with a dark and sinister appearance. But I never had suspicions about him at all. Hollis was sharp; he didn't ramble. There was never any indication that anything might be wrong. What is more Burke Trend was convinced there wasn't – and he's a very thorough man.[93]

Sir Patrick Reilly, who knew Hollis well throughout his professional career and also has no doubts about his loyalty, has confirmed Sherfield's analysis. Sir Patrick liked Hollis and was, indeed, a friend of his, but he recognised Hollis's mysterious side, as he recalled (with some relish):

> He certainly was an unusual man. His appearance was strange. There was always a vague impression of something odd. And he was very, very reserved.[94]

Sir Patrick has also pointed to the letter Roger Hollis sent him on 11 December 1956 on Reilly's appointment as HM Ambassador to Russia (see pp. 374–5). In it Hollis wrote:

> ... You will come up against many matters which interest me. If you have the time, I should very much like to discuss them with you before you go.

This letter could be seen by some as intrusive; indeed, there was something chilling about the head of MI5 asking to see someone going to Russia, if only because one might suspect one was being asked to do something very undiplomatic. Hollis's detractors would argue that his true purpose in wanting to see Sir Patrick was that he wished to discover precisely what Reilly would be looking at when he got to Moscow. Others, however, would argue that an alert MI5 boss ought certainly to have exchanged views with a prospective Ambassador to Moscow. After all, Communism in Britain and the colonies was indeed controlled from the Kremlin, and it was an indication of Hollis's thoroughness that he should pay due regard to this. In addition, of course, Hollis and Sir Patrick had known each other ever since the latter's wartime days in MI6. Those who knew him as well as Sir Patrick naturally met Hollis in the awareness that he carried within him the secrets of a nation.

There was an interesting sequel to this letter. In June 1960 Roger Hollis's son was invited to attend a chess tournament in Leningrad and Sir Patrick was asked whether he believed it safe for him to go. On 15 June Sir Patrick replied:

> I can see no reason to advise against your son's visit. If the Russians take note of his parentage it is, if anything, more likely to make them treat him with the extra respect due to the son of an important if hidden member of the Establishment.[95]

It also seems plausible to believe that Hollis, who had gone down

11.   12.   56

My dear Patrick.

I was in America or the Caribbean when your new appointment was announced, and the tasks of resettling myself here since my return have caused me to overlook it. May I now send you my congratulations on this very distinguished promotion.

One would sympathise with some trouble on such an appointment for I fear it will bring much toil and frustration with it, but you are a brave and resolute fighter and will not need sympathy. I hope you will be strengthened by the belief of all your friends that you will do the job splendidly.

You will come up against many matters which interest me. If you have the time I should very much like to discuss them with you before you go.

Yours ever,

Roger Hollis.

2 A letter from the Director General of MI5. Roger Hollis asks to see Sir Patrick Reilly before the latter's departure for Moscow

from Oxford without a degree, may have felt some unease in the company of the 'best and the brightest'. Sir Patrick's own intellectual ability (he was elected a Fellow of All Souls after completing an undergraduate degree) might well have daunted Hollis.

Sir Patrick contrasted Hollis with Philby, Maclean and Blunt, all of whom he had also known. Hollis was quite unlike them. Sir Patrick differentiates him in particular from Blunt, whom he could still see today 'standing there in his Captain's uniform, very cold, very aloof'. After the war he had once met Blunt at a party; much to his surprise, Blunt had cut him totally dead as if he wished to deny that he had ever known him. Subsequently, Sir Patrick was to learn why. Blunt had a lot about his time in MI5 that he wished to forget.

Those who saw Hollis out of the office, as it were, had yet another perspective on him. An early golfing friend, who was related to Hollis's first wife and knew him throughout his adult life, found him rather like an overgrown schoolboy. He was very competitive; he liked winning. He never talked about his job or about politics except to say things like 'one ought to buy British'. As for his home life: Hollis's marriage was difficult. In his friend's view, Hollis's first wife was:

> An intellectual and a pinch-penny. She served terrible food and got very cross when Roger got silly after drink. She complained every single evening about his coming home late; since he never came home until eight, there was always friction. Roger once said to me, 'I didn't know about girls before I got married. We were a family of boys; I then went out East. She was the first girl I ever had anything to do with.' When Hollis retired, he tried to make a go of his marriage but it was no good. One day he told me that after thirty years of marriage, he was going to divorce Eve [his wife]. He said, 'I made a mistake and I know you think I'm a shit. But it has to be done.'

This friend added:

> Roger never mentioned any foreign girls. He had a strong view that English things were best. His worst fault was that he could be lavatorial after a drink. And he was a very poor drinker; he did not have a good head. He never discussed his work. But I do remember that in 1956 I asked him about Suez. He replied, 'Eden's

policy is nonsense', but he was a Conservative. I also remember that when those two fellows [Burgess and Maclean] got away Roger was having a round of golf with two American generals. They were half way round the course when a messenger came with an urgent telegramme. Roger said he would have to break off. The Americans were furious; they said it had ruined the game. Roger was ordinary, quite witty and very amusing. He was a good Committee man and loved Committee work. He enjoyed a story about anyone who was unusual or absurd. He was entirely English, dyed-in-the-wool, hated lapses of procedure or sloppiness. And he loved golf.[96]

Hollis's brother, Bishop Michael Hollis, recalled a book that Hollis was proud of, inscribed by J. Edgar Hoover, the FBI boss, in his own hand, expressing 'friendship and admiration'. Hoover also gave Hollis a treasured golf putter. Once again, such evidence is circumstantial but by no means insignificant.[97]

It was not only Hollis's golfing friend who knew that his marriage to Evelyn Swayne was unhappy. His colleagues in the office knew about this, and some of them found the first Lady Hollis very difficult and always very anxious about money matters. Roger was, however, not a bad father: he was proud of his son Adrian (now an Oxford classics don) and his first granddaughter, Jennifer. Adrian Hollis was sent to Eton. Interestingly, he knew that his father worked in MI5 (and his housemaster at Eton was told as well). In public, however, he was told to say that his father was 'attached to the War Office'.

As Adrian Hollis grew older, his father persuaded him to take an interest in some aspects of his work. Adrian recalled being encouraged by his father to attend the Wraight trial; Adrian has written:

I think Wraight was a defector to the DDR who did not enjoy it very much and returned. My Father thought it would be educative for me to go to Court. He said Wraight deserved a few years prison but not too many because he had been stupid, rather than wicked.[98]

Adrian was also taken to dine in the House of Commons with Tony Courtney, MP. It was early in 1960 and Adrian recalled his father arguing that the prospect of unending Conservative Government (which Courtney favoured) would be detrimental to British democracy.

Yet Roger (not surprisingly) never told his son that he had himself been under investigation for allegedly being a mole. It was only in 1978 that an MI5 officer asked to see Adrian in Oxford in order to inform him about the various investigations that had taken place.

Another source of character references and testimonials has been provided via the columns of *The Times* from Sir Martin Furnival Jones and A. Simkins, who said:

Up to the time we retired [from MI5] there was not a shred of evidence that Sir Roger Hollis had been disloyal at any time or in any way, let alone evidence that he had been a spy. Moreover, throughout his career his positive contribution to security was outstandingly valuable and his wartime record makes ludicrous any suggestion that he might have been sympathetic to the USSR.[99]

A similar letter from one of the most senior Whitehall figures, Sir Charles Cunningham, appeared on 17 December 1981. Cunningham had seen Hollis, it has been reported, virtually weekly throughout his time as Permanent Under-Secretary at the Home Office. Another figure in a similar position who had, if anything, seen even more of Hollis at the Home Office but is, for obvious reasons, not able to comment on this matter by name, has stated that Sir Charles's recollections are entirely confirmed by his own.

It is, however, the case that not all the references were good ones. Sir Roger Fulford (despite being convinced that Hollis was not a mole; see p. 329) specifically mentioned Hollis's 'rather dissipated' time at Oxford, and the fact that he left without taking a degree. And one former colleague who had originally believed in Hollis's virtue changed her mind after discussions with other former colleagues.

The books and allegations that have been made since 1981 have taken their toll on the reputation of Roger Hollis. Other former colleagues have not, however, changed their minds and one reaffirmed:

He was exceedingly well-informed about Communist subversion. He knew they had money. Whilst knowing about international Communism, his main concern was Communism in the UK although he did know about 'sources and origins'. He was clued up about the Comintern directives; he was loyal.[100]

Some of these character references carry more weight than others; clearly none of them is conclusive. Added together they suggest that Hollis was a deeply secretive but not illiberal man; his marriage was not happy although it was, perhaps, not as disastrous as has sometimes been alleged. His failure to take a degree indicated that as a young man he was somewhat dissolute. According to his son, his tutor at Worcester believed he might have got a First Class degree had he pulled himself together.

Yet it is quite plain that there was nothing corrupt or sinister about Hollis's character. Former MI5 and MI6 officers who had experience of the moles have confirmed Sir Patrick Reilly's opinion: Hollis was an ordinary, decent and honest, if very secretive, member of the British Establishment.

Chinese days

This, then, was Hollis's character: careful examination gives no cause either for believing that he was a mole or even that he had a motive for wishing to become one. Hollis was a rather conventional, if of necessity highly secretive, example of an upper-middle-class Englishman of his time. If we now turn to Hollis's own account of the first stage of his adult life, the period spent in China from 1928 until 1936, we can see that it amply confirms what others said about his character. When we examine the documentary evidence of Hollis's Chinese days we can see that they are light years away from the elaborate concoction served up by Chapman Pincher.

Chapman Pincher's thesis, as outlined in detail in *Too Secret, Too Long*, is that while Hollis was in China he was converted to Communism and formed an association with three Communist agents, Agnes Smedley, Arthur Ewert and Sonia Kuczynski. The first and the last of these remained close to Hollis during the period when he was at Blenheim and thus represent, he alleges, the direct link which binds Hollis to Communism.

It is, of course, perfectly true that these three were Communist agents in China at this time. Arthur Ewert was a leading member of the German Communist Party. From 1935 until 1945 he was interned in Brazil, and in the Weimar Republic he played a role in the internecine feuding about Stalinism (he was a 'moderate' and opposed the line taken by Ulbricht which explains why, until his death in the DDR in 1959, he played no active part in politics). Agnes Smedley, a legendary character, worked as a journalist and Comintern agent in China. She died in England in 1949. Sonia Kuczynski, as we have seen, was also a leading Soviet agent, working for the GRU; after leaving England in the late 1940s for East Germany, she published her memoirs there in 1982.[101]

Despite Chapman Pincher's allegations, however, there is not a shred of evidence to link Hollis with either Arthur Ewert or Sonia Kuczynski, and there is no proper confirmation that Hollis ever even met Agnes Smedley (although some MI5 officers have told Chapman Pincher that he admitted that he had), despite the fact that a meeting with her was something that many Europeans in China seem to have had. Philip Knightley has argued that 'it would be unusual if Hollis had not known her; everyone in Shanghai knew Agnes Smedley'.[102]

Thanks to the memoirs of Major General Willoughby, who was General MacArthur's intelligence chief from 1941 until 1951, we have a good record of Communist activities in China in the 1930s.[103] Willoughby's account is largely concerned with Richard Sorge (who was hanged by the Japanese) and his Shanghai network. Agnes Smedley, who was in fact a German, was his recruiting officer. The people in whom Sorge was interested were those with Communist sympathies; they had to possess a 'loyalty and devotion' to the Soviet Union and they had to have a good cover. Journalism was one of the best, since it allowed people to have a good alibi for being in sensitive locations.

Willoughby added, however, that a knowledge of Sorge's activities ought not to make one feel too insecure. For Communist agents could be tracked; with sufficient care, it would always be possible to identify Communist agents, Willoughby argued, because they would always leave a trail. One needed to examine their activities in China and sooner or later one would come across a definite connection between the network and the individual members of it.

Had Hollis 'left a trail' while in China? It is true that he appears to have worked as a journalist for a time, and we know that he hoped to gain a job working for *The Times* on his return from China. Beyond this, Hollis's China period appeared to fuel speculation only because so little was known about it. At the end of 1981, however, important new evidence about Hollis's time in the Far East came to light in the form of personal letters written by him, both during his time as an employee of the British American Tobacco Company in China and then during his time in Wells and London, right up to and including his recruitment into MI5. They were addressed mainly to his mother, the wife of the Bishop of Taunton. These letters were discovered after the death of the first Lady Hollis. As we shall see, the real trail left by Roger Hollis was not merely quite different from the trail Chapman Pincher alleges he left, but the letters also provide prima-facie evidence of Hollis's complete loyalty to Britain while he was in China.

If the letters are a genuine account of Hollis's Chinese days (as I believe them to be) then Chapman Pincher's case as far as China is concerned must turn to dust. If, on the other hand, these letters are false, then Hollis must be considered not merely suspect but one of the most ingenious liars of the twentieth century.

For if these letters are what they seem, intended simply for his family at the time, to be read and not necessarily preserved for posterity, they prove that Hollis was not converted to Communism while in China. Chapman Pincher has argued that it is perfectly possible that these letters were a deliberate falsification designed to conceal from his mother the truth of his Communist involvements. But the letters are more than just an account of time spent in China; they are also a record of his character and his political views.

Why should anyone deliberately want to falsify their political views to their own family? Not, it seems, because they were proposing to become moles, for most of the moles appear to have told their families about their conversions to Communism. In his letters, however, Hollis shows himself to be a very conventional ex-public school boy, loyal to what might be called the British way of life. In short, if this picture of him is considered untrue, the reason has to be that Hollis was deliberately trying to lay a false trail which was intended to confuse anyone subsequently investigating him. Such a proposition seems totally ludicrous.

For one thing, it would have meant that Hollis, while under investigation at the end of his life, would have used the letters in his own defence (which he did not). Not only did he not use them (suggesting that he did not know they still existed), but they have never been examined either by his detractors in MI5 or by his supporters. These letters were truly the forgotten remnants of a bygone age, concealed in boxes under an old lady's bed, which only came to light because the death of the lady coincided with the public denunciation of Hollis by Chapman Pincher in 1981.

These letters must therefore be considered genuine evidence, and it is perhaps because some of them were published in *The Times*[104] that Wright and some of his supporters later shifted their ground from the Chinese days theory to the 'missing two years'. Chapman Pincher, however, sticks by his original (and I believe untenable) thesis. What, then, do the letters show? First of all, they give a further indication of Hollis's character at the time. Second, they demonstrate the nature of his political views at a time when, to be sure, many of his fellow Englishmen and women were turning radically and dramatically to the left.

Those letters which throw light on Hollis's character range in topic from accounts of hazardous journeys to the recurrence of TB, an illness which continued to plague him. On 4 December 1934, Roger wrote to his father (rather than his mother) from Chungking:

> I've had rather an unpleasant experience. After a strenuous weekend climbing I woke up on Monday morning with an attack of bleeding like the one I had after the West of England golf championship. This afternoon, I had another attack only worse and called the naval doctor who was a little alarmed and ordered me to bed where I now am. He doesn't know what the matter is but thinks it is no more than just a blood vessel in my throat. Anyhow, I'm going to be X Rayed as soon as we can arrange it and I will let you know the worst as soon as I hear it . . .

He did hear the worst three days later:

> The result of the X Ray examination has come through and I'm afraid it is rather bad though it might be a lot worse. There are definite signs of tuberculosis in my left lung and I'm now resting in the Canadian mission hospital before being shipped down river. Don't get Mother worried, I'm perfectly alright and have never felt better in my life. I seem like a complete fraud.

To his mother he wrote:

> I hope you don't picture me as white cheeked with a nasty 'acking corf because that's far from so. Actually you couldn't possibly tell there was anything the matter with me except that I'm in bed.

Thus it was that Hollis, a young man of twenty-nine, suddenly contracted the killer disease of TB on the other side of the world. He did not panic and he did not upset his mother. A little while later it was decided that Hollis needed urgent medical attention at a bigger hospital and he left Chungking for Hankow:

> My colleague and I flew down from Chungking last Thursday. It was rather a thrilling trip through the gorges. As the weather was very bad and misty we had to fly just ten feet above the water while our wing tips seemed to touch the cliffs. We were roaring through 1700 chasms at 100 miles an hour and it was terribly exciting.

It must have been.

Hollis's sense of humour (mentioned later by several friends) is also evident in these letters. After recuperating at the Fairy Glen Hotel in Kuling, high in the mountains, he went to Dairen for a holiday:

> One of this place's main claims to fame is its English language newspaper which practically keeps *Punch* supplied with misprints. Some visiting General was described as 'bottle-scarred' which was later corrected to 'battle-scared'. Mr Jones whilst travelling alone from Shanghai was announced in the arrival list as 'Mr and Mrs Jones'. As he had left a perfectly respectable wife in Shanghai and didn't want any misunderstanding, he asked to have it corrected. The next day appeared, 'We have been asked to state that the lady travelling with Mr Jones is not his wife.' Do you find that vulgar, Mother?

There is also proof of Hollis's social life in these letters. Needless to say, there is no mention of Richard Sorge, Agnes Smedley or even Sonia Kuczynski. Bearing in mind who Hollis was and what his background was, this is hardly surprising. The sort of people Hollis liked were people like himself from his own sort of background:

> Yesterday I went on a picnic with the very charming wife of the British consul at Dairen, the wife of one of our directors who has a son at Clifton [Roger's school], a pleasant local couple and a couple of wealthy but leisurely globe trotters ... it was a pleasant change. There is a pleasant English couple staying at my hotel called Quick who turned up from Shanghai. He is a schoolmaster whom I knew in earlier days in Hong Kong. They have a six month old baby but they are so apologetic about it that I'm

prepared to admit I was once six months old myself . . .

I'm having a mild battle with Mrs Napier, a good hearted person who daily fills me with the most libellous gossip. I do like her and she's a glorious snob which is all to her advantage. I saw both the Napiers at a cocktail party a day or two ago and I'm going to have lunch with them next week.

Hollis's view of the non-English contingent in China is also recorded. It is entirely predictable. Curiously, in one letter there is a description of people who might well have included Arthur Ewert and his crew. But does Hollis actually meet them?

This hotel is filling up with Japanese, blousy Russians and a sprinkling of rather un-Aryan looking Germans. Completely unexciting people. There is also rather a large colony of Russians here who go down to the beach every day to sunbathe in the most attenuated costumes. They are flamboyant, bright-red with raw patches. Not very beautiful. As for the Japanese, they'll move us all out of North China unless something is done to stop them. I am so sick of these filthy little people . . .

Those 'rather un-Aryan looking Germans' might have included Smedley and Kuczynski. But even if they were staying in the same hotel, they were still a world away from the real Roger Hollis.

As far as Hollis's political attitudes are concerned, the picture the letters give is entirely predictable. In January 1936 he wrote to his mother that he had just read a book by Lion Feuchtwanger entitled *The Oppermanns*:

I've read *The Oppermanns*. Have you? It's not the sort of book to leave lying around when Hitler comes to lunch but then I hope he never will . . .

Another letter proves that to the Englishman Hollis, Communism and Fascism were equally alien, as he wrote in October 1934:

And now for the journey on the Trans Siberian Express of which I could tell you little before as the Russians have a way of reading letters and criticism is not encouraged. Berlin struck me as a wonderful city but I didn't at all like the militaristic Hitlerism which one found everywhere. Uniforms, strutting self-importance and fantastic salutations on all sides. The poor plain clothes civilian is apparently very small beer ...

The next morning we arrived in Moscow where we were met by a representative of Intourist who drove us to their HQ in a very luxurious Lincoln car with a young lady as a guide. We drove round extensively but they would not let us into the various buildings or even drive through the Kremlin which looked fine – from the outside. Lenin's tomb looked rather like a high-class public lavatory without any dignity or artistic merit. Our guide was most enthusiastic as was to be expected but I have never seen anything which depressed me as unutterably as Moscow. It was like driving through a huge drab slum of three and a half million people, everyone ill-dressed in the most deplorable ready-mades, though not in rags, I must admit, and the younger people looked cheerful enough. Everywhere empty shop windows, an almost indecent sight when seen singly but unspeakable in rows with only an occasional dirty poster in them.

Three things are very striking about this letter. The first is how alien both Russia and Germany are to the young Hollis. He was not violently anti-Soviet or violently anti-Nazi; he plainly thought neither of these creeds had any relevance to his own situation. He hoped simply that Hitler would not be coming to lunch, and one suspects he hoped Stalin would not be coming either. There is certainly not the slightest trace of any admiration for Communism or any sign that it provides an example for Britain in any way whatsoever.

Second, of course, in order to argue that Hollis was a secret Communist at this time (which was only two years before he returned from China) one has to assume that Hollis was lying about his impressions of Russia. Chapman Pincher has argued that many Communists thought Moscow was an ugly city, but Hollis is saying far more than just this in his letter. He is talking about an entire system, one from which he feels quite distant and one which does not touch him personally. There is further evidence of this in another reference to Communism in China, made in March 1936 when he wrote:

We're beginning to forget about the Japanese troubles in the North for the Communists have suddenly crossed the Yellow River and are getting a stronghold in the province next to this. Their main plank is national solidarity against the Japanese. It is not very logical, I know, but it is so and there is no doubt that all this recent student trouble here is connected with it. One can't really help but sympathise with them in a way though really they are playing into Japan's hands.

The third thing to note about the Moscow letter is, of course, that there is no allusion to any recruitment of Hollis into the KGB or the GRU, not the slightest hint of any situation conducive to one; not even any mention of a sexual encounter with the attractive girl from the Intourist office. Hollis's detractors would argue that he would, of course, not reveal something like this to his mother. That might seem a fair point; parents are rarely told everything by their sons. But if this pretty girl had recruited him, Hollis would hardly have made any mention of her at all.

There is only one hint of anything untoward happening while Hollis was in Russia; a travelling companion by the name of Tebbs clearly told some lies about Hollis's behaviour at some stage on the Trans-Siberian Express, and Hollis was extremely cross that he should lie. There is no indication as to the incident itself; but one suspects that Hollis may have got drunk and perhaps a trifle 'lavatorial'. Tebbs (whose 'plebeian name' made Hollis laugh) was a schoolmaster in his friend Quick's school, the Cathedral School in Shanghai. Roger told his mother:

> I've been hearing quite a lot about that journey [from Tebbs's account to Quick], graphic descriptions of Lenin in his tomb, into which we were quite unable to penetrate, and many other incidents of the trip. I wonder if I am wrong to be, in general, so truthful. Practically all other people, as far as I can see, lie blatantly as soon as they get round the nearest corner. It doesn't seem to do much harm and in the case of people who have a real gift for it, like Peter Fleming [Ian Fleming's brother], exceedingly amusing. I think I would object to being found out ...

Those with doubts about Hollis's loyalty would, of course, point out that a scenario damaging to Hollis could easily be constructed out of this incident. They might suggest what had happened was that Tebbs had learned Hollis had laid himself open to blackmail in Moscow or even been recruited by the Russians, and that Tebbs had started talking about this; by virtue of Quick's position in the Cathedral School, the news might conceivably filter back to Wells and Hollis's mother. Yet there is no reason to believe that Hollis's strictures on honesty were not genuine.

Other letters testify to Hollis's political attitudes at the time and they seem true to form. About Hitler and Mussolini he wrote in 1936:

> If one could feel sure that Hitler was merely trying to adjust the provisions of a very unfair treaty, one might feel a good deal of sympathy with him. Unfortunately, it seems fairly clear that he is going a good deal further than that. Megalomania of the Mussolini type is extraordinarily unattractive. He almost forces one to hope that he will be beaten though I should not be surprised if the ultimate effect of that would be worse than if he wins.

This, too, is a very predictable British view: Fascists are a pretty rotten lot but probably better than the chaos that would take their place if they were pushed from power.

The picture which so clearly emerges from these letters is that Hollis was a typical public school boy of his era; he might be described as 'daring, decent and plucky' by those who admire this particular product of a 1930s' education. He was someone who liked people like himself and had no great affection for foreigners, although he plainly liked China, if not the Chinese.

This, then, was the trail he left in China. We should not forget that during the very years Hollis was trying to start a business career in China, Philby had gone to Vienna, where in 1933 he took up with his Litzi, a Communist and Jewess. His friends and indeed his mother knew fully he was a Communist, and his mother allegedly hoped that he would soon find a job to 'get him off his bloody Communism'. While the charmed Cambridge circle were learning to be moles, Hollis was fussing about his old school tie:

> If you happen to be near Clifton [he wrote to his mother on 22 October 1935] you might perhaps like to get me two Old Cliftonian ties ... it's so difficult to get decent ties out here that I've now got into the habit of wearing OC ties almost continuously.

On a different tack he wrote from Chungking in November 1935:

> I must have a statement about my shares. They're not quoted in *The Times* so I can't gloat over all the money I'm making. I think

I'll invest a little of it over here. We don't spend much for there's nothing to spend it on ...

As far as his shares are concerned, I suppose it is possible to imagine a Communist investing in stock, although they cannot be very good Communists if they do. Rather more telling, perhaps, is the fact that the shares prove that Hollis had ample funds in China; a factor of relevance when considering the charge that Hollis may have been bribed into Communism out of poverty.

Chapman Pincher goes to some lengths to try to ridicule the notion that these letters say anything significant about Hollis.[105] Yet it is hard to see how they can not be considered important evidence. Chapman Pincher argues that Burgess liked to wear his Old Etonian tie in Moscow, as if the point that was being made here was that Hollis could retain an affection for his old public school and still be a Communist. The actual argument is quite different. In Burgess's case, the tie and the clothes from London were an indication that despite his Communism he retained some affinity for England. In Hollis's case there never was any Communism; his old school ties are simply one further piece of proof of his loyalty to Britain. Like his golf, Hollis's ties are an integral part of the existing picture, not the exception which highlights the sinister side of a mole's double existence.

Hollis's final political statement was made after his return to England in 1936 in a letter to Eve Swayne, soon to be his fiancée:

This Abdication business is awful, isn't it? Hidden away in me I have always had a passionate loyalty to the monarchy and the ideal and the duties of the English gentleman. All my time abroad has strengthened that too because I've seen how much other people do respect our code. And now I cannot help but feel that Edward has let the side down utterly – just quit on us. I'm sorry to sound like a public school speech day but if there is any sense in our English training then one has to come back to those trite fundamentals when someone one trusts and admires suddenly cuts right across them. It seems to me so cryingly weak that any man should risk the whole future of the monarchy and the Empire for personal happiness. God knows it's a foul job to have to do but surely it is a job which inspires any real man to bigger things than personal happiness. Staunch Conservative that I am, I feel Edward has let us down as no other man on earth has the power to do ...

Here is yet another clear impression of the sort of person that Hollis was becoming and the kind of values that he truly possessed.

Let us now conclude our investigation into the question of Hollis's alleged Communist motivation by considering the theory of the 'Missing two years'.

The missing two years

As we have seen, there are no grounds for believing either that Hollis was converted to Communism in China or that he did anything untoward which might have made him a target for bribery or blackmail. He was not a homosexual. He cannot be shown to have been deeply involved with any known Communist agents, let alone Ewert or Sorge or Kuczynski. Far from being ordered to return to Britain, as Chapman Pincher has alleged, in order to 'worm his way' into MI5, it is clear from other passages in these letters that he was reluctant to leave China and return to England, where there were, after all, three million people without a job and Hollis's career (in which he had yet to establish himself) had been cut short by an illness which might make him unemployable in the future.

In short, there is absolutely no sign of any motive which might conceivably have led Hollis into becoming one of Stalin's Englishmen; his Chinese days provide no grounds at all for believing that it was there that he was recruited into Soviet Intelligence. What is more, it cannot even be doubted that on his return he continued to be the public school patriot that he was before he left. It is thus hardly surprising that Peter Wright has apparently changed his mind about Hollis's Chinese days, preferring instead the theory of the 'missing two years'. We must recall that in his Granada TV programme, Wright stated:

> Sir Roger dealt convincingly with questions about his career – except for a two year period immediately before joining MI5. We were of the opinion that he was hiding something. He seemed unprepared to tell us what went on. He avoided telling us exactly who he was meeting at that time, what he was doing [see p. 317].

It would therefore appear that for Hollis's detractors (unless they should wish to change their ground yet again) it is these two years that have now become crucial. Is there any evidence, apart from Sir Roger's apparent secrecy about them, which might lead one to suspect that anything sinister happened during this period? These were undoubtedly bad years for Hollis, of that one can be certain. From 1936 until 1938 he frantically sought a secure, and above all a challenging, post at a time when such jobs were scarce indeed. yet once again, it has to be categorically stated that there is absolutely no evidence that during those two years Hollis was ever 'turned' or that, with one possible exception, anything remotely peculiar befell Hollis at this time. There is actually no reason at all to accept Wright's suggestion that the missing two years hold the key to the alleged mystery of Roger Hollis; to believe that it was then that something happened to Hollis which turned him away from his earlier loyalty to the British way of life and towards Stalin.

Recently uncovered family records, including further letters from Roger to the first Lady Hollis until their engagement in February 1937, family diaries, Lady Hollis's accounts book, as well as Roger Hollis's visitors' book, allow one to reconstruct those two years. Two reasons immediately offer themselves for Hollis's reticence about them at the end of his career. They were a very unhappy time which he may quite genuinely have tried to forget; and they were also a time full of changes, and new (and usually false) starts, and also of changing abodes. There has been some suggestion that at some stage during this period Roger Hollis went to Switzerland (in order, it has been claimed, to re-establish contact with Sonia). The records do not indicate any such visit, although he may have gone there in 1934 before his final journey to China.[106]

Hollis returned to England in July 1936, coming back via Canada (and not Russia, as Chapman Pincher has alleged). On 26 August 1936 Roger Hollis is mentioned for the first time in his future mother-in-law's diary; they had met at a cricket match in which 'Arthur Wellard made history by hitting five sixes in one over'. Roger was seen as a most acceptable acquaintance, for on 31 August he came to stay with the Swayne family in Burnham-on-Sea. In November 1936 Hollis went to see Peter Fleming at *The Times*; *The Times* had published an article by him on China and he had hopes of a job. Chapman Pincher has argued that there is no trace of any such article; but there is.

In a letter to Eve, Hollis provides clear evidence of the link between his precarious job position and the chance for something better with *The Times*, with which he had already established a link. He wrote:

I saw my directors this morning in London. They were very nice about things and offered me a small accounts job, the only job the company have in this country. They smiled with obvious relief when I refused it and quite agreed that it would not suit me at all. In the afternoon, I saw Peter Fleming, who is an extremely charming person. My article really does seem to have made a hit with *The Times* and let's hope it raises a flicker of interest with the readers. It should come out in a week or two. Fleming has promised to look out for anything further I send him and has arranged for the *TLS* to send me a book or two for review ...

One does not have to have been along this road oneself to appreciate the complete genuineness and also the pathetically misplaced optimism of the young Roger Hollis trying to find an interesting job for himself. Hollis's failures compounded by his lack of degree (at a time when this was considered very poor, for even a Pass degree was infinitely more acceptable than none at all) must have taken their toll on his morale. He was not one of 'the best and the brightest'; was in indifferent health; and did not possess the brilliance of a Blunt or a Philby.

Thus it was that until 14 January 1937, Roger remained unemployed. During this period he went to visit Eve again and he offered her marriage. He was clearly depressed and cynical about his future. On one occasion he went to see his old friend Roger Fulford at *The Times* to enquire about another possible job; but that too fell through. Despite his decision to marry Eve, he did not wish his engagement to her to be made public because he had no steady job.

He then became rather frantic, putting in for all sorts of posts. His father, the Bishop, tried to get W.D. and H.O. Wills in Bristol to take an interest in him, and Roger managed to get an interview with Imperial Tobacco but the outcome was negative. They told him that his Chinese experience was of no relevance to the British tobacco industry. In March 1937 Roger completed a form for the Oxford Appointments Board (he was interviewed by them in September). He also applied to and was rejected by Cadbury, the chocolate company. He finally wrote to Ardath begging them for a job. Ardath agreed and he started work for them in their accounts department.

On 10 July 1937 Roger and Eve married at Wells Cathedral. They took a honeymoon in the New Forest and then moved into a flat at 87 Gloucester Road. In October, however, lack of money caused them to move out of the flat into digs. At the same time, Roger left

Ardath. He just could not bear it. The couple then moved to Wells where they lived with Roger's parents.

Then, perhaps a little mysteriously, on 26 November 1937 Roger and Eve drove to Bristol. They sold their car and went first to Paris and then to Loche where they both took French lessons. It would appear that Roger was employed on a short-term contract for three weeks by the Institute of Chartered Secretaries. They left Loche on 14 December and spent some time in Paris again before returning to Wells for the Christmas of 1937. On New Year's Eve, 1937, they went to the Wells Hunt Ball.

It was after this, but before 13 March 1938, that Roger Hollis was recruited into MI5. The full story of his recruitment is still unknown. All recruitment was on the basis of personal recommendation; applications for the security service were not invited, and those that came in the mail were a constant source of great mirth to serving officers. There is very strong evidence to suggest that the link was Ray Meldrum, who was related to Eve. It appears that at some time between December and March Roger Hollis and Ray Meldrum met at a family gathering; the Swayne family were clearly anxious that Hollis was married but jobless, and Meldrum decided to get him a job in MI5. Certainly, Roger always showed great kindness to the relatives who had put him in touch with Meldrum, and quite openly said he was indebted to Meldrum for having found him an interesting post. Meldrum had, according to one family version, been told to 'find poor Roger a job for he's too weak to be employable'.[107]

Roger and Eve then moved to 18 Elsham Road, London, W1, where they stayed until their move to 29A Charlbury Road, Oxford, on 1 October 1940. In October 1942 they moved into 2 Garford Road, Oxford, and on 1 February 1943 they began living at 6 Campden Hill Square. At first they leased the house and it was only some years later that they managed to buy the leasehold.

The family visitors' book is also extant. It does not depict an uproarious social life. Anthony Blunt dined with them once during the war. Hollis obviously knew him well (as he did Philby); but there is no record of their having remained on friendly terms after 1945. In 1949 Anthony Courtney of MI5 visited them from Minden, in West Germany. Tar Robertson, Adrian Hollis's godfather, was a guest. In August 1956 Dick White came for dinner. In addition, as Adrian Hollis recalled, MI5 office parties were held at Campden Hill Square on numerous occasions. This pattern of entertainment repeated itself until Sir Roger and Lady Evelyn split up in 1967.

We can see then that the 'Missing two years' by which Peter Wright sets such store are, in reality, not missing but merely depressing. It is true that Hollis was a secretive man and, because it had disappointed him, his early life was not something he wished to recall. He had not been a success in Oxford; his efforts to make good that failure by building up a career in tobacco in China were frustrated by severe ill health. He wanted to get married and he had no job; nor, by all accounts, much money when his Chinese savings had slipped away.

Yet he did not give up. It is said that when Hollis and MI5 first made contact, MI5 were impressed by Hollis's resilience. It is not hard to see why. Hollis was not the proverbial Establishment high-flyer. Although he may have wanted to have been one, his life had taken a different turning. But, and this is a very important but, to suggest that at any time from leaving Clifton College until entering MI5 it took a crooked turning is a total falsification of the record.

It has been possible to reconstruct this period of his life on the basis of documentary evidence, even if that evidence has been difficult to assemble. It is, perhaps, significant that when Peter Wright was asking himself the very questions we have posed in this part of our study, he failed to consider the evidence which has formed the basis for this chapter. We know this because neither he nor anyone else in MI5 ever asked to see Hollis's family papers, formerly in the possession of the first Lady Hollis. Was the effort too much for Wright? Or was he so obsessed with some deep urge to prove Hollis guilty that he was not interested in evidence which went against his theories? There is, of course, a third alternative: that in order to cast doubt upon Hollis's career, Wright deliberately chose to focus attention on what he believed would prove the most obscure and undocumented parts of his life.

For it should not be forgotten that apart from the assertion that Hollis was a mole, a score of other quite inaccurate misrepresentations were made about Hollis's career. Chapman Pincher insinuates that Hollis lied about minor details, such as having a half-blue for golf or going to America on a debating tour with the Oxford Union, claims never made by Hollis at any time. Actual achievements for which there is documentary evidence, such as writing for *The Times*, are, rather carelessly, called into question by Chapman Pincher who ascribes them to a Walter Mitty element in Hollis's character.

Other charges against Hollis made by Chapman Pincher are even more dubious. He accuses Hollis of grossly disreputable conduct over very detailed MI5 matters, even of destroying MI5 files during the Blitz, and of being hated by superiors and inferiors alike. Yet there is firm evidence that in 1940 Hollis was in fact the person responsible for the photocopying of MI5's files on Communists. In addition, Hollis was not hated; in particular Sillitoe, his boss, did not dislike him as Chapman Pincher suggests; Hollis was one of the few MI5 officers who tolerated Sillitoe, although he disapproved very much of what he and other officers saw as his professional shortcomings, in particular his disregard for secrecy. So, too, with Chapman Pincher's insistence that Macmillan could not recall having met Hollis. Adrian Hollis has confirmed that Macmillan remembered his father well and spoke warmly about him. Roger Hollis liked to recall Macmillan's remark about not wishing to know what MI5 did ('When my gamekeeper finds a fox, I like him to dispose of it without telling me'). It was one of the few things about his work that Hollis referred to at home.

It is also, according to family recollections, quite untrue that Hollis wished to have a Whitehall appointment after his retirement. Harold Wilson, the then Prime Minister, had asked him to stay on in 1965, but Hollis had not wished to accept this invitation. He was happy to be going to Somerset, to devote himself to country matters, such as his governorship of Wells Cathedral School.

No one doubts that Hollis made mistakes; some of them were to prove serious and damaging. But they can be explained in a variety of ways without needing to assume that he was a traitor. Everything we know about him suggests that although he did not catch the moles of the Second World War and although he ought, in theory, to have caught them, the reasons for his failure are perfectly honourable ones. Perhaps, subsequently, he showed too much compassion towards people he suspected (but could not prove) were moles. This may have been true when dealing with people like Blunt with whom he had been friends, and if this was so, then it was an unwise course of action. Yet he did not spare himself or a close friend like Graham Mitchell from intensive interrogation. However, we should not forget that Hollis's chief mistake was, given the constraints of high policy and British liberal traditions, hardly a gross dereliction of duty and hardly a terrible error.

So why has Hollis been put in the firing line? We have seen that, at the end of the day, those who have benefited most from the damage done to the morale and reputation of MI5 have been the

Soviets. Was it they who inspired Hollis's indictment? It must at once be said that very few of the former MI5 and MI6 officers to whom I spoke adduced any sinister reasons on Chapman Pincher's part. He did not invent the allegations against Hollis.

Yet it is true that what makes the case against him plausible is that it is so detailed and, apparently, so well-informed. And Hollis is implicated at almost every juncture. However, since the case is almost certainly quite wrong, it would seem to be the outcome of a most careful, but inherently inaccurate, reconstruction of the story of British Intelligence and Communist subversion, one which may have benefited not only from MI5's and MI6's resources, but from Soviet ones as well.

If, as I believe, the case against Hollis is, in essence, a fiction, then implanted into it may be several subverted threads. Who provided these is, of course, a matter for speculation. Kim Philby is alive and well in Moscow and he continues to take an active interest in British Intelligence. One might be forgiven for believing that he has supplied at least one of the leads, for after all we know that this was his special area of concern. Perhaps he was even its original author.

So what can be concluded about the unfortunate Roger Hollis? I believe that, at the end of the day, the hard truth is that during the war the moles were indeed undetectable; there was no way in which a man like Hollis could have even begun to unravel the evidence of Communist subversion in the high offices of the British State. Churchill's policy merged so fully (if unintentionally) with the aims and interests of the moles that the two could only be prised apart after very careful analysis over many years and, above all, with the benefit of hindsight. In reality, Hollis's duties were utterly daunting. And even when the Anglo-Soviet Alliance had fulfilled its role, the task was still daunting: Hollis must have shaken his head in disbelief as ever more evidence came to light showing that the penetration achieved by the secret Communists had been far deeper and far heavier than anyone had imagined.

The British national obsession with moles and agents, with Stalin's Englishmen and women, has a perfectly understandable basis. Even if I am right, and the case against Hollis is a sham, the questions that it has raised are legitimate ones. On learning about Communist subversion in Britain, many people quite understandably feared for the safety of liberal democracy and were anxious lest the great power that rests in Britain's political institutions had been abused from within to damage Britain. On the whole, these fears and anxieties were groundless; the damage that was done was not a great deal. But at the earliest stages the official policy of secrecy compounded the problem; people were not reassured by it, it served merely to fuel their apprehensions. This did damage of a different sort.

Hollis, White and others erred by keeping far too tight a grip on the secrets of the service. It became counter-productive and ultimately did almost as much to undermine MI5's national standing as the machinations of the moles. The full story about Hollis's failures was far less dramatic and sinister than the concocted story. But the desire to conceal the fact that failures had occurred helped those who had no interest in the truth. The secrecy which Hollis worked so hard to maintain ended up by engulfing him and his reputation.

There are, of course, still many questions to be answered. Mostly, though, they are very detailed. How did Philby get away? Why was Burgess so influential? Had the moles bred? As to the question of how many moles there really were, the most frightening thing, as we have said, is that no one has any firm idea. Certainly what is most surprising about the extent of Communist subversion from 1939 until 1951 is not its narrowness, but its breadth. Yet the very fact that its net effect was so minimal, and that Britain was spared the excesses of McCarthyite witch-hunts, is an important measure of the decent and sensible posture of Britain's security service.

In 1970 Hollis was recalled out of retirement to face a formal interrogation. In early 1973 he suffered a stroke; a second massive stroke later that year killed him. He died at Catcott in Somerset on 26 October 1973 in the full knowledge that some MI5 and MI6 officers continued to believe he was a Soviet mole. He also knew, however, that some of the most senior and respected figures in British Intelligence and in the Government of Britain were convinced that he was a loyal servant of the country.

On 26 March 1981 the then Prime Minister, Mrs Thatcher, made it clear that Chapman Pincher's account of the bizarre story of Roger Hollis was not an accurate one. Lord Trend, who had been asked in 1974 to provide a definitive judgment, had concluded, she said:

That Hollis was not an agent of the Russian intelligence service. The case for investigating Hollis was based on certain leads that suggested but did not prove that there had been a Russian intelligence service agent at a relatively senior level in British Counter-Intelligence in the last years of the war. None of these leads identified Sir Roger Hollis or pointed specifically or solely in his direction. Each of them could also be taken as pointing to Philby or Blunt.

But Sir Roger Hollis was among those that fitted some of them and he was therefore investigated. This took place after Sir Roger's retirement from the Security Service. It did not conclusively prove his innocence. Indeed, it is very often impossible to prove innocence. That is why, in our law, the burden of proof is placed upon those who seek to establish guilt and not on those who defend innocence.

No evidence was found which incriminated him and the conclusion reached at the end of the investigation was that he had not been an agent of Russian Intelligence. This view was challenged, however, by a very few of those concerned and in July 1974 Lord Trend, the former Secretary of the Cabinet, was asked to review in detail the investigations that had taken place into the case of Sir Roger and to say whether they had been done in a proper and thorough manner and whether in his view the conclusions reached were justified.

Lord Trend reviewed the investigations of the case and found that they had been carried out exhaustively and objectively. He was satisfied that nothing had been covered up. He agreed that none of the relevant leads identified Sir Roger Hollis as an agent of the Russian intelligence service and that each of them could be explained by reference to Philby or Blunt.[108]

The conclusions reached in this study confirm the conclusions referred to by Mrs Thatcher, with the possible exception of whether the references could all have applied as well to Blunt and Philby as to Hollis.[109] It is clear that the Prime Minister's statement was made on the very best advice and that it fully reflected the common view in the most senior sections of the intelligence community and Britain generally.

However, the enormous damage done to Hollis's good standing by the actions of Peter Wright and his helpers, Arthur Martin, Stephen de Mowbray and Harry Chapman Pincher, has not merely undermined an individual's reputation but also that of an institution. To this must be added the private distress caused to Roger Hollis's family. No one can ever be absolutely certain about anyone, least of all an intelligence chief who purposely cultivated great discretion and secrecy. But it is possible to be certain about the things that are visible; and they all point clearly in one direction, namely to Hollis's liberal interpretation of his duties and the difficulty of the task that confronted him. He may not have been the most brilliant of Britain's public servants, but he does not appear to have been a dishonourable one.

Hollis, like his colleague Dick White, stood for a certain sort of security service, one which tried to keep people away from situations where damage might be done, one which was passive and reactive, rather than invasive and interventionist. It would be a great tragedy if the secrets of the service, its failures and its shortcomings, were ever to cause this to change. For a passive security service is a far better safeguard of the democratic liberties of a State than an active one. The problems which Roger Hollis had to confront do not provide any grounds for altering the basic values which they helped to establish. That is why it is so important to put the secrets of the service into their genuine, historical perspective; to appreciate how difficult and how complicated reality actually was.

One could not do better than end with the testimony of an individual with great and intimate knowledge of this whole matter:

> The various Anglo-American moles no doubt tried to support a policy of leniency towards Russia but it was power politics that counted for most. It would obviously suit some people to depict our post-war ills which have followed the Russian take-over of Eastern Europe as the result of the influence on British and American policies of the moles. In the case of Britain, some people would like to attribute it to a conspiracy by Roger Hollis. You can reply to that in one word: balls.[110]

Postscript by a defector

In September 1985 it was announced that for more than fifteen years British Intelligence had possessed its own high-ranking mole within the KGB. His name was Oleg Gordievsky and he had been ordered to come over to the British authorities, for reasons not yet fully explained.

Gordievsky was asked to undergo intensive debriefing at a safe house somewhere in the south of England. One of the first questions that was put to him is of direct relevance to this study, not only because it shows that the questions we have posed are important, indeed plausible, ones, but because his answer confirms the conclusions of this study.

Gordievsky was asked whether Roger Hollis really had been a mole, a Soviet long-term penetration agent of many years' standing. His reply was unequivocal:

Of course not. But when the KGB saw the chaos caused by the allegations against Hollis, their laughter made Red Square shake.[111]

Notes

1 A National Obsession

1 Hansard, vols 483–94, 1951.
2 Ibid.
3 Ibid.
4 Ibid.
5 Ibid.
6 Ibid.
7 Ibid.
8 Quoted in Mather, J. (ed), *The Great Spy Scandal*, London, 1955, p. 154.
9 CAB 129/78.
10 Cmnd 9577.
11 Hansard, op. cit.
12 Ibid.
13 Ibid.
14 Cmnd 9715.
15 *The Times*, 21 November 1979.
16 Ibid.
17 Ibid.
18 BBC TV *Timewatch*, 27 July 1983.
19 Ibid.
20 Orwell, G., *Collected Essays, Journalism and Letters*, vol. 1, London, 1970, pp. 317–18.
21 Ibid., pp. 368–9.
22 Citrine, Lord, *I Search for Truth in Russia*, London, 1938.
23 Ibid., p. 363.
24 Gide, A., *Back from the USSR*, London, 1937.
25 Ibid., pp. 13, 45–63.

2 The Historical Context of Subversion

1 There is still a lively debate among historians as to when the Cold War really broke out: see Leffler, M. P., 'The American Conception of National Security and the Beginnings of the Cold War, 1945–8' in the *American Historical Review*, vol. 89, no. 2, 1984, pp. 346–81. Leffler's careful analysis shows that it was only after the spring of 1946 that the United States Government perceived Russia to constitute a real threat to itself which, if not countered, would lead to war.

2 The literature on this is enormous but see, for example, Knapp, W., *A History of War and Peace*, London, 1967, pp. 65 ff. Knapp argues that Churchill 'wished to resist the Communizing of Poland'. Yet Knapp also reminds us that, when in Moscow barely three months earlier, Churchill believed the Russians would stick to the agreement guaranteeing Polish political independence. He told Roosevelt, 'we found an extraordinary atmosphere of good will here'. Ibid., p. 61.

3 *The Times*, 13 September 1984.

4 Quoted in Charlton, M., *The Eagle and the Small Birds*, London, 1984, p. 14.

5 *Encounter*, September 1985.

6 Quoted in Foot, M. R. D., *SOE*, London, 1984, p. 155.

7 Ibid. (See also Chapter 3 of the present study.)

8 The task of providing documentary evidence has become considerably easier thanks to the labours of Dr Graham Ross who has uncovered and published a selection of Foreign Office documents about British policy towards the USSR from 1941–5. Ross, G., *The Foreign Office and the Kremlin, British Documents on Anglo-Soviet Relations 1941–45*, Cambridge, 1984. This wonderful collection possesses one major flaw: for inexplicable reasons it does not have an index.

9 Tolstoy, N., *Stalin's Secret War*, London, 1981.

10 See Gorodetsky, G., *Stafford Cripps's Mission to Moscow 1940–42*, Cambridge, 1985; Hanak, H., 'Sir S. Cripps as British Ambassador in Moscow', *English Historical Review*, 1982, pp. 332–44.

11 Whaley, B., *Codeword Barbarossa*, New Haven, 1973.

12 Quoted in Eden, Sir A., *The Reckoning*, London, 1965, p. 268.

13 Churchill, Sir W., *The Second World War*, 1949–54, vol. 3, p. 337.

14 Eden, op. cit., p. 270.
15 Quoted in Gilbert, M., *Finest Hour*, London, 1983, p. 137.
16 Ibid., pp. 1118–19.
17 Ibid., p. 1121.
18 Ibid., p. 1120.
19 Not papers included by Dr Ross in his collection.
20 FO 371 1829465.
21 Ibid.
22 Ross, op. cit., p. 100.
23 Ibid.
24 FO 371 29470.
25 Ross, op. cit., p. 81.
26 Ibid.
27 Ibid.
28 Ibid.
29 See Kettenacker, L., 'The Anglo-Soviet Alliance and the Problem of Germany, 1941–45' in the *Journal of Contemporary History*, vol. 17, 1982.
30 Ross, op. cit., p. 115.
31 Ibid.
32 Ibid., pp. 117–18.
33 Ibid.
34 Ibid., pp. 120–1.
35 Ibid., p. 121.
36 Ibid., p. 124.
37 Ibid., pp. 129–30.
38 See the *Observer*, 10 November 1985. Spender suggests this might have been written by Eden at the time of Yalta.
39 See Geyer, D., 'Deutschland als Problem der sowjetischen Europapolitik am Ende des zweiten Weltkriegs' in Foschepoth, J. (ed.), *Kalter Krieg und Deutsche Frage*, Göttingen, 1985; Fischer, A., *Sowjetische Deutschlandpolitik im Zweiten Weltkrieg, 1941–45*, Stuttgart, 1975.
40 Ross, op. cit., pp. 134–5.
41 Ibid., p. 140.
42 Ibid., p. 144.
43 Interview with Christopher Hill, 9 September 1985.
44 Ross, op. cit., p. 146.
45 Ibid., p. 152. (See also p. 192 of the present study.)
46 Ibid. The phrase 'strong and independent Poland' had been used by Stalin himself in his interview in the *New York Times*

of 4 May 1943. See Garlinski, J., *Poland in the Second World War*, London, 1985, p. 191.

47 Ross, op. cit., p. 160.
48 Ibid., p. 163.
49 Ibid., p. 50.
50 Ibid., pp. 199–201.
51 Ibid., pp. 210–14.
52 See Geyer, D., op. cit., especially pp. 54–5, 58, 60–65.
53 Ross, op. cit., p. 226.
54 See, in particular, Gilbert, M., *Road to Victory: Churchill 1941–45*, London, 1986; also Martin Gilbert's essay in *The Times*, 24 September 1986, in which (rightly, in my view) he describes Churchill as a 'victim not a villain' of Yalta and of the Communist take-over in Poland. For a different view see, for example, David Carlton's review of Gilbert's book in *The Times Higher Education Supplement*, 3 October 1986. Carlton, one of Eden's biographers, argues (quite unconvincingly) that Churchill was a moral hypocrite 'guilty [inter alia] of endorsing the transportation of Rumanian citizens to the Soviet Union for slave labour purposes'. Similar allegations have, of course, been made against Eden and, repeatedly, against Harold Macmillan for his part in returning pro-German Russians (and others) to the USSR after the end of the war.
55 See, for example, Wheeler-Bennett, John and Nicholls, A.J., *The Semblance of Peace*, London, 1972, pp. 189, 290–2.
56 See Churchill, Sir W., *The Second World War*, vol. 6, p. 198.
57 Ibid., pp. 201–4.
58 Colville, J., *Fringes of Power*, London, 1985, p. 555.
59 Hansard, vol. 408, 1945.
60 Ibid.
61 Quoted in Rothwell, V., *Britain and the Cold War*, London, 1982, p. 125.
62 Ibid., p. 167.
63 Ibid., p. 170.
64 Churchill, Sir W., *The Second World War*, vol. 4, p. 444.

3 The Special Operations Executive

1 See Foot, M.R.D., *SOE*, p. 145; Andrew, C., *The Secret Service*, London, 1985, p. 408.
2 See Howe, E., *The Black Game*, 1982, pp. 31, 105–6;

Foot, op. cit., p. 146.
3 Trevor-Roper, H., *The Philby Affair*, London, 1968.
4 Interview, 8 May 1986.
5 Foot, op. cit.
6 Stafford, D., *Britain and European Resistance, 1940–45*: A Survey of the Special Operations Executive with Documents, London, 1980.
7 For a comprehensive account of how SOE was formed and by whom see Foot, op. cit., pp. 12–27.
8 Interview, 1 November 1985.
9 See Foot, op. cit., pp. 12–27.
10 Howe, op. cit., pp. 32, 33.
11 Foot, op. cit., p. 15.
12 Ibid.
13 Ibid., p. 21.
14 Ibid., p. 20.
15 See Foot, M. R. D., *Resistance*, London, 1977; *SOE in France*, London, 1966, 1968; *Six Faces of Courage*, London, 1978; and *SOE*, London, 1984. Also, Garlinski, J., *Poland, SOE and the Allies*, London, 1969.
16 For a compelling introduction to this aspect of SOE's work see Schulz, G., *Geheimdienste und Widerstandsbewegungen im Zweiten Weltkrieg*, Göttingen, 1982.
17 There has always been some confusion about this department and it might therefore be helpful to outline the position here. For security reasons, PWE was never referred to as PWE but as PID, the Political Intelligence Department of the Foreign Office. In reality, however, a Political Intelligence Department of the Foreign Office already existed and continued to exist until 1943 when it became FORD, the Foreign Office Research Department. In July 1941, Robert Bruce Lockhart restructured PWE and it was placed under the control of a committee formed by three Ministries, the Foreign Office, the Ministry of Economic Warfare and the Ministry of Information. After November 1941, PWE's non-subversive propaganda work (called its 'white' work) was transferred from Woburn Abbey to Bush House in the Strand. When in February 1942 the Earl of Selborne took over the Ministry for Economic Warfare, the Foreign Secretary and the Minister of Information divided PWE between the two of them. Bruce Lockhart was put in charge of this, and SOE no longer had

any say in it. See Balfour, M., *Propaganda in War 1939–45*, London, 1979, pp. 91–100.

18 See Stafford, op. cit., p. 67.

19 See Foot, *SOE*, p. 29.

20 See Dalton, H., *Memoirs*, 3 vols, in particular vol. 2, *The Fateful Years*, London, 1957; Pimlott, B., *Hugh Dalton*, London, 1985, and Pimlott, B. (ed.), *The Second World War Diary of Hugh Dalton*, London, 1986. The last is an edited version of Dalton's diary. Dalton appears to have recorded comparatively little about his SOE's work, doubtless to preserve its secrecy.

21 See Gilbert, M., *Finest Hour*, pp. 306 ff., 315.

22 Ibid., p. 667; Dalton, op. cit., p. 366.

23 Gilbert, op. cit., p. 667.

24 Dalton, op. cit., p. 366.

25 Stafford, op. cit., pp. 1 ff.

26 Ibid., pp. ix–xi.

27 Ibid., p. 8.

28 Ibid.

29 See Amery, J., *Approach March*, London, 1973.

30 Ibid., pp. 239, 240.

31 Stafford, op. cit., p. 9.

32 Pimlott, B., *Hugh Dalton*, p. 317.

33 Stafford, op. cit., p. 24.

34 Ibid., p. 29.

35 Howe, op. cit., p. 34.

36 Schulz, op. cit., p. 45.

37 Foot, op. cit., p. 29.

38 Ibid.

39 Ibid., p. 46.

40 Ibid., p. 47.

41 Stafford, op. cit., p. 29.

42 Foot, op. cit., p. 36.

43 Stafford, op. cit., p. 28.

44 Pimlott, B. (ed), *The Second World War Diary of Hugh Dalton*, p. 60.

45 See Elliott, M. R., *Pawns of Yalta*, Chicago, 1982; Bethel, N., *The Last Secret*, London, 1974.

46 See Schulz, G., *Revolutions and Peace Treaties*, London, 1972, which is a brilliant account of what may be termed subversion in the First World War, of which the most notorious example

is, of course, Lenin's arrival at the Finland Station in Moscow in 1917 in the sealed train, by courtesy of the German Empire.

47 Dodds-Parker, D., *Setting Europe Ablaze*, London, 1984, p. 37.

48 Stafford, op. cit., p. 42.

49 Dodds-Parker, op. cit., p. 24.

50 Ibid., p. 35.

51 Ibid., pp. 35–6.

52 Ibid., p. 37.

53 See Howe, op. cit.

54 See Glees, A., *Exile Politics During the Second World War*, Oxford, 1982, p. 55, and, in particular, Balfour, M., *Propaganda in War*.

55 Howe, op cit., p. 39.

56 Ibid., p. 72.

57 Ibid., p. 243.

58 Dodds-Parker, op. cit., pp. 25–6.

59 Ibid., p. 16. Jaksch later came to Britain where until 1942 he was treated with great kindness by the British authorities. He returned to West Germany after 1945, becoming a prominent politician.

60 Howe, op. cit., p. 40.

61 Barman, T., *Diplomatic Correspondent*, London, 1968, p. 49. I am indebted to Professor Michael Balfour for telling me about Barman and his account.

62 Amery, op. cit.

63 Ibid., p. 160.

64 Ibid., p. 211.

65 Ibid., pp. 211–12. As Barman said: when Dalton made a joke, it was no laughing matter.

66 Ibid., p. 212.

67 Ibid., p. 222.

68 Ibid., pp. 223–4.

69 Bullock, A., *Hitler*, London, 1971, p. 712.

70 Quoted in Bullock, op. cit., p. 774.

71 See Stafford, op. cit., p. 183.

72 Ibid., p. 63; Foot, M. R. D., *SOE in France*, pp. 164–5.

73 Dalton, op. cit., p. 367.

74 Ibid.

75 Ibid., p. 368.

76 Ibid.

77 Ibid., p. 384.

78 Lord Gladwyn adds that there were a number of people in 10 Downing Street who disliked Dalton, not to mention the dislike of him felt by Eden and Bracken. Interview, 1 November 1985.

79 Pimlott, B., op. cit., p. 374.

80 Ibid., p. 354.

81 Dalton, H., *Hitler's War*, London, 1940, p. 109.

82 Ibid., pp. 110, 121.

83 Ibid., p. 188.

84 Dalton, H., *The Fateful Years*, p. 26.

85 Amery, op. cit., p. 262.

86 Ibid.

87 Ibid., p. 239.

88 Pimlott, op. cit., pp. 317–19.

89 Pimlott, B., letter to me, 21 June 1985.

90 Amery, op. cit., pp. 312–13.

91 Interview, 1 November 1985.

92 Stafford, op. cit., p. 33.

93 Ibid., p. 35.

94 Ibid., p. 16.

95 Amery, op. cit.

96 Ibid., pp. 240–1.

97 Interview, 12 October 1982.

98 Foot, M. R. D., *SOE*, pp. 130–5.

99 Ibid.

100 Ibid.

101 Ibid., p. 133.

102 Ibid., p. 134.

103 Ibid.

104 Woods, C., letter to *The Times*, 28 September 1984.

105 Rusbridger, J., letter to *The Times*.

106 See 'Private War on SOE cost 400 Lives' by Laurence Marks, *Observer*, 27 April 1986.

107 Ibid. See also Boyle, A., *The Climate of Treason*, London, 1980, pp. 246 ff.

108 *Guardian*, 14 June 1985.

109 Quoted in Kettenacker, L. (ed.), *Das 'Andere Deutschland'*, Stuttgart, 1977, pp. 112–13.

110 Ibid.

111 Quoted in Stafford, op. cit., p. 17.

112 Dodds-Parker, op. cit., p. 36.

113 Glees, A., op. cit.; 'The German Political Exile in London, 1939–45' in Hirschfeld, G. (ed.), *Exile in Great Britain*, Leamington, 1984.

4 Moles in the Special Operations and Political Warfare Executives

1 See Chapman Pincher, H., *Too Secret, Too Long*, London, 1984.
2 Interview, 1 November 1985.
3 See also Delmer's autobiography: Delmer, S., *Trail Sinister*, London, 1962.
4 Quoted in Howe, E., *The Black Game*, p. 261. (See also p. 214 of the present study.)
5 Dalton, H., *The Fateful Years*, p. 380.
6 Howe, op. cit., p. 100.
7 See Tracey, M. A., *Hugh Greene: A Variety of Lives*, London, 1983; Puetter, C., 'Deutsche Emigranten und Britische Propaganda' in Hirschfeld, G. (ed.) *Exil in Grossbritannien*, Stuttgart, 1984.
8 Roeder, W., *Die Deutschen Sozialistischen Exilgruppen in Grossbritannien*, Hanover, 1969; Glees, A., *Exile Politics During the Second World War*.
9 FO 371 24419.
10 Stafford, D., *Britain and European Resistance, 1940–45*, p. 29.
11 Dalton, *The Fateful Years*, e.g. pp. 37–8, 60–1.
12 Dalton, H., *Hitler's War*.
13 Ibid., p. 22.
14 Quoted in *Der Spiegel*, 7 May 1956.
15 Dalton, *Hitler's War*, pp. 133, 146–7, 149–50.
16 FO 371 25247. (See also p. 173 of the present study.)
17 Bruce Lockhart, R., *Comes the Reckoning*, London, 1947.
18 See Balfour, M., *Propaganda in War*, pp. 91, 100.
19 Quoted in Howe, op. cit., pp. 84, 85.
20 Glees, op. cit., p. 72. Gordon Walker also became a senior Cabinet minister after 1964.
21 Howe, op. cit., p. 106.
22 Glees, op. cit., p. 73.
23 Bruce Lockhart, op. cit., p. 134.
24 Howe, op. cit., p. 262.
25 FO 371 26559.
26 See Amery, J., *Approach March*, especially pp. 236–9.
27 Glees, A., 'Hugh Dalton und Friedrich Stampfer' in Radkau,

J. (ed.), *Exilforschung*, vol. 2, Munich, 1984.

28 Bruce Lockhart, op. cit., pp. 158–9, 184.

29 Barman, T., *Diplomatic Correspondent*.

30 Delmer's subsequent employer, Lord Beaverbrook, apparently tried unsuccessfully to get more recognition for him than the OBE with which he was issued. Information from Chapman Pincher.

31 Howe, op. cit., p. 244.

32 See Frederik, H., *Gezeichnet vom Zwielicht seiner Zeit*, Munich, 1972; Glees, A., op. cit., especially Chapters IX and X; Krivitsky, W., *I Was Stalin's Agent*, London, 1939; Poretsky, E., *Our Own People*, Oxford, 1969.

33 Tracey, M., *Hugh Greene: A Variety of Lives*, pp. 71 ff.

34 Ibid.

35 Ibid.

36 Boyle, A., *The Climate of Treason*.

37 See Cecil, R., 'The Cambridge Comintern' in Andrew, C. and Dilks, D. (eds), *The Missing Dimension*, London, 1984.

38 Both Leo Long and John Cairncross came from poorer backgrounds. Ibid., p. 173.

39 Dodds-Parker, D., *Setting Europe Ablaze*, p. 36.

40 Ibid., p. 31. Although here, as elsewhere, Mr Dodds-Parker is inclined to be cryptic, it is plain that for him the Communists were, quite justifiably perhaps, acceptable bedfellows.

41 Howe, op. cit., p. 31.

42 Ibid., p. 105.

43 Ibid., pp. 105–6. Part of this testimony relates to a later period, dealt with on p. 213 of the present study, but it seemed wise to include the passage in its logical context. Howe may have spoken to the same SOE officer who wished to report off the record to me. (See p. 244 of this study.)

44 Amery, op. cit., pp. 312–13. Amery's interesting final comment is worth recalling later on. (See p. 96 of the present study.)

45 Foot, M. R. D., *SOE*, p. 146.

46 Ibid., p. 145.

47 Hansard, vols 483–94, 1951. (See p. 13 of the present study.)

48 Page, B. *et al.*, *The Philby Conspiracy*, New York, 1968, p. 102.

49 Foot, op. cit., p. 146.

50 Ibid. Uren's imprisonment for subversion in SOE is something to which we shall return. (See p. 335 of the present study.)

51 Stafford, op. cit., p. 143.

52 Ibid.
53 Prompted by a Radio 3 talk given by me. (See p. 192 of the present study.)
54 *Listener*, January 1982.
55 Foot, op. cit., p. 146.
56 Ibid., p. 147.
57 Ibid., p. 149.
58 Ibid.
59 See Blunt's interview in *The Times*, 21 November 1979.
60 Philby, H. A. R., *My Silent War*, London, 1968, 2nd edn, pp. 19 ff.
61 Ibid.
62 See Howarth, P., *Intelligence Chief Extraordinary*, London, 1986, p. 163.
63 Philby, op. cit., pp. 19 ff.
64 Amery, op. cit., p. 212. (See also p. 87 of the present study.)
65 Ibid., p. 224. (See also p. 87 of the present study.)
66 Philby, op. cit., pp. 46, 50, 80.
67 The term was Dalton's own. See Dalton, H., *The Fateful Years*, p. 327.
68 Ibid., p. 381.
69 Williams, P., *Hugh Gaitskell*, London, 1982, pp. 89–90.
70 Ibid., p. 95.
71 Dalton, op. cit., p. 368.
72 Howe, op. cit., pp. 237–8.
73 Putlitz, W., *The Putlitz Dossier*, London, 1957. I am indebted to Mr Nigel West for drawing my attention to this book. (See p. 220 of the present study.)
74 Ibid., preface.
75 Nicolson, H., *Diaries and Letters, 1939–45*, London, 1967, p. 435.
76 Pimlott, B., *Hugh Dalton*, p. 345.
77 Letter to me, 21 June 1985.
78 FO 371 29465.

5 MI5 and MI6 on the Outbreak of War

1 See le Carré, J., *The Spy Who Came in from the Cold*, London, 1963.
2 Chapman Pincher, H., *Too Secret, Too Long*, pp. 1–2.
3 See, in particular, Andrew, C., *The Secret Service*; West, N.,

MI6 1909–1945, London, 1983; West, N., *MI5*, London, 1981; Page, B. *et al.*, *The Philby Conspiracy*; Deacon, R., *'C':* *A Biography of Sir Maurice Oldfield*, London, 1985.

4 Andrew, op. cit., pp. 58–9.

5 Ibid.; West, N., *MI5*, p. 34, *MI6*, p. 6.

6 West, *MI6*, pp. 4 ff.; Page, op. cit., p. 112.

7 West, *MI6*, pp. 4 ff.; Deacon, op. cit., p. 6; Page, op. cit., p. 109.

8 Andrew claims that all 'C's have gone so far as to use the 'special green ink' used by Smith-Cumming, which seems a little hard to believe. Andrew, op. cit., p. 73.

9 Page, op. cit., p. 118.

10 Andrew, op. cit., pp. 240, 345–6; West, *MI6*, pp. 21–2.

11 West, *MI5*, p. 23.

12 Andrew, op. cit., p. 478; West, *MI5*, facing p. 96; Page, op. cit., p. 136.

13 West, *MI5*, p. 40.

14 For the best account of Liddell, see Andrew, op. cit., p. 363 and elsewhere; for Dick White, p. 384 and elsewhere.

15 Verrier, A., *Through the Looking Glass*: British Foreign Policy in the Age of Illusions, London, 1983, p. 27.

16 See West, *MI6* and *MI5*.

17 Deacon, op. cit., p. 10.

18 Ibid., p. 8. (See also p. 167 of the present study.) The remark about Churchill is a trifle misleading for the period during which he did not hold Government office: there was no reason for him to have access to MI6 information. Yet he did seek his own sources of intelligence, as did another potential user with an unqualified right of access to MI6, Sir Robert Vansittart who possessed, rather grandly, his own secret agent, Colonel Christie. See Andrew, op. cit., pp. 382–3 and elsewhere; also p. 148 of the present study.

19 Page, op. cit., pp. 124 ff.

20 See Andrew, op. cit., pp. 461–2.

21 West, *MI5*, pp. 44–5; Andrew, op. cit., pp. 459–60.

22 There is, perhaps, some irony in the fact that in the 1930s an assistant editor of the *Listener* could enter MI5; in the 1980s, however, MI5 was apparently in a position to advise that a potential editor of the *Listener* be turned down on 'security grounds'. Yet that is as much a reflection of changed mores as it is of the people involved. See the *Observer*, 18 August 1985.

23 West, *MI5*, pp. 159–60.

24 Interview, 7 November 1983.

25 A number of former MI5 and MI6 officers have now stated that they are highly sceptical about the wisdom of recruiting 'high-flyers' straight from universities. Several mentioned the fact that fresh-faced graduates were often unsuitable intelligence officers, a view confirmed by the history of Michael Bettaney, the MI5 officer who received twenty-three years in prison in 1984 for passing secrets to the Russians.

26 Page, op. cit., p. 136. Rothschild and Hart were both remarkably intimate with people subsequently proven to be secret Communists, and Blunt was a major Communist mole. (See p. 20 of the present study.)

27 See Payne Best, S., *The Venlo Incident*, London, 1949 – Payne Best's enthralling, if probably not entirely accurate, account of the abduction; Andrew, op. cit., pp. 433–9; and West, *MI6*, pp. 72 ff.

28 West, *MI6*, p. 77.

29 Andrew, op. cit., p. 467. Hankey reported that 'all the service departments complained about the shortage and imprecision of SIS reports'. One result of this dissatisfaction was the appointment of a young and gifted diplomat, Patrick Reilly, as Menzies's assistant. (See p. 249 of the present study).

30 See West, *MI6*, pp. 80–1; Page, op. cit., pp. 123 ff. Page makes the point that Vivian, despite his ex-Indian police background, gained a reputation for wanting more sophisticated recruits to enter MI6. He was a friend of Kim Philby's father. Page, op. cit., pp. 124, 160 ff.

31 Lewin, R., *Ultra Goes to War*, London, 1978; Jones, R. V., *Most Secret War*, London, 1978; Andrew, op. cit., pp. 449–51; Welchman, G., *The Hut Six Story*, London, 1982; and Kahn, D., *The Codebreakers*, London, 1973.

32 Andrew, op. cit., pp. 449–51. He offers a different account: in August 1939 the Poles sent two of their 'reconstructions' of the Enigma machine to Paris from where one was sent to Britain. Gordon Welchman's obituary in *The Times*, 17 October 1985, would appear to confirm this version.

33 Lewin, op. cit., pp. 30 ff., 42.

34 West, *MI6*, p. 108.

35 Gilbert, M., *Finest Hour*, pp. 610–11; Colville, J., *Fringes of Power*, pp. 294–5; Andrew, op. cit., p. 451 and his somewhat

thin and pretentious chapter 'Winston Churchill and the making of the British Intelligence Community'. Colville reports that the first decrypts were produced early in 1940. By May, the Luftwaffe signals could be decoded, and by early spring 1941 the Germans' naval signals had also been broken. By 1942 all Wehrmacht wireless traffic could be decoded.

36 Gilbert, op. cit., p. 612.
37 Ibid., p. 814.
38 Ibid., p. 1146.
39 Andrew, op. cit., p. 451.
40 A quote Verrier takes from David Stafford's account of SOE. Verrier, op. cit., p. 37. (See also p. 74 of the present study.)
41 West, *MI6*, p. 60. West says Morton headed the 'Industrial Intelligence Centre', which appears to have been a private intelligence agency specialising in German economic intelligence.
42 See Howarth, P., *Intelligence Chief Extraordinary*, London, 1986, p. 144. Bentinck also confirms that both Blunt and Philby attended meetings of the JIC. Burgess he 'met twice'; see pp. 162 ff.
43 Gilbert, op. cit., p. 1184.
44 Ibid., pp. 1200–1.
45 Colville, op. cit., pp. 759–60.
46 Interview, 28 August 1985.
47 See Kahn, D., 'Codebreaking in World War One and Two' in Andrew, C. and Dilks, D. (eds), *The Missing Dimension*.
48 Lewin, op. cit., p. 22.
49 Ibid., p. 20.
50 Gilbert, op. cit., pp. 1209–10.
51 Ibid., p. 1201.
52 Verrier, op. cit., pp. 4, 9–10.
53 Dilks, D., 'Flashes of Intelligence' in Andrew, C. and Dilks, D., op. cit., p. 103.
54 Interview with Lord Sherfield, 16 July 1985.
55 See Andrew, C., 'Introduction' in Andrew, C. and Dilks, D., op. cit., p. 10.
56 Bethell, N., *The Great Betrayal*, London, 1984, p. 66.
57 West, *MI6*, p. 237.
58 West, *MI5*, pp. 152 ff.
59 Ibid., pp. 152–3; Boyle, A., *Climate of Treason*, p. 240.
60 West, *MI5*, p. 154.

61 Ibid., pp. 156–7.
62 See Seyfert, M., 'His Majesty's Most Loyal Internees' in Hirschfeld, G. (ed.), *Exile in Great Britain*, p. 164.
63 Ibid., p. 166; West, *MI5*, pp. 111 ff. West supplies an apparently more accurate figure of 71,600 enemy aliens.
64 West, *MI5*, p. 137.
65 Ibid., p. 30.
66 Ibid., p. 170; Andrew's account is pitiably scant on these matters as, indeed, on the whole problem of Communist subversion and even MI5 more generally. He is equivocal about Hollis himself, although he does group him with established traitors such as Blunt and Bettaney: 'one of the consequences of the Blunt, Hollis, Prime, Bettaney and other security scandals, real or alleged . . .' Andrew, op. cit., p. 504.
67 West, *MI5 1945–72*.
68 Ibid., p. 62.
69 Information from Sir Roger Fulford, March 1982.
70 Philby, H. A. R., *My Silent War*, p. 80.
71 *The Times*, 21 November 1979.
72 West, *MI5 1945–72*, p. 62.
73 Ibid., p. 142.
74 West, *MI5*, p. 276.
75 See, for example, the statements made to Christopher Andrew by Mrs Jennifer Hart and to *The Times* by Anthony Blunt. BBC *Timewatch* programme, 27 July 1983, *The Times*, 21 November 1979.
76 Interview, 28 August 1985.
77 Chapman Pincher, H., letter to me, 11 September 1983.

6 *MI6 as the Object of Communist Subversion, 1941–5*

1 Interviews, 28 August 1985; 13 September 1985.
2 Mastny, V., *Russia's Road to the Cold War*: Diplomacy, Warfare and the Politics of Communism, 1941–45, New York, 1979.
3 Ibid., pp. xv, xviii.
4 For a totally different view of East Germany, see Sandford, G. W., *From Hitler to Ulbricht*, who argues that the German Democratic Republic was not a state imposed by the Russians upon their zone of Germany, but an organic development created out of a bourgeois, rather than a Communist, republic. Many would treat such a thesis with considerable scepti-

cism. See too Geyer, D., 'Deutschland als Problem der sowjetischen Europapolitik' in Foschepoth, J. (ed.) *Kalter Krieg und Deutsche Frage*; Fischer, A., *Sowjetische Deutschlandpolitik im Zweiten Weltkrieg.*

5 Mastny, op. cit., p. 27.
6 Ibid., p. 28.
7 Ibid., p. 178.
8 Ibid., p. 167.
9 Churchill, Sir W., *The Second World War*, vol. 5, pp. 304 ff.
10 Ibid., p. 319.
11 Mastny, op. cit., p. 46.
12 Ibid., p. 53.
13 *Documents on Polish-Soviet Relations*, London, 1961–7, p. 116.
14 Ibid.
15 Ibid.
16 See Erickson, J., *The Road to Stalingrad*, London, 1985. Erickson's authoritative account of Stalin's activities during the first stage of the German attack on the Soviet Union certainly makes it seem remarkable that, contemporaneously with it, he should have begun to develop a plan for the Soviet domination of post-war Europe. On the other hand, the evidence of his policy-making speaks for itself. Certainly, the successful Soviet counter-attacks on Rostov on the Don in November 1941 and on the German positions before Moscow in December did, according to Erickson, produce euphoria in the Kremlin. Erickson speaks of 'vast new possibilities altogether beginning to gleam through the winter murk ... the scents of 1812 and La Grande Armée were in the air' (Ibid., pp. 383–7).
17 Information from Professor Robert Williams, Washington University, St Louis.
18 *Documents on Polish-Soviet Relations*, pp. 114–15.
19 See Glees, A., *Exile Politics During the Second World War*, pp. 188 ff; FO 371 34414, 34415 and 34416.
20 FO 371 34416.
21 FO 371 34415.
22 Ibid.
23 Ibid.
24 For a different interpretation, see Fischer, op. cit.
25 FO 371 34415.
26 See Glees, A., 'What Blunt and Philby Did', *Listener*, 29 October

1981. In this essay I argued that MI5 could have been more positive about procuring British support for the anti-Communist Social Democratic exiles in London, more accurate about the likely political importance of the post-war SPD, and more imaginative about postulating alternatives to British policy towards the anti-Communist exiles, and I argued that might have been the result of Blunt's formal influence in MI5 since it coincided so closely with what we know to be Communist aims. Although I still hold this view, I think that, in relative terms, when compared with other institutions in the intelligence community and with the Foreign Office, MI5 did well in trying to warn the authorities of the threat posed by Soviet subversion.

What I did not know at the time, but have since learned, was the extent to which those who argued that Communist subversion was a threat faced ridicule and worse. What I took as half-hearted and lack-lustre work on the part of MI5 appears today to be more impressive. Subsequent research and further disclosure, particularly about Hollis's role prompted me to look again at what his department did.

I have also since been told that Blunt's influence, while exercised as I suggested, was not expressed in the obvious shortcomings of the MI5 reports on this issue but on an informal basis. He used his considerable knowledge of these matters (gained not least from his surveillance of the diplomatic correspondence of various governments) to subvert policy wherever he could, but these MI5 reports are to be seen not, as I had surmised, as the direct result of his actions, but more correctly as an indirect result of them.

If MI5's reports were less insistent than they might have been, this appears to be the result of Hollis's caution. A head-on collision with official British policy would have opened Hollis's division to great ridicule. It might even have laid him open to the charge that he was doing Goebbels's work for him, since it was Goebbels's claim that the Russians were only interested in subversion (see p. 210 of the present study). Hollis was right to adopt a softly-softly approach even though, as we can see, it was just as ineffective as if he had taken the bull by the horns.

A reliable source has indicated that these reports, which were compiled by Hollis's office, were the work of a division

which was indeed alert to the dangers of Communist subversion in the exile movement in London, but had to struggle
against the attempts made by the moles and by an uncon-
vinced Foreign Office to downgrade the significance of its
intelligence (Interview, 28 August 1985). The fuller account
of these matters given in my previous book shows the extent
to which MI5 gave relatively accurate, if rather unimaginative
and one-dimensional, information to the Foreign Office (see
p. 326 of the present study and Glees, A., *Exile Politics During
the Second World War*, pp. 188 ff.)

27 *Encounter*, July/August 1984, vol. LXIII no. 2.
28 Chapman Pincher, H., *Their Trade is Treachery*, p. 32.
29 *Encounter*, July/August 1984, vol. LXIII no. 2.
30 Ibid.
31 Ibid.
32 Ibid.
33 Ibid.
34 Ibid.
35 Verrier, A., *Through the Looking Glass*.
36 Ibid., p. 3.
37 See Krausnick, H. and Wilhelm, *Die Truppe des Wel-
tanschauungskrieges*, Stuttgart, 1981.
38 See Colvin, I., *Canaris, Chief of Intelligence*, London, 1951,
whose findings were subsequently re-revealed by Nigel West:
West, *MI6*, p. 93 and elsewhere.
39 Interview, 7 November 1983.
40 See Page, B. *et al.*, *The Philby Conspiracy*; Trevor-Roper, H.,
The Philby Affair, London, 1968; Seale, P. and McConville,
M., *Philby, the Long Road to Moscow*, London, 1978;
Jones, R.V., *Most Secret War*; Cecil, R., 'The Cambridge
Comintern' in Andrew, C. and Dilks, D. (eds), *The Missing
Dimension*.
41 Memorandum prepared for me, 20 January 1985.
42 Ibid.
43 Interview with Lord Sherfield, 16 July 1985.
44 Interview, 7 November 1983.
45 Trevor-Roper, op. cit.
46 Ibid., p. 7.
47 E.g. Boyle, op. cit., pp. 261–2; Seale, P. and McConville, M.,
op. cit., p. 218.
48 Trevor-Roper, op. cit.

49 Interview, 7 November 1983.
50 Letter to *The Times*, 1 March 1944, sent by Frank Roberts for the Foreign Office. Quoted in Page, op. cit., p. 167.
51 Page *et al.*, op. cit., p. 169, for example, write: 'Philby was clearly working genuinely very hard at this period of his life for both the Russians and the West.'
52 See: *Die Zeit*, 6 September 1985; an article by me and Andrew Wilson in the *Observer*, 6 January 1985; Diels, R., *Der Fall Otto John*, Göttingen, 1954; Frischauer, W., *The Man Who Came Back*, London, 1958; John, O., *Zweimal Kam Ich Heim*, Düsseldorf, 1969 and the English version, *Twice Through the Lines*, trans. Baring, R., with an introduction by Hugh Trevor-Roper (copyright Hugh Trevor-Roper), London, 1972; John, O., *Falsch Und Zu Spät*, Munich, 1984; since British Government records about John are beginning to be released, however, it is now possible to add substantially to that story.
53 Trevor-Roper has written that John gave information of the Generals' Plot to MI6 *before* 20 July 1944, suggesting that John had been an MI6 agent well before the plot. This is at variance with John's own version of events.
54 John, *Zweimal Kam Ich Heim*, p. 168.
55 Ibid., p. 173.
56 John, *Twice Through the Lines*, pp. 314–15.
57 Ibid.
58 Deacon, R., *'C': A Biography of Sir Maurice Oldfield*, p. 143.
59 Ibid., p. 142.
60 Ibid., pp. 142–4.
61 Letter to me, 26 September 1984.
62 Amery, J., *Sons of the Eagle*, London, 1948, p. 334.
63 Trevor-Roper, H., 'Introduction' in John, *Twice Through the Lines*.
64 Ibid.
65 Interview, 28 August 1985.

7 *MI6 and Britain's Ignorance about Soviet Intentions, 1944–54*

1 This is also the explanation West advances. See West, N., *MI6*, p. 239. Page *et al.* argue that pressure from leading MI5 officers, notably Dick White, shamed MI6 into acting. Page *et al.*, *The Philby Conspiracy*, p. 170.
2 Cecil, R., 'The Cambridge Comintern', in Andrew, C. and Dilks, D. (eds), *The Missing Dimension*, p. 178.

3 Cecil, op. cit., p. 180. The reason why Philby understood more clearly than anyone else that the Cold War would break out was because he had the knowledge necessary to predict it. He had also, in his own way, helped it to occur.

4 See Boyle, A., *The Climate of Treason*, pp. 276–7 for one interpretation of events.

5 See West, op. cit., p. 239.

6 Boyle, op. cit., p. 282.

7 Page *et al.*, op. cit., p. 168.

8 Cecil, op. cit.

9 West, N., *MI5 1945–72*, pp. 26–7 appears to give the full story of why and how it was transferred from Philby to Hollis.

10 See Page *et al.*, op. cit., pp. 173 ff; Boyle, op. cit., pp. 289–91.

11 Interview, 28 August 1985.

12 See Bethell, N., *The Great Betrayal, the Untold (sic) Story of Kim Philby's Biggest Coup*, London, 1984.

13 See Amery, J., *Sons of the Eagle*, and Bethell, op. cit., pp. 34, 49.

14 Quoted in Bethell, op. cit., pp. 38–9.

15 Ibid., p. 16.

16 Ibid., pp. 93–4.

17 Ibid., p. 97.

18 Ibid., p. 105. (See also Chapter 3 of the present study.)

19 See Chapman Pincher, H., *Their Trade is Treachery*, London, 1981, pp. 246–7; West, N., *MI6*, pp. 49 ff. I am indebted to Chapman Pincher and Nigel West for suggesting to me that Putlitz warranted further study.

20 Putlitz, W., *The Putlitz Dossier*, London, 1957, p. 47.

21 Ibid., Chapter XXII.

22 Ibid., preface.

23 Ibid., Chapter XVI.

24 Ibid., pp. 217–18.

25 Ibid., pp. 225–6.

26 Patrick Dean of the Foreign Office (to whom Vansittart sent this letter) added, 'P. worked for the Allies during the war and has an excellent reputation here.' FO 371 55671.

27 Putlitz, op. cit., p. 244.

28 *Der Spiegel*, 22 September 1975. I am indebted to Fritz Heine for this and other documentary material relating to Putlitz and Otto John.

29 Information from Fritz Heine, 15 March 1983.

30 See Soltikow, M., *Ich War Mitten Drin*, Munich no date, pp. 42, 44. Soltikow also states that Hitler had personally berated Admiral Canaris for trusting Putlitz. Canaris, apparently, had told Hitler that Putlitz had been assassinated by Dutch Jews in 1939. A document from London dated 1940 and signed by Putlitz had then been presented to the Führer proving that Putlitz was still very much alive and working for the British. Ibid., p. 189.

31 Putlitz, op. cit., p. 247–8.

32 Ibid., p. 249.

33 Frederik, H., *Das Ende einer Legende*, Bonn, no date, pp. 72–3.

34 John, O., *Zweimal Kam Ich Heim*, pp. 251–2.

35 Thomas, M., *Deutschland, England Über Alles*, Munich, 1984, pp. 165–7. I am indebted to Professor G. Niedhart for this information.

36 West, N., *MI6*, p. 142. (See also p. 292 of the present study.)

37 One former MI6 officer has stated that John was employed as an MI6 agent; Deacon, R., *'C': A Biography of Sir Maurice Oldfield*, p. 143. Another has argued that in his recollection, although close to MI6, John was actually a temporary member of the Foreign Office; interview, 28 August 1985. Yet another has said that John worked first for MI6 and then for MI5; interview, 7 November 1983.

38 John, op. cit., pp. 212 ff.

39 Ibid., p. 215.

40 John's appointment surprised many friends, like Christabel Bielenberg. Interview, 7 May 1986.

41 Interview, 7 May 1986.

42 John, *Twice Through the Lines*, p. 198.

43 The German version of MI6 was the BND, the Bundes-nachrichtendienst, which at that time was still run as an offshoot of the American army, partly for historical reasons and partly because by 1950 the Americans had a very low regard for British secret intelligence about the major hostile power, the Soviet Union. The Americans seem to have resented the fact that MI6 had not done enough to provide good secret intelligence about the Soviet Union during the Second World War period. Indeed, one deeply regrettable corollary of this was that, in their thirst for intelligence about Russia, they turned to some of the most despicable specialists

available, who had themselves gained their knowledge of
Soviet affairs and methods while working for the Gestapo,
the SS and the Abwehr. This was how men such as Klaus
Barbie and Josef Mengele were recruited as agents by American Intelligence.

44 John, *Twice Through the Lines*.
45 Ibid.
46 Ibid.
47 Child, C., OBE, note prepared for me, 20 January 1985.
48 Communication, 11 January 1985.
49 FO 371 109323.
50 See the *Observer*, 6 January 1985.
51 FO 371 109323.
52 Deriabin, P. and Gibney, F., *The Secret World*, New York,
   1959.
53 Ibid., pp. 230–1.
54 FO 371 109323.
55 Ibid.
56 The latest is a secretary who had worked for Canaris and then
   for John. *Die Zeit*, 6 September 1985.
57 Interview, 28 August 1985.
58 A senior British official at the British headquarters at Wah-
   nerheide, in sending this view to the Foreign Office, added
   'this hardly makes sense'. FO 371 103842. The British High
   Commissioner, Ivone Kirkpatrick, himself felt forced to point
   out to London that the revolt had proved far more serious
   and widespread than West German Intelligence had
   suggested. Ibid.
59 FO 371 103843. John had one final go at justifying his thesis on
   18 June 1953. Frank Roberts himself ridiculed his notion that
   the 'revolt was a put-up job by the Russians to get rid of the
   SED leadership' but thought it should be noted. FO 371
   103838.
60 Tobias, F., note to me, 1 August 1985.
61 Felfe, H., *Im Dienst des Gegners*, Hamburg, 1986.
62 John, O., *Zweimal Kam Ich Heim*, pp. 312 ff.
63 See Trevor-Roper's introduction to John's autobiography.
64 Child, C., note for me, 20 January 1985.
65 E.g. Chapman Pincher, H., *Too Secret, Too Long*, pp. 70 ff.
66 Kahn, D., *The Codebreakers*, pp. 190 ff.
67 Colville, J., *Fringes of Power*.

68 Andrew, C., *The Secret Service*, pp. 488 ff.
69 Hinsley, F. H., *British Intelligence in the Second World War*, London, 1979, vol. 1, p. 199, footnote. What is more, the footnote has clearly been altered, presumably to remove a further reference initially inserted by Professor Hinsley. The footnote is not annotated or clarified; above all, no indication is given as to who gave the order or why.
70 Letter to me, 22 November 1984.
71 Interview, 7 November 1983.
72 Andrew, op. cit., p. 332.
73 Interviews, 24 September 1984, 28 August 1985.
74 Interview, 13 September 1985.
75 Howarth, P., *Intelligence Chief Extraordinary*, especially p. 179.
76 Chapman Pincher, op. cit., pp. 70–1. (See also p. 324 of the present study.)
77 Interviews, 28 August 1985; with Sir Patrick Reilly on 13 September 1985; and with Lord Sherfield on 16 July 1985.
78 Interview, 28 August 1985.
79 Interview, 13 September 1985.
80 Interview, 16 July 1985.
81 Interview, 7 November 1983.
82 See Andrew, op. cit., pp. 488 ff. Andrew suggests that Churchill not only believed that British Intelligence was the 'finest in the world', but he also set great store by it: 'He followed a wide range of intelligence activities with close attention and no section of the intelligence community captured his imagination more than Bletchley Park.'
83 Djilas, M., trans. Petrovich, M. B., *Conversations with Stalin*, London, 1962.
84 Ibid., p. 12.
85 Ibid., p. 26.
86 Ibid., p. 34.
87 Ibid.
88 Ibid., pp. 55–9. It is interesting to contrast Djilas's picture of Stalin with Amery's of Churchill – 'his face seemed very white, the skin clear but without colour, the eyes a watery blue'. He plainly also had the Kremlin complexion. Amery, J., *Approach March*, p. 309.
89 Djilas, op. cit., pp. 61–2.
90 Ibid., pp. 70–1.
91 Ibid., pp. 72–8.

92 Ibid., p. 99.
93 Ibid., p. 105.
94 Churchill, Sir W., *The Second World War*, vol. 4, p. 444.
95 Djilas, op. cit., p. 138.
96 Ibid., p. 139.
97 Channel 4 TV, 23 November 1983.
98 See Howarth, op. cit., pp. 179 ff., 182.
99 Bruce Lockhart, R., *Comes the Reckoning*, pp. 117, 152 ff., 289.
100 West, N., *MI6*, pp. 176–7.
101 Interview with Sir Patrick Reilly, 13 September 1985.
102 Rothwell, V., *Britain and the Cold War*, London, 1982, pp. 114–17.
103 Interview with Christopher Hill, 13 September 1985.
104 Rothwell, op. cit., p. 117; Ross, G., *The Foreign Office and the Kremlin*, pp. 50–1.
105 Interview with Sir Patrick Reilly, 13 September 1985.
106 Stafford, D., *Britain and European Resistance*, London, 1980, pp. 68–9; West, *MI6*, p. 176 states that Hill represented only SOE.
107 Smith, B., *The Shadow Warriors*, London, 1983, p. 334.
108 Ibid., p. 349.
109 Ibid., p. 330.
110 Ibid., p. 349.
111 Ibid., pp. 212–13. (See also p. 274 of the present study.)
112 Hill, G., *Go Spy the Land*, London, 1932.
113 Ibid., p. 7.
114 Ibid., pp. 94, 108.
115 Ibid., pp. 189–93.
116 Ibid., p. 210.
117 Ibid., p. 276.
118 Barman, T., *Diplomatic Correspondent*. I am indebted to Professor Michael Balfour, who was a friend and colleague of Barman's, for telling me about this book and providing much helpful detail for the writing of this chapter.
119 Ibid., p. 152.
120 Ibid., p. 153.
121 Ibid., p. 151.
122 Ibid., pp. 161–2.
123 Stafford, op. cit., pp. 68–9.
124 Interview with Sir Patrick Reilly, 13 September 1985.
125 Barman, op. cit., p. 163.

126 Ibid., p. 165.
127 Ibid.
128 Ibid., p. 177.
129 Yost was subsequently installed in the Washington Embassy. See Cecil, R., 'The Cambridge Comintern' in Andrew, C. and Dilks, D. (eds), *The Missing Dimension*, p. 186.
130 Chapman Pincher, H., *Their Trade is Treachery*, p. 139.
131 Ibid., pp. 174, 214.
132 Ibid., p. 264.
133 Ibid., p. 266.
134 Ibid., p. 267.
135 Information from Professor Michael Balfour, 7 September 1984.
136 FO 371 43322, 43395, 47911 in particular.
137 Balfour, M., letter to me, 16 September 1984.
138 FO 371 43322 and 43323.
139 Ibid.
140 Ibid.
141 Ibid.
142 Ibid.
143 Ibid.
144 FO 371 47911 N441.
145 Ibid.
146 Elliott, M. R., *Pawns of Yalta*, London, 1982.
147 See Howarth, P., op. cit., pp. 192 ff.
148 FO 371 47884.
149 Interview with Christopher Hill, 9 September 1985.
150 Hill remained a Communist Party member until 1957. See Kaye, H. J., *The British Marxist Historians*, London, 1984, p. 101, apparently based on an interview with Professor Hill.
151 Hill, C., letter to me, 13 July 1986.
152 Reilly, Sir P., letter to me, 10 July 1986.
153 Ibid.
154 Hill, C., letter to me, 13 July 1986. (See also p. 345 of the present study.)
155 Reilly, Sir P., letter to me, 10 July 1986.
156 FO 371 47884.
157 Hill, C., letter to me, 13 July 1986.
158 It is interesting to see that Orme Sargent crossed out the words 'Communist-infiltrated organisation' and inserted 'an organisation which should receive no support from HMG'.
159 Interview, 9 September 1985.

160 FO 371 47884.
161 Hill, C., letter to me, 22 June 1986.
162 Kaye, op. cit.
163 Interview, 9 September 1985.
164 Interview, 9 September 1985.
165 Holme, K. E., *The Soviets and Ourselves: Two Commonwealths*, London, 1945, p. 12.
166 Ibid., pp. 20–1.
167 Ibid., pp. 21–3.
168 Ibid., p. 28.
169 Ibid.
170 Ibid., p. 32.
171 Ibid., p. 63.
172 Ibid., p. 39.
173 See Glees, A. and Hall, R., *Observer*, 5 May 1985; also various files in the Public Records Office – e.g. FO 371 46748, 46749, 46714 and WO 208 3779–91.
174 Interview, 3 May 1985.
175 See Trevor-Roper, H., *The Last Days of Hitler*, London, 1947. This classic account in its first edition recorded Trevor-Roper's thanks to a 'Brigadier White'. Subsequent editions had White's name deleted for security reasons.

8 *The Secrets of the Service: MI5 and Communist Subversion*

1 Interview, 11 December 1984.
2 Interview, 28 August 1985.
3 *The Times*, 19 July 1984.
4 Chapman Pincher, H., *Too Secret, Too Long*.
5 Interview, 28 August 1985.
6 West confirms this. West, N., *MI5*, p. 143.
7 The briefest glance at Chapman Pincher's two studies shows what this can mean: particularly *Too Secret, Too Long* where 600 pages of text and notes are used to indict Hollis over a forty-year period, although there is no real evidence to connect Hollis improperly with any single KGB agent or indeed any Russian or German Communist.
8 Letter to me, 25 January 1985.
9 West, *MI5 1945–72*, p. 135.
10 See the programme about Wright's charges, Granada TV, 16 July 1984. At the time of writing, a book by Wright is the subject of a court action in Australia.

11 *The Times* has said 1958 and the *Observer* 1955.

12 West, N., *MI5 1945–72*, pp. 74 ff.

13 See Nigel Clive's excellent review of *Too Secret, Too Long* in *The Times Literary Supplement*, 14 December 1984.

14 West, N., *MI5 1945–72*, pp. 108 ff.

15 Chapman Pincher, H., *Too Secret, Too Long* discusses this on pp. 67–72. (His specific allegation about Hollis in this matter is dealt with later in the present study.)

16 Chapman Pincher, H., *Their Trade is Treachery*, p. 57. But here, rather strangely, he has not pointed out the origin of the material, thus underplaying its enormous significance. West, who refers to this all-important wireless traffic as 'U-Traffic' rather than Venona, also fails to make it clear that this was the wartime wireless traffic which the British Government refused to permit to be decoded. See West, *MI5*, pp. 28–9. Pincher adds that Fuchs's detection cannot therefore be considered an MI5 success since it did not result from 'any enquiries by MI5 but from a fluke'. This is clearly unfair; most discoveries are 'flukes' in any case.

17 Volkov wanted to sell his material; he would have been most foolish to give precise names and locations straight away for free. What is more, it is hard to see how if there had been names, even code names, Volkov's list would have presented the difficulties that it clearly did present.

18 Cecil, R., 'The Cambridge Comintern' in Andrew, C. and Dilks, D. (eds), *The Missing Dimension*, p. 179 states that Philby took up his post in November 1944.

19 Ibid., p. 179.

20 Fulford, Sir R., note to me, March 1982.

21 Gouzenko, I., *This Was My Choice*, London, 1948.

22 Gouzenko thus not only provided *post hoc* confirmation of the GRU's role in supporting the Communist bid for political control in Europe, he also explicitly drew attention to the Soviet policy of penetration into the high offices of State (see p. 20 of the present study). Ibid., pp. 137–8.

23 Ibid., p. 149.

24 *The Times*, no date. Later on, in 1972 when Wright came to interview him, Gouzenko added, 'It looks like somebody threw a stone in a pool 27 years ago and now, by the rings in the pond, they want to find out who ...'

25 Foote, A., *Handbook for Spies*, London, 1949.

26 Ibid., p. 61.
27 Report of the Royal Commission, 27 June 1946, Privy Council Order 411.
28 West, N., *MI5 1945–72*, p. 29.
29 Quoted in Chapman Pincher, H., *Too Secret, Too Long*, p. 625.
30 *Daily Express*, 13 June 1985.
31 West, *MI5 1945–72*, pp. 27–8. It is interesting that Chapman Pincher not only fails to make it clear that Nunn May was arrested as the outcome of MI5's investigation in the wake of the Gouzenko testimony, but also suggests that someone in MI5 had tipped off the KGB, because they failed to turn up for a rendezvous with Nunn May on three occasions. Chapman Pincher, *Too Secret, Too Long*, pp. 41–2. West, however, states that it was Nunn May who failed to turn up and not the KGB.
32 Gouzenko, op. cit., p. 282.
33 See Glees, A., *Exile Politics*, p. 216.
34 See Chapman Pincher, H., *Too Secret, Too Long*, pp. 138, 142. (Pincher's main propositions as expressed in this book are discussed later in the present study.)
35 *The Times*, 19 July 1984.
36 *The Times*, 26 July 1984.

9 *The Real Roger Hollis*

1 Interview, 19 November 1981.
2 Chapman Pincher, H., *Too Secret, Too Long*, p. 4.
3 Interview, 28 August 1985.
4 See *The Times* obituary, 3 January 1985.
5 Ibid.
6 According to West, Mitchell had prepared Macmillan's brief, exonerating Philby, for Parliament in 1955.
7 Chapman Pincher, H., *Their Trade is Treachery*, pp. 26 ff.
8 Private letter, 12 January 1982.
9 Private letter, 27 March 1981.
10 See the *Sunday Times*, 23 March 1986.
11 Chapman Pincher, H., *Too Secret, Too Long*, pp. 68 ff.
12 Interview, 13 September 1985.
13 Interview, 24 September 1984.
14 See the *Sunday Times*, 11 November 1984.
15 FO 371 34416 c 11608.

16 FO 371 34416 c 13941.
17 FO 371 46910 c 63445.
18 Chapman Pincher, H., *Too Secret, Too Long*, p. 125.
19 Fulford, Sir R., note prepared for me, March 1982.
20 Astor, Hon. H., letter to me, 19 September 1984.
21 Ibid.
22 See Andrew, C., *The Secret Service*, p. 332, quoted on p. 249 of the present study.
23 Interview, 28 August 1985.
24 Interview, 18 December 1981.
25 Interview, 24 September 1984.
26 West, N., *MI5*, pp. 278–80.
27 Communication, May 1985.
28 Krivitsky had been ordered back to Moscow and feared extermination. See Krivitsky, W., *I Was Stalin's Agent*.
29 Cecil, R., 'The Cambridge Comintern' in Andrew, C. and Dilks, D. (eds), *The Missing Dimension*, p. 174. Krivitsky was debriefed by Jane Archer. Boyle, A., *Climate of Treason*, p. 214; West, N., *MI5*, p. 73; Andrew, C., *The Secret Service*, pp. 432, 441. Andrew says that Krivitsky identified a Soviet mole, Captain John King, a cipher clerk in 1939. In January 1940 he met MI5 and MI6 officers and told Gladwyn Jebb about Maclean, although his clues were apparently 'vague'.
30 Interview, 7 November 1983.
31 Interview, 28 August 1985.
32 Phillip Knightley has quite erroneously contested Chapman Pincher's accurate statement that Hollis was the interviewer. *The Sunday Times*, 6 December 1981.
33 Interviews 28 August 1985, 18 December 1981, 24 September 1984.
34 Interview, 20 August 1985.
35 Interviews, 12 December 1981, 28 August 1985.
36 *The Times*, 21 November 1979.
37 Quoted in Mather, J., *The Great Spy Scandal*, p. 25.
38 Ibid., p. 28.
39 Ibid., p. 35.
40 Ibid., p. 38.
41 Letter to me, 13 June 1986.
42 Reilly, Sir P., letter to me, 10 July 1986.
43 Reilly, Sir P., letter to me, 17 July 1986.
44 Wilson, Sir G., letter to me, 20 August 1986.

45 Quoted in Boyle, op. cit., p. 242.
46 Interview, 7 November 1983.
47 Interview, 28 August 1985.
48 Foote, A., *Handbook for Spies*.
49 West states that Foote was in contact with Sonia Kuczynski and told MI5 about her when he was debriefed. West, N., *MI5*, p. 31. Sonia was Fuchs's contact in England.
50 Interview with Professor Williams, November 1985.
51 West, *MI5 1945–72*, pp. 31 ff.
52 See Morehead, A., *The Traitors*, London, 1952.
53 Interview, 16 July 1985.
54 This is Lord Sherfield's opinion. Interview, 16 July 1985.
55 Interview, 24 September 1983.
56 Interview, 28 August 1985.
57 Gowing, M., *Britain and Atomic Energy*, London, 1964, p. 53; Peierls, R., *Bird of Passage*, Princeton, 1985.
58 Gowing, M., *Independence and Deterrence*, 2 vols, London, 1974, vol. 2 pp. 144 ff.
59 Ibid., p. 141.
60 Ibid., p. 146.
61 Ibid., p. 147.
62 Ibid., p. 148.
63 Peierls, op. cit., p. 223.
64 Interview, 24 September 1984.
65 Document no. P1519 245 (copy held by Chapman Pincher).
66 Letter, 23 November 1981. Bishop Hollis died early in 1986.
67 Interview, 11 September 1985.
68 Interview with Lord Sherfield, 16 July 1985.
69 Chapman Pincher, H., *Too Secret, Too Long*, p. 191.
70 See Chapman Pincher, H., *Their Trade is Treachery*, p. 141.
71 *The Times*, 21 November 1979.
72 See Mather, J. (ed.), *The Great Spy Scandal*, p. 65.
73 Cecil, op. cit.
74 Boyle, op. cit., pp. 417 ff.
75 Lamphere, R. and Shachtman, T., *The FBI-KGB War, A Special Story*, New York, 1986.
76 *Daily Telegraph*, 17 June 1986.
77 Reilly, Sir P., letter to me, 10 July 1986.
78 Reilly, Sir P., letter to me, 10 August 1986.
79 Cecil, op. cit., p. 194.
80 Ibid., p. 191. Cecil held the post himself subsequently.

81 Sherfield, Lord, letter to me, 1 November 1985.

82 Interview with Lord Sherfield, 16 July 1985.

83 See Margaret Gowing's wonderful account of Bohr in Gowing, M., *Britain and Atomic Energy*. Bohr had been flown to Britain from neutral Sweden on a flight which almost killed him, since he forgot to inhale the oxygen he was provided with while hidden in a bomb deck. He never believed that nuclear fission either was, or could remain, the secret of any one nation.

84 Ibid., p. 358.

85 Ibid., p. 359.

86 Quoted in Mather, J., op. cit., p. 148.

87 Masterman, J., *The Double Cross System*, New Haven, 1972. This was a book that Hollis was said to have strongly disapproved of because he thought it betrayed MI5's secrets.

88 Chapman Pincher, H., *Too Secret, Too Long*, pp. 1–2.

89 Letter, 5 April, 1983.

90 Letter, 4 April 1983.

91 Letter, 7 May 1984.

92 Interview, 28 August 1985.

93 Interview with Lord Sherfield, 16 July 1985. Lord Trend conducted the review of the allegations against Hollis in July 1974.

94 Interview with Sir Patrick Reilly, 13 September 1985.

95 Reilly, Sir P., letter to Sir Roger Hollis, 15 June 1960. Oddly enough, Hollis's request appears to contradict any idea that he was working for the Russians. For if he had been, he would have had nothing to fear about his son's being in Leningrad. Alternatively, Hollis's detractors would argue that although this was true, not to ask Sir Patrick's advice might be seen as highly suspicious.

96 Interview, 19 November 1981.

97 Communication, 19 November 1981.

98 Letter, 17 March 1983.

99 Letter, 21 October 1981.

100 Interview, 24 September 1984.

101 Werner, S., *Sonias Rapport*, Berlin, 1982.

102 *Sunday Times*, 6 December 1981.

103 Willoughby, C. A., *Sorge: Soviet Master Spy*, London, 1952; *The Shanghai Conspiracy*, London, 1965.

104 *The Times*, 3 April 1982.

105 Chapman Pincher, H., *Too Secret, Too Long*, pp. 36 ff.
106 Information, 10 March 1986.
107 Moberly, Mrs P., letter to me, 17 November 1984.
108 Prime Minister's statement on security, 26 March 1981.
109 See Chapman Pincher, H., *Their Trade is Treachery*, especially pp. 283–91.
110 Letter, May 1985.
111 Communication, 2 October 1985.

Select Bibliography

Note on sources

This study has been based on published and unpublished sources as well as on interviews. As far as the unpublished sources are concerned, these consist chiefly of private records to which I was granted access and records freely obtainable in the Public Record Office at Kew. The Foreign Office and War Office files contain particularly interesting material.

Akhmedov, I., *In and Out of Stalin's GRU*, New York, 1984.
Amery, Julian, *Sons of the Eagle*, London, 1948.
—— *Approach March*, London, 1973.
Andrew, Christopher, *The Secret Service*, London, 1985.
—— and Dilks, David (eds), *The Missing Dimension*, London, 1984.
Auty, Phyllis and Clogg, Richard (eds), *British Policy towards Wartime Resistance in Yugoslavia and Greece*, London, 1975.
Avon, Earl of, *The Eden Memoirs: the Reckoning*, London, 1960.
Balfour, Michael, *Propaganda in War*, London, 1979.
Barman, Thomas, *Diplomatic Correspondent*, London, 1968.
Beaumont, Joan, *Comrades in Arms: British Aid to Russia 1941–45*, London, 1980.
Beevor, J. G., *SOE: Recollections and Reflections*, London, 1981.
Bethell, Nicholas, *The Great Betrayal*, London, 1984.
Boyle, Andrew, *The Climate of Treason*, London, (revised edn), 1980.
Brown, Anthony Cave, *Bodyguard of Lies*, London, 1979.
Bruce Lockhart, see Lockhart, Robert Bruce.
Bulloch, John, *MI5: the Origins and History of the British Counter-Espionage Service*, London, 1963.
Bullock, Alan, *Hitler*, London, 1971.
Carlton, David, *Anthony Eden*, London, 1981.
Caute, David, *The Fellow Travellers*, London, 1973.

Chapman Pincher, see Pincher, Harry Chapman.

Charlton, Michael, *The Eagle and the Small Birds*, London, 1984.

Churchill, Sir Winston, *The Second World War*, vol. 3, London, 1950; vol. 4, London, 1951; vol. 5, London, 1952; vol. 6, London, 1954.

Citrine, Lord, *I Search for Truth in Russia*, London, 1938.

Cockerill, A. W., *Sir Percy Sillitoe*, London, 1975.

Colville, Sir John, *Fringes of Power*, London, 1985.

Colvin, Ian, *Canaris, Chief of Intelligence*, London, 1951.

Conquest, Robert, *The Great Terror*, London, 1968.

Cooper, Duff, *Old Men Forget*, London, 1953.

Cruickshank, Charles, *The Fourth Arm*, London, 1977.

Dalton, Hugh, *Hitler's War*, London, 1940.

—— *The Fateful Years*, London, 1957.

Deacon, Richard, *'C': A Biography of Sir Maurice Oldfield*, London, 1984.

Deakin, F. W., *The Embattled Mountain*, Oxford, 1971.

Delmer, Denis Sefton, *Black Boomerang*, London, 1962.

—— *Trail Sinister*, London, 1962.

Diels, R., *Der Fall Otto John*, Göttingen, 1954.

Dilks, David (ed.), *The Diaries of Sir Alec Cadogan, 1938–45*, London, 1971.

Djilas, Milovan, *Conversations with Stalin*, London, 1962.

—— *Documents on Polish-Soviet Relations*, London, 1961–7.

Dodds-Parker, Douglas, *Setting Europe Ablaze*, London, 1984.

Douillet, Joseph, *Moscow Unmasked*, London, 1930.

Dulles, A. W., *The Craft of Intelligence*, London, 1963.

Eden, Sir Anthony, *The Reckoning*, London, 1965.

Edwards, Bob and Dunne, Kenneth, *Allen Dulles: A Study of a Master Spy*, London, no date.

Erickson, John, *The Road to Stalingrad*, London, 1985.

—— *The Road to Berlin*, London, 1983.

Feis, H., *Between War and Peace*, London, 1960.

Fischer, Alexander, *Sowjetische Deutschlandpolitik im Zweiten Weltkrieg, 1941–45*, Stuttgart, 1975.

Foot, M. R. D., *SOE in France*, London, 1966, 1968.

—— *Resistance*, London, 1977.

—— *Six Faces of Courage*, London, 1978.

—— *SOE*, London, 1984.

Foote, Alexander, *Handbook for Spies*, London, 1949.

Foschepoth, J. (ed.), *Kalter Krieg und Deutsche Frage*, Göttingen, 1985.

Frederik, Hans, *Gezeichnet vom Zwielicht seiner Zeit*, Munich, 1972.

Frischauer, Willi, *The Man Who Came Back*, London, 1958.

Gans, Wolfgang, Edler Herr zu Putlitz, *Unterwegs nach Deutschland*, no date.

—— *The Putlitz Dossier*, London, 1957.

Garlinski, Josef, *Poland, SOE and the Allies*, London, 1969.

—— *Poland in the Second World War*, London, 1985.

Gide, André, *Back from the USSR*, London, (2nd edn) 1937.

Gilbert, Martin, *Finest Hour*, London, 1983.

—— *Road to Victory*, London, 1986.

Gladwyn, Lord, *Memoirs*, London, 1972.

Glees, Anthony, *Exile Politics During the Second World War*, Oxford, 1982.

Golitsin, Anatoly, *New Lies for Old*, London, 1984.

Gorodetsky, Gabriel, *Stafford Cripps's Mission to Moscow, 1940–42*, Cambridge, 1984.

Gouzenko, Igor, *This Was My Choice*, London, 1948.

Gowing, Margaret, *Britain and Atomic Energy*, London, 1964.

—— *Independence and Deterrence*, 2 vols, London, 1974.

Hansard, vol. 408, 1945.

—— vols 483–94, 1951.

Hill, George A., *Go Spy the Land*, London, 1932.

—— *Dreaded Hour*, London, 1936.

Hinsley, F. H. *et al.*, *British Intelligence in the Second World War*, vols 1 and 2, London, 1979, 1981.

Hoehne, Heinz, *Canaris*, Munich, 1976.

Hoffmann, Peter, *The History of the German Resistance 1939–45*, London, 1977.

Holme, K. E. (pseud. Hill, Christopher), *The Soviets and Ourselves: Two Commonwealths*, London, 1945.

Howarth, Patrick, *Intelligence Chief Extraordinary*, London, 1986.

Howe, Ellic, *The Black Game*, London, 1982.

Hyde, Douglas, *I Believed*, London, 1952.

John, Otto, *Zweimal Kam ich Heim*, Düsseldorf, 1969.

—— *Twice Through the Lines*, London, 1972.

—— *Falsch Und Zu Spät*, Munich, 1984.

Jones, R. V., *Most Secret War*, London, 1978.

Kahn, David, *The Codebreakers*, London, 1968.

Kaye, H. J., *The British Marxist Historians*, London, 1984.

Kettenacker, Lothar (ed.), *Das 'Andere Deutschland' im Zweiten Weltkrieg*, Stuttgart, 1977.

Kimball, W. F. (ed.), *Winston Churchill and Franklin Delano Roosevelt: the Complete Correspondence*, London, 1985.

Krivitsky, Walter, *I Was Stalin's Agent*, London, 1939.

Lamphere, Robert and Shachtman, Tom, *The FBI–KGB War*, New York, 1986.

Lane, Arthur Bliss, *I Saw Poland Betrayed*, London, 1949.

Lewin, Ronald, *Ultra Goes to War*, London, 1978.

Lockhart, Robert Bruce, *Comes the Reckoning*, London, 1947.

Loftus, John, *The Belarus Secret*, London, 1983.

Luard, Evan, *The Cold War*, London, 1964.

Maclachlan, D. H., *Room 39*, London, 1968.

Macmillan, Harold, *War Diaries*, London, 1984.

Masterman, John, *The Double Cross System*, New Haven, 1972.

Mastny, Vojtech, *Russia's Road to the Cold War*, New York, 1979.

Mather, John (ed.), *The Great Spy Scandal*, London, 1955.

Mikolajczyk, S., *The Rape of Poland*, New York, 1948.

Morehead, Alan, *The Traitors*, London, 1952.

Nicolson, Sir Harold, *Diaries and Letters, 1939–45*, London, 1967.

Orwell, George, *Collected Essays, Journalism and Letters*, vol. 1, London, 1970.

Page, Bruce *et al.*, *The Philby Conspiracy*, New York, 1968.

Parker, Ralph, *Moscow Correspondent*, London, 1949.

Payne Best, S., *The Venlo Incident*, London, 1949.

Peierls, R., *Bird of Passage*, Princeton, 1985.

Philby, H. A. R. 'Kim', *My Silent War*, London, 1968.

Pimlott, Ben, *Hugh Dalton*, London, 1985.

—— (ed.), *The Second World War Diary of Hugh Dalton*, London, 1986.

Pincher, Harry Chapman, *Their Trade is Treachery*, London (revised edn), 1982.

—— *Too Secret, Too Long*, London, 1984.

Poretsky, Elizabeth, *Our Own People*, Oxford, 1969.

Putlitz, see Gans, Wolfgang.

Rees, Goronwy, *A Chapter of Accidents*, London, 1977.

Ross, Graham, *The Foreign Office and the Kremlin*, Cambridge, 1984.

Rothwell, V., *Britain and the Cold War*, London, 1982.

Schulz, Gerhard, *Geheimdienste und Widerstandsbewegungen im Zweiten Weltkrieg*, Göttingen, 1982.

Seale, Patrick and McConville, Maureen, *Philby*, London, 1978.

Sefton Delmer, see Delmer, Denis Sefton.

Serge, Victor, *Russia, Twenty Years After*, New York, 1937.

Sinclair, A., *The Red and the Blue: Intelligence, Treason and the Universities*, London, 1985.

Smith, Bradley, *The Shadow Warriors*, London, 1983.

Soltikow, Michael Graf, *Ich War Mitten Drin*, Munich, no date.

Stafford, David, *Britain and European Resistance, 1940–45*, London, 1980.

Stampfer, Friedrich, *Erfahrungen und Erkenntnisse*, Cologne, 1957.

——(ed. Matthias, E.), *Mit dem Gesicht nach Deutschland*, Düsseldorf, 1968.

Straight, Michael, *After Long Silence*, London, 1983.

Sweet-Escott, Bickham, *Baker Street Irregular*, London, 1965.

Thomas, Michael, *Deutschland, England Über Alles*, Munich, 1984.

Tracey, Michael, *Hugh Greene: A Variety of Lives*, London, 1983.

Trevor-Roper, Hugh (Lord Dacre), *The Last Days of Hitler*, London, 1947.

—— *The Philby Affair*, London, 1968.

Valtin, Jan, *Out of the Night*, London, no date (1941).

Verrier, Anthony, *Through the Looking Glass: British Foreign Policy in the Age of Illusions*, London, 1983.

Werner, Sonia, *Sonias Rapport*, East Berlin, 1982.

West, Nigel, *MI5 1909–45*, London, 1981.

—— *MI5 1945–72*, London, 1982.

—— *MI6 1909–45*, London, 1983.

Whaley, Barton, *Codeword Barbarossa*, New Haven, 1973.

Wheeler-Bennett, John and Nicholls, A. J., *The Semblance of Peace*, London, 1972.

Williams, Philip, *Hugh Gaitskell*, London, 1982.

Willoughby, C. A., *Sorge: Soviet Master Spy*, London, 1952.

—— *The Shanghai Conspiracy*, London, 1965.

Articles, television and newspaper features

Blunt, Anthony, Interview, *The Times*, 21 November 1979.

Carlton, David, 'The Raw Material', *The Times Higher Education Supplement*, 3 October 1986.

De Mowbray, Stephen, *Encounter*, vol. LXIII no. 2, July/August 1984.

Gilbert, Martin, 'Churchill: Victim or Villain', *The Times*, 24 September 1986.

Glees, Anthony, 'What Blunt and Philby Did', *Listener*, 29 October 1981.

—— 'The Hollis Letters', *The Times*, 3 April 1982.

—— and Wilson, Andrew, 'Otto John', *Observer*, 6 January 1985.

—— and Hall, Richard, 'The Secret Hunt for Hitler', *Observer*, 5 May 1985.

Hanak, H., 'Sir S. Cripps as British Ambassador in Moscow', *English Historical Review*, 1982, pp. 332–44.

Hart, Jennifer, Interview, *Timewatch* BBC TV, 27 July 1983.

Kettenacker, Lothar, 'The Anglo-Soviet Alliance and the Problem of Germany, 1941–45', *Journal of Contemporary History*, vol. 17, 1982, pp. 435–55.

Leffler, M. P., 'The American Conception of National Security and the Beginnings of the Cold War, 1945–8', *American Historical Review*, vol. 89 no. 2, 1984, pp. 346–81.

Leonhard, Wolfgang, Interview, Channel 4 TV, 23 November 1983.

Spender, Steven, Feature, *Observer*, 10 November 1985.

Wasserstein, Bernard, 'Whose history is it anyway?', *The Times Literary Supplement*, 25 July 1986.

Wright, Peter, Interview, Granada TV, 16 July 1984.

Index